# PRIZEFIGHTING AND CIVILIZATION

# PRIZEFIGHTING AND CIVILIZATION

A Cultural History of Boxing, Race, and Masculinity
in Mexico and Cuba, 1840–1940

David C. LaFevor

University of New Mexico Press | Albuquerque

© 2020 by the University of New Mexico Press
All rights reserved. Published 2020
Printed in the United States of America

First paperback edition, 2022

ISBN 978-0-8263-6158-5 (cloth)
ISBN 978-0-8263-6389-3 (paper)
ISBN 978-0-8263-6159-2 (e-book)

Library of Congress Control Number: 2020935086

Cover illustration: This image is drawn from the cover of a musical score for piano, titled "Blanco y Negro," published in 1898 in Mexico City. It likely illustrates the infamous boxing match between Billy Clarke and Billy Smith. Courtesy of Archivo General de la Nación, Mexico City.
Designed by Felicia Cedillos
Composed in Adobe Jenson Pro 10/13.5

# Contents

Preface vii

Acknowledgments
*Journeyman Research and the Sweet Science* ix

CHAPTER ONE. Introduction
*The Problem of Prizefighting in Cuba and Mexico* 1

CHAPTER TWO. Prizefighting and Civilization in
the Mexican Public Sphere in the Nineteenth Century 21

CHAPTER THREE. "Who Will Say We Are Not Progressing?"
*Cuba, Race, and Boxing in the Nineteenth and Early Twentieth Centuries* 77

CHAPTER FOUR. "Nigger Prizefighters" in Havana
*The Transnational Spectacle of Race and Boxing* 109

CHAPTER FIVE. "The Revolution Came and
Passed Out Gloves to Everyone" 133

CHAPTER SIX. Marching at the Head of Civilization 171

CONCLUSION. Legacies of Domesticating the Exotic
in Cuba and Mexico 209

Notes 213
Bibliography 259
Index 285

# Preface

Anyone who has watched boxing in the past few decades will know that Mexicans, Cubans, and other Latin Americans have held the lion's share of championship titles. What are the historical processes and coincidences that have yielded this outcome? How did an exotic and repugnant "Anglo-Saxon" diversion come to symbolize national identity and masculinity for millions across Latin America? The questions that led to this book arose from experiences in Cuba and Mexico when I was an undergraduate in 2001. During the summer and fall of that year, I worked as an intern for a large US-based shipping company in Mexico City and in the fall studied for a semester at the University of Havana. In Mexico City, I spent many afternoons training in the Tepito neighborhood at the Gimnasio Gloria, a boxing gym that had occupied a busy corner on what is now Eje 1 Norte since the 1930s. It has since closed, as more commercial and modern boxing gyms have rendered it obsolete. Tepito, located a few metro stops north of the *zócalo* (central plaza), is known as the *barrio bravo* (fierce neighborhood). I heard often that it was a part of Mexico City that, as a whole, was "very Mexican." Film directors, musicians, and writers have portrayed Tepito for decades in film, music, and literature as a setting in which the working class—indigenous migrants, mestizos, and others—fought for upward mobility and in the process molded this particular experience of modernity into a complex Mexican vernacular. Fittingly, the symbol for the Tepito metro station is a clinched boxing glove. One writer, recently reflecting on the many roles of the neighborhood in popular culture, characterized it in this manner: "Tepito was the most important bastion of boxing culture, a sport that has been an escape, spectacle, and aspiration for the people."[1] My initial question, as I read more deeply into the cultural history of Mexico, was simply: How and why did it become so?

When I was a student in Havana later that year, I located another boxing gym. The Gimnasio Rafael Trejo is situated in the neighborhood known as Old Havana. This *municipio* (municipal district) was contained within the city walls torn down by the 1860s to make way for urban growth. In 2001, Old Havana was experiencing the frenetic development of the tourist industry that the Cuban government promoted after the fall of the Soviet Union in order to fill budget deficits left by the cancellation of subsidies. At the Gimnasio Trejo, the entrance to which is flanked by a bust of Cuban national hero José Martí, I hoped to experience a microcosm of Cuban life outside the highly structured interactions that formed the daily routines of an exchange student. I also hoped that boxing would provide an avenue of interaction where I could be more of a participant observer than a curious gawker. I wanted to use this experience to better understand perceptions of the United States that resulted from the complicated and often tragic relationship with Cuba. At El Trejo, I quickly learned that boxing was an important source of national pride weighted with nostalgia. The illegality of professional sport since the early 1960s, however, created a starkly different context from that of professional boxing in Mexico. The Cuban state actively intervened in civil society to select the best fighters and to mold them, using scarce resources, into symbols of national achievement in a competitive transnational pursuit. With few punching bags, aspiring boxers in the Trejo punched car seats wired to the wall in the open-air gym.

After graduation from college, I was awarded a Thomas J. Watson Fellowship. The resulting yearlong project took me to a dozen countries in western and eastern Europe, North Africa, and Latin America. I lived with and trained among aspiring prizefighters. During that year, I followed what had become my routine introduction into a new environment. I found boxing gyms—most often in untouristed parts of town—made friends, and through those interactions studied the links between sport, nostalgia, transnational history, and national identities. After that year of solo travel, I began the formal graduate study of Latin American history and the research that forms this book.

# Acknowledgments
*Journeyman Research and the Sweet Science*

This book is the product of much professional and personal collaboration and debt. The greatest of these debts stems from the time colleagues, friends, and family spent reading, listening, debating, critiquing, and shaping the ideas here recycled to fashion meaning out of so many ostensibly unrelated narratives, from so many countries, across so long a period of time. I can never repay this time, but only acknowledge that generosity that has benefited me enormously and made this book possible.

The Thomas J. Watson Fellowship, the Fulbright Garcia-Robles Fellowship, the Helguera Fellowship, and multiple Vanderbilt University History Department grants provided vital research funding in the early stages of this project. That funding allowed me to pursue leads in Argentina, Cuba, Spain, and Mexico. At Vanderbilt and beyond, Marshall Eakin, Jane Landers, Edward Wright-Rios, Gary Gerstle, Michael LaRosa, Pablo Gómez, David Wheat, William Luis, Nicholas Villanueva, and others pushed me to ask deeper questions of the narratives. The Department of History at Berry College provided valuable time and support for the first stages of revision. The Center for Mexican American Studies, the College of Liberal Arts, and the Department of History at the University of Texas at Arlington supported final research trips to multiple archives in Mexico, Spain, and Cuba. At UTA, in particular, I'd like to thank Cristina Salinas and Christian Zlolniski for patiently reading and commenting on multiple drafts. Finally, several anonymous reviewers provided critical readings and suggestions.

Historian Marc Bloch wrote that most historians begin with a "simple liking [that] precedes the yearning for knowledge." For Bloch, this affinity stemmed from the same impulse to wander the streets in a new city, to study a foreign language, and to meld the abstract and the concrete, ideally, into a narrative that doesn't too greatly reduce the complexities of the past. This book evolved from gaps in the narrative and analytical histories of Mexico and Cuba in the existing literature.

Research in multiple archives also creates debts of time, patience, and knowledge. The staff in the Archivo General de la Nación, the Archivo Histórico de la Ciudad de Mexico, the Archivo General del Estado de Veracruz, Archivo Historicó Municipal de Oaxaca, the Hemeroteca and Biblioteca Nacional de Mexico, and the Biblioteca Lerdo Tejada provided insightful assistance and support in Mexico. In Cuba, the staff of the Archivo Nacional de Cuba, the Biblioteca Nacional José Martí, and the Archivo Histórico Municipal de Trinidad interpreted the rules in my favor and showed great patience. In Buenos Aires, the professionals in the Biblioteca Nacional Mariano Moreno allowed me unfettered access to rare periodicals, and in Spain the staff of the Archivo Historicó Nacional helped me along. In the United States, I'd like to thank the staff of the Nettie Lee Benson Collection at the University of Texas at Austin, the National Archives at College Park, and the Library of Congress. To those anonymous colleagues who have digitized millions of pages of newspapers—too many of which are only available through expensive databases—thank you for saving these undervalued documents.

Finally, a warm thank you and abrazo to those Mexicans and Cubans who have made years of life outside the archives such a pleasure. I'd like to thank, in particular, the former 1950s bantamweight boxing champion of Cuba, Enrique Hitchman, whom I met by chance on one of my extended stays in Havana. After the Revolution, Hitchman chose to stay in Cuba, sacrificed a promising career as a professional boxer, and worked as a security guard for decades. Within a few hours of meeting him, he showed me a massive scrapbook that detailed his life and travels as a prizefighter in the 1950s. I stood with him for hours as I photographed each page of his story. Though his narrative is outside the chronological scope of this book, my friendship with him and his willingness to humor my endless questions is typical of the reception I have enjoyed, luckily, at all stages of my work in Cuba and Mexico.

Most importantly, my family, Adam and Matt LaFevor (fellow scholars), Guillermo (Bill) and Chris LaFevor, made all this work possible and rewarding. Tara, Jack, and Elena LaFevor, this book is dedicated to you.

CHAPTER ONE

# Introduction

*The Problem of Prizefighting in Cuba and Mexico*

WHEN JACK JOHNSON, the African American heavyweight champion, arrived in Havana in 1915 to defend his title against the "White Hope" Jess Willard, Cuban cartoonists were ready. For years, artists such as Conrado Massaguer had followed the often picaresque and racist depictions of Johnson and his profession in the Cuban and American presses. The title defense had been scheduled to take place in Ciudad Juárez, Mexico, but the rapidly changing power balance during the Revolution altered his travel. He feared deportation from Mexico to the United States as a fugitive from justice.

Massaguer and other cartoonists rendered Johnson in Havana in dramatic and meaningful portraits. He was a priapic ape, suggestively pushing his large banana into the face of the viewer.[1] Accompanying text chided that Johnson looked like a "Zulu tourist" or a "King of the Congo." The writer mused the only way Johnson could attain such wealth in Cuba would be to harvest an entire field of sugar cane *every day*. Johnson was not just an exotic oddity in the port. His presence illustrated, by juxtaposition, the labor that Afro-descended people were *supposed* to conduct in Cuba in 1915, at least in the mind of that observer. Despite being a "glorious champion . . . poor Johnson" had been denied a room in most of the city's elite hotels, whose staffs "rejected him like a bubonic rat."

In episodes such as this, Johnson experienced the complex racial politics that were "the reality of life" in Havana. Even if there was something spectacular in Johnson's celebrity, the ubiquitous tropes of dangerous black male sexuality still applied to him: "when he sees a woman, he flashes his teeth like a shark when it sees white meat." Johnson, as a practitioner of violence, "the king of punches," arrived in Cuba less than three years after the massacre of the Afro-Cuban Partido Independiente de Color (Independent Party of Color), during which the same cartoonists depicted Afro-Cubans as bloodthirsty rapists and murderers. As historian Aline Helg illustrated, these depictions both reflected and molded public perceptions of race and violence.[2] Johnson, and boxing, entered Cuba loaded with and received among contested meanings of race, empire, and masculinity.

Other cartoonists, assigning Johnson a less threatening valence, depicted him as a larger-than-life bon vivant, dressed in an expensive suit, ambling with his cane down a Havana street while Afro-Cuban laborers, newspaper boys, and Sino-Cuban water carriers marveled with expressions of admiration.[3] In yet another image, Johnson and his opponent straddle the island while the warring powers of Europe call an imaginary truce in order to watch the outcome of this historic battle for racial supremacy in the boxing ring. One writer, Victor Muñoz, pretended to observe the reception of Willard in the United States after his victory over Johnson. He used that imagining to impugn the delirious racism that the fighter evoked in the United States while writing of Johnson as a cosmopolitan family man at home in Cuba. The fighter's reception in Cuba, and later in Mexico, illustrated the uncertainties of race, class, and transnational identities that surrounded the enormously popular and controversial cultural practice of prizefighting.

*Prizefighting and Civilization* is the first transnational study of the gendered, racial, and nationalist dimensions of boxing in Cuba and Mexico during the century between 1840 and 1940. It examines the movement of ideas, cultural practices, and individuals to the United States's closest Latin American neighbors. Cuba and Mexico confronted the challenges of expanding US cultural, territorial, military, and economic expansion in the last half of the nineteenth century. US power, broadly conceived, was experienced there first and most dynamically. The confrontation with prizefighting—a divisive subculture that was both profitable blood sport and contentious public spectacle—provides a unique vantage point to examine the deeper evolution of cosmopolitan nationalisms, everyday normative concepts of masculinity, and an expanding and democratizing public sphere.

The public sphere was and is the locus of deliberation in which public opinion is formed and debated.[4] Print culture—the growing vibrancy of the press in both countries during this period—served as a crucial forum for the creation of consensus around novel cultural forms. Writers debating in the public sphere resisted and digested the popularization of prizefighting. But the public sphere was more than a neutral site to express opinion; it could take on a life of its own beyond the intentions of writers and artists. As the above cartoons illustrated, creating meaning from such images was the role of the viewer. The creative appropriation of boxing entailed cultural exchanges with marginal foreigners and a troubled reckoning over the valence of imported practices. Opponents of boxing, especially in the nineteenth century, cited it as proof of US social and racial degeneracy and as an example of hypocritical pretensions of US civilization. It evinced the potential perils of unfiltered mass culture and was a dangerous extravagance of too much democracy. Within a few decades, Cubans and Mexicans transformed prizefighting into an enunciation of local working-class masculinity. This transformation did not follow a neat trajectory and, to be sure, was contingent on the interplay between local, national, and transnational contexts.

Prizefighting was propagated in both nations by a transnational and interracial group of athletes and entrepreneurs, who, opponents feared, were purveyors of low culture, hucksters who took advantage of local youths in the thrall of novel and disreputable celebrity. Others imbued it with meanings detached from, but often analogous to, its origins in England and the United States. They viewed the success of Mexican and Cuban boxers in international competitions as vehicles for popular nationalism and aspirational masculinity. Boxing was cathartic. It created divisive and meaningful narratives that fueled the sensational press of the era. For proponents of the sport, training the male body and appropriating norms of behavior became a method of proving and cultivating one's cosmopolitan manliness. Being a modern man increasingly included a knowledge of popular cultures both beyond and amid the confines of immediate and local experience.

The dissemination of boxing accompanied and exemplified the growth and democratization of civil society in Cuba and Mexico.[5] As Mexican intellectuals celebrated *indigenismo* in the 1920s, their Cuban counterparts similarly re-evaluated their "folk" in a movement known as *afrocubanismo*.[6] Both these elite-driven cultural programs valorized the respective racial and social underclasses as essential and historical elements of national uniqueness and legitimacy, but they did so while seeking to control a narrative that defined, and often denigrated, the place of these people in the present.

In the late nineteenth century, boxing was outlawed and repressed in both nations. As Cubans waged a thirty-year struggle for independence from Spain (1868–1898) and Mexican discontent with the dictatorship of Porfirio Díaz grew, boxing and boxers engaged the politicized field of popular culture. By the 1930s, however, boxing helped create a new social phenomenon: the hero-athlete from the margins of society.[7] There were few more dramatic forums for individual achievement than physically overcoming a matched opponent. As a meritocratic practice, sport challenged class hierarchies within "hegemonic masculinities." As R. W. Connell and J. Messerschmidt observe, historical studies of hegemonic masculinity seek to uncover "the currently most honored way of being a man . . . it meant ascendency achieved through culture, institutions, and persuasion."[8] Prizefighting as culture, its interaction with and the resulting creation of new institutions, and the "persuasions" evident in celebrity and fandom, destabilized local expressions of manliness by framing that identity within transnational vernaculars of prizefighting.

Boxers and boxing matches formed the narrative subject matter for pulp fiction, literature, and films in which Mexicans and Cubans assessed and created new heroes to inhabit the national pantheon. Boxers from the lower ranges of social and racial hierarchies with evocative and hybrid ring names such as Kid Chocolate (Cuba), Kid Charol (Cuba), Black Bill, Young Jack Johnson (Cuba) and Kid Azteca, Chango Casanova, Baby Arizmendi (Mexico), became embodiments of *cubanidad* and *mexicanidad*. This phenomenon, which later expanded to the rest of Latin America, occurred first and most controversially in Mexico and Cuba.

Before these transformations occurred, boxing was more contentious than any of the sports that Cubans and Mexicans encountered in the nineteenth and early twentieth centuries. It was foreign and violent, yet it was a rule-based practice that, ideally, contained that exotic violence within a regulated and leveling space. Ethnic and racial minorities excelled in this meritocratic field whose defenders posed it as a positivist and eugenic practice propelled by "scientific ideas" about corporeal and national development. The debates in the public sphere driven by prizefighting were a symptom of broader anxiety over the quickening pace of cultural change. This ever-increasing flow of ideas and symbols was amplified by the novel ease of international travel and the flows of information that challenged elite control of national self-definition.

In the late nineteenth century, writers, artists, and politicians seized upon *el pugilato* as insidious US barbarism. Yet it was also a cultural peculiarity that helped explain the militant and self-assured neoimperialism of Anglo-Saxons; it was often explained as a transcendent symbol of the "race." Boxing and lynching were often paired in this imaginary. They became twin rhetorical tools deployed to critique US pretensions of cultural modernity and broader racial and civilizational superiority. Nationalist intellectuals including Justo Sierra (Mexico) and José Martí (Cuba), and dozens of writers of lesser renown, argued that prizefighting was antimodern, illegal, and the degraded detritus of US society. Both Sierra and Martí observed the United States in person between the end of the US Civil War and the quickening of US expansion into Latin America at the end of the nineteenth century. Both writers evinced concerns similar to those of many US reformers about prizefighting: this cultural problem was symptomatic of militant US expansionism as increasingly experienced in Latin America.[9]

After a train journey through the United States in 1898, Justo Sierra reported his experiences in the north: "If I could personify this people, I would paint them as an athlete, a pugilist, ready to break bones."¹⁰ For Sierra and other contemporary intellectuals such as Rubén Darío, US Americans worshiped coercive physical power, and boxing exemplified troubling features of US democracy that its soldiers, missionaries, and diplomats conspired to impose upon Latin America.¹¹ Boxing was a metaphor for anti-intellectualism and gender confusion that evoked "women wishing to be men, to struggle for life . . . without a soul." It challenged traditional ideas of how good men and women should interact in public. For Sierra, the culture that supported prizefighting was alien and uncivilized. And it was a potential contagion. Despite these misgivings, pugilism in Mexico developed into an early example of a transnational cultural industry the proponents of which ridiculed elite fears and concepts of propriety. It paralleled and exemplified the increasing confrontation of Euro-American-derived meanings of gender and the content of popular culture with the carefully constructed model of civilization that Sierra and other Porfirians envisioned for Mexico.¹²

Writing as a newspaper correspondent in 1882, the Cuban nationalist intellectual José Martí was fascinated and repulsed by the uproar over an illegal heavyweight prizefight in the United States: "the whole nation is a cock fighting pit."¹³ Much of Martí's writing focused on constructing a cohesive and racially inclusive Cuban identity, distinct from Spain and apprehensive of the United States. He explained prizefighting as a powerful symbol of the uncouth character of US society. Martí's opinions were seconded by a correspondent for the conservative and pro-Spanish Havana newspaper *Diario de la Marina*: "They [US Americans] call this the manly art . . . because among that race that is supposed to carry the torch of modern civilization, human perfection consists in being able to flatten another person."¹⁴ Twenty years after Martí penned those lines, Cuban impresarios regularly hired US boxers and showed films of boxing matches in the Havana theater named for him, the Teatro Martí.¹⁵ While Martí's vision for the nation was the guiding rhetorical justification for many nationalist ideas after independence (1902), his warning about prizefighting failed to take root. The early years of the Cuban Republic were a crucial period for the invention of new cultural norms. As historian Marial Iglesias Utset has argued, writers and politicians, often working alongside US occupying forces, sought to inculcate nationalist (anticolonialist) traditions and plot a path toward an ideal civilization.¹⁶ Popular appropriation of boxing presented a challenge to this project.

*Prizefighting and Civilization* builds on a growing historiography of cultural hybridity in the region.¹⁷ Much of this work eschews the notion that unequal power relations, between nations and among individuals, can adequately account for the appropriation of novel cultural forms. Politicians and intellectuals in Cuba and Mexico sought to carefully incorporate the lessons of martial culture that had helped US Americans to defeat Spain (1898) and had helped the Japanese in their victory over Russia (1905). These rising powers provided intriguing examples of New World (United States) and non-European (Japan) societies whose fundamental cultural characteristics were, perhaps, worth examination.

Attempts to segregate boxing to the upper classes and its transformation into a mass spectacle occurred simultaneously. While cross-class *aficionados* imported prizefighting into Mexico in the early years of the twentieth century, Salvador Esperón, a Nahuatl-speaking early boxer from Oaxaca City, instructed cadets at the most prestigious military academy in Mexico City on the finer points of scientific boxing as a means to develop stoic masculinity and discipline.[18] Though he mentored the future leaders of the nation, police in Mexico City fined Esperón for fighting in illegal underground matches. This ambivalence was closely linked to social class and place. Fighting in public, even in members-only clubs, was far from pedagogical, or so reasoned the police and local government. Such debate became a leitmotif in battles over problematic popular culture.

The Cuban government outlawed films of interracial prizefights in 1910. Cubans had begun to re-create, using transnational newspaper coverage as their guide, the boxing matches of Jack Johnson. Theater critics, as they had since the 1840s, bemoaned that the boxing matches turned theaters and circuses into venues of violence that spilled over into the streets. Legislators feared that such powerful and meaningful images—African Americans pummeling and mocking "white hopes"—would heighten racial tensions as a crisis grew over Afro-Cuban struggles to achieve political power and social equality.[19] Cultural nationalists, reacting to the fad of boxing, argued that if it were legalized, other pursuits that many viewed as barbaric should likewise be permissible. Cockfighting, outlawed under the first US intervention (1898–1902) and, they argued, the essential Cuban pastime, was "closely linked to a tradition of *cubanía* [Cuban identity] with deep popular roots." Accordingly, it should be defended and even encouraged.[20]

By the 1920s, however, most of these debates had been settled. Cubans published celebratory treatises on the brief history and legalization of boxing that focused on the meritocracy of interracial prizefighting as a practice that demonstrated Cuban "racelessness." This idea drew on the dominant representations of the interracial alliance to overthrow Spain two decades before. According to historian Ada Ferrer, the interracial nature of the rebel army, along with the innovative ideas of José Martí, "gave rise to one of the most powerful ideas in Cuban history—the conception . . . of a raceless nationality."[21] In part, this nationalist allegory served as a point of resistance to the Jim Crow culture of the United States that was clearly evident in social and legal prohibitions of interracial matches in the north. Cuban writers cited the legalization of prizefighting—for all Cuban boxers—as an achievement of civic and political activism waged in the public sphere. It was not an insidious imposition of cultural imperialism from the north; it was an edifying display of Cuban racial equality. The former boxer Bernardo San Martín penned a series of editorials extolling the "scientific" and "masculine" lessons Cuban youths learned through prizefighting. Politicians, he argued, proclaimed racial equality while previously trying to prohibit this manifestation of racelessness.[22]

This activism helped legitimize spaces where new celebrities challenged racial and gendered cultural norms. Eligio "Kid Chocolate" Sardiñas, the local *negrito* as he was affectionately or degradingly known, defied social taboos by having sexual relationships with white women while becoming one of the first Afro-Cuban international celebrities.[23] US newspapers, reprinted in Cuba, carried glowing accounts of "the Kid," and this international acclaim became a factor in the cross-class acceptance of prizefighting.[24] This process, as is well known for other cultural forms such as popular music in the same period, followed the same informational circuits—radio and newspapers—that marginal musical forms such as tango (Argentina) and samba (Brazil) had followed.[25] In similar form, boxing was nationalized, ironically, as an enunciation of the Cuban and Mexican folk. This occurred while US newspaper publishers in Cuba bemoaned the "nigger lovers" and "race traitors" who pioneered interracial boxing in the 1910s.[26]

The act of being a fan, and including the modern values of organized sport into one's masculine identity, expanded the geography of affinity beyond the confines of the local. Men compared themselves *as men* to international symbols of manliness not just through reading coverage of boxing celebrities in the prize ring. Local advertisers seized upon didactic images of boxers to pitch products from cigarettes to elixirs to formal men's suits. As historian Peter Beattie contends for Brazil in this period, "The public servant, patriot, frontiersman, explorer, *sportsman*, statesman, humanitarian, and warrior became an archetype of Belle Époque manhood."[27] The appropriation of the honorific title of "sportsman" in particular, as Brenda Elsey has shown for Chile, became a cross-class signifier and a means through which working-class citizens and civic-social associations sought to expand their presence in the public sphere and in politics.[28] Louis Pérez Jr., in his study on baseball during the late colonial period in Cuba, likewise contends that preference for the US import over traditional Spanish pastimes was a political statement recognized by the colonial government as a threat to its cultural and political hegemony.[29] Playing a US American game and organizing into competitive teams, Spanish administrators feared, eroded the ties of affection that underpinned loyalty to the metropole. It attenuated the direct and exclusive link between the government and the governed by creating alternative forms of self-identification. Everyday citizens increasingly attended boxing matches and viewed films that vied for cultural space alongside traditional and state-sanctioned practices such as bullfighting and cockfighting. Culture, in Geertz's famous construction, is composed of the "webs of significance" that create a context for the production of meaning and the rational guidance of action.[30] These webs, constantly and increasingly stressed by competing practices from abroad, were becoming more complex and less responsive to management from above.

This study of prizefighting joins recent scholarship on race, national identity, and popular culture in national and transnational contexts in Latin America. Louis Pérez Jr.'s broad body of work has been particularly important.[31] Pérez argues that Cubans, from as early as the mid-nineteenth century, seized upon US ideas of cultural modernity. This translation took the form of practices such as anglicizing one's name, altering one's style of dress, and voraciously consuming popular culture, which became normative benchmarks for thousands of Cubans. These cultural alignments were intensely political. Pérez's argument, extended over the course of the Cuban Republic (1902–1959), helps explain the widespread discontent that resulted in Fidel Castro's revolution: Cubans aspired to living standards exemplified by US popular culture that were unattainable given the economic and political realities by the 1940s and 50s. The examination of boxing in Cuba during the Republic extends his analysis of cultural hybridity to examine an important counterpoint: boxing was racially fraught, and this dimension of the practice delayed its popularization for decades. African American athletes and their Afro-Cuban counterparts engendered often vitriolic resistance to the mimetic tendencies that Pérez suggests.

Pablo Piccato's work on the public sphere in Mexico provides welcome attention to the growth and importance of the popular press as a locus of cultural debates in late nineteenth- and early twentieth-century Mexico. Though much of his analysis focuses on elite feuds over honor that employed mass media, he shows how such enunciations of threatened masculine honor portrayed broader social conflicts over fundamental cultural and political ideals. Robert Buffington extends Piccato's study to argue that the penny-press and broadsides, such as those penned by the artist José Guadalupe Posada, both expressed and molded working-class ideas of manhood, often in satirical opposition to the pretensions of upper-class exclusivity.[32]

This study is also informed by scholarship from the past forty years that has revolutionized the study of the nation and nationalism. These ideas are most succinct in the work of Benedict Anderson and his compelling arguments that nations are constructed, or "imagined."[33] The style of their imagination as discrete and exclusive historical entities, with a generally agreed upon trajectory into the future, leaves a paper trail and can be traced, examined, and deconstructed. Nationalists often envision the nation both as what *we are*, but, as importantly, what *we are not*. Conflicts over exclusion were and are prime sites for debate over the fundamentals of nationhood. Prizefighting served as a nationalist parable, first for exclusion of foreignness and later as a democratizing expansion of the inclusive social boundaries of the national body.[34]

## Boxing's Golden Age in Cuba and Mexico

Elite attempts to prevent the popularization of prizefighting in Mexico and Cuba in the late nineteenth and early twentieth centuries failed. By the late 1920s, Mexicans and Cubans rejected elite fears of cultural decadence, racial antagonism, and foreign contamination. The fear of traditional culture under assault was not new, but the context of US imperialism heightened tensions and exposed fault lines. Tens of thousands of fans regularly attended boxing matches and listened to transnational radio broadcasts of distant bouts. Mexicans and Cubans constructed massive public venues for boxing, altering cityscapes and broadening the parameters of mass culture.[35] Arenas offered popular prices so that "the poor class amid which boxing counts thousands of enthusiastic admirers" could mingle with the self-styled cosmopolitan elite.[36] These spaces, often built with foreign capital that exemplified corrupt governance, were ground zero in these culture wars.

Many of these fault lines centered on language, especially the incorporation into Spanish of English-derived phrases, and they also manifested in the visual sphere. Realist and documentary photographers across Latin America, such as Gustavo Casasola (Mexico), Enrique Díaz (Mexico), Manuel Álvarez Bravo (Mexico), Martín Chambi (Peru), Walker Evans (United States/Cuba) and Aladar Hajdu (Hungary/Cuba) captured the gritty and sometimes erotic visual cultures associated with pugilism as part of the experience of urban life.[37] Hajdu's publication, for example, of a seminude image of the Afro-Cuban boxer Eligio "Kid Chocolate" Sardiñas, in the Havana magazine *Social* in 1931, would have been unthinkable twenty years before. Sport, and boxing in particular, had opened new and complex avenues for representation in the public sphere for Afro-Cubans.[38]

Cubans and Mexicans aligned themselves with boxers in matches thousands of miles away that, it might seem, had little direct effect on their lives. Some wrote poetry about boxers, pawned household goods to gamble on bouts, and expressed fealty to Latin or negrito fighters whom they imagined as racial brothers, especially when they met a US American in the prize ring. Athletes from the lower classes appropriated as nomes de guerre the stage names of transnational celebrity athletes. The owners of *pulquerias* (working-class bars in Mexico) rechristened their businesses after boxers. Mexican film directors produced biopics of *chilango* (from Mexico City) prizefighters who bootstrapped their way to wealth, celebrity, and masculine idolization. These paralleled the growth of cities, urban slums, and mass culture and played alongside imported films that dramatized the biographies of American and European sporting idols.

As film historian Carl Mora has argued, by the 1940s movies presenting lower-class boxers as Mexican heroes were among the first to use and popularize "authentic street dialogue from the slums of Mexico City."[39] Moviegoers viewed dramatizations of working-class prizefighters as paragons of Mexican masculinity, and, as historian Steve Allen argues, they became contentious symbols of upward social mobility.[40] Boxing films from the golden age of Mexican cinema are still deployed by the Mexican government to celebrate important national holidays.[41]

Cubans and Mexicans lauded the carefully crafted image of the rough Argentine cowboy from the interior, Luis Ángel "Wild Bull of the Pampas" Firpo, during and after his 1923 bout against American Jack Dempsey in New York.[42] As historian Theresa Runstedtler argues in her study of the global career of Jack Johnson, prizefighters as mobile case studies of race and international politics served as "a bellwether of racial and imperial conflicts in the early twentieth century."[43] *Prizefighting and Civilization* extends her important work by focusing on the reception and reconfiguration in Mexico and Cuba of these ideas.

Mexican and Cuban boxers confronted and symbolically defeated racial slurs in the democratic space of the prize ring. They refashioned these ideas simultaneously on local, national, and transnational stages. To be a *firpista* (a supporter of Firpo) and a sportsman was more than admiring the skill of a particular athlete. It was to express meaningful solidarities contingent on the convergence of diverse ideological factors that held meaning for thousands. The new technologies of film and radio made nearly real-time coverage of distant events possible, feeding the growth of transnational identities and cultural preferences beyond the local. New possibilities for imaging the self and the nation entered into even the smallest towns via the images, sounds, and ideas associated with modern celebrity and masculinity in the prize ring.[44] In Cuba and Mexico, individuals in rural towns kept abreast of daily reports on prizefighting. They wrote to national newspapers to express their opinions of certain prizefighters and to prove that they, too, had mastered the modern vernaculars of sport.

Being a "sportsman" in this period entailed the mastery of intricate new forms of knowledge and the expenditure, in many cases, of enormous amounts of emotional energy. The meaning of the imported term *sportsman* shifted during the late nineteenth century. When it first appeared in print in the 1840s in Cuba it was italicized and explained in newspapers.[45] In Mexico, the introduction of the term was footnoted for readers as "*Aficionado* of horses, bullfights, hunting, and other similar pleasures, as in the adjective *sport* it expresses the grouping of said exercises." It was deployed to describe aristocratic pursuits, but by the late nineteenth century it had morphed into a more popular association with sports such as boxing and baseball.[46] The use of the English word *sportsman* or, more often, *sportman*, appearing in Spanish-language publications peaked in the 1890s and again in early 1920s.[47] These transliterations were an important marker for this process of cultural translation and they suggest moments when the public sphere was most inundated with discussions of athletes and sport.

In the early 1920s, the Cuban and Mexican governments established regulatory agencies—commissions on boxing—to set rules and eligibility and to collect taxes on ticket sales. Government functionaries continued to intervene in the sport in sometimes farcical ways, refashioning established boxing rules in an effort to impose their stamp and commissioning censors to report any scandals provoked by the masses that attended prizefights.[48] These moves toward legalization and regularization garnered the approbation of such paternalistic US institutions as the Hispanic Society of America, which lauded the new "influences" within Latin American nations evident in their rapid mastery of modern sport. Jacob Warshaw, a professor at the University of Nebraska, wrote in 1922 that most US readers would be "surpris[ed] to find urban conditions in Latin America so similar to those of the United States." Modern sport, for Warshaw, was proof that Latin Americans were part of modernity: "England and the United States, from whom the fondness for athletics is taken, are thus remodeling... the scheme of Latin American existence... [and displacing] antiquated Latinity."[49] As Nancy Stepan has argued, this idea of modern civilization focused on a confrontation of the decadent forces of urban life in Latin America; "sports and physical fitness could be claimed to be eugenic because they 'improved the race.'"[50]

## Framing Public Spectacle and Masculinity in Transnational History

Historian Eric Hobsbawm posited that the transnational spread of sport in the late nineteenth and early twentieth centuries was a primary example of cultural transfer from the supposedly "civilized" British (and Americans).[51] But this center/

periphery model is overly deterministic. This book illustrates, in the case of boxing, that Latin Americans remade and reimagined the sport, fitting it into complex local environments. Mexicans and Cubans were not waiting on sport to arrive, but when it did, it displaced and augmented local practices. As historian Akira Iriye observed, the "fundamental transnational drive . . . [is about] defining the culture of people living in an international society."[52] Guy Debord, in a critical vein, identified the emergence of spectacles such as sport carried by mass media as a fundamental mirror of social relationships: "The spectacle is not a collection of images; but a social relationship among people mediated by images."[53] Debord's seminal work on spectacle and spectatorship, along with Gramsci's notions of cultural hegemony, tended to pose spectators as nearly devoid of agency, as unwitting victims of imposed norms, as subjects devoid of critical thought. While recognizing that all social relationships occur in the context of unequal power relations, this study focuses on how thinking individuals created meaning out of the events, celebrities, and processes that inhabit the narrative. Those meanings were not preordained, but they did carry a similar valence across borders.

Prizefighting, as a transnational popular culture, provided a dramatic range of images often detached from the immediate and local but made meaningful within them. These images drew Cubans and Mexicans into a competitive transnational marketplace of ideas. Boxing could easily be added to the list of popular diversions identified by Vanessa Schwartz that gave fin de siècle cities such as Paris (and Havana and Mexico City) their self-consciously modern identities. Boxing matches in Cuba and Mexico came to symbolize modernity: "Their consumption became one of the means by which mass culture and a new urban crowd became a society of spectators."[54] Joining thousands of others as boxing fans in celebration of national and international heroes was simultaneously an act of cultural nationalism and cosmopolitanism. As historian Theresa Runstedtler contends, "boxing lay at the intersection of these modern developments . . . by the turn of the twentieth century Victorian notions of manliness . . . were beginning to fall by the wayside." The rise of modern spectator sport, and boxing in particular, facilitated these formulations transmitted by "the conspicuous consumption of mass-marketed commodities, and the public display of bodily strength."[55]

As anthropologist Matthew C. Gutmann observes, the study of masculinity, of "men as men," has received increasing scholarly attention over the past twenty years. He identifies four main conceptual trajectories. First, masculinity is anything that men thought, said, or did. Second, masculinity is anything that men thought, said, or did to distinguish themselves as men. Third, masculinity was understood as either inborn as a quality that some had more than others, or as a quality that could be achieved and increased. Fourth, many scholars have sought to emphasize the centrality of women, or ideas about femininity, in the construction of masculinity for most if not all men at most if not all points of their lives.[56]

This book illustrates how men self-defined as men. It argues that aspirations for showing and proving virility were molded by the ideas that circulated around prizefighting. As historians Víctor Macías-González and Anne Rubenstein observed, "Individuals learn to express their genders through interactions with other people, social institutions, and physical spaces. As societies and landscapes change over time, so do the constraints and parameters of gender. Gender is in constant flux, never static, always unstable."[57] Being masculine, or, more importantly, becoming masculine, was a primary function of being a sportsman. As historian George Mosse observed, the "steeling" of the male body through sport and physical culture became a crucial enunciation of male beauty and masculine virtue in the late nineteenth and early twentieth centuries.[58] Historian Gail Bederman, writing on the links between ideas of race, sport, and masculinity in the imperial context of the late nineteenth and twentieth centuries, shows convincingly that "turn-of-century manhood constructed bodily strength and social power as identical."[59] She argues that Jack Johnson's challenge to white masculinity generated a crisis that resulted in his infamy and legislation to discipline and contain his sexuality. His refusal to conform to established racial and gender norms became a leitmotif of the era, a particular conflict still current more than one hundred years later.[60] Black celebrity and representations of the black male body as both enviable and dangerous existed simultaneously, straddling the global color line.

In Mexico and Cuba by the 1920s, boxing celebrities from racial and economic underclasses successfully challenged the amorphous racial line. They became national icons despite the nearly uniform representations of most people of their class as servile, provincial, and lacking in respectable masculinity. These constructions of masculine national identity filled the pages of public documents such as newspapers and *revistas* (specialized reviews), which increasingly promoted athletics as modern behavior, attained knowledge, and entertainment. Within the public sphere, the *juventud dorada* (golden youth) defended their affinities to the older generation of intellectuals. Taking up the debate were such writers as José Sixto de Sola and Nicolás Guillén of Cuba, José Juan Tablada, Federico Gamboa, and Ireneo and Octavio Paz of Mexico. Many writers in the younger generation—Tablada and Guillén among them—befriended and admired journeyman African American athletes who made their homes in the rapidly modernizing capital cities.[61]

By the late 1920s, hero-athletes from the marginal classes forged a novel sort of celebrity in Cuba and Mexico. Images of their bodies and their popular biographies filled the public sphere. Critics of boxing had scorned its presence in Mexico and Cuba as an invasive annoyance; now the sport provided a stage for the performance of working-class masculinity. It was also, in theory and often in practice, a meritocratic means to engage and reconfigure the valences and meanings of cultural currents from abroad.

### Why Cuba and Mexico? Why Sport, Why Boxing?

Mexico and Cuba were among the first countries to directly experience growing US imperialism—military, economic, cultural—in the late eighteenth and early nineteenth centuries. The appropriations of US- and British-based popular cultures of sport in Latin America have been explored by a number of scholars since the 1980s as a part of the broader cultural and social turn.[62] Despite several groundbreaking studies by scholars such as Joseph Arbena and J. A. Mangan, we still need detailed case studies of local, national, and regional histories.[63] Though US power and influence would not eclipse European prominence in most of Latin America until after World War I, Cuba and Mexico underwent an onslaught of images, ideas, and practices carried by soldiers, tourists, businessmen, athletes, and other expatriates throughout the nineteenth century. They were the first sites in Latin America to host dozens of journeyman prizefighters and the first two nations to have direct telegraph and telephone links that carried news to and from the United States. The relative ease of travel to Cuba and Mexico also facilitated these intercultural transfers. This early cross-pollination had clear results in the field of prizefighting: Cuba and Mexico produced the first Latin American world boxing champions. Unlike other Latin American countries where boxing took root in this period, such as Argentina and Chile, Cuba and Mexico were under nearly constant threat of imperial expansion and violence from the United States, and this context helps explain the ambiguity and intensity of public debate. Though other important areas of US expansion and influence developed rich boxing cultures, few emerged before the 1930s.[64]

Boxing generated debate in Cuba and Mexico long before the introduction of any other modern sport.[65] In Mexico as early as 1806, social commentators presented their readers with accounts of English boxing as a barbaric and bizarre spectacle relegated to the vulgar public (*populacho*) and as a peculiarity of the British "race."[66] From the mid-nineteenth century onward, boxing (*el box, boxeo,* or *pugilato* as it was variously transliterated into Spanish) was one of the first truly global cultural/sport industries, and it was a site where diverse conceptions of a range of cultural ideas underwent divisive discussion and debate, revealing much about the manners in which Cubans and Mexicans gauged their capacities for assimilation and distinction amid increasingly visible cultural flows from abroad.[67]

International celebrities such as Jack Johnson, Jack Dempsey, George Carpentier, and Luis Ángel Firpo (all of whom staged tours in both Cuba and Mexico) enjoyed massive followings in Latin America. Print media presented them as superior embodiments of their respective nationalities, representing stereotyped images of the "bad nigger," "the self-made American," "the elegant Frenchman," and the "Argentine cowboy." Havana and Mexico City became home to dozens of civil-social clubs and organizations explicitly dedicated to prizefighting. The scale of membership and the spread of these types of voluntary organizations provide more insight into evolving ideas about the body, modernity, and the organization of citizens along the lines of common cultural affinities. These were not solely aristocratic groups like the famous Jockey Club in Mexico City or the Vedado Tennis Club in Havana.[68] Several of these upstart organizations represented a cross-section of social classes from dockworkers in the Cuban port to railroad workers and miners in the mountainous interior of Mexico. These clubs were an important locus of cross-cultural and interracial contact, as US, British, Australian, Japanese, Ottoman, German, Russian, and other foreign nationals worked alongside Mexicans and Cubans to incorporate their mutual interests into national repertoires of popular culture.

### A Note on Sources: Prizefighting in the Archives and Public Sphere

This study draws on traditional archival sources including petitions, legal decrees, court cases, patents, and permit applications from Mexico, Cuba, Spain, the United States, and Argentina. The conflicts that generated those documents reveal some of the legal and social barriers to boxing. But in most instances before the 1920s, boxing matches took place clandestinely or with extraordinary dispensations from local governments. They were improvisational. It was only when authorities were tipped to covert activities that prizefighting entered the archives. Writers in the most prolific public documents of the day produced the bulk of extant documentary sources: newspapers and revistas.

Two examples illustrate some of the complementarity of using these diverse documents in tandem with archival sources. While the events surrounding the foundation of a new social-athletic club might surface in a brief petition to the Mexico City or Havana *ayuntamientos* (city governments), most of the careful justifications for these actions are drawn from the concerted attempts to change the public perception of prizefighting written by club members, journalists, and other social commentators. These narratives, carefully toned and reasoned to appeal to politicians and bureaucrats, filled the growing coverage of sport from the end of the nineteenth century. The publication of images of shirtless local youths had an air of triumph, manliness achieved and yet still persecuted under outdated policies.

In another example, Mexican newspapers from 1905 to the mid-1920s carried dozens of articles on a mysterious Afro-descended individual named Jim "Black Diamond" Smith, who taught boxing and Japanese jujitsu to elite and middle-class Mexicans. He performed alongside Japanese martial artists before admiring crowds. Journalists touted him as a proponent of "manly science," and provocative images of him were reproduced in thousands of print pages in a period when such pictures were extremely rare. Writers identified him as Australian, Jamaican, South American, or American. It wasn't until his immigration, marriage, and death records surfaced in the Archivo General de la Nación in Mexico City that it became clear that he was a Dutch national, that he had entered Mexico through the United States, spoke Dutch, Spanish, and English, and had been born on the Dutch island of Sint Eustatius in the Caribbean. Beyond the establishment of his origin, Smith's importance for this study lies in the meanings that Mexicans gave to his presence and controversial profession in the period that spanned the late Porfiriato and the Mexican Revolution. After becoming a successful gym owner and entrepreneur, Smith married a Mexican woman, trained Mexican and foreign boxers, and lived the rest of his life in a relatively affluent neighborhood of Mexico City. Jim Smith's life is emblematic of the unexpected oppositions that drive this study.

As historian Pablo Piccato argues, this type of history must rely heavily on periodical and other media sources.[69] The digitization of millions of pages of newspapers and revistas in the past ten years has yielded enormous new datasets. As historian Isaac Campos illustrates in his study of the cultures of marijuana use and repression in nineteenth- and twentieth-century Mexico, the ability to search such massive troves enables historians to establish the contours of social practices often scattered across time and space. His analysis of Mexican print culture holds equally true for Cuba: after about 1880 newspapers were "characterized by modern publishing technology, yellow journalism, and a division between official, subsidized newspapers and independent papers of both liberal and conservative leaning."[70] Coverage of marijuana use, in general, portrayed its users as threatening denizens of the urban demimonde, the indigenous, soldiers, and slumming elites. Marijuana, like prizefighting, made good copy. The establishment of relative freedom of the press in Cuba during the 1880s likewise created expanded spaces for social and cultural commentary that added to the contraband Cuban exile press clandestinely imported and disseminated on the island.[71]

The use of these documents allows both a recreation of public discourse and an examination of the mundane and shifting boundaries of the public sphere. As Juan Carlos Portantiero has argued, the public sphere is "the locus for the autonomous organization of a self-managed or cooperative society."[72] Writers reflected and created democratic civil society in newspapers. All social groups did not obtain just or proportional representation. Campos clearly illustrates that the Mexican press's paranoid depiction of marijuana users was often a highly inventive interpretation of reality. What is important for his (and this) study is to explain how this consensus created meanings that led to political and social action and cultural change.

Benedict Anderson argued that writing and reading newspapers in the nineteenth century was an act of bourgeois self-definition.[73] But that generalization holds truer for early periods before the relative democratization of news coverage that, as a commercial enterprise, expanded and shaped a broader audience of readers. As with any documentary source, newspapers must be weighed, dissected, and contextualized in order to determine broader contextual meanings. As Piccato has shown, two processes were integral to the creation of the "bourgeois public sphere." First, print culture and literacy, dependent on consumers of information, had to be relatively stable. Second, "the emergence of spaces of social life, media, and themes of discussion . . . courts, salons, newspapers and cafes organized debates where public men and women used their taste to judge theater, literature," and so forth.[74] These two factors emerged in Cuba and Mexico during this period. The evolving public sphere bridged three areas of social life: the private and domestic realm, the public spaces necessary to exchange and debate opinion (media and civic social organizations), and those interventions by and rhetoric of government.

The majority of people residing in the capitals, Mexico City and Havana, in the early twentieth century were literate. By contemporary accounts, there were more than a hundred newspapers and other periodicals in Havana alone in 1900.[75] Literacy rates, however, varied widely across regions and between urban and rural settings. By 1910, Mexico City boasted over 50 percent literacy and the newspaper *El Imparcial* had a daily circulation of more than 100,000. Its price of one centavo put it easily within reach of working-class readers.[76] By 1940, the country as a whole was still only 43.2 percent literate and it wasn't until 1950 that literacy climbed over 50 percent.[77]

Cuba during the same period had higher literacy rates for both men and women. The period following the Cuban wars for independence (1895–98), especially the 1920s, saw a dramatic rise in literacy rates across the island.[78] By 1919, 61.6 percent of the population as a whole was literate, with that figure rising to over 71 percent by the latter part of the period under consideration.[79] Given the geography of literacy and the events that form the narrative subject matter of this book, it is largely a history of urban Mexico and Cuba, especially Mexico City and Havana.

Beginning in the late nineteenth century, urban intellectuals (*letrados*) incorporated transnational popular cultures into their writings. As Ángel Rama posits, by the twentieth century "the lettered city had itself been transformed . . . from a handful of elite letrados designing government policies in their own image, into a socially more heterogeneous group that retained a vision of itself as a cultural aristocracy but incorporated powerful democratizing cross-currents."[80] This generalization holds true for the popular press.

### How the Narrative Unfolds

Chapter 2, "Prizefighting and Civilization in the Mexican Public Sphere in the Nineteenth Century," argues that Mexican writers and social critics sought to portray the nation as virile and progressive through their carefully calibrated celebration or rejection of boxing in the mid- to late nineteenth century. They compared themselves to other "civilized" nations before, during, and after the Mexican Revolution and evoked boxing alongside other barbarous aspects of US culture that should be rejected or carefully controlled. This tumultuous era saw boxing outlawed and legalized several times as local power changed hands and national policy vacillated between xenophobia and xenophilia. This chapter examines the petitions of intellectuals, social clubs, and entrepreneurs who sought to influence policy on public entertainment and the meanings they attributed to growing US power and presence in Mexico. They often argued their positions in the language of positive eugenics and national regeneration that drew heavily from positivist intellectual currents that pervaded Mexican society during the Porfirian and Revolutionary periods (1876–1920). This section also unearths and examines the transnational journeys of racially marginalized prizefighters such as Billy Clarke, Jim Smith, and Kid Mitchell (African American, Afro-Dutch, and African Mexican American, respectively) as they sought to profit by and implant boxing in Mexico.

Chapter 2 is followed by a photo and image essay that reproduces the many ways in which photographers, artists, and advertisers represented boxing and boxers in the public sphere. Chapter 3, "'Who Will Say We Are Not Progressing?': Cuba, Race, and Boxing in the Nineteenth and Early Twentieth Centuries," moves to the streets, clubs, and theaters of Havana. It begins with the first boxing matches in traveling circuses in the 1840s and culminates with the controversy over Jack Johnson. This chapter also examines the legal and cultural debates that coalesced around the earliest professional prizefights in Cuba (1910). Cubans were divided over the role that modern sport, with its racial, gendered, and national inflections, should play within their rapidly changing postcolonial and neocolonial society. Boxing's transnational reach and the high degree of mobility of boxers presented Cubans with a problematic decision: How would Cubans define the culture of the new republic (1902–1959) amid growing American influence?

Chapter 4, "'Nigger Prizefighters' in Havana: The Transnational Spectacle of Race and Boxing," focuses on the global and local significance of the 1915 heavyweight championship bout between Jack Johnson and Jess Willard. The fight took place in a suburb of Havana and was a proxy race war in the context of World War I. In Cuba, the bout focused attention on the importation of US racial norms and formed an important moment revealing a range of Cuban responses to growing US influence.

Chapter 5, "The Revolution Came and Passed Out Gloves to Everyone," examines the rise of the first Mexican boxing celebrities in the 1920s and 1930s. These popular icons spawned a cultural industry in film and print that celebrated working-class men as paragons of Mexican cultural values and masculinity. Chapter 6, "Marching at the Head of Civilization," returns to Cuba and examines the legalization and regulation of boxing on the island. It focuses on the shifting racial, gendered, and nationalist language deployed to celebrate the rise of Cuban boxers to international prominence in the 1920s and 30s. It traces how the once exotic was nationalized and became a part of everyday expressions of *lo cubano* amid the intellectual and artistic re-evaluation of Afro-Cuban life known as afrocubanismo.

## Conclusions

This study began by seeking to contextualize individuals and processes that did not fit easily into the existing historiography in Mexico and Cuba: the sons of slaves who became world traveling athletes and masculine symbols, Japanese professors of physical culture and jujitsu who circulated at the highest level of government, Cubans from the slums of Havana who became controversial national icons and traded boxing lessons for French classes in fin de siècle Paris, Mexicans from the barrio bravo of Tepito who defended "national honor" in arenas in the United States, all of this forming a part of an early strain of cultural globalization. By fleshing out some of the concrete manifestations situated at the margins of such abstract ideas as race, nation, and gender, this book contributes to our understanding of the cultural perceptions and social realities during this period of decolonization, revolution, and democratization.

CHAPTER TWO

# Prizefighting and Civilization in the Mexican Public Sphere in the Nineteenth Century

THE INTRODUCTION OF interracial prizefighting in the late nineteenth century challenged notions of civilization, gender, and cultural sovereignty during a formative moment in the development of the Mexican public sphere.[1] Positivist modernizers during the rule of Porfirio Díaz (1876–1911) sought to import foreign ideas, technologies, and cultural practices to remedy what they perceived as backwardness and underdevelopment. Despite this preference for foreign novelty, labeled by historian William Beezley as the "Porfirian Persuasion," critics infused this particular public spectacle with meanings that mirrored local anxieties over increasing American influence.[2] Many observers designated pugilism as a barbaric practice of the Anglo-Saxon "race" and its rejection a point of resistance to Euro-American modernity.

The dramatic discourses contained in these critiques in the 1890s exposed fear among the elites that their role as the arbiters of modernization was under challenge, both by exotic cultural imports and from a growing diversity of cross-class affinities in urban areas such as Mexico City. The popular classes, many Porfirians reasoned, were already barbarous enough that they needed protection from the detritus of American and British lowbrow culture: two men pummeling each other for money in a front of a crowd. They feared that spectatorship would spread violence as entertainment and reverse progress toward their ideal of an ordered and peaceful urban life. The celebrity of lower-class American boxers challenged ideas of bourgeois masculinity as sedate, controlled, sober, and nonviolent. Public approbation of racially diverse entertainers was the antithesis of their attempts to inculcate these precepts of manhood among the *pelados* (working-class men), whom they viewed as inherently disordered, drunken, and prone to violence.[3] Critics called for legal injunctions and the denial of permits to hold bouts. From editorial columns they sought to mold public opinion about boxing, labeling it as a contagion. Not only did they advocate censorship of public spectacle, they ridiculed American detractors who asserted that traditional practices such as bullfighting were evidence of Mexican atavism.

The elite of the 1890s, however, allowed and encouraged pugilism among their class in carefully controlled and exclusive venues. They prohibited participation by and attendance of the masses, however, in prizefighting. This was the context of an interracial boxing match in the 1890s. It explains why such an unusual event generated such controversy and defensive nationalistic reaction. Illegal boxing matches challenged the ability of the government to regulate public spectacle, and they undermined the elite's prerogative to define permissible behaviors. Ambiguous rules governing unusual genres of entertainment created confusion among civil functionaries as they applied their ideas of sophistication to the constantly changing tastes of the public.[4] Some politicians defied the explicit orders of Porfirio Díaz and allowed boxing matches in bullrings and theaters. Such individuals received public shaming by the press.

Those who opposed prizefighting wrote outraged satires in defensive nationalist terms. The illustrator José Guadalupe Posada sketched boxing matches as dangerously exotic, barbaric, and ill-fitting Mexican temperaments.[5] The interracial nature of these spectacles created outrage that resulted in public calls for the deportation of African American journeyman fighter Billy A. Clarke based on Article 33 of the 1857 Mexican Constitution, which permitted the removal of "pernicious foreigners."[6] Though several Americans, such as James Carroll, paralleled the attempts of Clarke to implant pugilism in this period, there were no calls for their expulsion. Compared with post-Revolutionary deportations of foreigners, the Porfirian era saw few expulsions, and most occurred in cases of political and religious challenges to sovereignty. Coverage of Clarke in the dailies focused on his public scandals and his marriage to a Mexican woman from the better classes. Detractors saw Clarke as a doubly pernicious challenge: he was a member of a racial underclass from the United States and he publicly undermined attempts to control exhibitions of his muscular body and his profession.

## The Porfirian Press and the Public Sphere

Media attention to pugilism surged in the late nineteenth century due to three factors. First, the Pax Porfiriana led to a new predictability in daily life that translated into a more vibrant, varied, and complex public sphere.[7] After sixty years of chronic instability, foreign occupation, and the amputation of half of Mexico's territory, the Porfirian Era represented relative stability and peace.

Drawing on the ideas of Jürgen Habermas, historian Pablo Piccato argues that this newly invigorated locus of public deliberation, driven by the daily press, was a shared space of debate and arbitration of opinion that mirrored, created, and disseminated ideas of modernity. Recently, several studies of the public sphere in the late Porfirian era draw attention to the mainstream and "penny press," as mediators of class-based definitions of honor, masculinity, and citizenship. Historian Robert Buffington argues that writers in newspapers such as *El Imparcial* and *El País* saw themselves as definers of decency.[8] Doña Carmen, wife of the dictator Porfirio Díaz, accepted the honorary presidency of the American-organized Society for the Prevention of Cruelty to Animals, even though that civic social group inveighed against the bullfights that she and her sisters attended.[9] These and other instances call for a re-evaluation of the complexity and contingency of the public sphere that places defensive cultural nationalism alongside and often in opposition to Anglophile preferences.

Secondly, Porfirian policies led to important advances in transportation and communication from the 1870s onward.[10] Newspapers were cheaper to produce and purchase. Railroad construction eased the difficulty of travel. This facilitated a dramatic surge in US travel to Mexico City.[11] Writers often criticized the growing pluralism of cultural life in the capital, where news reached a population that was overwhelming literate and that consumed dozens of newspapers and specialized revistas (weekly and monthly magazines).[12]

The third factor that explains the timing of these novel encounters was the quantitative increase of all media and qualitative changes in subject matter in international coverage available to Mexican readers. Narratives of illegal and controversial boxing matches in the United States and elsewhere surfaced increasingly in the largest daily newspapers and revistas. There was a dramatic expansion of the popular press as a vehicle for and a focal point of public opinion across Latin America in the late nineteenth century.[13] Newspaper writing was central to the development of political and cultural consensus. The largest dailies in Mexico accepted patronage and de facto editorial guidance from the national government, but disputes about certain cultural practices were allowed space for dissent and challenge. Pugilism fit well within the sensationalization of daily life, with lurid details of crime and the dangers of city life. Mexican readers were aware of the notoriety of working-class Americans, such as the boxer John L. Sullivan, as symbols of masculinity in the United States.

Critiques of boxing were not unique to the Porfiriato. During the late colonial era, polemicists argued that pugilism was either a disgraceful and uncivilized practice of the rabble (populacho) in England or a positive attribute for the Darwinian competitiveness of nationalized masculine bodies. English soldiers, many writers argued, dominated warfare partly because of the martial nature of their peculiar quotidian culture. The transfer of boxing's commercialized center to the United States in the late nineteenth century only increased the proximity of this threat to Mexico.[14] Prizefighting was still illegal in most of the United States in the late nineteenth and early twentieth centuries, and its reputation as an illicit pursuit can be traced in part to this legal prohibition. Boxers and their admirers openly flouted these laws, and the demimonde nature of their tastes was evoked in the Mexican public sphere.[15] Many argued that this fact alone was reason to prevent the practice in Mexico. Some cited it as proof that the United States should not be viewed as worthy of emulation. Racism and lynching became popular counterpoints in a press that admonished against the adaptation of Yankee values: "Some Mexicans ... guided by the spirit of imitation, have established boxing.... We'll see when it awakens in them the desire to lynch a fellow human being."[16] These musings show ambivalence surrounding the evolution of urban modernity and, ultimately, the inability of the Porfirian government to control the multiple challenges emanating from abroad.

### The Roots of Mexican Engagement with *El Pugilato* in the Nineteenth Century

For most of the nineteenth century, commentary on pugilism in Mexico manifested in press accounts of the exotic in England and the United States. As European immigration saturated the United States and Latin America, boxing flourished in saloons and rural areas, away from the control of government, and thriving on the public's fascination with violence, ethnic nationalism(s), and displays of masculinity.

As early as 1806, writers cited pugilism as evidence of Anglo-Saxon barbarism.[17] These critiques illustrated the peculiar, "modern" (yet simultaneously barbarous) tastes of Americans and Europeans.[18] Foreign observers of Mexico were hypocritical: not only did they flock to bullfights, they allowed bloody contests between rational beings. The discourses on pugilism, and the use of the term "pugilato," and neologisms such as "el box," "ring," "round," and "second," appeared increasingly throughout the nineteenth century.[19]

For some, the practice held the potential to help civilize the rabble by supplying a benign forum to settle disputes. Instead of inebriated peons drawing knives to kill an enemy, Englishmen, an 1848 almanac writer mused, used pugilism to transform emotion into "regulated scientific principles" of self-defense. A further novelty was that both the high (nobility) and low classes (populacho) participated in boxing as a locus for honor and masculinity.[20] The writer's surprise at the cross-class nature of such spectacles evoked further hesitation for a local elite focused on strict segregation by class. Mexican spectacles, such as bullfighting, featured segregation by economic class reflected in varying ticket prices for seats in the shade (expensive) and seats in the sun (economical). The masses were supposed to learn from their social betters while simultaneously remaining spatially and socially segregated.[21]

In May of 1887, police intervened to prevent a boxing match in the town of Huizachal (outside of Mexico City) between "two foreigners" that promised to draw a large crowd.[22] The match was planned for Mexico City but was moved to the neighboring town, a few miles west of the city limits. Matches such as this were forced underground or carefully staged in private, members-only clubs. Satirizing the event, the liberal writer Juvenal (Enrique Chávarri) praised the "humane, poetic, sensible, and romantic" police for stopping the match. They did so, Juvenal opined, while still allowing even children to take part in bullfights. Francisco González echoed Juvenal, pairing the fascination with boxing and other "barbarous spectacles" that were "invading all of [their] social classes" with the general cultural decadence that gave rise to such mass entertainments.[23] The lifestyle that surrounded pugilism also contributed to what González identified as "clandestine prostitution," or sex out of wedlock, which "steals peace from honorable families," takes the most "precious jewel" from women, "robs men of their virility," and is the greatest "cancer" on Mexican society.[24]

*La Voz de México*, a conservative daily, seconded González and Chávarri against the Mexican appropriation of prizefighting. In addition to being "barbaric," "homicidal," "bestial," and "grotesque," the Anglo diversion, while suited to their "robust" bodies, would injure fragile Mexican men, who on the whole had "no robustness."[25] Tropical climates, the author posited, were not suited to this type of sport. It was inconceivable that the Mexico City government would permit such a spectacle to take place. Underground boxing matches and the stealth with which they were organized and carried out amazed one columnist writing for *El Monitor Republicano* in June of 1892.[26] The popularity of this new "genre of diversion" was growing despite its "repugnance." Even though there were few announcements and no public advertisement, the seats in the Teatro de Invierno were filled, mostly with members of the "*Colonia norte-americana.*"

Despite a nearly uniform disdain for pugilism in the press, boxing was permitted among the elite in venues under their control. On December 1, 1894, President Díaz and his secretary of state, Romero Rubio, attended an athletic exhibition at the YMCA on San Juan Letrán Street.[27] Díaz, as was "well known," was a proponent of "exercises of muscular force."[28] The atmosphere surrounding the event was markedly cosmopolitan. In addition to Japanese parasols, the gymnasium was decorated with French and British flags while the Mexican and American colors were displayed interlaced as "proof of the confraternity that exists." The presence of numerous women enhanced the propriety of the event. The president of the republic presided over an audience of the "best families" on a raised platform.

President Díaz ordered that on this occasion, a boxing match between the instructors Emilio Lobato and Ángel Escudero was legal.[29] Elite families in the presence of the president did not constitute a risk to morals or an increase in barbarism as feared by Díaz on other occasions. The authorities allowed boxing in the highest levels of civil society; spectatorship was laudable, as boxing exhibitions took place at retreats such as the exclusive Lakeside Club.[30] The most prestigious preparatory school in the nation, the Escuela Nacional Preparatoria, proudly advertised that it offered classes in boxing and military exercises, giving "the greatest guarantee [of success]" for fathers who considered enrolling their children.[31]

The pugilistic exhibitions at the YMCA and the inclusion of boxing in the curriculum of the most elite preparatory schools represented a cosmopolitan embrace of novel ideas about the vigorous male body, physicality, and its centrality for exhibitions of national virility and aspirations for the behavioral trappings of modernity.[32] One of the boxers who took part in the boxing exhibition approved by Díaz, Emilio Lobato, was a proponent of physical culture who supported new ideas about the body and its development for the good of the Mexican race.

Díaz endorsed the ideas of Lobato by allowing him both to stage otherwise prohibited pugilistic exercises for select audiences and to play an integral role in the preparation and indoctrination of the juventud dorada (the golden youth).[33] Lobato was an astute political operator and one of the founding members of the "Porfirio Díaz Central Circle of Mexican Gymnastics" in 1890.[34] This private club was dedicated to "modern teaching" of body culture and depended on Díaz's patronage. Lobato was later assigned the post of professor of gymnastics at the Colegio Militar located on the grounds of the Presidential Palace.[35] Lobato wrote about the "modern science" of gymnastics in Lombrosian and positivist terms. He argued that the new practices of physical culture were fundamentally important to the "regeneration and enhancement of [our] race."[36] Acceptance of these norms of behavior would be a boon to the "the individual, the family, and the state."[37]

The generation formed by the Escuela Nacional Preparatoria and the Colegio Militar, youths destined to continue the Porfirian project, would perform physical culture in well-ordered classes where they would chant in unison the mantras, "moral and military," that "grew the soul of man" and propelled him toward the realization of virtues such as heroism, charity, and philanthropy. Creating muscular bodies would yield "mature fruits of virility." Thus developed, bodies would benefit the nation. Lobato reasoned, "We are in an epoch of transition between the routine, ancient principles [of bodily development] and modern, clear and irresistible dogmas. In México, pedagogical science is evolving actively to acquire the *forms that are presented in the most advanced countries.*"[38]

Scientific corporeal training would alleviate defects that leached the vitality of the Mexican national body: "it will notably reduce the number of rachitic and sickly individuals (*raquíticos y enfermos*) and also the number of the insane and idiots (*locos e idiotas*)." The excessive urbanization that "subjugated" the brain was to be moderated by physical exercise, yielding "grace and beauty to the two sexes, making them strong, at the same time, against all classes of struggle and privations that often the human race suffers." Lobato's influence on the teaching of body culture was long-standing. Even after the beginning of the Revolution in 1910, he taught educators from around Mexico on boxing and physical culture in primary and secondary schools.[39]

## Billy Clarke, Boxing, and Race

The first public prizefight in Mexico to generate substantial public attention and critical examination took place in 1895. Cultural nationalists in the press were outraged at this egregious violation of Mexican sovereignty. One of the boxers, Billy Clarke, posed an unusual threat to public decency: he was African American, his muscular body was admired by his Mexican fans, and he courted and married a young Mexican woman. He advertised his services as a boxing professor in the *Mexican Sportsman*, the first serial publication dedicated to modern spectator sport in Mexico. Clarke was an ambiguous standard bearer for the publishers of the *Sportsman*, which sought to "preach the gospel" of sport in Mexico; his risqué life outside the ring provided constant fodder for the press.[40] He had boxed and taught boxing in Guatemala and had likely arrived there to work on railroad construction projects.[41] In Mexico, he gave lessons starting in early 1895 from his "Olympic Club of Mexico," located one block from the zócalo. Advertising "scientific exhibitions" (no money would change hands), Clarke was, for a time, able to avoid needing permits from the local ayuntamiento. More than an attempt to gain clients for his gym, he was testing the waters for staging prizefights in Mexico.[42]

Later in 1895, while American promoters searched for a place on the US-Mexico border to hold an illegal boxing match for the world heavyweight championship, two boxers shocked the public by holding a prizefight fifty miles north of Mexico

City. Though Díaz dispatched troops to prevent the Maher-Fitzsimmons bout from crossing the Río Bravo (Grande), another bout, interracial and "barbaric," took place less than a two-hour train ride from the metropolis. The enraged reactions in the Mexican press illustrate the public sphere's rejection of the barbaric imposition of foreign pastimes.

James F. "Jimmy" Carroll, the former light-heavyweight champion of the world, opened a second boxing academy in Mexico City in early 1895. Carroll was an internationally recognized boxer and established himself in Mexico in an effort to extend the lucrative trade that had flourished along the Mexican-American border but which had become increasingly difficult due to the crusade of Texas governor Charles Culberson against prizefighting. Carroll sought to legalize boxing in Mexico by appealing directly to patriotic and "virile" sentiments.[43] In early 1895, he petitioned the Mexico City Ayuntamiento to hold boxing exhibitions at any theater in the city.[44]

His petition to hold a match in any theater showed his frustration with the intransigence of the Mexico City government. As the manager of the National Athletic Club ("The only place to attain health and strength in Mexico" and a competitor for Billy Clarke), he promised to introduce the Mexican public to "this essentially manly, useful and hygienic class of exercises that contribute to muscular development."[45] He offered members of the city government a private showing to convince them of the benefits of his instruction. His attempts to overturn these prohibitions were followed attentively in the press.[46] Failing to gain the blessing of the city government on the merits of pugilism (and the taxes to be paid on gate receipts), Carroll ventured to the state of Hidalgo, north of Mexico City, where he found the governor, General Rafael Cravioto, willing to grant the concession. Likely induced by both tax revenue for the fight and hoping to satiate the large foreign mining interests in Hidalgo, Cravioto also insisted that the bout would teach Mexicans how to settle disputes in a civilized manner, without the use of weapons.[47]

On the morning of November 25, 1895, an express train of the Hidalgo Railroad left Mexico City with six special wagons carrying hundreds of spectators from Mexico City to the bullring in Pachuca to attend the boxing match between Billy Clarke (the "Colored Champion of Central America") and the white Englishman Billy Smith ("Champion of Texas").[48] For two months, the boxing promoter, Jimmy Carroll, had assured the public they would be able to see a clean and scientific match in Mexico, and it appeared he was finally making good on his promise.[49]

"Reporters" (the English-language term used to denote a new type of journalistic coverage) for all the major Mexico City dailies scrambled to attend the bout. One observer was captivated and astonished by the atmosphere on the train. He mused about such individual combats throughout history. Boxing was descended from medieval tournaments, duels, and "patriotic warfare." But it shared none of the virtues of these pursuits. Boxers labored for the sum of two or three thousand pesos instead of the exaltation of honor, the saints, family, or country.[50] The din on the train was full of neologisms to describe rules, regulations, and "academic" boxing. The extraordinary levels of enthusiasm and the drama anticipated for such a bloody and barbaric spectacle both disturbed and intrigued reporters.

The columnist was also alarmed by what he understood as an unhealthy decline in the quality of legitimate public entertainments. The resulting invigoration of the lower classes that this type of match encouraged created angst. Among the traditional and nobler pursuits of comedy, music, work, and science, there was little chance of encountering the "sensations of the epoch: drinking much, and yelling even more with eyes injected with drunkenness and violence, attending the agony of a man between the bull's horns or under the knees of a fellow rational being; all this being a bit less barbarous than the public that applauds its triumph." The drunken, barbarized masses freely imbibing of ritualized violence should be feared.

At stake here was more than erosion in the standards of public spectacle. Though the columnist argued that bullfighters had long been celebrated as the glory of "the race," the current levels of celebrity were shameful. Bullfights had become excuses to drink, yell, and cause public scandal. The author reacted to a perceived shift in the cultural consensus, and he bemoaned decadence and Americanization. Pugilism, much more than baseball or other foreign athletic imports, retained a hint of "tawdriness," danger, and an association with what one author has called "underworld flavor."[51]

Mexican observers were horrified at the beating "el negro Clark [sic]" received.[52] It left him unconscious and bloodied. While his opponent was carried off on the shoulders of several intoxicated fans, Clarke was transported to the infirmary. There Clarke met and later became engaged to a "local lass" from the town of Teoloyucan, near Pachuca.[53] The posters used to advertise the match, which exhibited the boxer's muscular body, had supposedly enamored the innocent young woman. She was attracted to the "burly and sinewy form of the colored pugilist." Clarke admitted that he was not thrilled at the prospect of converting to Catholicism, but he acquiesced because his future bride's family demanded it. After the wedding he hoped to honeymoon in his hometown of Philadelphia.[54]

After the bout, Clarke visited the offices of several Mexico City newspapers and alleged that Smith had imbibed illegal substances that gave him an advantage in the contest and that his seconds had unfairly intervened in his favor. A rumor later circulated on the streets that Clarke had accused Smith to his face and that both men then drew pistols in public and had to be separated by those around them.[55] These "scandals" contributed to the outrage in the Mexican press.

Porfirio Díaz, angered that the mayor of Pachuca, Trinidad Vázquez, and the governor, General Cravioto, had not intervened to prohibit the bout, wrote a letter berating them for allowing such "a spectacle that signifies a great attack on civilization."[56] Editorialists for *El Globo* and *La Voz de México* lauded this action by the president (the private letter had been leaked to the press), stressing that "we celebrate the clear and energetic attitude with which the executive of the union is against the unsuitable spectacle of pugilism these days in a country that calls itself civilized."[57] Díaz would again pronounce his judgment that boxing in Mexico threatened the civilization he had helped bring to the country. A few months later, he instructed the governor of Chihuahua to prevent a boxing match from taking place there; it would be an "attack on civilization."[58]

Echoing editorial disdain, a cartoon by the artist José Guadalupe Posada appeared shortly after the match in Pachuca.[59] It mirrored the outraged press reactions and portrayed a Porfirian man, likely the governor of Hidalgo who had controversially permitted the bout, delivering a knockout punch to a stock racist depiction of Clarke. The body of the African American boxer, in apparent irony, is emblazoned with the word "civilization." In a mocking double entendre, the cartoon Clarke exclaims "Me moro," likely belittling his imperfect Spanish and referring to his dark skin as "Moorish."[60] Curiously absent is the recognition that most of the Porfirian press understood boxing as the worst aspect of an invasive "Anglo-Saxon" culture. Billy Clarke certainly did not fit the racial aspects of that amorphous definition.

Under the title "This Week's Savagery," *El Mundo* shamed the public with a description of what the editorialists deemed the combination of national vices with imported barbaric behavior. While it had taken decades and even centuries for Mexicans to discover basic hygiene and how to use an oven instead of an open fire in the kitchen, Mexicans still clamored to see "the pornographic exhibitions of Lilly Clay, and the imbecilic fight of rational versus irrational beings, and of two human entities [fighting each other] in the bullring."[61] He continued: "It seems incredible that in a civilized country such repugnant spectacles are permitted."[62] Mexicans held ideological double standards. While they fulminated against the practice of lynching *"aplicada a los negros"* (applied to Negroes) and cried out against the savage practices of "errant tribes," or of whipping petty thieves (*rateros*), they applauded when a bull disemboweled a man or when "a *macho* of our species smashes the skull of another of us in the a bullring."[63] Boxing was no better than dueling and all of the thousands that attended the match were guilty of violating the law.[64] *La Voz de México* seconded the judgment:

> What we should be talking about is decadence in our customs ... you will see how the chronicles, today frivolous and adulating in the newspapers, will not talk about these scandalous matters; but only of intense emotions, of enthusiasm for the struggle for life, of combat with the elements of nature and not against brothers; of industrial and mercantile contests and not for those wandering women who go in search for customers; of the learned who win prizes and not of geniuses who go to prison; of women who give sons to the patria and not of shameless ones that dishonor it, of scientific inventions and not of robberies, of heroic acts and not of vile murders, of applause for intelligence and not of ovations for brute force.[65]

After the Pachuca bout, critics monitored Billy Clarke and labeled him a public nuisance, but they ignored white boxers in Mexico City. Though he married Manuela Barron and began to establish a social support network in Mexico City, he was involved in a number of minor legal disputes involving nonpayment of debts.[66] In one instance, police dispatched to bring the boxer to testify noted with surprise that Barron lived in his home, but she denied knowing his current whereabouts.[67] Clarke sought to defend his honor in public. On one occasion he stopped his bicycle ride to question why men on the street were mocking him. This attempt to defend his reputation landed him in Belém Prison. The subsequent interview with his wife impressed the journalist, who was amazed that such a respectable woman "evidently loves her husband."[68] The governor of the Federal District of Mexico, who envisioned such detentions as part of the "first oven of moral disinfection," made the persecution of Clarke a focal point, invoking his potential expulsion from the country under Article 33 of the constitution.[69]

Despite public outcry against him, Clarke sought to circumvent norms on various types of public spectacle. Between 1895 and 1900 he traveled to dozens of cities and towns throughout the country. He became a focus of ridicule and derision, a brainless *negro* who represented the hubris and the imbecility of such entertainments. He fought bears and lions, performed feats of strength on stage, and wrestled other performers in bullrings. *El Contemporaneo*, a daily published in San Luis Potosí, suggested that Clarke's public exhibitions of strength were really more pornographic than scientific. The writer ironically observed that it was "a great show, seeing this black Adam *zapote*."[70] Reporters covered any news generated around Clarke, the more comical and ironic the better, such as when he was hit by a carriage while riding a bike near his residence in the center of Mexico City.[71] After a failed attempt to wrestle a bull in Toluca in 1897, indigenous market women capitalized on Clarke's fiasco. They made clay effigies that depicted him desperately clinging to a bull's tail. These astute businesswomen positioned themselves at the door of the Iturbide Hotel—the former mansion of the first Mexican emperor—where Jimmy Carroll managed the bar. They likely chose this location because of its US American clientele, where "everyone who passed . . . stopped and had a laugh, for he recognized at once the design."[72] These dolls were sold a few blocks from Billy Clarke's house, two days after the sudden death of his infant daughter. He likely saw them on his morning walks around downtown.

As an African American, Clarke had few defenders in the public sphere. White Americans and other foreigners who staged similar performances received at worst a light upbraiding from the press. A writer for *El Popular*, the satirical newspaper directed by Francisco Montes de Oca, was enraged at the prospect of Clarke's continued presence in the country. The editorialist taunted the police for their inability to end Clarke's offenses to public morals. Clarke's clandestine boxing matches were an open secret and an assault on decency. Repeated attempts to imprison him for months at a time in the Belém Prison had failed due to the boxer's ability to pay what Montes de Oca deemed a nominal fine.[73]

In late 1896, Clarke staged a series of matches in his home and in other secret locations without a license from the city government.[74] His opponent in these bouts was another African American, Benny Chapman. Police arrested Clark and Chapman and brought them in front of a judge.[75] Clarke was charged with assault and sentenced to thirty days in jail. Chapman, since he had lost the bout and been injured much worse than had Clarke, was considered the victim of the crime and was freed without penalty. Theo Eggers, a US American who had arranged illegal prizefights in the New Mexico territory, was also jailed for promoting the bout. Surprisingly, Oscar Braniff, a banker and the brother of one of the most important Mexican industrialists, was also jailed for fifteen days for helping to arrange the match.[76] Those in attendance were dismissed with a warning, but had to promise they would inform the authorities if they had knowledge of any similar illegal spectacles in the future. A writer for *La Voz de México* hoped that these sentences would teach the *negros* a lesson: those who outraged social norms would be punished. The English-language press also relished being outraged by Clarke; they ridiculed the lavish receptions he staged in his home. They mocked his flamboyant dress, expensive tastes, and his accent.[77] Yet some Mexican advertisers appropriated his image as a "strong and robust man." *La Flor de Cuba*, a cigarette brand, claimed that Billy Clarke only smoked its products and that he "knew how to live."[78]

Clarke ignored judicial injunctions. He organized secret boxing matches, placing bets and charging admission, fighting other black fighters in his home, blocks from the national palace. Angry writers called Clarke an animal.[79] In February of 1897, newspapers called for his expulsion from national territory. Critics argued that his actions were a blatant attack on law and order, the hallmark of Porfirian accomplishments. His continued presence in the capital was an example of the weakness of Mexican institutions and their inability to confront "barbarous and repugnant" foreigners who impudently tried to change the "manners and customs of the country" (*los modos y costumbres del pais*). Repeating the oft-expounded argument, it showed a "disdain for the civilization and the culture of all people."[80]

The polemics against boxing in general and Clarke in particular indicate the public reaction of the late Porfirian press when encountering both rapid urbanization and the concomitant democratization of public spaces and entertainments. Such events created obstacles to the flow of bureaucratic authority. A boxing exhibition in front of the president was one thing, but the drunken masses' celebration of violence was not to be tolerated. These disturbing trends were impelled by irresponsible newspaper coverage that lauded an "apotheosis" of brute force over the intellect.[81]

Mexicans, the columnist continued, already enjoyed cockfighting, bullfighting, and duels, the characteristic activities of what the author called *"nuestra raza"* (our race). To these cultural markers were added baseball, horse racing, and other pursuits from the "saxon race." Mexican men were lacking in knowledge of pugilism, and yet they still blindly craved it. The recent public disorders (near riots) in the bullrings worried many, convincing those who purportedly controlled public discourse that the popular masses were too full of themselves. The increasing incidents of public disorder and violence would lead to the end of bullfighting and the "elevation of '*box americano*' to the throne of popular admiration." The writer insinuated that modern sport was better organized and less chaotic than its more traditional and more Mexican counterpart. But "It was not possible, in only one country, to unite all of the entertainments of the globe. Our *civilización sportica* is not up to it, pardon the neologism."[82] The author added a hint of irony. He explained that when commenting on an interracial bout, mentioning a black *before* a white would be a crime according to the "perverted Yankee civilization." He ended with a further broadside against those who attended the match in Pachuca:

"Neither the sacrifice of the martyrs and the combats of the slaves for the ancients; nor the tournaments of the middle ages, nor duels, nor anything, can be comparable to this diversion, according to the elegant youths of today." In tandem with a generational shift marked by a growing affinity for prizefighting, a reaction was peaking against affinities for imported leisure, fast living, and a taste for dangerous pastimes among Mexican youths. Scant progress took place in the realm of culture, and the youth traded the backward behaviors of the past for more modern forms of barbarity:

> It shames us to admit that we are civilized. We contradict this when in the middle of the day amid a crowd drunk with savage emotions, two men—better yet two beasts—degenerated by their idiocy, two cretins that have no worldliness other than the purely physical and their herculean claws, go forth in the middle of a circus and there, almost naked, trade blows that swell the face, redden their jaws and threaten to destroy, annihilate and turn to ashes those muscles weakened by the fight and most times are covered in the blood that flows from their wounds.[83]

Such spectacles in Mexico were particularly dangerous for public morals because the mass of Mexicans had not reached that cultural level enjoyed by Europeans. They were apt to lose even "common sense." More than entertainment, the result of such public savagery was that Mexican culture lay "in the sand" alongside the fallen boxer, and the public enthusiasm was proof of Mexican inhumanity.

Other intellectuals commented on the public uproar caused by the Billy Clarke match. On December 16, 1895, two weeks after the bout, Federico Gamboa, the Mexican modernist writer and diplomat, entered his thoughts on the boxing match in Pachuca in his diary:

> After having attended—what a shame!—the pugilistic fight which, twenty days ago reached a horrible end—between a yankee negro, Billy Clark, and a white Irishman, Billy Smith, I went tonight to the Club Atlético de México, where the very same Billy Clark gives practice lessons on boxing. It's a ferocious thing, this science of the fists, and learning it demands that they slap you in the face! I'll probably never learn it.[84]

Echoing Gamboa, another prominent critic, Ireneo Paz—novelist, journalist, politician—editorialized on the front page of his newspaper *La Patria*:

> A bull rolling around in his blood, wounded by a matador's rapier and a

horse dragging its intestines through the sand, like a cock with its jugular cut by a spur. The same we'll say about pugilism. Two men of crude appearance, in whose countenance there is not even a hint of intelligence, punch each other for two hours—blows capable of demolishing a bull, fall in turn to the ground, covered in blood, faces inflamed, eyes bursting with the blows they have suffered, with a broken rib, and both retire to spend long days in bed, before finding themselves well enough to go back out onto the street to receive the ovations that are offered them in the taverns.[85]

Another anonymous observer present at the Clarke fight further reacted to the importation of prizefight films from the United States into Mexico. This piece is worthy of a lengthy quotation, as it is exemplary of the debates, evoking concrete and abstract ideas of civilization, between perceptions of barbarism and cultural perceptions that emerged around the seemingly isolated prizefight:

All of the Anglo Saxon race is impassioned by and adept at sport and boxing; and one can measure the distance between two races comparing their favorite diversions. Bull fighting is elegant, aesthetic, and focuses on the almost intangible movement of the bullfighter, like a dance. Boxing is no more than a hammer and an anvil. It is devoid of aesthetics. The movements of the boxers are inelegant . . . like a "tango de negros." Boxing is barbarous and savage yet insipid and monotonous. In bullfighting, man fights against savagery, Latins have not conquered nature (as the Anglo Saxons have) and they struggle against it still; in pugilism the Anglo Saxon struggles with man and tries in the arena, like in politics, to dominate and subjugate. In the bullfight, each fighter helps, assists, he protects the rest, and el quite [a movement of the cloak from in front of the charging bull] is a philanthropic manifestation, an act of gentlemanly abnegation, characteristic of the race. In boxing, none of the fighters have anyone's help, no protection, no defense, he has to base himself in his own skill, symbol of the individualism of the Anglo Saxon. . . . Within this is enclosed the secret to colossal success, in science, in industry, in war, in dominating the world which has been the patrimony and will be the future of the Anglo Saxon race.[86]

The reaction of the Mexican public sphere to the first inroads of pugilism in the late nineteenth century was largely one of repugnance. It exposed perceptions of cultural barbarity, Anglo brutishness, and resistance to the imposition of American cultural peculiarities on an unwilling Mexican cultural elite. Reading between the lines of these worried narratives, however, yields important insights into the growing fascination of the populacho with these imported spectacles of marginally modern masculinity. Beyond a refutation of American cultural influence in Mexico, these writers evince a greater concern with the Mexican masses whose tastes they perceived as increasingly detached from those of their social betters.

While the many quotations cited above may strike the reader as overblown, reactionary, and almost pathological responses to a marginal and innocuous voluntary practice, they must be contextualized as part of a rational response to an identity crisis in late Porfirian Mexico. The dramatic increase in the presence of foreign individuals and their cultural practices alarmed those writers in the public sphere who called, often unsuccessfully, on politicians to rid the republic of pernicious foreign influences. What made boxing significant in this period is that it polarized so many cultural intermediaries and became a focal point for enunciations of Mexican civilization under attack from modernity. American influence, in particular, was multivalent. It encompassed what most commentators viewed as the positive material benefits of modernization: telegraphs, railroads, foreign capital investment, and other innovations in late nineteenth-century Mexico. Rather than swallowing the modernizing pill whole, the public sphere was a sounding board for inclusions and exclusions in the name of ambivalent and defensive definitions of civilization.

Billy Clarke lived in Mexico for almost five years. His wife, Manuela Barrón de Clarke, gave birth to their daughter in 1897.[87] Despite his multiple conflicts with the authorities and the continuous racist mocking, especially by the US press in Mexico City, it seemed he had settled into a relatively comfortable middle-class life. In September, his eight-month-old daughter, Ana, died of an intestinal obstruction in his home on Calle Rebelde.[88] Less than a month later, Clarke attended a play at the Teatro Principal. Unexpectedly, one of the actors recited a poem about him that was "not exactly complimentary of Billy's bravery." When he took issue and sought to defend his honor, the incident became fodder for the *Mexican Herald*. In an article titled "He Say he Aint Gwine to Let no Man Put Him in Poetry [sic]," the American writers continued their long racist campaign against him.[89] The *Evening Telegram*, published in Mexico City, notified its readers that even the bulls in Toluca, where Clarke was scheduled to perform, "evidently did not want to get mixed up with a nigger . . . it is said that valiant animal possesses a keen sense of smell."[90]

After about 1900, Billy A. Clarke disappears from the historical record. It seems that efforts to expel him from Mexico had been successful. He surfaced once in Texas where he performed as the "Peruvian" strongman, alongside magicians and vaudevillian actors. A crowd in Fort Worth, after discovering that the weights he had lifted to entertain them were hollow, almost lynched him in broad daylight.[91] Elsewhere in Texas, Clark was introduced as "the colored prize fighter and wrestler from Mexico" and as "Professor Billy Clarke." The African American from Pennsylvania was now a specimen of muscular development from Peru and Mexico City.[92] His long-term impact in Mexico outlasted the memory of him in his native United States. As late as the 1950s, aging Mexican prizefighters remembered their time in his gym in Mexico City, where they learned their trade.[93]

**"Regenerating the Race" through the "religion of the biceps": Mexico City, 1905**

A decade after the outrage inspired by Billy A. Clarke, public perceptions about prizefighting had begun to shift toward greater acceptance. Mexican fighters challenged the growing interracial class of foreigners who claimed to be "champions of Mexico."[94] These early Mexican boxers were often from middle- and upper-class backgrounds and were supported by powerful voices in the press and a rising generation of well-placed Porfirians. These connections allowed for a degree of impunity, which opened spaces for increasing publicity and the systematic publication of laudatory accounts of gymnasiums as vital breeding grounds for virility. Their bouts were also rationalized in the public sphere as nationalistic acts that showed both Mexican achievement in a competitive transnational medium and the fortification of supposedly fragile Mexican bodies.

In the months leading up to November 15, 1905, Mexico City newspapers relayed the portentous gossip circulating on the streets of the capital. Two Mexican youths, Fernando Colín and Salvador Esperón, would hold a prizefight in the Cosmopolitan Club of Mexico City.[95] Advertisers pitched the spectacle as a fight to the finish, until one fighter was knocked out or for twenty rounds, whichever came first. This long duration made it potentially more dangerous for the boxers than the sporadic "scientific" exhibitions of boxing. Those events, held every few months in private clubs since around 1900, rarely exceeded five rounds. In these abbreviated matches, the boxers used oversized gloves to prevent injuries such as bloodied faces and broken bones, which would scandalize spectators who attended, supposedly, to receive scientific corporeal education. The coming prizefight, though, was different. It prompted several editorialists, among them writers for the *Gaceta de Policía*, to comment that Mexican bodies were incapable of resisting such a brutal test. Mexican men, unlike their counterparts in the "yankee race," lacked the bodily constitution to support such a sustained assault.[96]

For more than a decade preceding this bout, Mexican writers in the public sphere chastised young people for slavishly and foolishly imitating the vogue of sport. The ridiculous attempts to imitate foreign cultures were, the scholar Luis G. Urbina opined in 1892, characteristic of "weak races." "We give ourselves over" he reasoned, "to games of sport with laughable delirium. We are not trained, we are not agile, nor strong, nor healthy, but no matter, we still take on these new diversions with enthusiasm."[97] Other commenters promoted the Colín-Esperón bout as an indication that the city's youth could transform themselves into enviable physical specimens and compete with any race in the "virile sport" of boxing.

The match at the Cosmopolitan marked a shift in the public sphere. The rejection of boxing surrounding the Billy Clarke match of 1895 had defined the sport as alien and barbaric. A younger generation gaining a foothold in the press now posed it as a calculated and cultivated pursuit, scientifically justifiable, and as a potential tool for racial improvement.[98] Mexican athletes established private athletic clubs, such as the new Club Ugartechea and Club Olímpico, in the first years of the century to introduce "clean" prizefighting and *musculación* (bodybuilding) to a public eager to assimilate imported ideas. They joined a growing number of foreign and Mexican sport clubs that vied for members and sought to change the cultural consensus about the social utility of physicality. José Juan Tablada, the poet and journalist, enlisted fellow writers in the press and founded a boxing gym.[99] Tablada and his allies sought to explain prizefighting as a panacea for the perceived effeminacy of middle-class youth. Good sportsmen, they argued, would ultimately make good masculine citizens.[100]

This match was the first time Mexican-run organizations openly flouted legal prohibitions on boxing. They portrayed prizefighting as socially respectable and themselves as supplanting an older generation whose worldview was ossified in counterproductive dogmas of the past. Once again, two men meeting in a boxing ring crystallized competing ideas about the capaciousness of the public sphere in the capital and about which ideas deserved open discussion. Mexican athletes sought the expertise of US professors of boxing, especially the controversial African American Joe Maljoy and the "mulatto" Kid Levigne. This section examines the public and political reaction to these events and the evolving social context in which boxing in Mexico gained its first Mexican champions.

Thousands of pesos were at stake in wagers and ticket sales. These large sums alarmed and angered critics; they viewed it as a profligate waste. Despite these warnings, observers from cities around Mexico, such as Jalapa (Veracruz), anxiously followed the buildup and aftermath of the bout. Newspapers in the United States took notice and reported on police actions to prohibit it.[101] The *Mexican Herald*, the English-language newspaper in Mexico City, portrayed the fighters as unusually skilled . . . for Mexicans. This was to be, US and Mexican journalists agreed, the most important sporting event in the history of Mexico.[102]

*El Diario del Hogar*, a newspaper that defended bourgeois, gender-based ideas of domesticity, demanded that the government protect the public from this atrocity. During the preceding year, the newspaper had waged a campaign against public acceptance of prizefighting. It reprinted articles by the Venezuelan intellectual Nicanor Bolet Peraza, whose dispatches from the United States were widely published in Latin America. These articles focused on the racial aspects of prizefighting; it was a tawdry interracial spectacle that created "brown pancakes out of noses" and caused "civilization to cover its eyes."[103] An editorial in *El Diario del Hogar* called for legal injunctions, enforced by the police, to stop the bout. It commented disapprovingly that the public sphere of cafes, bars, streets, and sporting clubs was electrified by debate over the comparative merits of the fighters. Among proponents of sport, both Mexican fighters were hailed as the greatest examples of modern virility. One of the boxers, Fernando Colín, had fought and defeated an unnamed US American athlete. This fact lent credibility to his knowledge and scientific learning that, they argued, paired with his prodigious physical development. Colín was a paragon of the "golden youth" of the city. Mexican athletes no longer demurred to foreigners as the most virile men on the streets of the capital.

Manuel Carpio, a poet from Guadalajara, disagreed with the basis of Colín's celebrity. He mocked the members of the Ugartechea Club (a boxing, wrestling, and bodybuilding school) as pretentious and comical imitators:

> Look at the happy flock of gymnasts that Ugartechea leads: running and jumping like naughty boys (traviesos), athlete-lovers (atletófilos) and muscle worshippers (musculómanos) who try to box and profess in all its forms the religion of the biceps. A poet [Tablada] follows him [Colin] as well, who after being very solemn in the gardens of the Academy, admires Sandow, and tries to emulate him."[104]

The men Carpio mocked were part of a cross-class network of young urban men who trained with US journeymen fighters they employed in their sport clubs. African Americans such as Joe Maljoy, "Kid" Levigne, "Black Satin," and the Mexican American boxer Kid Mitchell received the honorific titles of "professors" of boxing. In custom-built gymnasiums they used imported exercise machines from the United States. Weekly magazines that normally chronicled high society began to print serial images of these curious novelties. For the first time in Mexico, they mass-reproduced images of shirtless African American and Mexican men and lauded the effects their training had on the development of muscular bodies.[105] Under the auspices of these new clubs, these athletes held scientific exhibitions of boxing, wrestling, and Japanese jujitsu. These skills, writers explained, were a means to cultivate the values of virility that constituted being modern and being manly.

These private spectacles were hybrid events. The agenda for an evening at the club might contain an exhibition of weightlifting, gymnastic workouts, orchestral performances, and poetry readings. Club managers such as José Juan Tablada of the Ugartechea paired accepted elements of high culture with more controversial displays of seminude male bodies enacting choreographed violence. Tablada, as a journalist, had sought to translate foreign ideas into the Mexican vernacular for several years, publishing hundreds of articles ranging from explanations of haiku and discourses on Buddhism to accounts of physical culture.[106] The sportsmen strategically dedicated these performances to high-ranking members of the political elite in hopes of protective patronage and as a way to self-advertise. This creative arrangement also served a more strategic and practical purpose: the police were less likely to intervene in an evening's entertainment if it formed part of respectable and legal spectacle. Such elevated diversions, by virtue of being private, also excluded the members of the populacho, whose presence would likely cause suspicion and unease.

One such "Athletic Exhibition" earlier in 1905 is an example of the dozens of similar events that took place in that year. In the Teatro Renacimiento, the Club Ugartechea de Cultura Física dedicated a performance to the secretary (Justo Sierra) and subsecretary of public instruction and *bellas artes*. Sierra's disgust over prizefighting in the United States and his important role in the Porfirian government made him a potentially critical observer. Enrique Ugartechea was from Veracruz and had represented Mexico as a wrestling judge during the Saint Louis exhibition of 1904. After months in the United States, he imported bodybuilding equipment, opening a gym in Mexico City near the zócalo in February. He was hired to teach bodybuilding and give boxing lessons, along with the Oaxacan Salvador Esperón, to the students of National School of Jurisprudence.[107] He also imported some of the racial ideas governing public spectacle in the United States.

The evening of June 29 began with a performance of orchestral music. The members of the club then took the stage to exhibit their mastery of the gymnastic rings. Following this, two members wrestled in Greco-Roman style. After intermission, there were several fencing bouts, punctuated by further musical interludes. All these preliminary performances were beyond reproach, even by conservative writers in attendance. The more unusual and risqué elements served as the climax for the exhibition. Enrique Ugartechea, shirtless, performed feats of strength leading into a five-round boxing match between Salvador Esperón and Gaspar López.[108]

A reviewer for the conservative daily *El Tiempo* lauded the evening as full of "virile and beautiful exercises" led by "professors" and their students. Though the secretary of public instruction, Justo Sierra, was unable to attend, his subsecretary, Ezequiel Chávez, occupied his place of honor by the stage. Ugartechea, the "great Mexican athlete," was the highlight of the evening. His "herculean" body amazed the crowd and they gave him multiple ovations when he lifted a two-hundred-pound dumbbell over his head (ironically an act for which Billy Clarke, the African American, had been mocked a decade earlier on a similar stage). Though Ugartechea was the most admired performer, the final boxing match between "Professor Don Salvador Esperón" and Don Gaspar López caused the most "anxiety" in the crowd. This anxiety was likely due to the understanding that the boxing was illegal, especially illegal if the boxers were Mexican. When the curtain rose on the fighters, the well-known "American sportman" Charles Keefe served as the referee. After five rounds, Keefe declared Esperón the winner. Given the carefully controlled and theatrical setting, the reviewer for *El Tiempo* summarized the evening as an example of Mexican advance in the "virile and useful" field of athletic exercises. No money changed hands and the crowd was composed of the best classes of people, supervised and presided over by a government official. The writer for *El Tiempo* portrayed the performers with honorific titles of respectability. Even in this sedate setting, though, the boxing match still caused angst.[109]

The exhibitions of the Ugartechea and Olympic Clubs grew in popularity through 1905. Members performed in front of sold-out crowds and were lauded for their patriotic labor: "Our publications, in patriotic eagerness publish [images], as eloquent proof of our development attained by such a well-organized *centro de sport*." The magazine *México Industrial*, normally dedicated to chronicling infrastructure projects so central to Porfirian political legitimacy, dedicated an entire page to images of the Ugartechea's virile young men. It labeled Ugartechea a "*científico*" for his use of "efficient systems" and his implantation of the Sandow Method to train Mexican bodies.[110] The appellation "scientific" coded Ugartechea as more than a mimetic worshipper of brute force. He used imported science to cultivate superior physical specimens. The goals of his club, in this instance, fit well into the positivist public sphere. The article explained his imported weightlifting machines in close detail. They provided rational systems to improve the Mexican race. Ugartechea subjected his members to regular bodily measurements. His instruction helped "obtain physical regeneration among our youths, an affinity which will be fruitful for the race."¹¹¹ In July, the boxers of the Olympic Club were similarly praised in the press: "Fernando Colín along with Salvador Esperón are genuine Mexican representatives in the pugilistic arts, which are the *most virile, most useful, the most passionate, and the most complete of all athletic exercises.*"¹¹²

The magazine *El Mundo Ilustrado* also published several pages of pictures of the Ugartechea Club, citing it as a catalyst for the explosion of interest in sport among Mexico City youth. One writer surmised that there was not a single vacant lot, even in the suburbs, that was not filled with novel sporting activity. One goal of the magazine was to encourage this phenomenon that would "vivify and regenerate" the nation. Much of this commentary conveyed the conviction that the Mexican race had degenerated, in part, due to backward ideas that governed the male body. These statements impugned the older generation of educators and implied that they should allow and encourage youth to assimilate these novel practices.

The reportage was echoed by one of the most respected intellectuals in Mexico City. Dr. Manuel Flores, director of the prestigious National Preparatory School, explained that learning these new ideas could extinguish the long-standing francophilia of the social elite. He criticized French body culture as concerned only with aesthetic outcomes. Better and more useful, he argued, were the Anglo-American cultures of sport, especially boxing. The practice of these sports promised to perfect and strengthen men as social actors in a precarious urban society. Flores contended that such sporting cultures augmented and protected national independence and dignity. He called for change: "Let's substitute the applied sports of the *anglosajones* for the decorative sport of the French or geometric gymnastics of the Swiss."¹¹³ In a subsequent plea, Flores claimed that attraction to dramatic and violent spectacle was a natural and useful instinct to "feel pleasure and pain, indignation and enthusiasm, love and hate, and to vibrate the chords of our passionate (bodily) lyre."¹¹⁴

Ugartechea, Colín, and Esperón, through public acclaim, emerged as idols for Mexican youths whose frames of reference for self-evaluation were increasingly international and experimental. For many positivist writers, their example promised a panacea for the decadent Mexican male body.¹¹⁵ Even *El País*, among the most culturally conservative dailies, was cautiously optimistic about the Ugartechea and Olympic Clubs' enormous popularity. But it still revealed anxiousness over the popularity of boxing among young people.¹¹⁶

The young boxers who were slated to fight at the Cosmopolitan, Salvador Esperón and Fernando Colín, bore little resemblance to Billy Clarke. Both men were born and came of age in Mexico during the Porfiriato. Esperón was the legitimate son of a storeowner from Oaxaca City in the majority indigenous southern state of the same name.[117] In 1894, Colín had moved to Mexico City from his native Monterrey, a booming industrial city near the US border. He had first trained in the gymnasium of US American Jimmy Carroll, who competed with Billy Clarke and also ran the saloon at the infamous Hotel Iturbide. Both Mexican boxers were members of the social elite known informally as the "Golden Youth."[118]

Colín instructed boxing at the Club Olímpico, which, the writer posited, was largely responsible for the novel popularity of sport over the preceding few years. Colín, unlike Billy Clarke, was not presented to the public as a brainless brute. He was "distinguished by his science, agility, and energy" and along with the Ugartechea, his Olympic Club "marches at the head of Mexican sport clubs that grow daily and whose impact on the regeneration of the race is undeniable." This regeneration, the critic implied, was central to the legitimate popularity of Colín, Esperón, and Ugartechea.[119]

Two weeks prior to the bout in Cosmopolitan, a reporter attended a private match in the Club Olímpico between Kid Mitchell and Joe Maljoy. These two US Americans trained Colín and Esperón and were central to the knowledge transfer that took place in these athletic clubs. Maljoy, like Clarke before him, was dogged by controversy in Mexico City. Like Clarke, he had sought to earn a living performing in any public spectacle that could draw a crowd. His race was constantly reiterated. Enrique Ugartechea, who primarily appeared in public spectacles as a wrestler and strongman, refused to accept a challenge for a Greco-Roman match with Maljoy because he was black and in a higher weight class.[120] In his response to Ugartechea's drawing the color line, Maljoy retorted that he was not black, but Cuban. He claimed to have been born in Cuba but educated in the United States.[121] This assertion is difficult to evaluate given the scarce information extant on Maljoy in Mexican, Cuban, or US archives. It does illustrate, however, that Ugartechea had imported not only the novel exercise machines from the United States, but some of the racial norms governing sport and public spectacle. This incident also illustrates Maljoy's use of a racial strategy that would be common in coming decades: dark-skinned Cubans claiming Castilian descent to argue that they should not be subject to the color line. Their relative whiteness should allow them to compete freely.[122] Despite the interracial nature of the exhibition between Mitchell and Maljoy, the reporter found the performance a "corporeal education" that was of "intense interest" for the city's youths.[123] An African American journeyman boxer exemplified the skills deemed necessary for the regeneration of the Mexican race.

On the day of the Colín-Esperon bout, November 15, the semiofficial newspaper *El Imparcial* reported that night's performance in the careful language of

Porfirian positivism. Though it was public knowledge that the boxers were fighting for a purse, the *Imparcial* stressed that they would only be rewarded with medals. The purpose of the bout was not to entertain the crowd but to showcase "all the advances in physical culture" visible in the bodies and the preparation of the boxers.[124] More conservative editorialists observed bitingly that the heavily subsidized de facto government newspaper twisted the truth in its support of breaking the law.[125]

That evening, while a sold-out crowd of more than a thousand people filled every seat at the Cosmopolitan Club, several policemen lined up to stop the bout. The governor of Mexico City, Guillermo de Landa y Escandón, ordered police to allow the wrestling matches scheduled for the lineup and to permit one boxing exhibition, but to arrest Esperón and Colín if they tried to enter the ring for a prizefight. Landa y Escandón, a "close confidant" of Porfirio Díaz, trusted this task to one of his lieutenants, José Rafael de Altamira, chief of police with jurisdiction over the Cosmopolitan.[126] The crowd booed the policemen and refused to disperse for more than two hours. They hoped the police/censors would lose interest and depart. The other performers slated for that night refused to take the stage in an act of solidarity and civil disobedience; in altering the program of an advertised public spectacle, they risked fines from the government.[127] The governor had tried to intervene selectively in the program, but they would not allow him to impose his will on the evening's entertainment.

The day following this police action, the conservative press hailed the governor's prudent decision as a defense of civilization. He acted with enlightened concern, a writer for *El País* implied, for the well-being of naïve Mexican boxers. Colín and Esperón had deluded themselves, through their training and admiration of their US American professors, to think that their Mexican bodies were capable of fighting for twenty rounds. That class of physical exertion was conceivable for the "yankee race, but not for us, because neither our physical makeup, nor our climate, allow for such a challenge between two native youths. If this bout had taken place, we can be sure that today we would be lamenting a tragedy."[128] These thoughts were reprinted the *Gaceta de Policía*.[129] They evoked a biological basis of culture. This melding mirrored the language and reasoning the US writer Jack London used to defend prizefighting as an element in the vitality of the "English speaking race."[130] The older generation of the political and social elite intervened to protect idealistic youths from themselves and to police the boundaries of racialized culture.

Despite the triumphant relief in the conservative press, the bout took place in secret a few days later, on November 17. The nephew of the governor of Mexico

City and son of the governor of the state of Morelos, Pablo Escandón Jr., disregarded his uncle's orders and held the bout in the patio of his home.[131] A writer for *El Imparcial* announced the following day the bout had taken place in front of a few dozens of the city's sportsmen. He defended the fight, arguing that it was clean and regulated and that no bets had been made and no money had changed hands. This report on the absence of wagers, likely false, was a proactive attempt to diffuse the anger and possible legal actions that were sure to follow.[132]

The conservative reaction was spearheaded by the newspaper *El Tiempo*. Since its founding in 1883, the paper's editor, Victoriano Agüeros, had "led the conservative opposition to the *yanqui invasión pacífica* that attended Porfirian defensive modernization."[133] The editorialist couched his commentary in irony. It angered him to be forced to write about the existence of such low and disreputable activities in a modern city. He only did so, he justified, out of patriotic concern over the amount of public attention the bout received. Without naming the younger Escandón directly, he excoriated the "elegant and rich sportmen [sic]" who had the audacity to disobey the governor's order. Esperón lost the bout and was badly beaten, his jaw dislocated and his nose "opened up." The quantity of public discourse led many to believe that it was the beginning of a "new and barbarous diversion that, without difficulty, will take root and extend in Mexico, as in England and the United States." If the decades-long resistance of the editorial staff of *El Tiempo* was not enough, the writer cited Juan Valera, the recently deceased Spanish intellectual and member of the Royal Spanish Academy. For Valera, boxing was a metaphor for the barbarous age's continuance in the modern present; "we cannot deny that it is brutal and alien to the civilized and philanthropic era in which we live." Cultures that supported such blood sport handicapped themselves in the pursuit of progress.[134]

*El Tiempo* represented the critical voice of conservative intellectuals. But newer publications such as *El Mundo*, edited by liberal politician Fausto Moguel, embraced cultural hybridity despite being subsidized by the government. Promoting athletics and the civic social groups that introduced them in the public sphere did not constitute a direct political challenge to the Porfirian regime. It did entail a series of actions that contested the cultural hegemony of the Porfirian elite and their very basis for authority. The appropriation and Mexicanization of sport was a hallmark of a rising generation of public intellectuals, such as José Juan Tablada, who worked to carve autonomous spaces within the authoritarian social confines of the era.

Along with its sister publication, *El Mundo Ilustrado*, the editorial staff of *El Mundo* and *El Imparcial* helped pioneer the model created in Mexico by the newspaper magnate Rafael Reyes Spíndola. His publications featured the latest imported technologies of image reproduction along with a focus on the spectacular, popular, and lucrative features of modern newspaper coverage: crime, violence, sport, and scandal.[135] These columns increased the size of newspapers from four to five dense pages of newsprint, to dozens of image-laden pages by the outbreak of the Revolution in 1910. The increasing reproduction of information of international popular culture, especially from the United States, enabled Mexican readers to consume narratives about transnational daily life. Boxing matches, given their global audience and the risqué underworld associated with them, fit well within these changing journalistic practices.[136] Mexicans simultaneously read minute details of the lives of athletes from abroad while recreating the medium of that fame in their clubs and theaters.

On November 21, 1905, four days after the illegal bout in the home Pablo Escandón Jr., *El Mundo* published images of the shirtless Colín and Esperón and a glowing yet cryptic account of their now infamous boxing match.[137] The bout was a milestone in the development of sport and had succeeded in drawing the attention of elements of society who had before been indifferent. Those Mexicans who celebrated bullfighting had to reconsider their belief that boxing was barbarous. Those Mexicans who admired bullfighters as masculine icons looked beyond national borders for genres of celebrity and public spectacle. Mexicans who were aficionados of modern sport did the same, but their heroes were of the present and they illustrated the struggles inherent in an urbanizing environment. The editorialist for *El Mundo* made this comparison explicit. Those who viewed boxing as barbaric and bullfighting as noble were mistaken: prizefighting was a modern "manifestation of the virility of those nations (*pueblos*) that take part in it."[138] Even though the bout had been illegal, the *Gaceta de Policía* was swept up the excitement of its aftermath. It published large portraits of the boxers.[139]

The terrain on which to prove and exhibit manliness underwent a generational shift from the Hispanic past to an imported Anglo present. The boxers' preparations for the bout in the months before—regular exercise in the countryside, intense physical training, learning from foreign professors of boxing—served as a parable for Mexican youths "despondent from physical inertia." The promoters surprised the public by staging such a match "with our own people, given our apathy for athletic exercises." In the ensuing lines the author relayed what he understood as the broader meaning and scope of the event:

> Trained with the utmost care, the boxers arrived at the ring. Their presence was magnificent, and when they exhibited their muscular forms, they seemed to symbolize a promise: that of a new race, vigorous and full of energies, that

might bring our country an era of marvelous greatness.... The fight was very clean and it highlighted the boxers' brilliant faculties of strength, ability, and endurance, qualities that should characterize the man who confronts struggles that must be defeated—great physical and mental force and mental activity. As those who know about such things said, this fight was so close and so clean, that it rivals any bout in a given year in the country of boxers [United States] where these matches are so common.[140]

Though this language may seem hyperbolic, such grandiose conclusions should be understood as strategic enunciations of purpose and an expression of a commonly held worldview. The language of positive eugenics—of means to improve the Mexican race and make it more competitive with foreigners—made sense and held clear directives for the generation coming of age during the Porfiriato. They saw themselves struggling to define their place within a public sphere and broader culture that restricted their pursuits and derided the means through which they sought to be modern.

Esperón threw in the towel in the patio of the Escandón mansion at the beginning of the eighth round. The new title "Lightweight Champion of the Republic" was awarded to Colín. His celebrity grew. He was immediately challenged by an African American boxer identified only as "Black Satin." The boxer had arrived in Mexico City, along with more than a dozen other journeyman boxers, to take advantage of what they hoped would be a lucrative uptick in legal boxing matches. Satin was arrested in mid-November for going on a "high lonesome," a drunken bender that allegedly led to his assaulting a number of police officers at the central railroad station. He was confined in Belém Prison for ten days. There he reportedly continued his training by lifting bricks and taking cold-water plunges, becoming a spectacle for his fellow prisoners and guards.[141] When Satin issued a challenge for the championship in the press, Colín drew the color line, refusing to risk his title to such a disreputable African American.[142]

In late November, the press announced that Colín, along with Esperón and Escandón, had been fined one hundred pesos each for their violation of the governor's orders. Colín, likely hoping that his political connections and newfound celebrity would make the fine disappear, presented a formal request to the governor to waive the penalty and potential jail time. No police or judicial record exists to determine whether this occurred. The *Mexican Herald* reported that given the actions of the Mexico City government, future matches would likely be held in the mining town of El Oro, outside his jurisdiction. Conservative papers continued to chastise *El Imparcial* for its encouragement of prizefighting.

Colín became the "man of the hour" for his victory over Esperón. Following the bout, his fans treated him to a weeklong celebration in bars and cantinas, lavishing dinners on him at the most expensive restaurants in the city. Colín's celebrity was furthered by an extravagant banquet in his honor hosted in the home of the one of the editors of *El Imparcial*, A. E. Lozano. Antonio Fuentes, the well-known bullfighter, was one of the admiring public in attendance.[143]

Colín's frenetic rise was short-lived. Within a few weeks of the bout, which newspapers from across the political spectrum had grudgingly or willing chronicled, mention of him and the bout disappeared from published documents. The popular fascination with the bout, extending to the United States, likely set in motion the censorship of the press common during the Porfirian era. Because no such orders remain in Mexican archives or were published in newspapers, it is impossible to determine what accounts for the glaring absence of coverage after the end of November. The only newspaper that reported on the postfight events was the English-language *Mexican Herald*.

To the chagrin of the authorities, the Colín-Esperón bout entrenched boxing as a mainstay in the private clubs of the city, spaces largely beyond the regulatory jurisdiction of the government. Dozens of journeyman prizefighters, most of them African Americans, arrived in Mexico City.[144] There would be no repeat, however, of a public prizefight between Mexicans in a commercial venue for several years.

One unintended consequence of this match was to introduce the color line in sport to Mexico City. Colín refused to fight black boxers. When Kid Mitchell, a Mexican American boxing instructor from the Olympic Club, was challenged by Black Satin, he was quoted in the press stating, "I'm not going to fight any niggers, but I will take on that Frenchman, Spinner, and for that matter am looking for any one but a black man."[145] The arrests of boxers for illegal boxing matches and drunken brawls, from Billy Clarke to Black Satin, and the importation of the US color line, likely provided clear justifications for the further prohibition of prizefighting in the capital. In the ensuing months, foreign boxers managed to contract bullrings and private clubs outside of Mexico City in nearby locations such as El Oro and Toluca, repeating the process that had led to the Clarke-Smith bout in 1895. The Cosmopolitan Club, where the abortive Colín-Esperón bout was to have taken place, continued to annoy the authorities and was the subject of numerous lawsuits in 1905 alone.[146] The attempts by proponents of modern sport in the Mexico City press to change the law and public opinion had faced an uphill battle. Their strategic plan failed for the moment; prizefighting remained outlawed among Mexicans in public venues, but was tolerated in private clubs where the golden youth continued to learn from, and draw the color line against, their foreign professors.

These efforts were not relegated to Mexico City. In January of 1906, a month after the Colín-Esperón bout, the Guadalajara-based journalist José B. Velasco reported on a boxing and strength exhibition held in the Centro Mercantíl of that city. The students of the Colegio Militar, many of them also members of the Olympic and Ugartechea Clubs, traveled to the coastal state of Jalisco to display their progress toward building modern bodies. Velasco was amazed at the large number of young women who attended the exhibition of the "strong and agile" youths displaying their science and their musculature. This spectacle, he explained, was entirely new to the city, and it held great meaning as the beginning of new and beautiful physical culture. The youth of the city were "degraded" by lives that transpired around the bar and the bullring. But they saw new possibilities of public spectacle and bodily renovation at the traveling exhibition. "Blond yankee girls" liked this new sort of ring (compared to the bullring) where "Robust and strong men, semi-naked and proud revolve upon the stage. Biceps jump, the chest seems to grow, and arms and legs, backs and necks, show proportions of one of those old statues that represent demigods and heroes." Velasco posited that this semierotic display of the male body would also be useful in the broader field of social life. It would lift the youth from the "fluffy pillows of pleasure and enervation in which they live prostrated with slavish languidness." Such a sea change in the valuation and celebration of vigorous masculinity would prepare them for success in three interrelated ares: "the patria, the struggle for existence, and honor." The writer closed by quoting José Juan Tablada as an expert about the virile outcomes of such cultural appropriations.

Fittingly, on the same page as Velasco's elegy, another writer expressed the perception that Mexico was being overrun by US culture, what he called the "Saxon absorption." English was spoken everywhere, he wrote, and in the last ten years US Americans had begun to inhabit all parts of Mexico. This "patriotic nightmare" was the "black mark on the horizon of our future." The "yankee penetration" of Mexico, he reasoned, was based on "ethnic superiority" and the energy and inherent expansionism of US society. His self-criticism ended with a rhetorical question: "Where might we find a remedy?" Writers such as José Juan Tablada and José Velasco had a clear answer: making the individual Mexican body stronger and more modern should serve as the first bastion for a defense of the nation in pursuit of defensive modernization.[147]

## Civil Society and Boxing at the End of the Porfiriato

Between 1905 and 1910, private sporting clubs flourished in Mexico City, but the city government still outlawed prizefighting. Despite this prohibition, entrepreneurs screened fight films of interracial boxing matches such as the 1908 Burns-Johnson bout. Mexicans watched the events unfold in Sydney, Australia, in which Jack Johnson became the first African American heavyweight champion. Journalists reported that important members of the Porfirian government, such as the vice president, Ramón Corral, attended these exhibitions. Outside of Mexico City, prizefights took place in locations such as Aguascalientes, where local newspapers contracted with fight promoters to advertise bouts in newsprint and by placing posters in public sites around the city.[148] Most prizefighting, though, was relegated to civic social clubs such as the Olympic and Ugartechea. Due to the prohibitions on public prizefights in Mexico City and the officially private nature of these organizations, they left few records behind. This section pieces together short biographical sketches from widely dispersed documents to recreate the context of these interactions. A picture emerges of a multinational and interracial subculture that rarely surfaces in the extant historiography of the Porfirian era.

Kid Mitchell arrived in Mexico City in 1905 and immediately gravitated to the Olympic Club.[149] The club managers employed him as a boxing professor and Mitchell attracted several Mexican students eager to learn from him. Even though Kid Mitchell was not his legal name, he appeared as such in both the press and in Mexican legal documents that outlined his many conflicts with the authorities. Mitchell's real name was Jesus Sótelo and he was a Mexican American from El Paso, Texas. The year before he arrived in Mexico City he had married an eighteen-year-old Mexican American woman named Tomasa Bernal in El Paso. The marriage was apparently not a happy one. An El Paso newspaper reported that Bernal de Sotelo committed suicide by drinking carbolic acid in the boarding house where she lived in December of 1905.[150] In one highly publicized incident in Mexico City, Mitchell, like many US boxers before him, was arrested for drunk and disorderly conduct, *ebrio escandaloso*.[151] In November of 1906, he was evicted by his landlord for being months behind on rent.[152]

Despite his notoriety, Mitchell seems to have remained purposely mysterious. At various times over the next decade, writers claimed he was from Denver, Colorado; Kentucky; or El Paso, Texas. Unlike Fernando Colín, whom he helped to train, Mitchell did not, in the long run, draw the color line. One early account claimed that the US boxer had "no prejudices of this kind." A writer for the newspaper *El Excelsior* would later remember Mitchell as a "darkie."[153]

Mitchell, along with the Afro-Dutch fighter Jim Smith, was one of the most conspicuous foreign athletes in the boxing subculture during the first decade of the twentieth century. The press detailed his life outside the ring; it made dramatic reading. While training in the countryside outside Mexico City for a club bout in

1907, Mitchell's nine-month-old son died of an undisclosed illness. He was buried in the American Cemetery. A few days later, Mitchell's friends at the Olympic Club, including Salvador Esperón, held a benefit match to help cover the costs of the infant's funeral. Despite this loss, he could not afford to take time off. He was in the ring within two weeks, even though in mourning he had been arrested for the drunken scandal mentioned above.

The Afro-Frenchman, Kid Levigne, was another mysterious and peripatetic journeyman prizefighter emblematic of this period of improvisation. Like Kid Mitchell, he arrived in Mexico City around 1905. According to his official record, he was born "at sea, under the French flag in 1880." He was likely a sailor who disembarked wherever he could make extra money as a prizefighter. He had boxed in the port cities of Manila, London, Liverpool, Sydney, and New York. In Mexico, he held dozens of matches in Acapulco, El Oro, Salina Cruz, Aguascalientes, and Mexico City. He trained a "disciple," the young boxer Carlos de la Tijera, who would be a proponent of boxing in Mexico after Lavigne's departure.[154]

Among the other less visible athletes was an African American known as Kid Kirkwood. He arrived in Mexico City after boxing on the US West Coast in 1907. He claimed to be a veteran of the famous black regiments of Buffalo Soldiers that fought alongside Theodore Roosevelt in the Spanish-Cuban-American War of 1898 and to have been a sergeant in the army.[155] Kirkwood was challenged in Mexico City by another African American prizefighter, Battling Mulligan, the "dusky whirlwind." Mulligan was employed as a miner in the American-owned copper mine in Cananea, Sonora, the site of the infamous massacre of striking miners in 1906.[156] He was likely present when this happened.

Jim "Diamante Negro" Smith would be among the few foreign boxers from this period who spent the rest of his life in Mexico. He made for an unusual sight as he jogged through the Mexico City zócalo alongside his French trainer, the fencer and wrestler Eugene Spinner, in the winter of 1907.[157] Smith was born in 1880 on the Dutch Caribbean island of Sint Eustatius. He was likely descended from the enslaved Africans and free blacks who toiled in the small yet cosmopolitan Dutch trading post.[158] He learned to box while living near the Mexican American border in the early twentieth century. In that zone of cultural confluence and conflict, he was exposed to the illegal underworld of prizefighting that generated transnational press coverage and public uproar greater than any other public spectacle of the late nineteenth and early twentieth centuries. In April of 1907, he crossed the border from El Paso, Texas, to Ciudad Juárez, Chihuahua, likely on the invitation of the wealthy American mining engineer, inventor, and "sportman," Andrew Ennis.[159] Ennis exploited the rich iron and silver deposits in the mining city of Guanajuato.

He also promoted and staged boxing matches there, becoming Smith's early benefactor and promoter.[160] Ennis, as a mechanical engineer and promoter of modern sport, was emblematic of the multifaceted technological, financial, and cultural impact of US Americans during the late Porfiriato.[161]

Smith arrived in Mexico City in August of 1907. He joined Kid Mitchell, Kid Levigne, the Puerto Rican boxer Kid Lavergne, the Turkish bodybuilder and wrestler Rahain, the Italian wrestler Romulus, Canadian boxer Jack Connell, the "Boer" (South African) Strongman "Otto," the Japanese jujitsu professor known as Conde Koma (Mitsuyo Maeda), and dozens of other foreign professors of boxing and wrestling.[162] Smith quickly took his place among a growing number of transnational athletes who plied their trade in the theaters, clubs, schools, and private homes of the Mexican elite.[163] The appropriation of the skills and culture brought by these marginal journeymen became part of what one scholar has called a "means to modernity" in an increasingly complex global marketplace for ideas and cultural alignments.[164]

Foreign investors such as Andrew Ennis colluded with Porfirian politicians to modernize the Mexican countryside through the construction of railroads, bridges, mines, and factories. Less visible and more marginal individuals such as Smith, through improvisation and seeking financial opportunity, laid the groundwork for the expanding boundaries of popular culture. Foreign economic interests often relied on the coercive power of American diplomacy. People such as Smith were self-promoters, relying more on personal charisma and showmanship to convince Mexicans of the importance of their ideas. They also fought to contain the nascent color line in public entertainment; beyond the few incidents mentioned above, it never became a significant feature of national life.

Mexico City on the eve of the centennial and the beginning of the Revolution (1910) was a cosmopolitan center of about five hundred thousand people and the showcase for the carefully constructed project of Mexican modernity.[165] Here the order and progress much vaunted by the científicos clashed with the informal and improvisational cultures taking root and expanding within civil society. The debates about prizefighting in this period, at their core, centered on issues of social control. Those whose writing reflected the public sphere and sought to define the boundaries of permissibility endeavored to create clear lines between what *was* and *was not Mexican*. But by the time Jim Smith sat for mandatory photographs to complete his file for the registry of foreigners in 1940, the culture of pugilism had been transformed from a cautious elite's sampling of foreign culture into an expression of working-class national identity and masculinity.[166]

As the nationalization of boxing took place in the public sphere, foreigners impugned Mexican manhood through stylized *retos* (challenges) published in the

Mexican press. They challenged anyone, of any nationality, to meet them in violent sport in front of curious and impassioned spectators. In response, Mexicans from across the class spectrum entered the ring. Patricio Martínez Arredondo, Cuauhtémoc Aguilar, Salvador Esperón, and Enrique Ugartechea: *relojero* (watch repair man), stage actor, scion of an Oaxacan family, and Veracruz-born "strongman" respectively, altered established careers to make a living in the lucrative and novel sport.[167] These cultural flows progressed via multiple channels as Mexican athletes increasingly ventured north to compete in the gymnasiums and prize rings in the United States.

Modernist writers like José Juan Tablada, Amado Nervo, and Federico Gamboa and the Mexican pianist Alberto Villaseñor explored whether the nascent popularity of boxing symbolized cultural regression or positivist progress. Tablada managed boxing gyms and Mexican and American boxers in the first decade of the twentieth century. He hoped to mold aristocratic young men into cosmopolitan, poetry-loving masculine ideals.[168]

The novel spaces created by modern sport within the public sphere grew in popularity and lucrative potential in tandem with urbanization, industrialization, and the development of entertainment industries. But Mexican boxing maintained its original association with the demimonde, scandal, and normative cultural change.[169] Due to its association with the lower classes, gambling, and "scandal," boxing was a cultural import that represented what historian Mauricio Tenorio-Trillo has called the "urban and even cultural anti-ideals."[170]

## Unearthing the Informal: Molding Tastes and *Afición* between the Private and Public Spheres

Historian Pablo Piccato's work channels Habermas on the evolution of the public sphere in late nineteenth-century Mexico and encourages a re-evaluation of the private/public dichotomy and the role of public opinion in understanding the era. In his studies on the elite practice of dueling, the press, and defense of individual honor, Piccato stresses that "we should focus less on stable ideals and concepts and more on the practical dimension of historically situated local and personal interactions."[171] His work examines representations in the expanding popular press. Those documents illustrate the creation of consensus through rational arguments that drew upon unstable cultural ideas in the late nineteenth and early twentieth centuries. These malleable and volatile concepts and behaviors, particularly the use of dueling to settle issues of aristocratic personal honor, illustrate the melding of foreign technologies of honor defense onto local conditions.

Journalists in the late Porfiriato wielded a high degree of "cultural capital" and served, through their editorial musings, as intermediaries who negotiated the impact of changing norms of behavior and cultural alignments in the realm of public opinion.[172] As Elías José Palti has posited, Mexican journalists generally fit into two interrelated models, the "juridical" and the "proselytist."[173] According to latter part of that model, journalists made normative judgments concerning the suitability of Mexicans to appropriate imported body culture and modern sport. Beyond mere descriptions of events, they conveyed to their readers a set of qualitative evaluations around events such as the Esperón-Colín bout. The language of that engagement was saturated with gendered and nationalist evaluations of the factors that made a man "good at being a man" within a cultural milieu in which "sporting prowess [was increasingly] a test for masculinity."[174]

The imagination of masculinity and its relationship to national identity were among the unstable ideas deployed around the Mexican appropriation of prizefighting. Though William Beezley characterized the "Porfirian Persuasion" as the attraction of elite Mexicans to foreign cultural practices due to their exoticism and status-exhibiting qualities, a close examination of the evidence reveals a more complex process at work.[175] The melding of diverse cultural inputs into the Mexican vernacular represented a profound and soul-searching encounter in which Mexicans contested and created fundamental bases of mexicanidad.[176] This process defies the traditional periodization of Mexican history into pre- and post-Revolutionary periods.

As Mauricio Tenorio-Trillo has shown, the Porfirian elite sought to harness foreign and positivist cultural influences by portraying Mexico as a modernizing nation while learning from other exemplar races during a series of world fairs in the nineteenth and the beginning of the twentieth centuries.[177] Controls on the press and the persecution by the government of individuals who portrayed Mexico in an unflattering light reflected this concern with the construction of Mexico as modern nation on par with the most advanced "races."[178]

## The Club Atlético Internacional: Baldomero Romero, José Juan Tablada, and the Logic behind Virile Action

Sportsmen wrote multiple petitions in the first decade of the twentieth century seeking to reverse the decisions of Mexico City mayor Guillermo de Landa y Escandón that prohibited public boxing matches. Petitioners argued in a register calculated to evoke national pride and often published their petitions in the press. Their language channeled science in an attempt to create an irrefutable discourse:

Darwin, and later Spencer, had provided a vocabulary and philosophy that guided their arguments.

In the few instances when exhibitions were allowed, the municipal government stipulated arbitrary rules, defining the length of rounds and mandating that combatants only strike each other with open hands.[179] When petitions for boxing matches were denied, and this occurred in the majority of cases, bureaucrats in the office of public spectacles cited the orders of the mayor. They replied to license seekers most often by simply stating that boxing had no place in Mexico City (*no ha(y) lugar*).[180] These prohibitions vacillated in their reasoning and on at least one occasion, when Luís Sarría was granted permission to open a boxing gym, that permission was revoked before he opened the doors.[181] When foreigners, especially US Americans, sought licenses under the Porfirian government, they were more likely to obtain them. One egregious example of this occurred in August of 1908, when US, French, Dutch, and Mexican boxers held a match at the "Pastime Athletic Club" in which one of the features was a Battle Royale, in which six or seven African American boxers fought blindfolded to the last fighter standing for a few coins.[182]

A further example of this improvisation was the match between Jim Smith and Cuauhtémoc Aguilar in 1908. An angry crowd rushed the stage and threatened to pummel Aguilar for his poor performance.[183] Though Mexicans were allowed to open clubs dedicated to physical culture, the government sought to limit the types of activities that took place there, denying the petition of the Centro Deportivo de México to serve alcoholic beverages at their location next to the zócalo on Calle San Francisco.[184]

Proponents of boxing and physical culture were angered by what they saw as the atavistic tastes of a small elite that governed the behavior of the masses. The pleas of socially concerned Mexicans for permission to stage bouts were penned by the leaders of these novel groupings who impugned "backward"-thinking public functionaries for their intransigence and misunderstanding of the goals of these displays of manliness. The press continued to play an important role for these petitioners as a legitimizing agent; they often included glowing accounts of club exhibitions as supporting evidence for their claim to be a virilizing public good.[185]

For those in favor of sport, this resistance was more than irresponsible; it was a pernicious attempt to retard national regeneration. Brothers Ireneo and Baldomero Romero, members of an aristocratic Mexico City family, wrote and circulated these petitions to the "sportmen" and newspapers of the metropolis, pushing the case for boxing as a crucial means of social and cultural advancement, a way to narrow the gap between Mexico and the "most advanced countries."[186] In the process, they collected hundreds of signatures from the like-minded who sought to influence public policy. To support their petitions, the members of the Club Atlético International included copies of the magazine they had published over the preceding years, *Revista de Sport y Cultura Física*, along with newspaper clippings in praise of their "manly" efforts.[187] The Romero brothers founded the club for the express purpose of bringing together people of all nations resident in Mexico. They were angered by exclusivity and segregation of sport clubs that only allowed members of the British, French, or US colonies; these clubs were provincial and did not embrace cosmopolitanism. The Romeros also argued that an open club gave the best chance of proving "which nation is most distinguished by its [physical] constitution and its ability to achieve physical development."[188]

The petitioners based their arguments on several interconnected ideas. First, they stressed, Mexico was a latecomer to the modern world where masculinity was increasingly mediated by practicing sport. But if permitted, an autonomous civil society would remedy the government's failures to promote these innovations. Vigorous, physically adept athletes were the force behind the well-known "triumph" of Anglo-Saxons over lesser races. History, as they interpreted it, demonstrated that the ascendance of national races was tied to their cultivation of manly virtues. Greeks and Romans, before falling to the more vigorous Germanic tribes, made physical education the focal point of childrearing and gave cultivation of the physical almost "cult-like" status. These lessons of history, accordingly, manifested in the recent accomplishments of superior races: "All the governments in the world, currently, allow their men to become sportmen [sic], to make robust and clear minded individuals, not to make *effeminate and rachitic men*."

The petitioners interpreted the charge of Theodore Roosevelt's "Rough Riders" in Cuba as the clear proof of their claims. The US victory over Spain proved that nations that promoted certain ideas of masculinity in the service of national regeneration rose to the top of the Social Darwinist ladder. Their cultures of the body, not their race alone, fueled their rise. This stress on the attainment of knowledge provided an escape hatch from racial determinism, an extension of Lombrosian ideas of eugenics then popular in Latin America.

They quoted Baron Harcourt, paragon of European martial nobility, as irrefutable support for these interpretations. Incorporating the ideas of foreign experts and intellectuals, they impugned those who, like Mayor Landa y Escandón, sought to stifle the forward-thinking elements in civil society. Such reliance on traditional cultural norms prevented Mexican success in the competitive struggle of nations. It was a *"crime of a weak country,"* the petitioners wrote, to pretend the "virile youth" should follow in the footsteps of those effeminate elements of Mexican society who "rode in carriages about the country" and celebrated bullfighting as the only national sport.[189] Who was the mayor of Mexico City, they implied, to question a thinker as elevated as Maurice Maeterlinck, who had just won the Nobel Prize for literature:

> They are ignorant of the precise forms of practice, rules, and severe discipline that characterize all "matches" of this virile sport in countries that are without a doubt more civilized than Mexico—even though as Mexicans it embarrasses us to say it—like France, England, the United States and others who enjoy powerful merit and about which have written in favor elevated personages of the intellectual world, that we won't resist the desire to transcribe, as the best defense of pugilism, the sage maxim of the celebrated poet Maeterlinck which says "It seems paradoxical; but it is easy to prove that the art of pugilism, where it is practiced, becomes a garment of meekness and of peace."

The Japanese, they further argued, were another case in point. Their defeat of the Russian empire in 1905 was due precisely to their cultivation of the virtues of physicality. Along with African American boxers, Japanese athletes taught the Mexican elite the "science" of jujitsu and other martial arts in which "small men" were able to conquer larger opponents through the deployment of the science of bodily combat.

In 1909, Mexican men and women attended open-air exhibitions where they were intrigued by Japanese sumo.[190] Sumo wrestlers and jujitsu martial artists gave exhibitions in front of the aging Porfirio Díaz and were incorporated into the training for the most elite Mexican youth: the cadets who attended class on the grounds of the Presidential Palace in Chapultepec park.[191] The excitement over new ideas about the body extended all the way to the National Agriculture School, where students appropriated sport into their curriculum as in American colleges.[192]

Conservative commentators raged against the inhumanity of violent sport and the base, mimetic tendency they identified as central to the implantation of boxing and Japanese martial arts in Mexico. The Catholic daily *El País*, after first congratulating the rapid increase in sporting clubs throughout the Republic, thundered against the perceived betrayal of Mexican values that threatened their civilization. In a front-page editorial, it proclaimed, "We will be more humane than our neighbors:"

> The American and Americanizing newspapers of this capital, like the injudicious public that systematically forgets all their own [customs] in order to

inculcate themselves with foreign "vices and virtues" in flushed mixtures, cry now for the loss of their favorite spectacle, *el box* [sic], as Yankee as it is savage.

The reporters crowded around the Señor Governor of the Federal District, Don Guillermo Landa y Escandón, inquiring why he had frustrated their great satisfaction in seeing two men crunch bones, denying them the permit to fight; to which our humanitarian Sr. Governor responded "You can announce, in my name, that boxing has reached its end in this District."

In the name of humanity: Bravo![193]

The official journalistic organs of the Porfirian government added to the complexity of the debate by offering their congratulation to the valuable initiatives of the Romero brothers. They offered youth "undoubtedly beneficial" effects that, in addition to other ameliorative benefits, would give their bodies "elegance and beauty."[194] *El Diario* congratulated the Romero brothers and encouraged their letter-writing campaign to the governors of all states of the Republic that offered instruction in combat sport for their citizens. *El Imparcial* threw its lot in with the Club Atlético Internacional, promising to report and assist in the "elevation of 'sport' in [their] nation."[195]

Not only was cultivating manly bodies essential to Mexico in time of war, but boxing was a panacea for number of other social concerns:

> It can offer to the motherland (madre patria) a contingent of serene and conditioned soldiers who in times of danger are not derailed before bloodshed nor before the glint of arms and that in peace time are not drained and exhausted working the machines in a factory. Today, now that our people are beginning to scrutinize the word "SPORT" and they start to understand its meaning we should help them like one helps a child when it takes its first steps, facilitating them by any means possible, leveling any obstacles that arise, so that with sure steps they advance to the ideal perfection of the race.[196]

## Crisis by Proxy: Jack Johnson and the Great White Hope in Mexico in 1910

On the eve of the Mexican centennial and controversial presidential election of 1910, the popularity of boxing continued to increase despite continued resistance from the government. Amid these epoch-defining events, the racially charged July 1910 boxing match between Jack Johnson and Jim Jeffries reached Mexican readers. Newspapers portrayed it as a global racial crisis. As in Cuba, writers endowed the bout with meanings that mirrored local conditions and broader critiques of US society. Though it occurred deep within US territory, in Reno, Nevada, Mexican newspapers published hundreds of stories and dozens of images that traced the buildup to the bout, its round-by-round details, and the race riots and lynching of African Americans that ensued after Jack Johnson's resounding victory.

These scandals became a focal point for critical discussions of US race relations and a means to define Mexico in opposition US barbarity and hypocrisy. The match also evoked broader discussions of white supremacy. For some writers, Johnson's victory signaled a blow to US pretensions of superiority over other nations. The long-standing narrative that posited Anglo-Saxons standing at the pinnacle of the racial hierarchy was exposed as meaningful irony. The national sport of the United States, long perceived in Mexico as a quintessential aspect of US culture, was the means through which long-degraded African Americans exposed the fallacy of all-encompassing white supremacy. Some Mexican and US American boxers in Mexico had recreated this context in Mexico City. They had publicly drawn the color line that was at stake in the match between the "Great White Hope" and the "Bad Nigger" in the United States.[197]

Johnson first won the heavyweight boxing title in 1908. His victory over the Canadian Noah Brusso (aka Tommy Burns) in Sydney, Australia, had begun a global search for a "white hope" that could win back the title. Films of the fight in Sydney played to large crowds in Mexico City theaters such as the Metropolitan Academy.[198] Readers were treated to multiple accounts of Johnson's risqué social and personal life, especially his marriages to white women. The angst created by Johnson's ownership of what one writer deemed the emperorship of masculinity was reflected in much of the public commentary over his life inside and outside the ring.[199]

*El Imparcial* asked its readers, "Are there any whites alive who can snatch the title away from Johnson?"[200] Newspapers translated and printed celebrity novelist Jack London's brooding account of the bout. London was certain that the events in Reno presaged a racial war. He grudgingly admitted Johnson had surprised white observers by not showing the "yellow streak" of cowardice that was supposedly the mark of all African Americans.[201] Johnson "demolished the chosen representative ... of the white race. ... He fought a white man and toyed with him in a white man's land and in front of a crowd of whites who did not wish him to win." Johnson's performance, London relayed to his readers, had been "a black man's monologue in front of 20,000 spectators."

Coverage of Johnson-Jeffries began in Mexico several months before the bout. Between 1904, when Johnson first gained global notice, and 1910, nearly five hundred articles recounted narratives about Johnson's rise and clash with the racial and gendered status quo. *El Diario*, a newspaper in which cartoons were uncommon, printed hopeful images of a muscular Jeffries standing ready to crush the stereotyped inflated lips of a bewildered Jack Johnson.[202] It published lengthy editorials that explained the racialized history of the color line and Jack Johnson's challenge to white dominance in the prize ring. In the aftermath of the bout, the novelist José Escofet mused, "It is real and serious, a punch from Jack Jhonson [sic] has shocked the world. This *upper cut* has a terrible transcendence; we have already seen that it has caused riots in the Republic of the North. It has awakened global anxiety."[203] Escofet used these events to criticize the United States more broadly. US Americans viewed Jeffries's loss as a "catastrophe for the white race" and a "deterioration of their [US] prestige." These grandiose conclusions, he implied, were easy to understand for anyone with knowledge of the debased nature of social prestige and white supremacy in US culture. This taste for brutality and fetish for violent performances of manhood over the refined pleasures of art and poetry, Escofet argued, were the leitmotif of American identity.[204]

*La Patria* reported on the hundreds of police officers necessary to keep jubilant *negros* in check after Johnson's victory.[205] Mexican readers learned of Johnson's every move, his white wife, his expensive tastes, and how he enraged white Americans. As one Mexican commentator phrased it, "this thing that a pugilist of the Ethiopian race dominates a Caucasian is depressing."[206] Mexicans read that Johnson was more than a simple and brutish athlete; he was a threat to white dominance over supposedly lesser races, his power directly tied to the medium of his celebrity. He planned to take a victory lap around the world, stopping in such places as British India, China, and Japan. There he would give boxing exhibitions and speeches about race relations. "Surely," one editorialist mused, the Negro pugilist would talk about how the "yellow" and "black races" should "dominate the white."[207] Johnson's example would impugn the racial and cultural basis of European colonialism and neocolonialism. As if to illustrate this fear, one weekly magazine published large pictures of a shirtless Johnson and detailed images of his clenched fist overshadowing that of Jeffries.[208]

The racial tensions that boiled over into violence on US streets after the bout caused anxiety outside the United States. Readers in Mexico learned that the governor of Havana, fearing "an upsurge in the race question" in Cuba, had outlawed films of the bout. Many cities in the United States had done the same. The film of Johnson-Jeffries was not outlawed in Mexico, but a writer for *El Abogado Cristiano* imagined scenes of barbarism if Mexican children were exposed to it:

> Here, among us, the governor of Federal District said he would not oppose the

exhibition of the film, given that here the negro problem does not exist. Brave reasoning! No, Sr. Governor, the negro problem does not exist in the country, but the moral problem implicated in this brutal fight between those boxers does exist and will continue to exist. And this problem (boxing matches in Mexico), deeper and more painful than the consequences of racial conflict in the north, deserves to be dealt with by our authorities. But in a country where bullfighting, cockfighting, and other such edifying things are tolerated: why not show film that is a brilliant example of brutality for our people whose blood needs so little to come to a boil? The fight between the black and the white took place on the fourth of July, anniversary of the independence of the United States, casting a stain on the glory of that day. We propose that we keep the film until the sixteenth of September [Mexican Independence Day and centenary] and exhibit it in front of thousands of boys and girls who are there to sing the Centenary Hymn?[209]

Despite these dire warnings, the hour-and-half-long film reached Mexico by sea and first played in the port of Veracruz in late July. *La Opinión* (Veracruz) reported that viewers were promised an imaginary trip to Reno. Local theaters advertised the "pleasure or displeasure" of witnessing the "sensational spectacle" that had "world-wide resonance." The writer warned that it was difficult to see emotion on the face of Johnson because he was the "color of pinkish tar," and black skin did not reproduce well on film.[210] Despite attempts by several groups to prevent theaters from showing it, another critic posited that the fight film was the best movie he had ever seen. This triumph of moviemaking, this commenter held, was aside from the fact that Johnson was both a slave and a despot whose sole aspiration was to anger whites.[211] The controversial film reached Mexico City by early August. One critic reported that the Salón Rojo cinema overflowed with spectators, "attracted by the novelty of a spectacle worthy of barbarous times."[212] The film was screened in numerous other cities in addition to Mexico City and Veracruz. In San Luis Potosí, a large crowd of African American laborers, the *colonia negra*, joined numerous Mexicans in the local cinema to watch the annihilation of Jeffries by Johnson. The *colonia americana*, by which the writer meant white Americans, was conspicuously absent.[213]

The film showed for several months in Mexico and helped keep the bout in the public sphere long after the postfight riots had subsided. The novelist Carlos González Peña reflected that Jeffries had lost his "manly glory." The massive public attention to this sad spectacle angered the writer. In the months before July, the telegraph wires had unceasingly vibrated with the details of the boxers' diets, their pulse rates, and the degree of darkness of Johnson's skin. "Never before was the cable so petty or so detailed." The entire world, he mocked, hung on these minutiae. The spectacle had ended with stabbings of Negroes, riots, and other scandals enacted by those "indignant because the white race had been beaten, because the white race had lost its prestige and superiority at the hands of a son of Africa." González Peña imagined these scenes as the antithesis of civilization and as a moment for pan-Latin solidarity against barbarous yankeedom: "Vibrating from the unison of our Latin sentiments, we want to scream at these men: No! It will not be the Jeffries or the Jhonsons [sic] who decide the destiny of the races."[214]

Johnson's challenges to the color line outside the ring were an ongoing topic of discussion and criticism of racial politics in the United States. In an article titled "The Black Hand in Action," a writer for *La Iberia*, a conservative newspaper, satirized the reaction of the "pseudo-aristocrats" of New York to Johnson's plan to buy a home in an all-white neighborhood of Brooklyn. *Blue Bloods* there, he reported, had goose bumps and were terrified at the prospect of living near the boxer: "This shows the North American hatred of the colored race and the falseness of the democratic ideals so vaunted in the colossal republic." The nightmare of white New Yorkers was "that shortly . . . the corpulent negro, who in the ring in Reno extinguished forever, in a single blow, the legendary pride of a race," would be a neighbor. Such an inflated sense of self and irrational fear, the writer reasoned, did not exist in Mexico to the same degree. "If Johnson had come to Mexico to live in *Colonia Roma* (a wealthy neighborhood of Mexico City), for example, the families would not have felt anything but curiosity, and this only at first, without ever thinking of running away or becoming indignant, and even then, they might think themselves *chic* enough to ask him for a lesson in the gymnasium."[215]

A critic for *El Diario del Hogar* summed up the conclusions of many writers. The Johnson-Jeffries bout had clearly established the "muscular superiority" of the black over the white race. Human supremacy had previously been gauged by the development of noble sentiments and artistic achievement. Negroes, he argued, had always figured in the second category of humanity and were "inferior beings in this sense." But with Johnson's victory:

> It seems like negroes in the United States don't wish to understand this, and wanting to change the established order . . . they have caused great disorder with which they want to impose themselves and force an accounting, even in public. And where will this new danger, darker than the yellow peril, stop?[216]

Though in 1910 Johnson had not yet set foot in Mexico, his image was appropriated and deployed to advertise products and as a sex symbol. La Tabaclera Mejicana, a cigarette company, published a short farcical piece that claimed the secret to his victory over Jeffries was due to his exclusively smoking its products. The satirical magazine *La Risa* printed an entire-page cartoon in which Johnson wears skimpy boxing shorts and has the inflated lips so common in caricatures of African Americans during this period. A fashionably dressed woman drapes herself over his heavily muscled chest and arms: "Oh, Jhonson! Jhonson!" she intones. "I seem so pale at your side!"[217] Despite the fear and disgust over Johnson, his image carried diverse meanings in popular culture.

Conservative observers, like their sportsmen counterparts, looked to the lessons of history and current events abroad. The interracial prizefight between African American Jack Johnson and the "white hope" Jim Jeffries in Reno on July 4, 1910, provided fodder for their excoriations. With the victory of Jack Johnson, the "arrogant and savage Yankee" had received his due.[218] Not only were the race riots after the fight proof of the danger of boxing for the public, they also dealt a blow to the "haughtiness of the white man of the north, who thinks himself superior to all men not born in the land of Linch [sic] and shows his vigor by cruelly abusing the weak and killing the unfortunate *negros* with repugnant impunity."[219]

Shortly after Johnson's victory, the Mexican boxer and actor Cuauhtémoc Aguilar set off on a tour of Mexico, starting on the Oaxacan coast. He traveled with his team of "mulatto" and "negro" boxers, including one crowd favorite named "Young Jack Johnson."[220] The public, it seemed, did not share the editorialists' fear that Johnson represented a threat to racial hierarchy. Or, perhaps, that fear did not outweigh the crowd's taste for spectacle that created such consternation among cultural critics. In the small port town of Salina Cruz (Oaxaca), during the saint's festival celebrated from "time immemorial," families came from all over the region to watch Young Jack Johnson take on the Mexican champion, Aguilar.[221]

Blurring the high-low cultural divide, Mexicans read boxing commentaries and the normative musings of such literary celebrities as Enrique Gómez Carrillo.[222] Gómez Carrillo portrayed boxing as the most fashionable and well-attended of all public spectacles in Paris, outstripping even the Paris Opera. Far from barbaric, boxing was essential for any modern urban man. Its practice was ennobling and it gave men control and security over their corporeal selves.[223] Stressing that the highly cultured French, along with the English and Americans, were devotees of pugilism likely lent Gómez Carrillo's assertions greater legitimacy. This transnational worldview was daily reading for Mexicans on the eve of the Revolution.

FIGURE 1. "Pugilism in Perspective." General Valeriano Weyler faces Uncle Sam in an allegorical boxing match on the eve of the Spanish-American War. The illustration appeared in a satirical Mexican magazine, *El Hijo de Ahuizote*, and it evoked the popular image of US militant expansion being fueled by cultural elements such as boxing. According to many Mexican commentators, boxing in the United States, like martial arts in Japan, created robust citizens that allowed for successful military conquest. *El Hijo de Ahuizote: Mexico para los mexicanos*, January 3, 1897.

FIGURE 2. "Fernando Colín and José Matjoy [sic] in a Boxing Match." Joe Maljoy was one of many African American journeymen prizefighters who made their living as "professors of boxing" in late nineteenth- and early twentieth-century Mexico. As a group, they constituted a highly visible subculture in Mexico City and beyond. Their classes and public performances prompted legal prohibitions on boxing, but they often worked around the laws by claiming that their craft was "scientific" and that it would elevate Mexican manhood to international standards of virility. *El Mundo Ilustrado*, November 5, 1905.

FIGURE 3. Voluntary associations, such as the Club Olimpico of Mexico City channeled novel international ideas about building and training the male body in an effort to fortify masculinity, which was threatened by the debilitating effects of modern urban life. These clubs often hired foreign professors, such as the African American Billy Clarke. They celebrated idols such as Eugene Sandow, the first celebrity bodybuilder, as exemplar specimens of manhood obtained through scientific training.

FIGURE 4. "[John Lester] Johnson and [Sam] McVea at the Beginning of One of Their Rounds." In 1915, Cuban cartoonists seized upon the interracial Jack Johnson vs. Jess Willard prizefight in Havana to present some African Americans and Afro-Cubans as enviable specimens of manhood. Physicians called in to examine these exotic boxers declared them to be in nearly perfect condition, a lesson to all Cuban men. Seldom before had laudatory depictions of African-descended individuals been serialized in this manner. In the immediate aftermath of the racial war known as the Massacre of the Independent Party of Color (1912), it was surprising to see approving depictions of black men engaging in violent behavior, especially in an interracial context. *El Mundo*, February 21, 1915.

FIGURE 5. "The Invincible Nestle." This image is one of dozens of illustrations from around the western hemisphere that drew on white angst and Jack Johnson's celebrity to sell products. In this Argentine poster, a white child, fortified by Nestle milk, reclaims the title of white supremacy from the "champion of the world," Jack Johnson. This image appeared in a magazine in Buenos Aires while Johnson was temporarily in exile there. *Caras y Caretas, Numero Almanaque*, 1915.

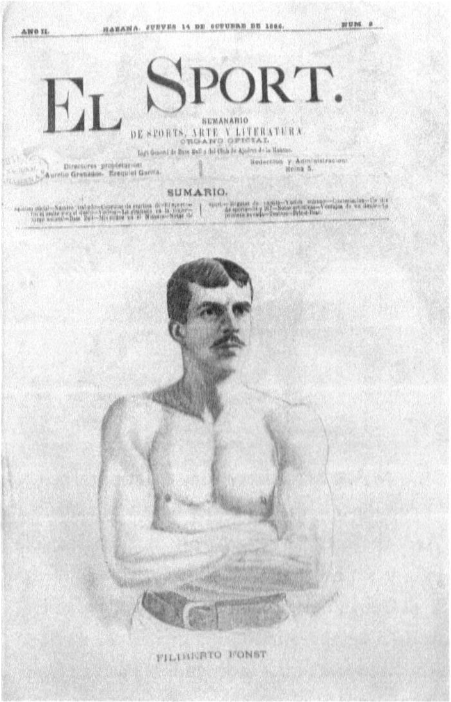

FIGURE 6. "Filiberto Fonst." This cover of the Cuban magazine *Sport* from 1886 depicts a young man celebrated as the epitome of the modern Cuban. Pictures of shirtless men were rare in this period, and though boxing was tenuously legal and associated with the US demimonde in Havana, he is depicted as a prizefighter. *El Sport*, October 14, 1886. Courtesy of the José Martí National Library, Havana.

FIGURE 7. "The Stadium." This image shows the ring and stadium built by the American publisher George Bradt, flanked by the Cuban and US flag flying at equal height. The first purpose-built boxing venue in Cuba, the stadium was the home of such racist American imports as the infamous Battle Royale, in which six to eight Afro-Cubans were blindfolded and then fought to the last person standing for the entertainment of Cuban and American audiences. The stadium lasted only a few months; Cubans did not have a taste for spectacles of this nature. *Pittsburgh Post Gazette*, April 4, 1915.

FIGURE 8. This is the cover of the Mexico City newspaper *El Demócrata*. All of the dozens of daily newspapers that served the capital and beyond chronicled the rise of the Argentine boxer Luis Ángel Firpo. As the headline conveys, Dempsey and Firpo were global "symbols of two opposing races."

FIGURE 9. This clipping, from the newspaper *El Mundo* (Havana), illustrates one of many boxing matches between the "Cuban Hope," Anastasio Peñalver, and African American heavyweights such as John Lester Johnson. These popular bouts surged during months surrounding Jack Johnson's 1915 loss of the heavyweight title in Havana. It also calls attention to the Battle Royale that forms part of the lineup.

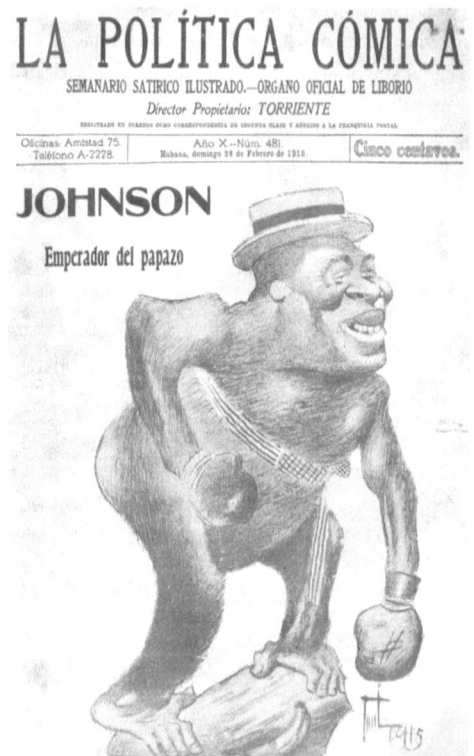

FIGURE 10. In this cover of a satirical magazine published in Havana, Jack Johnson is portrayed as an ape-like figure. Some images, like this one, mocked Johnson's race and his supposed pretentiousness. Others showed him as an admirable physical specimen and gentleman.

FIGURE 11. This full-page illustration shows Cuban perceptions of the global significance of the bout taking place in Havana. All the warring powers of Europe halt the war to watch the results of the racial drama unfolding in Cuba.

FIGURE 12. This cartoon by Cuban artist José Massaguer shows Johnson's effect on a cross-class and interracial group of Cubans when he arrived in the port in 1915. Chinese Cubans, Afro-Cubans, policemen, middle-class businessmen, and newspaper boys marvel at his self-confident presence. His expensive wardrobe and tastes were widely chronicled in the press.

No hay quien venza los precios fijos de "LA VERDAD".—*La caída fatal, Abril 5 de 1915.*

FIGURE 13. A hand-tinted postcard from Havana advertises a store. It also chronicles the triumph of the Great White Hope, Jess Willard, over Johnson. Johnson shields his eyes from sun, giving some credence to his later assertion that he had not been knocked out but had thrown the fight in order to be allowed back into the United States.

FIGURE 14. This image, from *La Política Cómica*, portrays Johnson as a "Zulu tourist traveling like a king of Congo." It also relays to readers that Johnson was in danger of being arrested and deported to the United States for violation of the Mann Act, for transporting a white woman across state lines for "immoral purposes."

FIGURE 15. This page from the Mexico City revista *El Tiempo Ilustrado* informs readers of the Johnson-Jeffries match in 1910. Readers learned that Johnson's victory over the former white champion led to race riots and lynchings in many cities in the United States. Johnson's complete mastery over his opponent set off an international search for a white boxer who could regain white supremacy in the ring.

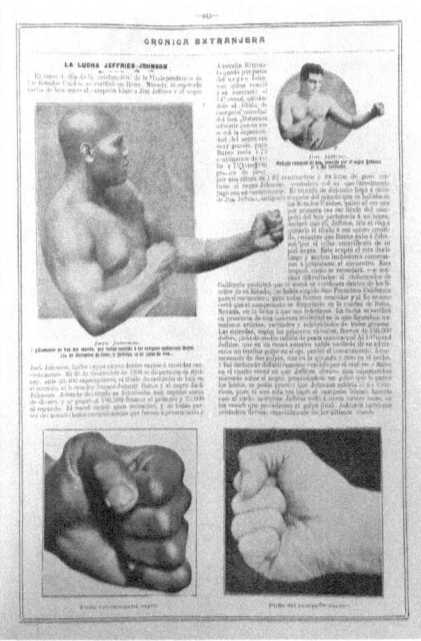

FIGURE 16. This image is the cover of a popular song for piano (1898) by the composer Dario Ramos Ortiz. His music often accompanied popular theater performances in Mexico City. It most likely features a rendering of Billy Smith and Billy Clarke's bout that so outraged the metropolitan press. Courtesy of the Archivo General de la Nación, Mexico. With many thanks to Professor Kevin Anzzolin.

FIGURE 18. A Cuban advertisement from 1923. It shows a corpulent white Cuban, empowered by patent elixir, defeating an anonymous boxer of African descent. Images such as this were widespread and evoked the fear of threatened masculinity that could be cultivated by boxing and the consumption of tonics and patent medicine.

FIGURE 19. A circa 1905 image from the match between the Afro-Dutchman Jim Smith and the Mexican boxer Cuauhtémoc Aguilar. The crowd rushed the ring after the bout, causing the police to intervene. They felt defrauded because the boxers had not fought hard enough.

FIGURE 20. This image from 1910 Mexico City portrays Johnson as a threatening sex symbol. Mexican readers were likely aware of the scandals that Johnson's interracial relationships caused in the United States. *La Risa*, November 26, 1910.

FIGURE 21. This image is from around 1906. On the left is Cuauhtémoc Aguilar, an actor, bullfighter, and boxer. He died during the Mexican Revolution fighting in Carranza's army. The fellow on the right is Jim Smith, who was born on the Caribbean island of Sint Eustatius, moved to Mexico as a boxing "professor," spoke Dutch, English, Spanish, and German, married a Mexican woman, and lived to ripe old age as a trainer for the Mexican military. They fought each other several times in the ring; their matches were often stopped by the police for obscenity and nudity. They helped make an exotic cultural import into something very Mexican. Courtesy of Fototeca Nacional de México, INAH.

FIGURE 22. "Champion of the Trompada." A drawing by the satirical artist José Guadalupe Posada in which the governor of the State of Hidalgo (perhaps) delivers a knockout blow to "civilization," represented by Billy Clarke. Boxing as civilization or barbarity figured often in discourse on the sport. *Gil Blas*, December 2, 1895.

FIGURE 23. "The Mote in Our Neighbor's Eye." A self-righteous Uncle Sam, as policeman and cultural imperialist during the first occupation of Cuba (1898–1902), tells Cubans that bullfighting is barbaric in the midst of violent US sports such as boxing and football. *Puck*, July 12, 1899.

CHAPTER THREE

# "Who Will Say We Are Not Progressing?"

*Cuba, Race, and Boxing in the Nineteenth and
Early Twentieth Centuries*

THIS CHAPTER EXAMINES the controversial importation of prizefighting to Cuba under three distinct political regimes: Spanish colonialism (until 1899), US military occupation (1899–1902; 1906–1909), and under the early independent Republic (1902–1915). It demonstrates that boxing, in particular, presented a symbolic and concrete challenge to cultural sovereignty, but that it was simultaneously a problematic site for the expression of aspirations for modernity and cosmopolitanism. As in Mexico, generational shifts in several interrelated social philosophies exposed important cultural fault lines. These divides evoked shifting expressions of proper masculinity, the content and scope of debate in the public sphere, and racialized practices governing public spectacle as an expression of cultural identity.

Beginning in the mid-nineteenth century, writing about boxing was a coded means of criticizing censorship of public spectacle. Prizefighting and bodybuilding were concrete and symbolic cultural practices that challenged the underlying norms of colonial and, later, neocolonial behavior. Engagement with prizefighting provided a potent metaphor to challenge powerful cultural currents emanating from the United States and Europe, and it provided spaces of oppositional self-definition. Cubans partially defined their nascent national culture against prizefighting, and later in an embrace of it.

## Cuba, Spain, and Public Spectacle in the Nineteenth Century

Cuba remained a colony of Spain until 1898. Wars for independence swept most of the hemisphere during the age of Atlantic revolutions in the late eighteenth and early nineteenth centuries, but Cuba remained under Spanish sovereignty.

Beginning with the American and Haitian Revolutions, these wars resulted in the loss of nearly all European colonies in the hemisphere. These movements led to the establishment of new nations constructed upon republican models of government.[1] In 1823, as these anticolonial battles reached a climax, the United States proclaimed the Monroe Doctrine. This controversial and unilateral declaration imposed US protection on the hemisphere. It also served to help preserve Cuba as a slave society under continued Spanish rule.[2] Using Monroe as a paradigm, the United States hoped to prohibit future European colonization.

In the aftermath of nineteenth-century political revolutions, Cuba's loyalty to the mother country resulted in its official title as the "Ever Faithful Isle." The Spanish crown rewarded its most loyal subjects, mainly slaveholding planters and merchants. It incentivized continued hegemony by granting economic freedoms unknown in nearly three hundred years of colonial economic policy. These policies of comparatively free trade resulted in the further expansion of slavery in Cuba.[3] Cuba's agro-industrial economy boomed in the early nineteenth century, due partially to access to new export markets, such as the United States. Cuban plantations produced enormous wealth based on sugar and tobacco harvested and processed by hundreds of thousands of enslaved Africans and, from the 1840s onward, Chinese indentured servants and indigenous Mexican laborers. Spain profited greatly from the income derived from this forced labor, especially after slavery was outlawed in British Caribbean colonies.[4] Though Cuban ports were intimately linked to cosmopolitan world trade, Spain sought to govern the terrain of culture and ideas by policing and censoring the growth of an independent Cuban identity.[5]

To maintain colonial loyalty, Spain cultivated and encouraged affective ties to bind Cubans to continued Spanish rule.[6] Colonial governors wanted Cubans to feel Spanish, yet they often denied them the rights of Iberian Spaniards. Protection was central in this relationship. Spain promised Cuban elites military defense against two interrelated sources of potential threat. First, the crown promised to protect against the ever-present threat of slave revolts that increased with the continued illegal (after 1820) importation of African slaves. The threatening example of the Haitian Revolution and the constant menace of slave revolts convinced planters that a permanent military force was necessary to protect their lives and investments.[7] Second, the Spanish crown sought to repress and defend against the spread of republican ideas from the rest of Latin America, especially the anticlerical and republican philosophies represented by leaders such as Benito Juárez in Mexico. Cuba would become an island bastion against nineteenth-century liberalism. It remained a counterweight to the political revolutions whose successor states formed the largest regional concentration of republican governments in the nineteenth century.

The relative economic autonomy Cuban planters enjoyed in the nineteenth century did not extend to freedom of the press, freedom of association, or effective representation in the Spanish Cortéz (legislative body). These political and social prohibitions were central to the development of a vibrant and autonomous public sphere.[8] The crown's representatives policed and censored the press and prohibited most autonomous civic social organizations. Colonial authorities carefully monitored any club or public gathering, even after free associations were legalized in the 1860s.[9] Though these attempts to control public opinion and political debate were never completely successful, they did retard the development of the public sphere, especially when compared to the relatively free press and contentious political and cultural debates that drove politics in Mexico in the same period. As historian Louis Pérez Jr. observes, despite these legislative attempts to quell the growth of Cuban identity, "Cubans registered their presence in the form of public display and social engagement. Something of a modern public sphere was in the making."[10] Spanish archives contain dozens of reports from the colonial government that detail attempts to prevent the introduction of Cuban exile newspapers and abolitionist literature from Britain and the United States.[11]

It was only in 1869 that the newly arrived captain general, Domingo Dulce (his title a reflection of the martial nature of colonial power), declared that Cubans would have the basic civil liberties of their counterparts on the peninsula. The declaration of freedom of the press coincided with the beginning of the thirty-year struggle for Cuban independence that would end in US intervention and occupation from 1898 to 1902. The period between 1869 and the defeat of Spain in 1898 witnessed a massive proliferation of newspapers and revistas along with newly legal but highly regulated civic social organizations. These new laws legalized private newspapers and revistas in theory, but the government still censored all publications and reserved the right to cancel or prohibit any newsprint, photograph, poster, or drawing. The new laws established press courts, *tribunales de imprenta*, with broad-ranging powers to censor speech.[12] The statutes also prohibited any publication that mocked the government or "Christian morals." Despite these narrow openings in the public sphere, several visitors to Havana in the last half of the nineteenth century commented on the large quantity and diversity, both Cuban and international, of newspapers in private reading rooms in the city.[13] The completion of the telegraph line between Havana and Key West and the growing frequency of steam travel to Cuba created informational flows that the Spanish crown could not effectively stanch. Maintaining cultural hegemony amid such novel and dynamic challenges proved impossible. Spaces for debate grew.

All associations had to be approved by the crown, and it reserved the right to enter the premises of a club without a warrant and dissolve it for any reason.[14] Any public spectacle or public diversion, including such events as bullfights, cockfights, theatrical shows, and any boxing matches, had to be licensed by the government and attended by state representatives. Foreign troupes of performers, since the early nineteenth century, were to be especially monitored by the police and heavily taxed.[15] One of the primary responsibilities of these censors, their manual stated, was to prevent any dangerous speech or association.[16] Colonial governors perceived the practice of imported sports such as baseball as a threat to the dominance of an aristocratic cultural elite and as a danger to continued sovereignty.[17] If Cubans, to borrow Louis Pérez's phrase, were becoming more Cuban, they held less loyalty to Spain.

Because these reforms came relatively late to Cuba, there are fewer documentary sources that illustrate the cultural debates on the behaviors of daily life so common in Mexico during the same period. Tracing discourse on popular culture is a painstaking process of reading between the lines. This lacuna challenges historians seeking to recreate the diverse viewpoints that are clearly evident in the Mexican media during this period. Despite these challenges, there are a few narratives that provide important vantage points on how Cubans perceived and created meaning out of imported public spectacle and blood sport in the nineteenth century. The truncated public sphere confronted novel spectacles such as boxing and male body culture and, as in Mexico, used them as a lens to describe themselves. Boxing in nineteenth-century Cuba was deployed to ridicule and delegitimize US pretensions to be the exemplar New World civilization. Criticism of boxing formed part of the growing social commentary on what was Cuban and what was not.

### Subversion and Abolition in a Nineteenth-Century Havana Gymnasium

In July of 1842, a clandestine government informant in Havana brought to Gerónimo Valdés alarming information about seditious speech behind closed doors.[18] As captain general, Valdés was the highest-ranking official in Cuba. His long career in defense of the Spanish empire made him apprehensive of the power of speech and free association to foment anticolonial uprisings. Two decades before, he had commanded Spanish loyalists against South American rebels during the wars for independence at the pivotal Battle of Ayacucho.[19] Those battles resulted in the loss of almost all of Spain's empire and the rise of antimonarchical republican governments in the former colonies. Valdés's primary responsibility was to ensure that these upheavals never materialized in Cuba. The rich, sugar-producing island was to remain Spanish, and its African slaves, the backbone of the colonial economy, were to continue in bondage. These two outcomes were mutually dependent. All other concerns were subordinate.[20]

Valdés's informant overheard seditious and abolitionist conversations in a gymnasium where young creoles (native-born Cubans) and foreigners gathered daily. There they strengthened their bodies and, he feared, plotted the overthrow of the colonial government and fomented the abolition of slavery.[21] In the foreign, exotic, and hence suspect environment of the gymnasium, wherein the members "propagate unwise, anti-political, and risky conversations, such as those that critique the operations of the Supreme Government and the authorities of the island . . . they promote ideas of independence from the metropolis, and also ideas about abolition and the freedom of slaves."[22] This was clearly a violation of the law. Any public discussion of the "slave question" was forbidden in Cuba.[23]

The gym was beyond Havana's city walls, outside the main precinct of surveillance and colonial power, in the neighborhoods where free blacks, mulattos, and poor whites formed the bulk of the population.[24] These classes, according to colonial authorities, were particularly vulnerable to such rabble-rousing. Anticolonial and abolitionist uprisings had occurred in this precinct before.[25]

Valdés responded to this threat by imposing arbitrary constraints on the gym and its director, the Cuban-born intellectual Rafael de Castro. The Gimnásio Normal would now be permitted to open its doors only three days a week. All sessions would be scrutinized and censored by a military chief. The doors would remain closed unless such official chaperones were present to prevent seditious speech or actions. Freedom of association was tightened.[26]

Though these violations had occurred under his watch, Valdés stressed to his superiors that the gym's existence was not his fault. The danger posed in that space and context might have been foreseen had his predecessor denied the license. The gym's permit had been granted even though de Castro had not provided the requisite list of rules and members' names for the approval and oversight of Havana's military police.[27] It was common knowledge, the captain general wrote, that in "these types of establishments a multitude of young people gather who, because of the inexperience of their few years, are susceptible to committing disorders." Several months later, a standard time lapse for transatlantic communication before the telegraph, the secretary of state in Madrid commended Valdés for his swift action in putting an end to "such abuses."[28]

Though this series of events may seem like an obscure act of municipal paranoia, the ideas that drove the establishment of a gymnasium in this period of growing Cuban nationalism, and the reaction to it, help explain changing concepts of masculinity, corporeality, and nationhood in Cuba. Surprisingly, the gymnasium survived until the end of the nineteenth century despite the apparent danger it posed to colonial order. This endurance over the chaotic nineteenth century—rare for any institution—was due to the concerted efforts of the foremost organization of intellectuals on the island, the Sociedad Económico del Amigos del País.

This society was also responsible for much of the early press in Cuba and ran several newspapers, all subject to prior censorship by law, in various cities on the island. For the Sociedad, the renovation and modernization of Cuban bodies was both a symbolic and practical resistance to the backwardness and decadence of colonial rule. It was also a patriotic act to import the latest ideas from Paris and the United States. Those peoples deployed the most modern understanding of how to create vigorous bodies and moral hygiene that resulted from training. Among the most renowned Cuban nationalist intellectuals of the day, José de la Luz y Caballero and Domingo del Monte, supported and patronized the effort to build a gymnasium to offer free training to "all classes" of Havana youth.[29] Del Monte wrote that he attended the gym regularly and that his four-year-old son had become "intrepid and courageous" due to his training there.[30] Before officials would permit such ideas to reach a broader public, Cuban creoles had to convince them in a language permissible for colonial subjects.

In September 1838, the Cuban anatomist and surgeon (and Rafael de Castro's brother) Vicente Antonio de Castro penned an article that challenged the constraints of colonial society in the name of the modern and "civilized" human body.[31] Rafael de Castro was a convincing writer. He was a medical doctor and boasted a foreign education that imbued him with social legitimacy. Despite these credentials, he later went into exile for his anticolonial activism typified by his protest against the expulsion of the British abolitionist David Turbull in 1842, roughly at the same time that the family gymnasium came under the suspicion of the captain general.[32]

The de Castro brothers attended school in Paris, where they were the "disciples" of the controversial Spanish exile Coronel Francisco Amorós.[33] As the director of the Military Gymnasium, Amorós theorized a positive correlation among cultures that esteemed the cultivation of vigorous bodies and the comparative robustness of those civilizations. Amorós's ideas were fundamentally democratic: he argued that horizontal citizenship, the antithesis of social and racial hierarchy, was the most important element of national greatness. He sought to implant physical training to elevate the body of the nation to health and robustness. Amorós was expelled from Spain after the restoration of monarchical rule following the Napoleonic occupation, but he had been allowed to return to his native Valencia. He was subsequently granted a title of nobility in the late 1830s.[34] After thus being rehabilitated in the eyes of the empire, Amorós's ideas were less controversial than they would have been had he still been in exile from Spain. They were safer for the de Castro brothers in Cuba to present to the censors.

In "Gimnástica," Vicente de Castro pleads with the Cuban public to embrace new ideas about the importance of the cultivation of individual bodies for national advancement. He argued that Cuban parents worsened the enervating island climate by rejecting imported ideas about the body. If emulated, new practices could counteract the debilitating effects of geography and climate. He pledged himself to work toward founding new institutions to teach corporeal development, instilling those "advances in civilization."[35]

De Castro impugned fellow Cubans. They were out of step with modernity. This atavism was not inevitable; his education and knowledge provided remedies that could transcend the weight of history and climate. The first and most obvious defect in national health was that Cubans were not a people in motion. Stasis was the enemy of progress. It symbolized the stagnation resulting from colonial rule. The scientific use of new machines to train and fortify the human body could counteract the negative effects of climate and colonization and rescue Cuban youths from lives of vice, dissipation, and premature death. This geographic determinism, de Castro reasoned, partly explained why Cubans were unable to rise to a higher level of civilization.

The author's social position and his history of political activism added gravity to his writing. De Castro, along with his younger brother Rafael, was a political agitator constantly at odds with Spanish authority. In his published writing he was, by necessity, inventive when critiquing the colonial government. They could prohibit publication or suppress any text that did not promote the continued legitimacy of colonial rule. They also imprisoned, fined, or exiled those editors who did not clear their manuscripts with the government, even if their articles were otherwise unobjectionable.[36] Several newspapers and reviews that communicated the de Castro brothers' writings were repressed or monitored by the Spanish authorities that dutifully reported to Madrid about such subversive threats.[37] Cautioned by Captain General Tacón in 1835, the Spanish government decided that Cubans, unlike Spaniards on the peninsula, were not ready for freedom of the press and that public opinion was not sturdy enough to withstand outside ideas.[38] This abstract language did little to hide the real fear of a free press in Cuba:

abolition and independence. The insinuation that Cuban intellectuals such as the de Castro brothers were not mature enough for the responsibility of their own thoughts likely added fuel to their desires for independence and their resistance to generalized paternalism that justified Spanish rule.

The year "Gimnástica" appeared, 1838, marked a climax in the colonial government's attempts to repress critical speech, making even de Castro's veiled attacks on colonial rule a calculated risk.[39] Censorship went beyond print and into the public spaces of theaters, circuses, and dance halls. The owners of these spaces of exchange were required to apply for expensive and often arbitrary permits and were also subject to strict vigilance by zealous loyalists who dissected each performance for its political and cultural correctness in the hope of being rewarded by the crown.[40]

At the center of "Gimnástica" are two interrelated arguments. First, the lack of institutional life and free civic society are the greatest hindrance to the betterment of Cuban society. He implied that Cuba was a nation, not a mercantilist territorial extension of Spain. The lack of educational institutions, in particular, drove parents to send their children abroad. Though wealthy parents were accustomed to educating their children in Europe and the United States, this sort of "degrading tribute to foreign nations" was no longer acceptable in a country that aspired to its own expression of civilization.[41] Though Cubans were quick to imitate even trifling practices from abroad, Castro bemoaned, they had been unwilling to embrace challenges to the sedate "complacency of [their] lives." Institutions should follow ideas, and foreigners were correct to mock the lack of modern education in Cuba.

The second argument derived from the first. Colonialism inscribed itself even on the bodies of Cubans, preventing them from evolving into something greater: citizens. The stifling of civic social institutions prevented them from battling the effects of their natural environment. As a physician, de Castro wrote with scientific authority. De Castro's nationalism, however, was an elite and exclusive idea justified by the complaints of the elite classes over their own lack of freedom. Absent was any notion of African-descended peoples whose labor was the central point of profit and the colonial raison d'être. De Castro's coded calls for independence, while a challenge to the political and cultural authority of Spain, did not break with the fundamental racial and social hierarchies that anchored the colonial system. While de Castro deployed his ideas by writing coded articles and building a gym to create spaces for discussion of politics and the cultivation of civilized bodies, other public venues challenged the boundaries of permissible public spectacle in Havana and the foundations of tradition upon which the colonial edifice stood.

In a broad sense, the above confrontations constituted the exploration and appropriation of novel forms of cultural identity. As Louis Pérez Jr. has argued, the increasing flow of ideas during the nineteenth century likely outweighed overtly political acts of rebellion and military resistance in the demise of the colonial empire in Cuba. "There is more than ample evidence to suggest that the political mobilizations of the nineteenth century were consequences—and not causes—of larger moral transformations by which the logic of the status quo could no longer sustain the claim of credibility."[42] In the nineteenth century:

> Cubans embraced the promise of modernity as a source of self-fulfillment and means of self-knowledge, a seemingly endless influx of new values that in the course of events and over the course of time contributed to the collapse of the moral infrastructure upon which the colonial system rested.... Some of the most significant transformations were experienced not as a matter of political circumstance but as a cultural condition, of moral structures being dissembled and reassembled in function of changing social needs, change that served to suggest what lo cubano might look like.[43]

## "Man Fighting" and the Public Sphere in the 1840s

On April 7, 1848, an editorialist for the newspaper *Diario de la Marina* took stock of an alarming new spectacle at the Circo Habanero (Havana Circus).[44] The Circo was on the waterfront just outside the defensive city walls that, increasingly, failed to contain the explosive growth and urbanization of the city.[45] Colonial authorities fixated on the supposed disorder outside city walls, and the circus was surrounded by symbols of the coercive power of the metropolis: the Royal Prison, two fortresses, and the military parade grounds. One of the few remaining images of the Circo, a lithograph from 1853, portrays it as a substantial building crowded with both light-skinned and dark-skinned Cubans.[46]

A man identified only as Mr. Charles, "the king of the pugilists or *boxers*," plastered posters in which he challenged any "men of strength" in Cuba to test their prowess against his. Mr. Charles was variously described as a performer from New Orleans, or a Frenchman, or both. His foreignness alone was not unusual in Havana. In the 1840s, Havana had a population of nearly two hundred thousand. Nearly 10 percent of those residents, not counting sailors temporarily in port, were foreigners, including almost seven hundred US Americans.[47]

The commercialized display of violence piqued the interest of the unidentified editorialist, but he looked on such practices with disdain. Pugilism was uncivilized, he had heard. Eyes were popped out of their sockets, men were killed, the drunken masses lost fortunes betting on the outcome. The fighters were bathed in *aguardiente* (a sugar-cane-based spirit). "Man-fighting" (*lucha de hombres*), the writer continued, was human cockfighting and spectators craved barbarity.[48]

Mr. Charles's first bout allayed many but confirmed some of the writer's fears. The performer struck him as admirable physical specimen, "over six feet tall and a yard wide," a foreign "colossus" in Havana. The audience, he reported, was mostly of the lower classes with "few tunics" among them. He mused that had not a military parade been taking place at the same time, the crowd would have been "more select."[49] The enthusiastic mob surprised the viewer by not rioting, even though they intervened in the performance. They screamed for more violence, threw sawdust at the combatants, and demanded that Mr. Charles speak to them in Spanish. The lack of a military guard (because of participation in the parade) to maintain order, the writer implied, had made him apprehensive of how the rabble would respond to such a spectacle; it was good luck, perhaps, that they had been able to constrain themselves with the example of violence in front of them.[50]

A week after the first bout, the newspaper *Advisador del Comercio* published communication between Mr. Charles and an anonymous Cuban challenger. This first Cuban opponent would defend national honor against the insinuation that no one on the island could best Charles, whom the challenger called a "king lion among irrational people." The challenger described his emotional response when learning of the opportunity to fight this foreigner. He had read the many newspaper advertisements and viewed the posters on the walls of the old city but had not been able to attend the first bout. These stylized public challenges to masculine and national honor—similar to notices of dueling—were calculated to draw interest and paying spectators to the circus.[51] The mysterious appeal of the novelty was further stoked when the challenger announced he would wear a mask to protect his identity. Writers heightened the drama, perhaps unknowingly, when they acclaimed the masked fighter as an "errant knight who shows his love of adventure" and who might meet a tragic end in the ring. The audience was encouraged to come and see for themselves the following Sunday.[52]

The publicity worked as planned. On the Sunday of the bout, the Circo was filled to capacity with more than five hundred spectators. Such a congregation in the afternoon sun caused the venue to "heat up like an oven" and turned half of the faces in the crowd pink; the other half, presumably, did not have skin given to turning pink. Mr. Charles fought against three amateurs, defeating them easily and evoking a satirical response from a writer who chided that no one who was not a "Hercules" should hazard a challenge. Afterward, the masked man entered the ring for main event. After some attempts to attack Mr. Charles, he ended up on his back, drawing charges of fraud from the crowd that had expected a longer and more equal engagement. As the audience grew more dissatisfied and unruly, a challenger emerged and, stripping to his waist to reveal "formidable musculature," challenged Mr. Charles to a match. Charles responded that he was too tired to take on a new comer. The public, the editorialist explained, would not allow this, and they screamed, "Fight!, Fight!, Fight!" The ring judge intervened and promised the crowd that the bout would take place on the next day, temporarily quelling their demands while guaranteeing massive attendance at another moneymaking spectacle. The newspaper promised its readers that, along with the well-muscled "new champion" challenger, León Elliser, a *guajiro* (Cuban peasant), a "herculean sailor," and a Basque and Catalan would also appear to challenge Mr. Charles. One observer mused, upon seeing the large sums bet against the foreigner and in favor of the local Elliser and Cuban strongman Santiago Jiménez, that Cubans were "changing [their] habits" due to the pandemonium created by the new public spectacle.[53]

Throughout April and into May of 1848, Mr. Charles drew attention and commentary in Havana. Challengers understood the need for dramatic spectacle, and the press assisted them by providing details of their enviable masculinity. Miguel Torrens, a sailor from the Balearic Islands, had proven himself by lifting and holding a full barrel of wine over his head while drinking from it. The masses, unaccustomed to spectacles of wrestling and prizefighting, were constantly reminded that there were rules to prevent them from claiming fraud and demanding a return of their money when they were dismayed by the outcome.[54] Disorder and the unleashing of their passions was a tangible threat to the military police that monitored such gatherings, especially when the events were followed immediately by late-night dances and heavy drinking in the circus. In response, a satirist from Cádiz, Juan Corrales Mateos, wrote a stinging parody of the newfound sensation of boxing and wrestling. Corrales Mateos's essay, titled "A Boxing-Bullfighting Dream" (*Sueño Boxi-Taurico*), lauded bullfighting while sarcastically recounting the barbarism of the weekly boxing and wrestling matches at the circus. Men transforming into savages in the boxing ring was the "metamorphosis of the epoch."[55]

Corrales Mateos was seconded by an anonymous writer alarmed by the growing popularity of the foreign import and what it meant for the city:

> The crowd in the Circus increases every Sunday while it diminishes at the bullfights, and in the presence of such facts one is tempted to think that the national spectacle, par excellence, is going to be dethroned—Gaviño [a popular

bullfighter], who is a man of the fists, and directly interested in the matter [should] present himself one afternoon to the theater of Mr. Nin y Pons [owners of the Circo], and make King Carlos [Charles] eat the dust, as he normally does with the most dangerous of animals."[56]

The city's symbol of masculinity in public spectacle was impugned and provoked to defend Cuban honor. The class of people that attended these "manful" exhibitions unnerved more sedate *habaneros*. The "stupendous racket" that arose from the Circo created chaos; no one could understand anyone else in the area around the venue. The "noise of the multitude that boiled within it [the circus] crashed like the waves against the wall of the Saint Lazarus tower during a hurricane."[57] The intensity of the spectacle was such that "a nervous woman could not hear it without fainting."

One afternoon, a Valencian man succeeding in besting other challengers in the ring. The crowd, a journalist recounted, showered him with coins because, unlike the professional foreigners who didn't speak Spanish, he had "nothing of the Hercules." He was the common peninsular (born in Spain) youth who worked in the shops of the port city. Mr. Charles then defeated this unnamed youth and the crowd booed the outcome until they spilled out onto the street, where they were nervously monitored by the authorities. The reporter was doubtful that the police would allow another match, given the tension and emotion and potential for disorder present in such public spectacles.

Matches continued throughout the first half of 1848. Grudgingly, newspaper reporters relayed the details of each encounter. Large crowds of Cubans and foreigners continued to attend the Circo, where they marveled at the "iron musculature" of Charles and his Cuban opponent León. Wrestling matches did not unsettle writers as much as boxing matches, which they still "could not tolerate" (*no podemos dar asiento*).[58] In one instance, a theater critic rechristened the circus the "Circo de Leon y Charles" and labeled the pleasure the crowd took in boxing matches a "glory of Lucifer."[59] Observers marveled at the income of the Circo, its "monstrous crowds," and catalogued the "rain of rivals," Cubans and Spaniards, who took up the lucrative challenge.[60] Being familiar with the new culture of spectacle and physicality became ambiguous shorthand for being modern and fashionable. One satirical article recounted a conversation between two strangers attending one of the bouts. A visitor from the town of Remedios (a sixteenth-century town in the province of Las Villas) is educated by a habanero on the finer points of the show, because those from the interior "are not very civilized."[61]

By mid-June of 1848, this theatrical violence spread to other cities and gave many writers in the public sphere a sort of outrage fatigue. Charles traveled by steamship around the coasts of the island, stopping in port cities to challenge locals. He was already a celebrity due to the circulation of Havana newspapers. One writer in Matanzas promised to serve as a prophylactic for his readers; he would attend the match and report back if it was "worthy of their attention" and to prevent their exposure to such potentially distasteful entertainment.[62]

Thousands of foreigners lived among Spaniards and Cubans in the confined space of the old city wall of Havana, and the importation of new genres of public spectacle were eroding elite prerogative to define entertainment preferences. US citizens had lived in Havana and other sites in Cuba since US independence, and many of them were directly involved in the illegal slave trade, smuggling, and other demimonde activities.[63] The importation of violence as entertainment, "man-fighting" as it was called, only added to the array of illicit or unsavory entertainment options in the cosmopolitan port city. Mr. Charles had rankled Cuban society by holding boxing matches in a theater that was being taken over by performances that catered to the international and multiracial lower classes. Known as a "theater of great disgraces" and "a disgusting citadel" for its risqué spectacles, the wooden Circo Habanero was a meeting place of Cubans and foreigners.[64] It was likely a site where poor creoles and peninsular Spaniards mixed with free people of color. The Circo, later renamed the Teatro Villanueva, was a few yards outside the old city wall that divided the respectable city from the growing *extramuro* neighborhoods.[65] It opened in April of 1847 and quickly filled with spectators drawn to see foreign prestidigitators, illusionists, acrobats, and strongmen, all acts calculated to amaze and entertain habaneros by giving them a taste of the exotic and modern outside world. Theatrical advertisements assured them they would be enthralled by the performers, just like in the United States, France, and elsewhere.[66] It hosted masked balls—on one occasion observers noted that the hit of the evening was a "negrito" (Cuban blackface stock character) who imitated a *bozal* (illegally imported and unacculturated African) by speaking in dialect and ridiculing those lowest on the social ladder.[67] The Havana public was promised entertainment and diversion in the same newspaper columns that sold "four active and agile negroes . . . from the countryside" and published runaway ads for those Africans and Afro-Cubans who had fled bondage. These two very different exhibitions of human bodies coexisted, inches apart on the printed page.

Defenders of high culture looked painfully on as foreign athletes and performers fought for an audience. A writer for *Diario de la Marina* worried that the new Bellini Opera, set to debut in Havana in the higher-class Tacón Theater, would have no chance at drawing a large enough audience to sustain production due to the popularity of Mr. Charles's boxing matches.[68] Charles likely added to the writer's angst by advertising himself as "the king of boxing and wrestling and the strongest man on the island of Cuba." While the violence and imperialism of the enlarged US empire was engulfing Mexico, a different type of US cultural imperialism of violence was piquing the interest of raffish theatergoers in Havana. Charles profited by these displays through sharing the revenue generated by ticket sales with the theater. His troupe of showmen demonstrated the transnational nature of these early bouts.[69]

Charles, one of a number of foreigner performers vying for public acclaim in mid-century Havana, was more successful than most. His performances struck a chord. Not only did the novelty and intensity of the spectacle attract attention, but the cultivated virility of performing bodies in the prize ring likely evoked the insecurities and growing national sentiment that were felt, as shown by the de Castro brothers, on the very bodies of Cubans. Mr. Charles's exhibitions were so lucrative over the course of a few months that he was able to funnel his earnings into property ownership in the capital. He opened a bar and billiards hall.[70] For years after his retirement, other boxers and wrestlers invoked his name to advertise their performances in the Circo Habanero.[71]

**Manliness and Femininity: The Science of Corporeal Modernity in Nineteenth-Century Havana**

In the same period when Mr. Charles drew crowds to the Circo Habanero, a different institution vied for public approbation through the language of respectability and pedagogy surrounding displays of modern virility. In 1853, Amadeo Chaumont, member of a large Havana family and respected professor of gymnastics at the Real Colegio Cubano (Royal Cuban College), opened the Normal Gymnastic School, designed to teach the elite youth of Havana.[72] Since 1850, he had held public exhibitions of his students' "physical development" from his gym on Neptuno Street outside the city walls.[73] He had carefully assured the public that his purpose was to "bring foreign innovations that benefited the patria (fatherland)."[74] He promised to demonstrate the latest trends in exercise and muscular development from Europe and the United States and to import machines for the scientific improvement of Cuban bodies. Rather than importing public spectacle, he promised a measured and purposeful education. In his advertisements, he explained the location of his gym, outside the city walls, as "the center of the city for the comfort of the members and the public." Adding to the legitimacy of his title, he stressed that the governor of Havana and the captain general had personally approved his instruction.⁷⁵ Compared to the reactions to Charles's exhibition, the first public spectacle given by the students of the Normal Gymnastic School could scarcely have been more laudatory. The "select crowd" cheered the "advances" taught by Professor Chaumont. He molded his students into admirable specimens of masculinity. One observer was effusive in his praise: "That intelligent professor. . . . We join the general celebration with our most cordial congratulation for the brilliant state of the Normal Gymnastic School."⁷⁶

It is likely that Afro-Cubans and poor creoles were denied entry and membership in his gym, even if they could pay for it. A year after opening, Chaumont was careful to announce that only "decent people" (*gente decente*) would be allowed to attend his sessions and become members. This coded phrase excluded people of color and those from the lower classes. In a bid to increase appeal and respectability, Chaumont enlisted the expertise of a physician, Dr. Ramón Zambrano, and rechristened it the "Normal, Medical, and Orthopedic Gymnastic School." He also set aside twelve slots for youths of the decent classes who could not afford the subscription. In addition to offering machines to remold and perfect the body, he offered classes on boxing. Special hours would be segregated from the normal schedule to allow women to use the machines.⁷⁷ Chaumont published editorials that celebrated the cultivation of masculine bodies as a prime directive of modern civilization. Carefully controlled sport, he implied, was not a threat to decency or public order if enacted within the confines of respectable establishments. He spoke the language of the educated classes by further justifying a focus on the body, citing Roman, Greek, and Spartan societies that celebrated the cultivation of physicality "because it gave society healthy and robust men, and gave the fatherland (patria) winning soldiers."⁷⁸ In hundreds of advertisements, he attempted to convince readers that a focus on educating the body was both healthy and decent.

He also sought to extend his ideas to young female bodies. This was more controversial; writing about women's bodies was rare, and in the mid-nineteenth century, decent Cuban women were seldom seen in public outside of their carriages, much less dressed in athletic clothing and moving freely in a venue designed to exhibit the corporeal development of its members.⁷⁹ One advertisement spoke in this carefully gendered language, offering to give private lessons: "Women who want to receive the benefits of gymnastics can indicate the place and time in which I can direct their exercises . . . they will be serviced with the decorum and delicacy that they merit."⁸⁰ Amadeo's brother, Prospero Chaumont, specialized in training female bodies at the Colegio de Señoritas de Santa Catalina within the city walls on Reina Street, where he assured fathers that he had calibrated the machinery so as not to damage delicate female constitutions. He also invited them to chaperon all sessions, "as they should."[81]

By 1856, the gymnasium occupied a visible enough position in the social life of the city to warrant selling lithographic prints of the interior, with its novel machines and bodies in uncommon motion.[82] Chaumont moved his gym to a more respectable location, backing up to the city walls, and it became a landmark for giving directions to nearby sites. It again changed names to complement its move toward respectability, becoming part of the military nomenclature of the capital as the "Military and Civil Gymnasium" by 1861.[83] In November of that year, editorialists gave hearty approval to Chaumont's mission: "The exhibition of strength and agility at the Chaumont gym ... attracted a large crowd. It gives the writer pleasure to see Cuban youths of both sexes exhibiting *amor propio* (self-respect) by rivaling the movements of the foreign acrobats so admired in Havana."[84]

Though Chaumont worked assiduously to gain support for his ideas on the cultivation of female bodies through modern exercise, he could not escape the satirical mockery of publications such as the conservative pro-Spanish *El Moro Muza*. In 1863, it published a cartoon of frock-coated men peering through cracks in the wall of the gym to glimpse the women under Chaumont's training.[85] The caption announced that no youths, whether married or single, would be allowed to attend, ostensibly because the performance was semipornographic. Disruption of gender and class norms warranted mockery in the public sphere.

Amadeo Chaumont's visibility as a local celebrity continued through the mid-1860s. Branches of his gymnasium opened in several Cuban cities. In Matanzas, Lorenzo López y Muñiz detailed the existence of two gymnasiums to teach physical culture in 1865 as a laudable achievement of the city, along with the opera, library, and the philharmonic.[86] He labeled these sites as emblems of a robust and modern civil society. In Havana, Chaumont's popularity with elite youths led private and religious schools, such as the Colegio de San Esteban, to establish programs of gymnastic training. Gymnastics was a shorthand phrase for virtually any sort of physical education and training of the body. In 1868, a teachers' manual described modern educational practices taught at the exclusive preparatory school, the Colegio Nacional y Extranjero San Francisco de Assís in the upper-class Cerro neighborhood of Havana. It contained a large gymnasium and was staffed with professors of gymnastics, who, along with classes in horsemanship, taught skills necessary to attain the status of a modern and educated gentleman.[87] One of its scholarship students that year, Raimundo Cabrera, later became one of the most well-known Cuban intellectuals of the late colonial and early republican periods.[88]

Alongside the popularization of bodily exercise in elite institutes and members-only gymnasiums, prizefighting exhibitions continued to link Cuban spectators to broad transnational currents of spectacle and male body culture. In 1860, the illegal boxing match between the US American John Heenan, an enforcer of rigged elections in San Francisco, and the British fighter Tom Sayers created international sensation. In a field near Farnsborough, England, the bout became the sport spectacle of the year and one of the first truly global spectacles of masculine popular culture.[89] Since 1858, Cubans had read in newspaper narratives details of Heenan's various bouts.[90] Ironically, *Diario de la Marina* both castigated and lauded the US press for its substantial coverage of boxing. The Cuban writers praised the technical advances represented by the speed of such publishing and found them worthy of imitation, but they fretted that mass communication was catering to the mob. While editorialists in the United States generally disdained boxing, they were responsible for its popularity. They fanned vulgar public passions for blood sport and created celebrities for the masses: "consulting the sales of the newspaper more than the cause of civilization."[91] Despite this judgment, the conservative *Diario* translated the blow-by-blow of the bout for its readers. The correspondent in New York cited the crowds attending boxing matches in that city as emblematic of the modern metropolis.

A bullfight critic, writing in 1860, cited the Heenan-Sayers bout, the *lucha internacional*, as emblematic of decadent lower-class culture that was crowding out the noble spectacles of opera. The bout provided an opportunity to critique the United States: "The people of the United States need constant agitation in order to live." Boxing was a symptom of degradation and the inability of democratic societies to properly constrain the tastes of its citizens.

Cubans watched as the sectional crisis that would become the US Civil War gained momentum. In the year that John Brown's raid on Harper's Ferry created sensational news, the excitement generated by the transatlantic Heenan-Sayers bout paralyzed commerce and brought US Americans together in solidarity against the English rival. Yankees degraded Cubans for attending dogfights and bullfights, yet they craved the spectacle of two men killing each other with their fists. Men, an ostensibly female writer named Felicia mused, would always attend such shows, even though discerning Cubans were horrified at mere descriptions of the bout.[92]

Despite this insistence in the press that Cubans found boxing repugnant, habaneros gathered to watch recreations of Heenan-Sayers staged in the bullring on Belascoín Street in the suburbs of the city. Nixon's Circus, a traveling troupe based in New York, staged a successful season of boxing, gymnastics, feats of strength, and horseback acrobatics over the winter of 1860–61 at the Havana Circus, by then known as the Teatro Villanueva.[93] As the final act of the season, they purchased advertising space in several newspapers to publicize a "simulacrum" of the Heenan-Sayers bout. For authenticity, the Nixon brought John Heenan's brother James and another boxer named Price to re-enact the contest. They built a boxing ring in the middle of the bullring and planned the re-enactment down to the clothing worn by each of the fighters. They stressed that unlike the bout in England, the boxers would wear gloves (boxing was still bareknuckle) and would not spill any blood. They emphasized that the show was educational and the boxers would teach the latest practices from elite academies of Europe and the United States.[94] Even with these strategic justifications, they had to donate a portion of their gate receipts to charity in order to obtain a permit from the Havana government.[95] The spectacle was so well-attended, it raised the ire of the reporter from the *Diario*. More than two thousand people filled the bullring, so many that ticket sales were stopped and the doors closed, leaving a large and disgruntled crowd outside. The writer stressed that it was beneath his dignity to attend but that as a journalist he was bound to describe the world as it was for his readers. Nixon's successes in the bullring led him to build a temporary tent outside the city walls and to travel to such interior cities as Puerto Príncipe (now Camagüey). A competing circus, the Circo de Chiarini, offered a similar array of feats of strength and gymnastics.[96]

These periodic events surface occasionally in the surviving press of the era, but the records of permits, advertisements, and other documentary sources have been lost or destroyed. There is no trace of them in Cuban archives. From the documents that remain, it is clear that before the wars for independence (1868–1898), Havana was integrated into transnational networks of performer-athletes that promoted these novel ideas of masculine body culture. These early stirrings of the popular culture of sport challenged class distinctions and drew curious crowds that were knowledgeable about transitional events and that recognized names of popular culture heroes from the United States and England. Clearly such entertainments, or "diversions" as they were classified by the colonial government, were politicized due to their foreignness and their overtly democratic nature. Such broad appeal challenged colonial pretensions of cultural hegemony and social hierarchy. Though boxing in particular was repugnant to conservative culture critics, many, such as those from the *Diario de la Marina*, were caught between their moralizing mission and satisfying the public demand for news of distant prizefights.

In 1866, an editorialist for the liberal daily *El Siglo* argued that boxing in Havana occupied a middling place on the hierarchy of public entertainments. At least, he argued, boxing, like bullfighting and cockfighting, was regulated by rules. The truly demoralizing public spectacles were the lascivious masked balls. They supposedly led to murder, nudity, and the loss of honor and virtue.[97] In 1874, under the title "Barbarous Spectacle," one editorialist commented on a prizefight in New York, reminding readers that he had frequently censored news on boxing as an inhumane spectacle during his career; this implied that boxing did occur, at least sporadically, in Cuba. He castigated an unnamed competitor, likely the liberal newspaper *El Siglo*, for covering the bout. He then printed a detailed, round-by-round account in his own newspaper.[98]

**Sport Magazines and Politics at the End of Empire**

After the declaration of freedom of the press in 1869, Cubans founded dozens of specialized magazines (revistas) to promote sport. By the 1880s, these complemented at least six gymnasiums dedicated to physical culture, in neighborhoods from the aristocratic precincts of the old walled city to Chinatown. Their titles often used English terms and their arguments hinged on a number of Spanish neologisms, a lexicon that presupposed knowledge of these new cultural forms. In 1886, for example, the magazine *Sport* published articles that criticized culture that celebrated the brain to the detriment of the body. "Refined civilization" produced "rachitic bodies," and sports such as baseball (by then wildly popular in Cuba) and boxing were a remedy to the outmoded colonial customs. As Louis Pérez Jr. has demonstrated for this period, these choices and affinities were anticolonial performances. They were also acts in defense of masculinity and the Cuban capacity to embrace modernity. As Julian Silveira argued in his 1886 article "Sports in Cuba," under elegant clothes Cubans hid modern muscular bodies as proof against "the firm belief of some that Cuban youths are completely effeminized."[99] Though the military domination of the Spanish empire remained, Cubans secretly formed themselves into robust individuals capable of independence.

Baseball was the most visible anticolonial sport. In one article in *Sport* titled straightforwardly "Bulls or Base Ball," an anonymous writer mocked the daily newspaper *La Voz* for its supposition that baseball was as barbaric as bullfighting. Liberals in Spain resisted the national sport, even in Seville—the birthplace of Spanish bullfighting. He printed a list of the social benefits of baseball and excoriated bullfighting, tacitly connecting it to the colonial project: "We will not set the clock back on this society anymore! No more causes of vice and degradation! We've had enough!" A later article called on Cubans to denounce bullfighting as a barbaric imposition: "We are neck-deep in this mud and we must elevate ourselves to not drown. Those who love this little piece of earth must unite and protest against this demoralizing factor that, even in Spain, sensible people combat." The anticolonial sentiment was further expressed in the metaphor of youthful Cubans resisting the "social manifestations" of the old regime: "In sport . . . the youth of today distances themselves with increasing disdain from the undignified diversions of yesteryear (*antaño*), and direct their exuberant fervor to bodily games that have made the mental and material greatness of modern England."

The Ten Year's War (1868–1878) scattered young Cubans abroad, and they returned with "elevated" concepts of the body and "social spectacles" that drew public attention amid the "disenchantment of the present." "Manly sport" was a reason for hope. Former censors in Havana likely regretted press freedom.[100] Such publications conveyed a political message and embarrassed the Spanish government beyond Cuba.

From Mexico, Nicolás Dominguez Cowan criticized the publishers of *Sport* for the English words they printed. Dominguez Cowan, the "grandson of an Englishman," wrote from Mexico City after reading an issue of the revista, facetiously questioning, "Is not Castilian the language spoken in Cuba?" He conceded that all advanced cities now had sport magazines and that Havana should be applauded for this, but not at the expense of becoming linguistic "beggars." The editors defended themselves. Yes, Castilian was their native tongue, but they also spoke "the language of *sports*." They refused to limit themselves to a vocabulary whose inelasticity made their writing unintelligible to their readers. Dominguez Cowan, a friend of José Martí, would later become a leader in the pro-independence Cuban exile community in Mexico City. He defended Cuban independence, but like Martí, he feared the onslaught of US culture.[101]

Antonio Prieto, writing the same year that José Martí reported on the barbarity of boxing in the United States (1882), called for a valorization of baseball and a rejection of atavistic "pagan" sports like boxing, bullfighting, and cockfighting in Cuba.[102] As early as 1886, an American boxing instructor offered classes at the Club Gimnástico on Havana's most fashionable thoroughfare, the Prado.

Amid these erosions of public decency, the Spanish government continued to subsidize writers who attacked boxing and lynching as proof of US cultural barbarism. The Spanish poet Felipe Pérez wrote the poem "Oh, What a Great Nation" in 1897. He chastised US fascination with boxing as proof of national idiocy and hypocrisy.[103] In 1898, the year the United States invaded Cuba, one pro-Spanish writer again cited the United States as an example of democracy run amok. In the United States, women were on the verge of gaining political rights (a barbarity, he implied) and men flocked to boxing matches and lynchings. Women dressing like men, having all-female orchestras, and the "savage distraction of boxing" were, apparently, what the exile Cuban independence movement in New York hoped to transplant to Cuba.[104]

In 1902, a public boxing match attended by five hundred spectators was held in the Teatro de Marianao (a new suburb of Havana). This spectacle occurred despite an 1899 order by the secretary of state and government that boxing matches not be permitted in any of the provinces. This prohibition, along with a ban on bullfighting under the US occupation, was similar to Military General Order 54 in Puerto Rico (which also covered Cuba), which decreed a prison term of from one to five years for anyone who would "voluntarily engage in a pugilistic encounter between a man and man or a man and a bull or any other animal." It was seconded by the newspaper *Patria*, which deplored boxing, pairing it with the debased game of jerking the head off of a duck while riding horseback (*corrida de patos*), cockfighting, and bullfighting, all "inhumane spectacles."[105] US Americans and Cubans were also made aware, starting the year after the invasion, that disreputable American businessmen (gamblers, bar owners, and boxers) were seeking to transfer illegal vices such as boxing and gambling to the newly "acquired" island of Cuba. In 1903, Cubans read that these underworld figures hoped to hold the heavyweight championship match between Jim Corbett and Jim Jeffries in Havana, a match that eventually took place in the United States.[106]

## Prizefighting and "Americanization" in the Early Cuban Republic

After the defeat of Spain in 1898 by Cuban and US forces, new challenges for Cuban cultural sovereignty arrived in force on the island. The US occupation forces demanded and obtained the insertion of the Platt Amendment into the Cuban Constitution of 1902. It ceded the right of intervention for US forces as a precondition of sovereignty. US political patronage was paired with massive private investment in sugar and infrastructure. The well-documented interventions in Cuban society were accompanied by a saturation of daily life with the ideas and popular culture emanating across the Florida Strait. Boxing was one of the most visible and controversial of those cultural features. The political transition between colony and republic did not replace convictions that despite the benefits of US intervention, central features of US popular culture remained inimical to visions of a modern Cuban republic. Boxing, as most Mexican commentators agreed in the same period, was antimodern amid flows of modernity. In 1899, the satirical illustrated magazine *Puck*, a critic of US imperialism, published a two-page lithographic cartoon titled "The mote in our neighbor's eye."[107] In this colorful image, Uncle Sam is a policeman and holds a cudgel to threaten a Spanish bullfighter in the bullring. Uncle Sam has arrived to end such atavism. On the borders of this central image, ironic renditions of US practices, such as football, hunting, and boxing, illustrate the hypocrisy and cultural chauvinism explicit in US critiques of Cuban and Spanish public spectacle. The US military government outlawed bullfighting and cockfighting as barbaric practices whose continuance signified a reversion to what they conceived as the atavism of Spanish culture. Meanwhile, full-length boxing films, among the first to be shown in Cuba, played in Havana theaters.[108] US soldiers, despite broad illegality in the United States, were allowed to stage matches in the first years of the Republic in theaters and on board US naval vessels. In February of 1900, newspapers announced a public boxing match in Havana between two US soldiers. The writer evinced irony in coded language. He wrote that, he supposed, permission would have to be obtained from the competent authority due to restrictions placed by the *American* government: "I mean, the United States government."[109]

A writer for *La Lucha*, a liberal and generally pro-US newspaper, satirized prizefighting as a ridiculous means to attain celebrity. "There are celebrities (rightly so) in science, in politics, in the arts, in literature . . . and there also celebrities on the crime pages, in boxing, and in the sport of [dogs'] killing rats . . . what is important is to take advantage of celebrity."[110] By 1904, Cuban entrepreneurs sought to capitalize on the growing US tourist trade in Havana. Alfredo Misa, a real estate developer, obtained permission from the Cuban government to build an amusement park and hotel on the outskirts of Havana that would feature boxing matches. Though the government promised to incentivize his venture by suspending taxes for ten years, it is uncertain whether the project came to fruition.[111]

Though the government recognized the lucrative potential of staging prizefights, the press continued to cite boxing as repugnant and foreign. In 1905, A. Rivero, a defender of Spanish culture and a critic of the United States, labeled boxing the "savage sport, par excellence" despite being very "manly" (*varonil*).[112] That same year, a critic reported that the state legislature of New York was considering making boxing mandatory instruction in schools. For him, this was idiocy: "the grand republic is preparing a future of morons (*chichones*)."[113]

In 1906, the writer G. A. de Caillavet imagined a conversation between two fashionable women in Havana. Unlike their more sedate counterparts, watching boxing and jujitsu thrilled them. They were disappointed that a particular match was not more dramatically violent: only a few ribs and teeth were broken.[114] That same year, the fad of automobile racing reached Cuba from the United States. There were several accidents and racing posed a danger to horse-drawn carriages and pedestrians. As one commenter saw it, "Car racing is barbaric . . . if we consent to it, being barbaric, the Government has no reason not to prevent boxing, cockfighting, and bullfighting from taking root."[115] Boxing, Cuban readers were further warned, led to deaths in the rings of the United States.[116]

The United States occupied Cuba a second time from 1906 to 1909 to quell an insurgency against the US-backed government of Tomás Estrada Palma. As during the occupation from 1898 to 1902, the second invasion served as a forced introduction of US cultural norms. In October of 1906, US naval commanders invited the liberal general Faustino "Pino" Guerra on board the battleship *Louisiana* to watch several boxing matches between US sailors.[117] Guerra was one of the leaders of the Liberal insurgency against the government, but after the intervention he colluded with the occupying forces. Several members of the press, from both liberal and conservative newspapers, accompanied Guerra and his entourage to watch six matches. Writing for *El Mundo*, Raul Marsans described the scene: "There was everything there: screams, bets, bloody noses ... delirium. And still, there are those who assure that boxing is more humane than bullfights or cockfights!"[118] For Marsans and other journalists, being forced to watch and report on a boxing match was a distasteful imposition of US culture in Cuba. He continued:

> My readers, surely you ask yourselves, since I write about sport, why I write this review. I ask myself the same question. But our good friends from the North call this sport, and since I am a grateful Cuban (un cubano agradecido) and since I am not political, I will call things by their names—or the name that the occupiers give them. I don't want to get in over my head (no me quería meter en camisa de once varas) and I'll leave it to those writers who are careful enough not to be too provocative ... and if they are, they know how to cover their tracks quickly.

A writer for *Diario de la Marina* lauded Marsans for his careful language, suggesting that "cooperation" with Washington was the easiest way to shorten the occupation. If allowing these types of spectacles guaranteed free protection against internal disorders, then it was a relatively small price to pay. Future interventions would alter many Cuban customs. But, the writer hoped, Cubans would negotiate the content and values embraced as national identity; a collective imagining was underway. Despite all the interventions—military, cultural, and political— Cubans hoped to continue: "Eating our *agiaco* [sic] when we want. That, for many, is the essential thing in this life."[119] After relaying the "bone crunching" details, one writer mused that Cubans who enjoyed the spectacle were sycophants.[120] In agreement, Enrique Fontanills hoped that when the Americans left, boxing would stop. Until then, there was little Cuban autonomy in the midst of American power.[121] These matches were illegal, but they happened anyway.

Sporadic boxing matches continued under US occupation. In December 1906, two US "champions" fought in front of crowds in Havana's Teatro Martí and Teatro Payret.[122] They advertised the match on street posters as a "simulacrum," a pretense of conforming to the laws.[123] Other matches between US soldiers publicly and illegally advertised prizefights with bets up to five hundred pesos, doing so with the impunity of occupying forces.[124]

J. N. Aramburu, a cultural critic for *Diario de la Marina*, published a manifesto from petitioners in Cienfuegos that called upon the provisional US government to legalize cockfighting. *Lidias de gallos*, they argued, was the national sport and cultural patrimony. Aramburu mocked them for asserting it as the "most important national question," but he sympathized that cultural preferences were under attack.[125] His satirization of cockfighting was attacked by provincial politicians. They labeled him "anti-patriotic" for not vehemently defending traditional Cuban pastimes. He responded, reminding critics that "I have not denied that this game is part of the Cuban's customs. I maintain that now is not the time to spend energy to re-establish cockfighting, but to save the country . . . the love of roosters, corresponds within the US to a state of political inferiority. This Cuban vice was developed when a Spanish General governed us." Gabriel Camps, a planter in Havana Province, offered a more straightforward defense of cockfighting and attack on boxing in Cuba. Cockfighting was a distillation of national life. It would continue despite the admonitions of "hypocritical foreigners" and their allies who sought to ape imported ideas of proper public spectacle.[126]

Alfredo Zayas, the future president, wrote a letter to the editor in February of 1907 in which he agreed that cockfighting was a leitmotif of the Cuban nation. Compared to Spanish bullfighting, English dogfighting, and [US] American boxing, it was an innocuous and honorable practice.[127] In dozens of editorials on cockfighting, the politics of popular culture created divisions over the nature of Cuban culture and society. For some, prizefighting was the US version of cockfighting; its essential foreignness and its imposition raised the most ire.

US soldiers organized boxing matches outside of Havana. In Matanzas, two Afro-Cuban amateurs (*dos negritos cubanos aficionados*) fought as a preliminary match. Two marines then fought, both bleeding from their faces. Even more egregious for one observer, Cuban police stood by. This inaction was "the worst of scandals."[128] In Santiago de Cuba, US sailors from the battleship *Des Moines* fought in front of a "disgusted" public at the *glorieta Americana*. The shocked crowd promised to never again attend such a repugnant spectacle.[129]

In the early Republican period, boxing emerged as a contentious symbol of cultural imposition. Some critics viewed the sporadic matches as an act of coercive cultural imperialism. The celebration of cockfighting, in this formulation, served to counter the denigration of Cuban public spectacles and the appropriation of US culture. As in Mexico, the Jack Johnson vs. Jim Jeffries match of 1910 served as a critical moment for Cubans to take stock of the increasing flows of popular culture and to discuss the boundaries of national identity.

**Presence by Proxy: Cubanidad and the Fight of the Century in 1910**

In the weeks surrounding the 1910 prizefight between Jack Johnson and Jim Jeffries, Havana readers devoured daily news of the distant racial spectacle unfolding in Reno, Nevada. They debated US racial norms in the public sphere and Jack Johnson's unique threat to white manhood. Johnson, the notorious bon vivant, actor, and boxer, occupied the Cuban public sphere as a symbol of the peculiar cultural and racial "problems" of the United States that demonstrated the barbarity of American culture and the limits of its democratic pretension. These representations of Jim Crow were connected in the press with a neologism disseminated widely throughout the Spanish speaking world, the "ley lynch." Since the 1850s, Cubans had known of the practice of lynching in the United States, and it was often hailed as proof of American backwardness.[130] Joaquín Aramburu, alarmed by the popularity of boxing during the latest US intervention (1906–1909) and the hype over the Johnson-Jeffries match, made the association of boxing and lynching explicit as two uniquely barbaric American customs. How did the United States pose as a teacher of civilization when these two specimens of American culture were the most uncivilized behaviors known to man?[131]

The *negro* Johnson was a practitioner of an illegal profession. It bridged elite and popular culture. He reveled in the international fame resulting from often picaresque pursuit of a leading symbol of white virility, the heavyweight boxing championship of the world.[132] Johnson, as one of the first globally visible African American celebrities, violated a number of US cultural prohibitions: He mocked white pretensions to physical dominance over blacks. He openly had sexual relationships with and married white women. He was one of the most hated figures in the American press in an era when lynching of African Americans was lauded in the public sphere. He was a focal point for white fears of black social mobility and sexuality, and a lens through which a global audience viewed race in the United States.[133] In Cuba, journalists portrayed Johnson's challenge to US race and gender norms in vivid detail. As Aline Helg has shown in her examination of the Cuban media surrounding the racist massacre of the Partido Independiente de Color in 1912, Cuban journalists wielded enormous power to shape and inform public opinion, especially when commenting on racial issues.[134] As Louis Pérez Jr. demonstrates, Cuban culture in this period evolved in close connection to popular culture currents emanating from the United States.[135]

Reporter Abel Linares chronicled details of legal battles and attempts by religious and social leaders to prevent the bout from taking place.[136] Cubans, reached throughout the island through the pages of the most prominent daily newspapers, *Diario de la Marina*, *La Lucha*, *El Triunfo*, and *Heraldo de Cuba*, were exposed to even the corporeal measurements of the "terrible boxer" Jim Jeffries, whose explicit goal was to win back the title for white male supremacy.[137]

This imagination of the savior of white masculinity was reproduced visually for the Cuban public. Before boxing films were outlawed, Havana theaters screened films of the boxers preparing for the bout, deepening the inundation of the Cuban public sphere with narratives of the drama. Films represented both a threat to racial stability and lucrative new means to profit through the rising cultural phenomenon of athletics. As an entrepreneur, Johnson managed distribution rights and, in the case of Cuba after 1915, sued over the illegal reproduction of moving pictures of his bouts. One film scholar has showed that "Fight pictures pricked at the fabric of American social order to such an extent that their dissemination was halted by nothing less than an act of Congress."[138] Cuban critics shared this apprehension.

From independence onward, "becoming Cuban" was both an inward- and outward-oriented process largely defined by and sometimes in opposition to foreign gender and racial norms disseminated on a massive scale.[139] The nascent Cuban state, like its colonial predecessor, regulated novel behaviors, justifying state action in positive and negative (oppositional) terms; the early importation of boxing served as a divisive point of contention between entrepreneurs and "sportsmen" and conservative commentators determined to censure and prevent Cuban appropriation of American barbarism.[140] In response to prohibitions on fight films, many writers argued that legislators were succumbing to American racial norms and were ignorant of the historical trajectory of "racial harmony" on the island. Their assimilation of omnipresent American norms, largely through the media, warped their understanding of cubanidad. Consumption of "Americanism" was compounded by the ease and frequency of travel to the United States.[141]

Cubans had intimate experience of the United States through travel and residence there. They also read daily generalizations of US culture in the press. Abel Linares had observed Negro League baseball and followed the first mixed-race

Cuban teams to travel to the United States. His narratives were infused with arguments about civilization that coalesced, reminiscent of those in Mexico, around Jack Johnson.[142] Simultaneously, boxing was transposed onto Cuban soil and consciousness in the language of national identity, honor, and manliness. The press treatment contributed to the visibility of boxing, framing it as a nationalist defense of Cuban masculinity. Cubans such as Santiago Agramonte challenged upstart foreign boxers resident in Havana in order to defend "the colors of the nation," accepting challenges in public via letters published in the press that drew on the older language of dueling and the defense of Cuban dignity.[143]

Extending access to the bout for even illiterate Cubans, a cartoon appeared in *La Lucha* titled "The Man of the Week." A rendering of Jack Johnson holds the Earth on his hip. A brittle and weak Uncle Sam (*Tío Sam*) looks on in helpless disgust.[144] The cartoonist portrayed Jack Johnson as muscular, confident, and victorious despite the dominant racial norms of the United States.[145] The Cuban experience of US invasion and occupation was paired with massive American buyouts of lucrative agricultural properties and urban utilities in this period, and it gave Cubans a multifaceted knowledge of the growing power of the "Colossus of the North."[146] Boxing was one manner in which those emergent cultural norms were both disseminated and contested.[147]

Characterizing the immediate impact of the distant bout, a writer for the liberal daily *El Triunfo*, after admitting surprise that the attention of the entire country (Cuba) had been "monopolized" by "anxiety" over the events in Reno, told readers that "more than a pugilistic battle, this is a battle of the races."[148] He continued, "This transcendental struggle ... [that reaches beyond] natural sporting interest is much more, because Jim Jeffries is going to demonstrate the superiority of the white race, while Johnson will demonstrate just how far the potency of the black race can lead."[149]

In Reno, on July 4, while a band played the "patriotic" song "All Coons Look Alike to Me," Jack Johnson humiliated the Great White Hope, taunting him physically and verbally throughout the bout.[150] The evening and day after, Havana newspapers reported that race riots had broken out in a number of US cities. Dozens of African Americans were killed or injured. *La Lucha* portrayed "insolent Negros," celebrating the triumph of the black fighter, positing that they "seemed to think that Johnson's victory extended to them."[151] This insolence, another Cuban reported, had been greater among blacks in the US South. Police were dispatched to the "black areas" of cities to prevent further eruptions of violence.[152] In this chaotic aftermath, readers learned, the enormously valuable film of the bout was banned in the United States, South Africa, and England because of "the fear that such spectacles promote disorders of a racial character."[153] South African theater owners, fearing the impact of visual reproductions of an African-descended individual pummeling a white man, uniformly refused to show the film due to the "offensive attitude" taken on by local black South Africans.[154] The small stage of Reno became a threatening counternarrative to "Anglo-Saxon" dominance writ large in the Cuban public sphere.

On July 9, five days after the bout, the Cuban secretary of the interior, López-Leiva, likely after reading reports of racial violence in the United States, ordered police to prevent the exhibition of moving pictures of the bout in theaters anywhere on the island.[155] The government argued showing the films would have the same effect on blacks in Cuba that it did in the United States, and in the interest of "public order and good feeling between whites and blacks the pictures will be excluded, not only in Havana, but in all points of the island."[156] López-Leiva also reasoned that the film was pornographic, another basis for its exclusion.[157] The nascent symbol of Cuban national unity, the "raceless Republic," was not sufficiently implanted to withstand such images.[158]

The idea of Cuban racelessness was a political construct from the wars for independence and served as a powerful tool for nation building. It was also a justification for the massacre of the Partido Independiente de Color in 1912. Under these rationalizations, an Afro-Cuban political party, by merely citing racial disparities in public life, was fomenting racism. José Martí, the Spanish-descended intellectual, and Antonio Maceo, the "Bronze (colored) Titan," had provided a potent example of racial cooperation in waging war against Spanish colonialism, and the importation of the racially charged popular culture seemed like retrogression. In the aftermath of Johnson-Jeffries, Afro-Cuban boxers fought each other in local theaters while white "mercenary" boxers refereed and instructed them. Children held impromptu boxing matches in the street, running from the police when discovered. This was disconcerting for Cubans who defended the racial status quo.[159]

In the years before 1910, underground boxing matches, like duels, engaged elite society but were seldom commented upon in the media. In one rare example the poet and social satirist Ignacio Rivero, writing for the conservative *Diario de la Marina*, mocked the pilgrimages to rural areas where Cubans watched the "prohibited" boxing matches similar to those illegal acts of their counterparts in the United States.[160] Though Cuban authorities, in the aftermath of Johnson-Jeffries, sought once again to prohibit the extension of boxing, these attempts failed. There were ways around this censorship for creative, if disreputable, theater impresarios in the capital. Several Havana showmen, recognizing the lucrative potential, rushed to hire Cuban and foreign athletes, offering them positions as performers on their staff, and drawing foreign boxers from Mexico City, where the local ayuntamiento had moved to outlaw boxing in 1910.[161]

The first sustained series of boxing exhibitions in Cuba since the 1840s were initiated by an unlikely journeyman boxer and journalist who was emblematic of the transnational origins of prizefighting across Latin America. A Chilean, Juan "John" Budinich had studied physical education at the Teacher's College of Columbia University in New York and had left there in 1909.[162] He began staging boxing matches in Havana in September of that year.[163] Budinich shortly ingratiated himself across the social spectrum. He became the boxing instructor for the son of President José Miguel Gómez and trained the first generation of Cuban boxers, among them the journalist and boxer Bernardino San Martín, the Afro-Cuban Anastasio Peñalver, and the Chinese-Cuban boxer Victor "El Chino" Achán.[164]

From the date of these bouts, despite the preferences of the government, interracial boxing was the norm in Havana. In September of 1909, Budinich plastered Havana columns with posters advertising his exhibitions to any Cuban or foreigner who wished to accept his challenge to box in front of audiences at the Teatro Actualidades. Budinich fought African-descended boxers in Panama and Chile and refused to draw the color line as so often occurred in the United States. The Actualidades was an apt choice for Budinich to introduce novel practices to the Havana public. The Actualidades opened in 1906 and was the first purpose-built cinema in Havana, seeking to expand the novelty of moving pictures to the Cuban public.[165] By 1909, when Budinich debuted in Havana, the theater was under the direction of Pablo Santos and Jesús Artigas, better known as the popular entertainment (cinema, boxing, theater, carnival) entrepreneur team Santos y Artigas. They had a keen business sense that focused on importing and appropriating new technologies of popular entertainment and using these novel media to express Cuban national identity.[166] It is likely on their initiative and invitation that Budinich made the trip to Cuba with the express purpose of promoting boxing in Havana as a moneymaking venture.

As early as 1908, the editorialist Gabriel Camps called for the implantation of boxing in Cuba to be funded by the Ayuntamiento in an effort to modernize and Westernize the city and to attract tourism.[167] Camps explained that boxing, along with cockfighting and bullfighting, should not be viewed through a moral lens (he did not approve of them on ethical and aesthetic grounds). Such spectacles were an established characteristic of modern nations that Cubans should emulate in order to become modern and to make the island attractive to the growing tourist industry. Writing "as if [he] were the Mayor," he called for "new men for new times." Camps did not envision the popularization of boxing in theaters, but called for new public venues to be constructed under careful government regulation as part of a campaign to modernize the capital.[168]

Camps's calls to action through the popular press were seconded in the highest levels of academia. In his inaugural address to the Faculty of Letters and Science at the University of Havana on October 1, 1908, Dr. Gabriel Caruso, a surgeon, called for an emulation of the physical and "corporeal" education in the United States.[169] As head of the medical school, he posited that "Today, we judge the strength of a nation through its *desarollo sportivo* (sporting development)."[170] The spread of boxing and other sports prepared US men for a vigorous life. Such preparation accounted for the strength of the US military and the overall *fitness* (in the Darwinian/Spencerian sense) of the nation. Reciting the call to action, Caruso repeated the Latin phrase most often spoken at similar events: *mens sano en corpore sano*. In his wide-ranging speech, he cited several exemplar individuals who promoted physical culture and modern manliness, from Theodore Roosevelt to Pope Pius X. Caruso's point was clear: If Cubans did not allow and actively promote the cultivation of Rooseveltian masculinity through every means available, they would slip further behind in the competitive race to create and maintain civilization. Caruso demanded that educators incorporate this variant of masculinity and physical education so their students would be less "sterile" and "so that the graduates of our University will enter into life as disposed to fight with their intellects as they are with their fists."[171]

Joaquín Nicolás Aramburu disagreed with Camps and Caruso on the benefits of the "new physicality" in Cuba.[172] The aping of American customs, he argued in 1907, was destroying everything that was *criollo* (native Cuban). Not only in the cities were Cubans losing the fundamentals of their culture, but even in the countryside the guajiro was taking to American fashions and modern behaviors: now "the guajiro also dances *two-step*, rides a bicycle, and puts on boxing shows (*hace ensayos de boxeo*)." The result of these transformations, for Aramburu, was devastating: "There remains nothing criollo in our distractions, and nothing Cuban in our feelings."[173]

In the first years of the Republic, Aramburu was one of the most vocal critics of new popular culture. He wrote that the "yanqui intervention" was part of a plan to "de-Hispanicize" Cubans. Mindlessly copying US "vices and stupidity . . . lynching and boxing" was not really to Americanize or modernize Cuban customs. Such imitation was to knowingly degrade one's nation.[174]

Adding to Aramburu's argument and Caruso's list of bicycle riding and two-stepping, a Havana editorialist argued that if the government were to allow automobiles on the streets of the capital, why not allow "the implantation of boxing" and all other things that are "prohibited" and encourage "license and gambling."[175] These novelties should all be permitted if Cubans would admit, "once and for all," that they "are barbarous."[176] Boxing, the "savage sport par excellence," Enrique Fontanills added, was little more than an exercise in inflated "manliness and brutality." *El Mundo* commented that teaching boxing in the United States did little for the nation other than create a future full of "ruffians."[177] An unnamed poet, writing in 1910, mused that "We are already becoming like Yankees (*Ya nos vamos yankizando* [sic]). Shopkeepers, in imitation of their US counterparts, were starting to close their doors at six in the afternoon. Perhaps boxing will become our national sport."[178]

As in Mexico in the same period, these debates engaged competing visions of national progress and masculinity constructed within the public sphere.[179] The image of the boxing president Roosevelt, counter to the emphatic rejection of what he represented by the Nicaraguan poet Rubén Darío, was widely hailed in Latin America as a paradigm of modern manhood. But many commentators disagreed over the valence of the US as a symbol and whether it was worthy of emulation.[180] In Buenos Aires, by 1909 there existed a "Club Roosevelt," formed by aficionados of "sport, art, and theater . . . which delegated to its boxers the mission of [national] regeneration."[181] Despite these often forceful calls, justified in the lofty prose of nationalism and using virile transnational symbols, these controversial boxing matches took place in risqué theaters under private control, and the globetrotting Budinich was an unlikely yet pivotal figure in this improvisational introduction.[182]

CHAPTER FOUR

# "Nigger Prizefighters" in Havana

*The Transnational Spectacle of Race and Boxing*

THIS CHAPTER EXAMINES the 1915 prizefight between Jack Johnson and Jess Willard in Havana and the reception of Jack Johnson in Latin America while he traveled from Argentina to Cuba. Cubans experienced this infamous prizefight amid intense and often emotional debate over the content of popular culture. These events became a primary point of negotiation of new cultural forms alongside the historical roots of Cuban nationalism. The bout also became a catalyst for the enactment of US racial politics in Cuba in a context of political instability and strengthening transnational foundations for Cuban identity.[1]

On April 5, 1915, the Great White Hope, Jess Willard, knocked out Jack Johnson in a suburb of Havana. The match took place at an American-owned horseracing track, Oriental Park, that was newly constructed in order to attract foreign tourists to the rapidly growing city. It was by chance and necessary improvisation that this boxing match occurred in Cuba. That accident was driven by Johnson's status as a fugitive from justice for transgressing the social and legal color line in the United States (Mann Act). The bout focused considerable international attention on the island. It became a focal point for Cuban commentary on the meaning of US racial practices and attempts to implant them in Cuba. It also created context for Cubans to discuss, more generally, the significance of American expatriates and their cultural, economic, and political power. Newspapers, as "one-day bestsellers," were particularly important for the public discussion of these ideas.[2] Cubans imagined scenes of Jack Johnson and the White Hope in their cafes, streets, and bars. They were keenly aware that a global audience of readers was simultaneously envisioning their nation.

Amid unequal power relations, the Cuban political class yielded a meaningful portion of its cultural sovereignty in the hope of increasing economic prosperity.

They also allowed the public to choose which forms of entertainment would flourish on the island. Writers and artists seized upon the Johnson-Willard bout to gauge the nation's place within the ascribed hierarchy of civilizations. It evoked latent arguments about cultural nationalism deployed around blood sports such as cockfighting and bullfighting that had been outlawed during the first US occupation.

In early 1915, President Mario Menocal temporarily legalized boxing, arguing that such spectacles would attract tourists to Havana. He placed bets on Johnson's victory in the presence of reporters and attended the fighter's training camp on the grounds of the Maine Park, a public space dedicated to the US sailors whose deaths had provoked US intervention in Cuba's anticolonial war against Spain. Cuba's first dedicated boxing ring was built in that memorial space by George Bradt, an expatriate from Chattanooga, Tennessee, and the publisher of the largest English-language daily in Cuba, the *Havana Post*. These events, along with the provocative presence of Jack Johnson, illustrate the mundane complexities intersecting race, neoimperialism, and the politics of popular culture in early Republican Cuba.

During the months leading up to the April bout, an "invasion" of US boxers performed in multiple newly built stadiums and popular theaters in Havana. In these venues, Cubans debated the content of their social life. The patterns of thought evident in previous confrontations with the notorious sport were honed and intensified, and the immense public attention resulted in further political and legal action against prizefighting. Some writers inveighed against the cultures of public spectacle in the United States and Europe and pointed out the hypocrisy inherent in the cliché criticism of Cuban civilization as a farcical mirror of foreign ideas groping toward self-government. Along with such ruminations on the quality of Cuban society, the bout prompted discussions of African American (and Afro-Cuban) male bodies on public display. Some writers lauded attempts by Afro-Cubans to challenge African American heavyweights in the ring; others mocked them. Racist portrayals labeled Afro-Cubans "capitalists" for naïvely risking their safety in an attempt to earn meager livings as athletic performers.

Coverage of this event saturated newspapers and fueled discussion on race and masculinity on every populated continent.[3] Johnson was the most notorious Afro-descended individual in the world. Writers seized on this status and employed it as a baseline point of debate on such broad ideas as Social Darwinism, racial superiority, and eugenics. Johnson's image as a threatening and violent specimen of black manhood reached far beyond the boxing ring. Soldiers in the trenches of World War I nicknamed large cannons "Jack Johnsons."[4] The context of world war provided other visual depictions that portrayed the global resonance of the bout and its broader meaning. A cartoon by the Cuban artist Conrado Massaguer represented Johnson and Willard facing off as giant figures, standing upon and dwarfing the island, while the warring powers of Europe and Asia halted their slaughter to focus on the spectacle of race war.[5] The match also exhibited, in stark language, attempts by US Americans living in Havana to transfer racial norms of the Jim Crow South, and it showed diverse Cuban reactions to these impositions.

Cuban and US entrepreneurs had tried, unsuccessfully, to transplant boxing to Cuba since the mid-nineteenth century. In 1905, Cuban entrepreneur Alfredo Misa obtained a license from the Havana government to build a sport complex in the outskirts of the capital. His proposal focused on making the city a tourist attraction by hosting boxing and other athletic spectacles.[6] The alteration of social norms on the island was implicit in his petition, but he further implied that the attraction of tourist dollars outweighed the imposition of interracial spectacle. He applied for an exception to laws banning boxing by citing U.S. Military Order 124 (1900), which gave ultimate jurisdiction over "public amusements" to municipal governments. A separate order had banned boxing on a national level. Given these two conflicting directives, there was ample space for debate on the legality of the sport and jurisdiction over the permissibility of public spectacles.[7] The mild winter climate and the fact that prizefighting was illegal in much of the United States, he hoped, would make Havana into a winter sport mecca to attract US tourists.[8]

The April 1915 bout had been scheduled for the month before, in Ciudad Juárez, Mexico. The Mexican Revolution, along with Johnson's legal status as a fugitive, made a journey from the Gulf Coast city of Tampico to Juárez too risky. The easiest path, via rail from New Orleans or Galveston, would have resulted in his arrest once on US soil. He was also unable to book passage on any US-owned steamships, which constituted the majority of maritime passenger traffic in the Gulf of Mexico and the Caribbean. Before his arrival in Cuba, he had traveled exclusively on ships sailing under Dutch or British flags; these mobile sovereign units did not include violation of the Mann Act as an extraditable offense. When shielded travel was impossible, he spent large amounts of his diminishing savings to charter private boats whose nationalities also protected him from arrest and rendition.[9] In Mexico, the ongoing struggle for the northern port city of Tampico between the forces of Francisco "Pancho" Villa and Venustiano Carranza made it impossible for Johnson to land there.[10] Given these threats and the city's proximity to the United States, Havana became the best potential location to stage the lucrative championship.

Thousands of newspapers articles in the United States traced Johnson's journey from Europe to Argentina to the Bahamas to Cuba. He became a peripatetic case study on race and broader perceptions of US culture. While in Havana preparing to sail for Tampico, Johnson learned that Carranza, then the US-recognized president of Mexico, had threatened to facilitate his arrest and rendition to the United States if he set foot in Mexico.[11] Pancho Villa, Carranza's opponent during this phase of the Mexican Revolution, had reportedly promised Johnson protection. Villa, Carranza feared, would deploy the revenue generated by the bout to fund his army's continued insurgency against the constitutionalist forces.[12] Given this uncertainty, Johnson chose to remain in Havana. The US district attorney in Chicago told reporters from Johnson's hometown newspaper, the *Chicago Tribune*, that the extradition treaty with Cuba did not extend to violations of the Mann Act for white slavery. The boxer would be safe from deportation in Cuba, but he still faced US racial politics in Havana. He was barred from US-owned hotels, and American newspapers published there repeatedly called him a "nigger criminal" and a threat to white womanhood.[13]

Within weeks of his arrival in late February, Jess Willard and the dozens of promoters, managers, and press people had decamped from Ciudad Juárez to Havana. The city thus became an unexpected and improvisational proxy stage. Cuban entrepreneurs and social commentators seized on the bout as a potentially lucrative venture that would establish the capital as a global sport city. They promoted the performance of a fugitive from the United States in the hope that a successful spectacle would enhance the attractiveness of Cuba as a destination for American tourists. With the legal imprimatur of the government, entrepreneurs and social activists moved to capitalize on the global attention. A successful spectacle of violence would bode well for the development of Cuban civilization.

On the afternoon of the bout, Enrique Díaz Quesada, a pioneer of Cuban cinema, stood ready at his camera on a platform above the audience. He planned to film the bout for distribution in Cuba and beyond. The director had agreed to partner with Johnson and share the profits from the film.[14] Afro-Cubans, called to action by a local black politician, Eligio Madán, waited anxiously to hear news of the bout. They occupied the cheap seats far from the ring, and they gathered on the small hill outside the racetrack to catch a glimpse of Johnson, and black celebrity, in action.[15]

Twenty-six rounds later, the seven-year international search for the Great White Hope was over. Jess Willard, a tall and awkward cowboy from Kansas, upset the thirty-seven-year-old champion. White Americans, and many white Cubans, reveled in Johnson's defeat. The knockout resulted in one of the most famous pictures of early twentieth-century sport: the white Jess Willard standing over the prostrate Jack Johnson.[16] The meaning of the image to critics of Johnson was clear: white manhood was resurgent and once again in safe hands. This image appeared in thousands of newspapers around the world. The film of Johnson's defeat, after facing legal injunctions in several countries, eventually played in theaters across the United States, Cuba, Mexico, and beyond for years after the bout.[17] The theatrical specter of racial violence in the boxing ring in 1915 drew audiences to the same screens that showed D. W. Griffith's film *Birth of Nation* (1915).[18] Willard, like the Ku Klux Klan, was romanticized as a savior of white male supremacy.[19]

For two months before the bout, Jack Johnson and a retinue of journeymen African American boxers lived in Havana. Before Johnson's arrival, advertisers for a health elixir claimed that Johnson was able to fend off the effects of age by consuming its product. These sorts of advertisements, using Johnson's name in bold print to attract the attention of the reader, seldom had the boxer's approval or consent to use his name or image.[20] For many Cuban writers, Johnson was both a picaresque and a tragic character. Cuban cartoonists, led by the prolific artist Conrado Massaguer, portrayed him as either a respectable and cosmopolitan gentleman or as a hirsute ape wielding a large and phallic banana.[21] For critics of US culture in Cuba over the preceding fifteen years, his treatment at the hands of US authorities and private citizens exposed the hypocrisy of the civilizing mission through which the occupying forces had sought to mold society in its image. American editorialists in Havana congratulated their compatriots in the city for denying Johnson lodging and other services, even though such racist actions were illegal under Cuban law.[22]

The Johnson-Willard bout has received its due amount of attention from historians of the United States.[23] This section explores the meanings of this bout in Cuba, where the politics and significance of race were as central to the formation of Cuban identity as they were in the contemporary United States. Jack Johnson evoked sympathy in the Cuban public sphere. Cubans were exposed to the full drama of Johnson's peripatetic career years before his arrival in Havana.[24]

### The Path to Havana

On December 14, 1914, Jack Johnson disembarked from the Dutch steamer *Zeelandia* in the port city of Santos, Brazil, after a two-week voyage across the Atlantic. As was his routine, he drove off the ship in one of his expensive cars to tour the city.[25] Journalist regretted that he would not be permitted to box in Brazil because of the legal prohibitions against prizefighting.[26] This prohibition did not extend to films of the Johnson-Jeffries bout (1910), and they later played in theaters in Rio de

Janeiro and São Paulo. Later in the decade, Brazilians also attended Jack Johnson's feature-length movie made in Spain: *Fuerza y Noblesa* (Force and Nobility).[27]

Though he did not know it at the time, his eventual destination was Havana. Over the previous two years in self-exile, Johnson had boxed and performed on stage in several European countries. His world travels gained momentum in 1908 when he became the first African American to win the heavyweight boxing championship title from a Canadian, Tommy Burns (Noah Brusso), in Sydney, Australia.[28] From that moment, Johnson was the focus of a frantic search for a white man capable of taking back the title of white supremacy in the ring. With no successful opponents on the horizon, the US Bureau of Investigation sought to imprison Johnson to avoid the further embarrassment to white supremacy.[29] In late 1912, the federal government trumped up charges that Johnson had transported a white woman across state lines for "immoral purposes" and sentenced him to a year in prison. Though he later married the same woman, he was found guilty of promoting her for prostitution.[30] The Bureau of Investigation would continue to shadow Johnson for nearly a decade in exile.[31] Several agents would be ringside at the bout in Havana.[32]

In Chicago in 1913, Johnson skipped bail disguised as a Negro League baseball player and fled the one-year prison sentence through Canada to Europe. In prewar Europe, he found a ready audience for his boxing and vaudeville acts, and for a time his stage career provided him with a comfortable living in Paris. There, his wife felt able to escape disparaging opinions, both among whites and African Americans, of their interracial marriage.[33] The outbreak of World War I, paired with increasingly unpleasant brushes with European authorities and an offer from boxing promoter Jack Curley for a lucrative defense of his heavyweight title in Mexico, led him to leave Europe in search of more stable and lucrative venues. Johnson, and the dozens of other boxers who made a living as performers, fighters, and boxing professors, looked for work in the more stable environment of the Western Hemisphere. In most Latin America countries, no national laws prohibited prizefighting, and a skillful negotiator could convince municipal authorities to allow them to stage "scientific exhibitions." But, as in Brazil, this was not always the case.

The commercial introduction of boxing in Latin America responded to both pushes and pulls. The war in Europe and the tenuous legality of boxing in the United States sent performers looking for cities where their craft might draw a crowd. They were aided by the growth of transnational media coverage of sport, which increased steadily from the late nineteenth century. Latin American audiences were attracted to, and often repulsed by, the novelty of boxing. They now had the opportunity to witness, in person, that which they had read and collectively imagined as a disreputable and yet intriguing oddity.

While living in London four months after the beginning of World War I, Johnson signed to fight Jess Willard. The most important stipulations in the contract were that the bout would take place somewhere in Latin America and that Johnson would receive the enormous sum of thirty thousand dollars.[34] Willard, known as the "Pottawatomie County Kansas Giant," was the most promising white prizefighter. But few observers of boxing believed he could compete with Johnson if the champion were even a shadow of his former self. The sporting press imagined that Johnson's life in bohemian Paris had dissipated his skills and enervated his body; they hoped this might provide an opening for his defeat.[35]

The location of the proposed bout was necessarily uncertain; the promoters needed a location where enough spectators would make the fight profitable and in a country where Johnson would be allowed to disembark. He researched ahead of departure from Europe to assure that countries where he landed had no extradition treaties with the United States that would apply to the technicalities of his fugitive status. Before the match in February or March of 1915, Johnson planned a theatrical and boxing tour of South America and the Caribbean to ascertain the potential for prizefighting in the region. He intended to travel north from Buenos Aires with his wife, cousin, and a few hangers-on that were drawn to his wealth and celebrity. The tour was to end with a defense of his title in Juárez, from where he hoped to return to France. In Mexico, the fight promoters anticipated, a large enough crowd from the United States would cross the border to be present at Johnson's potential defeat.[36]

Johnson was constantly in search of opportunities to fund his extravagant tastes. He had agreed with New York promoter Billy Gibson to meet another African American heavyweight, Sam McVea, in Havana in March.[37] Accordingly, he left a Europe mobilizing for war to entertain, travel, and, vague rumors held, become a permanent resident in one of the many rapidly modernizing cities of Latin America.[38] In late November, he bought passage from London to Buenos Aires.

Johnson's arrival in Argentina generated a prodigious response in the *porteño* press. Social critics lamented and satirized the celebration of brute force over calm reflective masculinity that, they held, Johnson's image evoked. Boxing (black boxers in particular) and the "extreme emotions" they aroused were a danger to what one writer deemed the "peaceful environment" of the port city. A cartoon drawing of Johnson's face, smiling to emphasize his gold-capped teeth, was superimposed above a warning in *La Crítica*: "At least we hope that the feverous enthusiasm for the sport that Johnson cultivates will not carry us to the deplorable extremes of the descendants of Linch [sic]." Johnson, the "glory of his black race," carried the stigma of racialized violence that threatened, this writer warned, to convert Argentines into their violent and racist counterparts in the United States.[39]

Journalists in Buenos Aires commented on incidents that had little to do with boxing. They published details of his biography and observed how crowds followed him through the city. Masses of Argentines and foreigners erupted in spontaneous applause after waiting for him outside of a clothing store. Johnson would stop, remove his hat, and thank his admirers, sometimes making a brief speech in his dramatic vaudevillian intonations. To their delight, journalists recorded how he commented that Buenos Aires shared the cosmopolitan ambiance of European cities where he had lived and performed. This calculated flattery was designed to ingratiate him among skeptical audiences; it was a skill he had honed over his years performing in front of wary crowds.[40]

The illustrated magazine *Caras y Caretas* published images and accounts of Johnson. In one photograph, taken on board the steamship that brought him to Buenos Aires, Johnson appears surrounded by young Argentine children. A boy sits in his lap. He traveled with families who, like the boxer, were fleeing the war in Europe. Johnson, the caption read, was a "good friend of childhood" (*un buen amigo de la niñez*).[41] These images and captions provided counterpoints to Johnson's threatening and belittling reputation in the United States that Argentines had read about.

After meeting him, the Argentine press generally portrayed him as an affable and even erudite gentleman, but he could not escape the usual racist depictions. In the same issue of *Caras y Caretas* that claimed Johnson was a friend to children, a full-page advertisement for Nestle powdered milk depicts a cherubic white child wearing boxing gloves and standing with his foot on a prostrate black boxer identified only as "the world champion."[42] The caption declared that parents who fed their children this product would assure "health, power, and vigor." The white child of the future, fortified by Nestle, would be "invincible" and would win back the title of champion for the white race. Another series of photographs portrayed a shirtless Johnson whose gaze directs the viewer to his large flexed biceps. Battlefield photos and maps from the war in Europe surrounded these images in serial publications, linking Johnson to these global conflicts. There was not a person on earth, one caption read, who didn't know about Jack Johnson, "who had become the symbol of his race . . . and the empire of force over the globe."[43]

A writer for the satirical magazine *Fray Mocho* attended an exhibition match staged outdoors in Buenos Aires. He captioned a series of photographs by lauding Johnson's skill in the ring, but he relayed that relatively few spectators had attended. Newspapers, the writer mused, had convinced the public that boxing was a "dangerous sport."⁴⁴ One writer for the magazine *Nosotros* commented that Johnson's exhibitions had violated public ordinances, but that his celebrity overcame "public decorum."⁴⁵ Though most of the satirical representations mocked the medium of Johnson's celebrity, they acknowledged that his global popularity and his image as a symbol of masculinity transcended sport. In 1916, after Johnson had lost the title, the magazine *PBT* published a picture of Johnson standing in his car in London, giving a speech to an enormous crowd encouraging them to volunteer for the British army.⁴⁶

Johnson's celebrity furnished opportunity for political satire during his short stay in Argentina. The night after his press interview at the Casino Theater, the boxer unintentionally terrified an elderly Argentine politician from the provinces. Johnson was lodged in the same hotel, and when the minister emerged from his room late in the evening, he encountered Johnson returning from a night at the bar in the dim gaslight of the hallway. The minister was threatened by the large black figure with shining teeth, and his shrieks woke the guests and staff of the hotel. The minister, one reporter mocked, must have mistaken Johnson for a "Mandinga," or a "devil."⁴⁷ The minister, "*el viejito Ortiz*" (the little old man Ortiz), was chided as comically old-fashioned, effeminate, and out of touch with modern life. Not only was he uncomfortable amid the cosmopolitan bustle of the port city, he didn't recognize Johnson.

On the 26th of December, Johnson made his Buenos Aires debut at the Casino Theater.⁴⁸ His performance in front of "numerous boxing fans" consisted of exercises with a medicine ball, shadow boxing, and a demonstration of his famous uppercut with a sparring partner. Due to legal prohibitions on boxing enacted by the municipal government and the lack of a suitable opponent, the show was limited to this relatively anodyne performance. In response, one spectator penned an open letter to Johnson. He was disappointed by what he perceived as a third-rate spectacle. He explained that he had followed Johnson's career in the United States and Europe through the cable dispatches printed in newspapers and had watched films of his matches. The writer envied the champion for his luck, his achievements, and his wealth. When the boxer appeared at the Casino Theater, the fan applauded him, further admiring his muscular body and his powerful physical presence.⁴⁹ In one of the mainstays of his performance and the climax of his act, Johnson hit an inflated bag with enough force to break the cord and send it flying into the crowd. Despite the excitement stirred by his finale and the ovation of the two thousand spectators in attendance, the author of the letter felt cheated.⁵⁰ It was a question of respect. Johnson, he contended, treated Argentines as an inferior audience and, by extension, an inferior and naïve people. His presence in Buenos Aires, after European audiences were "tired of being happy about having to put up with the terrible Negro," was like a charitable offering. He was angered by the Negro's audacity in treating him like an uncultured observer. The image of Johnson, created by the press and moving pictures, was far from reality as experienced at the Casino Theater. Giving vent to his dissatisfaction with seething satire, the writer ended by informing Johnson that despite his fame he was still "just like a Negro."

A subsection of the porteño press used the opportunity of his stay in the capital to hold forth on the dangers of what Johnson, the man, and boxing in general represented to modern civilization. Writers evoked the familiar terms of barbarity versus civilization and low versus high culture that pervaded the Latin American public responses to boxing in the early twentieth century.[51] The Socialist Party's daily, *La Vanguardia*, dedicated space on the front page to ask if such disreputable entertainments had a place in the "times of culture and progress."[52] In an article titled "The Rise of Barbarism," the author assailed those who attended boxing matches. He asserted that the crowd in attendance proved itself more "atavistic" than the boxers. The enthusiasm for watching shows of "muscular force" was more debased than the performance of those who profited by it. For some time, Argentines had had to countenance those "muscular gangsters" who exalted the cult of physical force over reflection. The popularity of boxing spurred by Johnson's presence, though, was cause for alarm. The author lamented damage to Argentine culture: "Today we will debase ourselves and the culture of our great city under official auspices [the Ayuntamiento had granted Johnson unusual license], and seat ourselves before the disastrous precedent of glorifying barbarity."[53] Johnson, as in many instances before, served as a mirror for the construction of local identities. Argentine writers viewed him, paradoxically, as both an amiable individual and as a vector of barbarism.

## Johnson's Cuban Period Begins

As Jack Johnson arrived in Cuba, his celebrity generated a similar fascination in the media. The more critical responses evident in Argentina were subsumed by the immediacy and the elation of having so many foreigners and international celebrities in the city at once. Journalists, such as the prolific writer Victor Muñoz, covered every detail of Johnson's movements. More than a dozen newspapers and magazines published news on his diet, he and his wife's attire and dozens of trunks and suitcases, his views on Cuba, and minute descriptions of his home life. This left little time to reflect upon the abstractions of boxing's impact on Cuban civilization that had been such a clear impulse during the preceding years.

Hundreds and later thousands of journeymen pugilists, American and Cuban socialites, gamblers, and fight fans packed the hotels, cafes, and bars of Havana from February to April. Beginning a week and a half before his arrival on the 21st of February, cables reached Cuba from the Bahamas that Johnson had chartered a ship and would arrive at the southern port of Cienfuegos.[54] The nascent Havana sporting press scrambled for opinions, took offense at slights by American tourists, and ruminated about how far Cuba had come in the eyes of international public opinion. President Menocal attended the training camps of both Johnson and Willard, bet on the victory of the black champion, and declared the day of the fight a public holiday so that Cubans could "see the scientific exchange between the challenger Willard and the Colossus Johnson."[55] Congress delayed its opening session, public transport was rerouted to the suburb of Marianao where the ring was located, and Menocal cancelled his plans so that he could attend the fight, sitting with his entire cabinet in a presidential ringside box.[56] Tailors advertised new "Panama Suits" available on Obispo Street to keep spectators cool and fresh during the match.[57] Writers were amazed at the size of Jess Willard (he stood six feet six inches tall). One female observer, hired by *El Mundo* to write to Cuban women about the bout, admired that Willard was like a "giant carved from marble."[58] He strode the streets of Havana, "causing little earthquakes." Amid the pervasive sense of awe, the press reported Willard's mission: "I've come to Havana to destroy that Negro."[59]

Amid the general excitement, some writers were angry that the authorities permitted such a depraved spectacle. It was an example of Cuba's moral and "intellectual backwardness."[60] This permissiveness threatened to stigmatize the young republic in the eyes of civilized nations. Boxing, along with bullfighting, belonged to a more primitive age. Both boxers—the black celebrity and the white challenger—were equally barbarous in the eyes of one critic. The United States had shared so much of the "light of civilization" with Cuba. It was now exporting, in the form of boxing, the refuse of its culture.[61]

Amid chaotic media coverage, American entrepreneurs saw a chance to profit. They partnered with Cuban businessmen to transform some of the most visible public spaces in Havana into venues for prizefighting. George Bradt, the Jewish American financier (his religious and ethnic identity was often stressed by his detractors) was the editor and owner of the *Havana Post*. He invested thousands of dollars to construct a boxing arena on the grounds of the Parque Maine at the entrance to the wealthy suburb of Vedado.[62] Bradt hoped his new "Stadium" would popularize boxing, and he promised the government that it would bring an avalanche of tourists from the United States. It would also serve as a site where

Americans would re-enact some of the most palpably racist entertainments that had fallen out of favor in the United States.

Two miles from the new stadium, on the border between Old and Central Havana, another US businessman constructed a second boxing arena. John Robinson, the director of publicity for the Johnson-Willard match, partnered with Abel Du Breuil, the sports editor of the liberal daily *La Lucha*. They inaugurated the Arena Colón on March 25, 1915. This outdoor boxing arena and cafe was on the grounds of the Teatro Martí, on the corner of Zulueta and Dragones. Ironically, the theater was where, in 1910, Cuban playwrights had presented original plays that mocked the "boxeomania," then prevalent in Havana. The match that garned the most headlines that evening was between Miguel "Mike" Febles and a New Yorker named Smith. It was easy to note the "superiority of the criollo (native-born Cuban)" Febles over the American. Febles knocked him out in the third round. Jack Johnson, Havana mayor Fernando Freyre de Andrade, and a number of other celebrities attended. New boxing arenas had the tacit imprimatur of the Cuban political elite.[63]

The Arena Colón also promised to popularize the sport more broadly among aspiring athletes and spectators. Robinson vowed to host a championship among the many amateur athletic clubs, including the Club Atlético de Cuba and the Vedado Tennis Club, that had taken root across the city in the preceding decade.[64] From the beginning, it promised to be more attuned to Cuban sensitivities than Bradt's Stadium. Not only would it hold professional matches for the "popular prices" of fifty cents, it would serve the community by organizing an amateur championship for local clubs.[65] Cuban journalists seized on the arrival of prizefighting in Cuba to promote the modernizing project of the Club Atlético de Cuba. One writer described its gym, located on Havana's fashionable Prado, as a "glorious club ... overflowing with life, with young life, healthy and enterprising."[66] The city government, citing the social and patriotic value of such organizations, funded the expansion of the club's gymnasium.

The most controversial new construction that resulted from the boom of boxing and physical culture in Havana was Bradt's fifteen-thousand-seat "Estadio de Habana."[67] Bradt was an odd choice to introduce the Havana public to interracial boxing. He was, according to the nascent NAACP, a force for evil in the fight for equal rights for African Americans and he viewed Afro-Cubans as "niggers."[68] He was a "wild animal" sent abroad by the government of the United States to represent them. From the pages of his newspaper, Bradt fulminated against the members of the Afro-Cuban social and political Club Ateneo, who had the audacity to compare the Haitian leader Toussaint L'Ouverture with

George Washington. L'Ouverture, Bradt seethed, "was just a bad nigger who ran amok in Haiti." The general, Bradt estimated, was no better than Evaristo Esténoz (a leader of the Partido Independiente de Color) and others "happily dead in Cuba."[69] Bradt, the NAACP worried, "spoke for America."[70]

Bradt, despite his clear racial hatred of a sizable portion of the Cuban population, was a central actor in the development of the tourist industry in Havana. He had obtained, over the previous years, a monopoly on sport entertainment in the city. He negotiated grants from the Havana City Council to advertise and entice American tourists to vacation in Havana.[71] Given the restrictive laws in most of the United States on boxing, and Havana's year-round sunshine, Bradt and the city council envisioned the city as a prime venue for athletic tourism.[72] Abel Linares, writing for *Diario de la Marina*, predicted that Bradt's new stadium would bring a much-needed "invasion of tourists."[73] With Mexico in the turmoil of revolution, Havana, they hoped, would enjoy a healthy income from pleasure seekers from the north.

The most raucous resistance to Bradt's project to import interracial prizefighting came from another US American, Asa Daniel Roberds. Roberds owned the rival English-language newspaper the *Cuba News*. He was a veteran journalist who had worked in Kansas and Florida. He arrived in Havana in 1905 and immediately became a focal point in the social life of the growing American expatriate community.[74] In Havana, he worked for the English-language section of the liberal daily *La Lucha* before briefly collaborating with Bradt on the *Havana Post*. For Roberds, the initiative to bring boxing to Cuba and implant it as a permanent fixture in the cultural life of the capital was a farce doomed to failure. He focused on Bradt: "The publisher of the *Havana Post* may be a nigger-lover and enjoy such spectacles," but unlike Bradt, most Americans did not wish to see African Americans in their adopted city.[75] Bradt's Havana Commercial Association sought to debase Cubans by importing boxing with the false promise that US Americans would spend tourist dollars to view such public spectacles. Roberds warned his readers in the "American colony" of the threats that Johnson and other "nigger prizefighters" embodied:

> Jack Johnson, negro pug, former brothel keeper, white slaver, and fugitive from justice from the United States . . . landed in Havana last Monday morning with his white wife. . . . A father does not want his boy to be fired with the ambition of becoming as great as a negro pugilist and fugitive from justice, whose every act is extolled and made much of by some publications. A mother does not want her daughter to read praises of the alleged beauty who was so wanton as

to run away with a negro.... It is too vile a thing, really, for the Cuba News to even mention in order to denounce, going as it does to be read by those who know of no such evil things and who should be kept in ignorance.[76]

Despite Roberds's trepidation over publishing information on Johnson and that innocent women and children might be exposed to such damaging words, he published a torrent of pieces against Johnson and other black boxers. His most seething anger, however, was reserved for the white US expatriates who purportedly bore blame for the athletes' presence. Roberds's reasoning constituted an attempt to recreate US racial norms in Cuba: "Rather funny to hear the nigger fighters to be described as being 'in the pink of condition.'" He lauded US hotel owners, especially those at the Plaza, the first hotel to deny Johnson lodging: "Perhaps it made the black fellow think he was getting back home when was turned down because of his color."[77] Roberds was clear why Johnson was refused a room. Hotel owners, likely knowing that overt racism of this sort was illegal in Cuba, stated that Johnson had been refused a room due to his low character, or had told him no rooms were available.[78] Hotel managers denied the racially motivated intent of their actions and avoided potential conflict with the authorities. Given the long-standing attempts by the Cuban government to attract US tourism, this avoidance of conflict over de facto segregation by US Americans likely relieved Cuban politicians.

One Cuban observer, Victor Muñoz, followed Johnson from his arrival at the train station in Havana to the Hotel Plaza. In a long article, illustrated by two full-length photographs of Johnson and his wife, Muñoz recounted fighting through the crowds to get a look at Johnson. The boxer's "great negro head" stuck out above the masses. It was the head of a man "who with his intelligently deployed fists has known how to scale the highest summits of universal celebrity." As many observers were, Muñoz was particularly intrigued by Johnson's wife, Lucille Cameron, whom the fighter introduced as "a prolongation of my person." Muñoz was star struck:

> She is a delicious type of woman, beautiful and elegant, with the chic of a Parisian, and with the graceful self-confidence of an American woman. She is as white as a snowflake, and her blond hair shines under her black velvet hat, her blue eyes shining on the crowd that had surrounded her celebrity husband.[79]

The crowds followed them as they made their way to the Hotel Plaza. Johnson's walk through the city was captured by the cartoonist Conrado Massaguer. His playful image portrayed a cross-section of Cubans marveling at the boxer.[80] Muñoz shared the crowd's enchantment. He wrote that Johnson treated his wife as if they were on "perpetual honeymoon," wiping grapefruit juice from her face with a napkin at breakfast in the cafe of the Plaza. A crowd of managers and businessmen eager for Johnson's ear surrounded his table. The writer took the time to speak further with Cameron. She told him that she no longer liked the United States. She preferred Paris, where the couple was treated better. The past few years had been a constant adventure in Moscow, Berlin, Paris, Brussels, London, and most recently in Buenos Aires. Amid this conversation, the manager of the hotel approached Johnson and engaged him in a conversation that Muñoz could not hear. Johnson "smiled sardonically" and announced that his retinue would have to look for other lodging. Shortly afterwards, Johnson drove to Bradt's new stadium. Word of his presence preceded him and streetcars slowed for their passengers to get a look at him. Another writer summed up the importance of Johnson's presence on the same day as Muñoz's observations:

> Havana, born yesterday to the life of boxing, will have the privilege of seeing Johnson, the world champion, in action—when its great Stadium is not even a month old. The sportmen of the United States have fixed their sight on Havana, and the arrival of Johnson to our beaches, as with the horseraces and our good baseball players, serves to announce our country to the whole world.[81]

Despite the notoriety that Johnson might lend the city, *El Mundo* reported that Johnson had failed to find lodging at any hotel in the city, but this story was underplayed in the Cuban press when compared to their US counterparts. Though US capitalists succeeded in treating Johnson like "he was getting back home," his reception by Cubans in the public sphere was markedly different from his experiences in his native country. Compared to the reaction of the English-language press, many Cuban journalists looked upon Johnson more as an intriguing curiosity and as an intelligent manipulator of US racial politics.

Cubans interested in sport had followed boxing abroad but had never been able to obtain licenses to hold matches on the island. They eagerly followed Johnson's journey to Cuba, reporting on rumors of his arrival and noting that he had "escaped Judge Lynch" in the United States.[82] Despite the pleasure they likely derived in reporting Johnson's embarrassment of US racial norms, some, such as Bernardino San Martín, were angered by what they saw as foreign interlopers in Havana. With the collusion of the Cuban government and the advantage of ready capital, US businessmen were stealing the impetus to develop sport. Boxing had been illegal in Cuba since 1910, largely due to the specter of Johnson's celebrity. In several instances, boxing matches were impeded or reported to the police on the grounds of indecency. In agreeing to allow a foreigner to stage lucrative matches at the stadium in the wealthy neighborhood of Vedado, the authorities were willfully stifling local initiative.[83]

When news broke that boxing was to be held in Havana, George Bradt acted. He dusted off one of his many concessions and constructed the stadium. He was spurred to action by the arrival of Billy Gibson, a fight promoter from the Bronx, New York, who also planned to build venues to accommodate the growing popularity of prizefighting.[84] Boxing in Cuba, the New York Times printed, would finally allow championship matches "to a finish," a feature that was not widely permitted in the United States.[85] Bradt held a long meeting with Havana mayor General Freyre de Andrade, who promised his "sincere help" and approved boxing matches.[86] Freyre de Andrade's approval was seconded by the governor of Havana Province, Pedro Bustillo, even though boxing was still illegal in Cuba.[87] The Havana City Council also voted to award Bradt permission to build the stadium, first in Maceo Park, closer to downtown, before revoking that concession out of respect for the Afro-Cuban war hero Antonio Maceo.[88] A presidential resolution from Mario Menocal temporarily revoked permission for Bradt to build there. The president's decree did not prevent boxing matches, it only called for a change of location because builders were about to break ground on a large equestrian statue of Antonio Maceo.[89]

To soften the blow to Cuban prohibitions on prizefighting and make such spectacles more palatable to those who objected, Bradt agreed to hold two benefit matches, one for the local orphans' home (Casa de Benefica y Asilo de Huérfanos de la Patria) and another in which the gate receipts would be donated to the mayor to spend as he saw fit.[90] A writer for the liberal daily El Mundo lauded the grand opening of the stadium, writing that "The Stadium has placed the final seal of cosmopolitan importance on Havana." Bradt contracted two veteran boxers, the British-born fighter from Brooklyn, Young Ahearn (Jacob K. Woodward), and another New Yorker, Willie Lewis, to feature in the opening night. Bradt introduced both boxers to the Havana public as experienced performers who had fought in the United States and Europe. The promoters pitched performances at the stadium as vaudevillian spectacles that recreated racist entertainment in the United States. Together with an array of acts, including a trained monkey, a transvestite singer, and burlesque performances, Bradt presented dozens of "Battle Royales."[91]

In these spectacles, once common in the US South, six to eight African Americans fought until one remained standing. The fighters, often with little or no training, mounted the ring and were blindfolded. On the sound of the bell, the crowd cheered them on to strike, grapple, and kick the other men until they could no longer lift themselves from the canvas. The promoters advertised the spectacle as the greatest amusement in all of Havana. In the evenings, after the horse races in Marianao, Americans in their finest attire joined Cubans to see and be seen in the sea air and the electric lights and to watch Afro-Cubans and African Americans beat each other into submission. These shows were more frequent in the weeks leading up to the Johnson-Willard bout. Some Cuban journalists applauded these spectacles. The poet Enrique Ruiz de la Serna satirically dubbed Afro-Cuban participants "capitalists" and "citizens," implying that they participated out of greed and were less than full Cubans.[92] One journalist, observing that the same unnamed Afro-Cuban man had won the Battle Royale on several occasions, dubbed him "King Shoe Polish."[93]

On the day of the much-anticipated Johnson-Willard bout, three squadrons of the Cuban army, wielding machetes, guarded the ring to keep the crowd back. They were accompanied by plain-clothed US federal agents dispatched to shadow Johnson.[94] The spectators waved white flags to show their racial preference. In the over one-hundred-degree heat, Jess Willard knocked out Jack Johnson in the twenty-sixth round, regaining the heavyweight title for the white race. Shortly thereafter, Willard announced that he would draw the color line and refused to fight other black boxers.[95] After the match, while white America celebrated and toasted Willard's health, Cuban journalists tried to explain to their audience the "ethnic intransigence of the country of lynching."[96] Willard had regained the title for the "racists among the Yankees."[97]

This understanding of Johnson as victim of hypocritical racial politics pervaded the popular reception of the dozens of boxers who arrived in Havana in 1915. Writing under the pseudonym "Frangiopane," Victor Muñoz asked his readers, "We have Jack Johnson in Havana: it is said that our city might host a fight for the championship of the world . . . there are daily horse races . . . a Stadium where there are weekly boxing matches, in the exterior circus of the new Colón theater they will effect other competitions of this nature . . . *who says we are not progressing?*"[98] The way the people of Havana handled the pressure of being a focal point of world attention was encouraging to journalists who covered these scenes. The intensity and discernment with which thousands of Cubans followed the developing plans for the fight, even buying tickets ahead of time (this was, they argued, very un-Cuban), was proof of "how our character is changing and how we are learning good things from other peoples."[99]

Beyond the simple fetishization of masculine strength or admiration of a well-muscled body, the Havana press saw in modern athletes important values that, they stressed, should be a goal for all Cubans. These values were displayed by athletes from a number of countries and were not necessarily tied to one national culture. As professionals, these men pursued wealth through the deployment of skill, intelligence, and strength. Few if any of these individuals were born into wealth. Central to their success was dedication, "science," and hard work. The boxer, as an archetype of masculinity, abstained from smoking, drinking and drugs, and displayed "good customs [buenos costumbres]."[100]

While in Havana, Johnson took advantage of his celebrity to support causes that, seemingly, little related to him. He agreed to appear in a benefit for the Comite Central de Torcedores de la Habana (Central Committee of Cigar Makers of Havana) at the Payret Theater on Central Park.[101] The war in Europe decreased demand for Cuban cigars and the majority of cigar rollers were out of work. The committee was formed as a mutual aid society and collective bargaining organization to negotiate and disperse charity from the Cuban government and the Catholic Church for the thousands out of work. Johnson had appeared in hundreds such variety shows and afterwards the committee published a formal thank-you letter.[102]

Johnson, the consummate businessman, wasted no time in negotiating endorsement deals with expensive tailors who sought to use his notoriety to attract clients.[103] He also ingratiated himself with the working classes by refusing to charge admission for the thousands of onlookers who gathered daily to watch him train for the match in the Havana stadium. Johnson appeared in dozens of shows in theatrical venues, was introduced in theaters, racetracks, and other public spaces, and generally drew a crowd wherever he went in Havana. Accounts of his risqué and unapologetic lifestyle, one journalist commented, had given him enormous popularity in Havana.[104] On February 23, the announcement that the Willard-Johnson fight would be held there received larger headlines than the death of famous independence-era leader Gonzalo de Quesada.[105]

On hearing that Johnson had been repeatedly refused lodging at all the best hotels in the city (Inglaterra, Plaza, and Pasaje), an Afro-Cuban member of the Ayuntamiento de la Habana, Eligio Madán, announced that he would offer his home to the boxer.[106] Madán published a letter detailing his outrage at the attempts by American-owned hotels to re-enact their racism in Havana: "It is impossible that a famous man of my race will not find, here in Cuba, a stay worthy of him." The next day, the *Heraldo de Cuba* carried a picture of Johnson at a reception party at Madán's home. Johnson appears in the center of a group of several Afro-Cuban men. He stands out due to his size, and among dark-suited

Afro-Cubans he is dressed in white. His white wife sits next to him and is erroneously identified as a Frenchwoman.[107] There are few other images that paired Afro-Cuban men with white women from this period. Further commentary by Madán, who served as the unofficial link between the Afro-Cuban community and Jack Johnson, continued in the weeks leading up to the fight. For the politician and activist, the implications of the bout for Afro-Cubans were clear: "Yes my race brothers . . . anticipate this! Soon we will see the white hope against black reality!"[108] Johnson, son of former slaves from Galveston, Texas, was a transnational symbol of that black reality in Cuba.

Though little is known about Eligio Madán, anecdotal evidence suggests that he was secretly a "bablawo," a religious leader in the Afro-Cuban tradition of Santería that was officially repressed by the same government he served in this period.[109] As a local political and religious leader with roots in autonomous Afro-Cuban associations, Madán's outrage was strategic and purposeful. Though few Afro-Cuban publications from 1915 have survived (they had become increasingly untenable after the massacre of the Partido Independiente in 1912), Madán's call for racial solidarity and his offering of his home to his "race brother" was an act of resistance in an extraordinarily tenuous racial environment with fresh memories of race war. Though there are few extant sources to gauge the response of Afro-Cubans to Johnson, impressionist evidence comes from one American reporter, who relayed to his readers that "hundreds of negroes, the best sports on the island, are anxious to attend the fight" but could not afford it, and were "scraping together pennies" to attend.[110]

Other politicians, among them V. Morales, Gonzalo Pérez, and Fernández Guevara y Alberdi, clashed with Madán and renewed their objections to both boxing and Jack Johnson. They penned a petition before the Ayuntamiento to enforce the practically defunct ban on boxing.[111] Their demand was seconded by the prestigious National Association of Veterans of the Wars for Independence, of which President Menocal was a member.[112] The association wrote the president beseeching him, in the name of the sacrifices made by so many veterans to "regenerate the country," that he not allow boxing in Cuba. Letters from abroad also crossed the president's desk. Albert Doogan, claiming to be the president of the University of Michigan, feared that with the popularity of boxing, bullfighting would soon be relegalized, and he pressed the president not to allow it.[113] The Association of Baptist Churches of Eastern Cuba, claiming more than two thousand members, also made clear their opposition to these brutalizing customs.[114] These isolated sources are the only archival records pertaining to these seminal events of 1915 in Cuba; they were not enough to prevent the bout.

Boosters claimed that the fight would bring enormous amounts of money to the city. This, paired with Menocal's embrace of boxing in Cuba, made impotent these attempts to censure public spectacle.[115] Though few Cuban newspapers mentioned that Menocal placed bets on the fight, US journalists reported that Menocal had bet one hundred dollars on Johnson and that the police commissioner of Havana had wagered five hundred dollars on the black champion.[116]

Cuban women, argued one journalist, had a role to play in encouraging the appropriation of boxing. Muñoz, writing for *El Mundo*, contended that women should be allowed to attend boxing matches, especially those staged with such international attention. The editor hired the British vaudevillian singer and writer Cecilia Wright to convince the Cuban public that respectable women could be boxing fans. She became the first female sportswriter for a Cuban newspaper. In her articles, she astutely predicted the outcome of the match and argued that Cuban women should be encouraged to attend so that they could best understand how to educate the future generation of men.[117]

Three days after the Johnson-Willard bout, the films produced by Santos y Artigas taken illegally at the match debuted in Havana. This was despite Johnson's desperate attempts to sue the entertainers for the outlandish sum of 500,000 pesos and appealing to the secret police to aid him.[118] George Bradt's newspaper, the *Havana Post*, used the opportunity to mock Cubans and Jack Johnson, stating that the boxer was too ignorant to understand the custom of Cuban "mañana" and that he would not be able to get an injunction to stop the exhibition of the film.[119] Johnson had shown himself to be ridiculous yet again, Bradt chided, in trying to fraudulently obtain an American passport after the bout. He was able to convince an embassy worker to grant him one, but when the head of legation was made aware he had it immediately revoked. US secretary of state William Jennings Bryan ordered the head of the US legation in Havana not to issue Johnson a passport due to his status as a fugitive from justice.[120]

Cuban readers also learned that after the bout, groups of white vigilantes had gone to the "black belt" of Chicago to mock *negros* and taunt Jack Johnson's elderly mother. That same day, a lawyer and senator from Oriente, a proponent of American missionary work in Cuba, Erasmo Regueiferos, presented his initiative to ban boxing in Cuba once and for all.[121] The law was drafted by fellow senator Antonio Gonzalo Pérez, and after "prolonged study" Regueiferos endorsed the proposal. The disgust evident in the wording of the law was compounded by the fraudulent actions of American fight promoters in Cuba. As they hurriedly fled the island, the fight's US organizers left behind a series of unpaid debts ranging from hotel bills to the daily wages of the carpenters who had constructed the ring.[122] The legislators moved "to stop the acclimatization of boxing in Cuba, which was a custom so improper for the generous and elevated sentiments . . . that characterizes the Cuban people." The proposed law reasoned that in the United States, "the country that marches at the head of civilization," boxing was rejected by the vast majority of people. This explained why unscrupulous promoters had landed in Cuba. Boxing had been illegal under Spanish rule, illegal under both American occupations, and had been illegal in the Republic since 1910. Those politicians who allowed the recent bouts had done potentially irreparable harm to the "civilization and humanity in Cuba." This law did not mention President Menocal by name, but it did state that any public functionary who approved a boxing match would be subject to a fine and would be unable to hold office for a year. Greater penalties, in line with the American prohibition of boxing during the first military intervention, were levied on managers and promoters: a fine of up to five thousand pesos and year in prison.[123] The law was a success, and boxing disappeared, for a while, from Havana.

The essayist Mario Muñoz Bustamante shared the sentiment that the Cuban government had debased itself to American promoters by allowing the bout, and boxing in general. Though Muñoz Bustamante admired the US educational system that "paired physical and intellectual culture that serves as the base of their existence," he viewed boxing as indecent.[124] A week after the bout he published an open letter to the US American Jeannette Ryder, the president of the Bando de Piedad.[125] This women's organization fought against animal cruelty in Cuba and rebuked Cubans as backwards for their customs of bullfighting and cockfighting. Ryder staged a demonstration in a bullring in a Havana suburb to stop a mock bullfight on April 4, the day before the bout. Muñoz Bustamante chided that, in keeping with her pious and protective sentiments, he fully expected her to repeat these actions and to stop the boxing match the following day. "You weren't there," he wrote, stressing that her pious sentiments did not extend to humans. He continued, "A few days ago a moralist friend asked me to write something about what has happened this winter in Havana. We had boxing, horse racing, cockfighting, gambling and more gambling . . . we are almost a capital of vice." A young and rich nation, he argued, need not be a center of vice to attract tourists by offering risqué and taboo spectacles. He implied that US tourists, in collusion with the Cuban government, were assaulting Cuban national honor.

At the root of this new law against boxing and in the public reactions to prizefighting were racial fears and nationalist sentiments. Legislators and some journalists expressed apprehension over the rising ambitions of Cubans from the working classes who flocked to these types of spectacles and saw in them an avenue of social advancement and new cultural alignments. It was no coincidence that this was one of the few times that the Afro-Cuban male body was reproduced photographically, in public, and printed in thousands of newsprint pages. These images of boxers such as "the Cuban Jack Johnson" Anastasio Peñalver, a dockworker, portrayed them as enviable physical specimens who excelled in a meritocratic and competitive profession. Peñalver was trained by the African American journeyman boxer Sam McVea, a longtime friend and competitor of Jack Johnson, and McVea reported the Cuban was an astute and quick learner.[126] McVea noted that with further training, Peñalver would "exalt the name of Cuba in the ring." A pharmacy in Centro Habana seized on the potential of the Cuban Jack Johnson, urging customers that "to have power and energy [like Peñalver], and not be impotent, you need to take our special vitamins."[127] Beyond mere entertainment, boxing culture entered Cuba as a means of advancement for the thousands of working-class men who gathered daily to watch Johnson train on the *malecón* (seafront drive).

Victor Muñoz gave a fitting coda to much of the frenetic coverage during the months of February, March, and April 1915. He visited Johnson's temporary home, in the white suburb of Vedado, home to hundreds of expatriate Americans. From there he reported on Johnson's idyllic home life: his wife and friends singing around a piano in the parlor while Johnson rested after a day of training. The day after Johnson lost the match reporters relayed Johnson's "chivalrous" behavior toward his wife: when he had realized he was about to lose the bout, he asked his trainer to escort her from the stadium so she would not see him beaten.[128] After the bout, Johnson attended a celebration in honor of Willard, who had immediately announced that he would draw the color line and never risk the title again to a black man. Johnson took the center of the ring at the stadium in front of a capacity crowd of thousands and accepted his loss "with ease and notable words." Johnson spoke eloquently compared to Willard, who was not accustomed to public speaking.[129]

That same day, Muñoz again visited Johnson at his home. "His house was like a crypt," while a subdued crowd waited outside for him to speak or to catch another glimpse of him. "I was beaten fair and square," Johnson told Muñoz, trying to force a smile. Muñoz was clearly shaken upon seeing Johnson so cowed, but he noted that in his loss he was dignified: "We said goodbye to him. Yesterday, on a day that would be so memorable for him, he was the same man as always, affably polite, worldly, and likeable."[130] Johnson later took leave of them, "shining on his face the eternal smile that is his good nature."

A week after the bout, Roberds gloated in the *Cuba News*. His ominous prediction had come true. Cubans were naïve. They were tricked by greedy and dishonest fight promoters.[131] He claimed the bout had been a net financial loss for the city and that the crooked businessmen involved had skipped town without paying their debts. Roberds's racist rants during the months leading up to the bout were never directly challenged.

One dissenting voice took a longer view of what the bout and its aftermath meant for Cubans and how they should learn from the American treatment of Johnson. Victor Muñoz, writing from the basement office of *El Mundo*, used the pen name "Attache" and relayed news from the United States as if he were a reporter on-site in Washington DC. He read US newspapers daily and then, feigning a lag time for dispatches to reach Havana from Washington, relayed news from the United States to his Cuban readers. Ten days after the bout, he wrote an article called "El Campeón" (The Champion), in which he detailed the elated reception Willard, the champion of the white race, received upon his return from Cuba. On his train journey from Key West to New York, thousands of people came to train stations, in small and large towns, to see and touch the new champion. Women held their children up to the train window to be kissed by Willard. Muñoz explained to his readers what this all meant:

> Willard had returned prestige to the white race. This ... shows the extent of race hatred. How is it that in the twentieth century, the era of the intellect, physical appearance is so important! ... They treated him like some sort of Messiah ... placing huge signs for him to see and trying to find some sort of relic of him. ... These people have some sort of defect.[132]

Johnson remained a bit longer in Cuba. He tried to prohibit the illegal showing of fight films taken surreptitiously, but he was unsuccessful and the films showed in almost every theater in the city. Within two weeks of the bout, Cubans were dancing to the famous Enrique Peña orchestra's new composition "Jack Johnson."[133] Years after the match, when Johnson tried to regain the limelight by claiming he had been deceived into willfully losing in Havana, many Cubans were all too eager to believe him. He had been swindled by greedy American promoters with the promise that he would be allowed to again enter the United States if he willingly lost to a white man.[134]

The unique American relationship with Cuba, intensified and further intertwined by military occupation and an economic stranglehold over the sugar monoculture, was also mirrored in the events of 1915.[135] American businessmen enjoyed relatively free rein in Havana, abridged national sovereignty at will by undermining laws with impunity and in collusion with the government, and treated the island as a staging ground in their quest for profit. Boxing, after a brief period of illegality and the first ring death of a Cuban boxer in 1919, would return to the national prominence in the early 1920s.

CHAPTER FIVE

# "The Revolution Came and Passed Out Gloves to Everyone"

THIS CHAPTER TRACES the evolution of prizefighting in Mexico after its beginnings as a controversial, imported, and meaningful practice to its nationalization as part of the cultural symbolism of post-Revolutionary working-class identity by the 1930s. This shift entailed the popular appropriation and redefinition of boxing as part of the larger democratization of culture in the 1920s. It also focuses on the racial dimension of prizefighting celebrity, in Mexico and beyond, surrounding the 1923 bout between Luis Ángel Firpo and Jack Dempsey. The bout provoked incisive commentary on the racial, nationalist, and gendered meanings of prizefighting in Mexico and how Mexicans viewed the meanings of race in a comparative context. These events, and how they are constituted in popular memory, are visible through an examination of mass-produced media, such as newspapers, popular histories, film, and interviews, along with archival sources that reveal the confusion, contestation, and clashes between civil society and the government. These conflicts erupted over who would define the boundaries of Mexican culture during and after the revolutionary era. Mexican and Cuban boxers traveled a circuit between Havana and Mexico City, and they read new serial publications that detailed the subculture of boxing in each others' countries.[1]

## Boxing in the Chamber of Deputies

In late November 1929, Luis F. Sotelo Regil, a historian and member of the Chamber of Deputies from Campeche, introduced a motion at the last legislative session of the 1920s. He knew his proposal had little likelihood of passing. Sotelo had written to President Emilio Portes Gil to explain his desire that blood sports such as boxing, bullfighting, and cockfighting be outlawed in every state in the nation.

He hoped to halt and reverse the popularization of boxing in Mexico and its rapidly evolving association with working-class masculinity.[2] The 1920s and 1930s, despite Sotelo's misgivings, witnessed what subsequent cultural commentators and historians would label the "golden age" of Mexican prizefighting.[3]

The wording of Sotelo's resolution evoked the common pre-Revolutionary defense of progressive and elite Mexican civilization against popular barbarism in the public sphere. Sotelo linked the prohibition of prizefight spectacles to the national campaign against alcoholism then underway. Like boxing, reformers viewed excessive alcohol consumption as a remediable affliction of working-class Mexicans.[4] Blood sports, such arguments held, did not foster the types of modern affinities preferred by the government as a means of diminishing alcoholism and redirecting the energies of the masses. Prizefighting, especially among the working classes, was too plebian to be embraced by government reformers and public intellectuals such as José Juan Tablada, despite the post-Revolutionary democratization of popular culture.[5] The inability of the government to impose its preferences on cultural alignments of Mexicans despite an interventionist and activist state in the 1920s and beyond illustrates the growing dynamism of the urban public sphere.

Sotelo's moralizations were booed by the other deputies and he was nearly laughed out of the chamber. Few legislators or writers came to his defense. Among the minority in favor of his ideas was a writer for the *Abogado Cristiano*, who invoked the out-of-fashion argument that blood sports injected Mexican blood with barbarity and pushed them into centers of vice and drunkenness. Boxing and bullfighting were not "virile and picturesque" as proponents claimed.[6]

The clear majority, both in the Chamber of Deputies and in the press, argued that Sotelo's admonitions were anachronistic in modern Mexico.[7] One deputy reportedly commented that Sotelo should be "buried standing up" for his "foolishness."[8] The biting sarcasm greeting his bill forced the secretary to stop reading it on the floor. Senator Gamio Coloca spoke for the consensus view, arguing that civilized people, far from a prudish abhorrence of such spectacles, drew virility, bravery, strength, and gallantry from the embrace of "games more or less barbarous."[9] A controlled sampling of barbarism was inherent in modernity, he implied, and should not be denied to the nation if it were to continue as both masculine and pluralistic. Those who profited from the growing popularity of prizefighting as a national industry vigorously agreed. The narrative through which Sotelo attempted to outlaw this popular pastime was deemed so ridiculous that the account was carried in newspapers in Europe and in every region of the United States where readers learned that Sotelo had been treated to a "storm of boos, sprinkled with laughter."[10] Boxing, as this and subsequent events illustrate, had been nationalized as an integral feature of Mexican popular culture.

## Death in the Ring: Paco Sotelo, 1936, and the Mundane Exoticism of Prizefighting

With fifteen seconds remaining in the tenth and final round of a featherweight bout, Jesús "Chucho" Nájera delivered a straight right hand to the face of seventeen-year-old Francisco "Paco" Sotelo. On this June evening, thousands of working-class Mexicans had gathered near the Alameda Central in the Arena Nacional to attend this spectacle. On the count of five, Sotelo tried to rise, but fell face-first on the canvas.[11] The "half-drunk" crowd called him a coward. They were convinced the fight was fixed. The ringside doctor, Gilberto Bolaños Cacho, stepped into the ring as Sotelo's manager carried the unconscious boxer to his corner.[12] As the victorious Nájera was lifted on the shoulders of his fans, the doctor gave Sotelo two adrenaline injections. When the fighter's pupils failed to contract in reaction to the flashlight, he called for an ambulance. Sotelo's unconscious body was taken to the Puesto Central de Socorros a few blocks away.

Alejandro Aguilar Reyes (1902–1961), better known by his pen name "Fray Nano," reported these details on the front page of his boxing newspaper, *Afición*. Reyes was honored by his contemporaries as "a world authority (on sport) and perhaps the best sportswriter in the Spanish language."[13] With daily print runs in the tens of thousands, the newspaper was dedicated to boxing but also covered other spectator sports. It had enough subscribers from Mexico and around Latin America to fund ten pages covering local and international prizefighting. Boxing venues such as the Arena Nacional, specially built for prizefighting and later adapted for *lucha libre*, had replaced the private clubs, improvised theaters, *carpas* (tents), and bullrings of the late nineteenth and early twentieth centuries. They constituted an infrastructure that by the 1920s accommodated tens of thousands of fans and generated enormous revenue for boxing promoters. As the capacity of these public spaces grew, they continued to host interracial and transnational athletes from as far abroad as the Philippines. African American boxers such as Sam Langford and Harry Wills were welcomed and fêted in Mexico in the 1920s, as was Joe Louis in the 1930s. The Arena Nacional also served the working class as more than a sporting venue; it doubled as a meeting hall for workers and labor unions during the populist regime of President Lazaro Cardenas (1934–1940), further linking prizefighting and working-class culture.[14]

The staff of *Afición* promoted boxing and transnational sport for more than thirty years. Reyes began publication in 1930, and *Afición* was one of the first Mexican daily newspapers dedicated to the international coverage of sport. Its editorial staff fervently supported Mexican athletes, especially when they traveled for bouts to the United States or Europe. From the late 1920s and into the 1940s, it joined dozens of comic books and films using the image of the Mexican boxer as a parable to narrate mexicanidad.[15] Fray Nano is remembered annually in Mexico: the award for the best sport journalism bears his name.[16] Popular sporting magazines like *Afición* (1930), *Ring* (1936), and *Futból* (1936) operated at odds with state-led educational attempts to foment certain types of athletics as benevolent forms of social organization that taught the values of hygiene and modernity, especially in rural areas.[17] These efforts were meant to stem vices such as drinking, gambling, and unregulated violence through the constructive and community-building activities of team sports such as baseball and basketball. *Afición* competed with these attempts. The magazine employed dozens of photographers and caricaturists who captured the personalities of local boxing celebrities and brought visual accounts of local and foreign boxing culture to even illiterate spectators. In the process, they created a valuable graphic and narrative record of the subculture that it both reflected and nurtured.

Drawings of Paco Sotelo's and Nájera's faces adorned the front page for several days leading up to the fatal bout. *Afición* reported that the day after being knocked unconscious, Sótelo never awoke from his coma and died in the arms of his manager at around four in the morning. No legal charges were filed against Nájera since his fight with Sotelo occurred under the jurisdiction of the nascent and controversial Mexican Boxing Commission.[18] More than twenty thousand people, a cross-section of Mexican society, filed by his coffin at the Agencia Gayosso funeral home, a few blocks from the Mexico City zócalo.[19] Sotelo's parents could not pay for such a sumptuous wake. Wealthy Mexican boxing fans, such as revolutionary veteran General Gustavo Arévalo Vera, a member of the Boxing Commission, and the Mexican American and Puerto Rican impresarios of the Arena Nacional, Jimmie Fitten and Carlos "Kid" Lavergne, paid the expenses.[20] Fitten, whose full name was Luís James Fitten y Sarmiento, tried to hold an interview but was overcome by grief. He had not slept since the bout, where he was pictured sobbing by the side of the boxer as the doctors had worked to revive him through the night.[21] Fitten was originally from San Francisco. He had come to Mexico in 1926 after a mediocre career as a journeyman boxer in the United States and had presided over the increasing popularity of boxing as a promoter, matchmaker, and importer of American boxing talent.[22] Fitten was one in a long line of cross-cultural brokers who were instrumental in the popularization of prizefighting.

During the funeral, fellow boxers and other athletes and managers covered the cost of the police service that was necessary to maintain order among the massive crowd.²³ The procession stopped at the Nacional. Fray Nano gave a short and emotional oration that centered on bravery and youth. Guilt-ridden and faint, Nájera was relieved of his post on the honor guard escorting the casket for fear he would collapse. He was taken home by his fans, "broken by emotion." Sotelo's father, speaking to reporters in the rain, said that he didn't blame anyone for the death of his son, that he was "resigned to it."²⁴ Taxi drivers offered their services for free and wealthier individuals gave rides in private cars to those who could not walk. As the newspapers expressed it, the scene was a cross-class enunciation of solidarity in a very natural and Mexican context.

The long procession led from the Nacional to the gravesite in Sotelo's home neighborhood. The youth was a "favorite son" of the small town formerly known San Ángel, which had recently been rechristened, after the former Revolutionary general and president, as Villa Obregón. An "enormous multitude ... contrite and somber" began the long march to the cemetery. Among them were "people from all ages and social classes ... aristocrats, professionals, laborers, students, shoe-shiners, paper boys, youngsters—all passed in front of his coffin and accompanied him to the distant *panteón*." In Villa Obregón, businesses closed and government offices shut. Thousands more people joined the procession. At the graveside, a member of the cemetery staff opened the coffin so Sotelo's mother could have a last look at her son. When the first shovelful of dirt landed, the chronicler for *Afición* waxed philosophical: "That sound touches the deepest recess of the soul and reminds us that, some sooner, some later, we all end there."²⁵

The dramatic language of this eulogy, mirrored in most Mexico City dailies, reflected the intensity of emotion that surrounded not just Paco Sótelo, but the subculture of boxing in Mexico City in the 1930s. The circumstance held intense meaning for those who experienced it. It was especially meaningful for those from the lower classes who, like Sotelo, saw prizefighting as a vehicle of upward mobility. It also made good copy. *Afición* and all the major dailies in Mexico City carried news of Sotelo's death and funeral. None of them questioned the manner in which he died. Boxing had become an established element of national life. It was not only an important form of entertainment for the hundreds of thousands of Mexicans who attended matches, it was a vehicle for performing and representing a hardscrabble, modern, and urban identity. Attendance at boxing matches, one US observer in Mexico surmised, now outstripped bullfighting as the most attended blood sport.²⁶ The famous matador from Guanajuato, Rodolfo Gaona, relayed his fear to a reporter that the popularity of boxing among Mexican audiences was displacing the centuries-old tradition of bullfighting. The only remedy was to "keep prizefighters out of Mexico."[27]

Before Sotelo's death, boxing had spread through the country by means of radio and newspaper coverage, specialized sport magazines, and the travels of transnational boxers who held exhibitions in virtually every part of Mexican territory.[28] In provincial cities such as Oaxaca, local elites embraced sport as a signifier of the ideal virile and bourgeois man and as a vector for the values of civilization and progress during the Porfiriato.[29] By the 1920s, local boxers from rural pueblos had appropriated and transformed these ideas; they held bouts during the Revolution and throughout the decade of the 1920s. Documents from municipal archives in the cities of Xalapa and Oaxaca show a similar willingness on the part of the authorities to allow boxing matches (and tax them) in this period, though in both cities, authorities clearly preferred that their citizens attend baseball games.[30] In Xalapa, boxing posters advertised regular matches in the Teatro Lerdo. These events, often accompanied by variety shows, advertised free seats for women and featured female wrestlers and boxers. Advertisers informed female viewers that they should bring their daughters to learn about modern body culture so they could "cast off the title of the 'weaker sex.'"[31]

These events occurred and surfaced in the press alongside international pugilistic events, which, Mexican commentators argued, had worldwide and local resonance.[32] Mexicans took on the names of foreign sport celebrities through the common appellation of "Kid." Before international television broadcasts, thousands of fans attended re-enactments of distant bouts that were charged with racial and ethnic significance. For example, weeks after Sotelo's death, a large crowd gathered at the Arena Nacional to watch two boxers acting the parts of the African American Joe Louis against the pride of Adolf Hitler, German boxer Max Schmeling. In the weeks leading up the event, a writer for *Afición* explained that this "epic" bout was a war for racial supremacy between the "the Detroit Brown Bomber" and "the Hun from the Rhine."[33] Boxing narratives and personalities served to localize and distill international politics and race.

Images of boxers and boxing illustrated the experience of urban life. Twenty-foot-tall signs for boxing gyms, advertisements for a vast array of products from cigarettes to panacea tonics, movies, and serialized images formed part of the backdrop of urbanization and the post-Revolutionary democratization of popular culture.[34] In Mexico, as in Europe between the wars, sport became "an expression of national struggle, [with] sportsmen representing their nation or state, [as] primary expressions of their imagined communities."[35] Often unacknowledged in these observations was that nearly all the athletes who would become standard bearers were from the margins of urban society. They were among the first lower-class heroes and antiheroes in a crowded field of masculine idols whose rise in the meritocratic field of sport led to their embrace by millions of spectators. Renowned photojournalists like Gustavo Casasola, Enrique Díaz, and avant-garde photographers such as Manuel Álvarez Bravo documented the popularization of boxing as simultaneously exotic and embedded in the experience of mexicanidad. Manuel Álvarez Bravo's 1930 picture "Boxeador," for example, depicts a modern street scene in which a two-story-tall rendering of a boxer in fighting stance is fixed within a chaotic array of power lines over a decaying cantina.[36] The Fondo Enrique Díaz collection, housed in the Archivo General de la Nación, contains hundreds of photographic plates of boxers and boxing from the 1910s through the 1940s. The Fototeca Nacional contains more than 1,400 boxing images—athletes, crowds, celebrities, venues—thus far catalogued from this period.[37] The private Gustavo Casasola collection, in Coyoacán, likewise contains many images from the late nineteenth century to the 1970s. All collections contain numerous images of African American boxers, most of them unidentified, in Mexican rings.

Newspapers such as *Afición* published nationalist accounts of Mexican boxers in the United States. These accounts often stressed the difficulty a Mexican fighter had to overcome to win a decision due to the racist and parochial attitudes of American judges, who viewed Mexicans as "Negroes." US Americans, Fray Nano posited, feared that if a Mexican were to become champion local Chicanos would become insolent and "unbearable." Fray Nano followed Mexican boxers to their bouts in Los Angles, California. He observed that even though most of the crowd was Mexican, US referees made it impossible for Mexican boxers to win a fair fight. One letter to the editor argued that despite this perception, boxers traveling to the United States should be praised as "virile" patriots who "know how to put the Mexican flag on high."[38]

*Afición* served as a forum for expressions of national honor defended through the medium of boxing. Its editors published hundreds of letters written in forcefully nationalist terms. International sport was a means to tame the outside world and to participate in and dominate, through the consumption of popular narratives and biographies, a transnational culture with its own rituals, language, rules, and symbols.[39] The rapid extension of media coverage of sport culture was initiated and consumed by Mexicans, whose affinities ranged beyond the confines of the traditional and the local: their interests and allegiances as aficionados created cultural spaces in which the exotic was domesticated and imbued with meaning. Though writing of more modern means of communication and media, Jorge Larraín's explanation of the centrality of these newly mediated subcultures captures the impact of this strain of transnational identity formation:

> The process of globalization ... has an important effect on cultural identities for three main reasons. First, because in the formation or construction of any cultural identity the idea of the "other" is crucial, and globalization puts individuals, groups and nations in contact with a series of new "others" in relation to whom they can define themselves. This can only happen through the media. As [John B.] Thompson has noted, "the process of self-formation is increasingly nourished by mediated symbolic materials." The construction of personal identities has become more complex and open-ended because the media increasingly mediate it. The globalization of communications by means of electronic signals has allowed the separation of social relations from the local contexts.[40]

Readers, based on the letters to the editor published in *Afición*, were aware of the cultural stereotypes surrounding Mexican boxers in the United States. Bob Edgren, the most widely published American boxing commentator of the 1920s and 1930s, argued that the "Aztec race" had put forth many "physically superior" boxers who had potentially lucrative capabilities. Their fatal flaw, according to Edgren, was being headstrong, given to drunkenness, and, in general, being "mentally inferior." Fray Nano, reprinting the article for the readers of *Afición*, agreed "unfortunately" that Edgren was correct. Given their lack of formal education and sudden wealth, Mexican boxers often sunk under the weight of their new status. Luis "Kid Azteca" Villanueva and Rodolfo "Chango" Casanova imbibed the patriotic rhetoric of their "paisanos" who dreamed of a "champion of their race," but failed to manage their notoriety into long-term stability.[41]

Depicting these expanding boundaries of *lo mexicano*, Talán's narratives, cinematic portrayals, and popular literature are composed of boxers, hustlers, businessmen, doctors, wives and girlfriends, drunks, immigrants, African Americans, "blonds," and mestizos. The antagonists are greedy businessmen, Mexican Americans who are not quite Mexican but not quite American, and dishonest and materialistic yanquis who exploit Mexican talent. The protagonists are often impoverished Mexican laborers turned athletes who, from the *arrabales* (poor neighborhoods) of Mexico City, rise to fame and (all too often) temporary wealth.[42] Boxers in these representations perform clichéd *machista* behaviors and are often cast as embodiments of Mexican stereotypes and self-perceptions.[43] For example, the Mexico City newspapers *Excelsior* and *Universal* reported on the death of Paco Sotelo and the benefit match held in his honor. The match was intended to raise funds for an elaborate monument for Sotelo's grave. The best boxers of Mexico had also agreed to fight to raise money for the deceased boxer's family, but Sotelo's father, a man "who followed the bible and lived by the sweat of his brow," refused to accept charity. In the space of few weeks, the seventeen-year-old boxer and his family became representatives of the "bravest Mexicans of all time," who proved that "A brave death is the most notable act a human can accomplish. All brave acts disappear in the face of a single cowardly moment. Bravery is for men what virginity is for women." The Sotelos, father and son, became paragons of Mexican manhood. The narrative of masculine honor simultaneously defined the characteristics of proper femininity.[44]

Rodolfo "Chango" Casanova, the popular boxing idol, sold ice cream in the working-class neighborhood of Tepito before becoming a boxer. He offered to box free of charge to raise money for Sotelo's family.[45] A long list of pugilists from around Mexico had likewise agreed to waive their normal fee. *Excelsior* juxtaposed this as common decency, a very Mexican trait (*un rasgo muy nuestro*), against another boxer, Kid Azteca (Luis Villanueva), who refused to appear for free. The observer implied that Azteca was acting dishonorably. He assailed the boxer as a parvenu, mocking him for his defeat by the more popular and lighter boxer, Chango Casanova. Not only was Casanova a better boxer and generous with his talent within the community; he was humble. He honored his working-class roots after his rise to fame. The reporter drew on popular stereotypes regarding those who comically put on airs by disdaining Mexican culinary nationalism: instead of tortillas, Azteca was one of those "boys who eats bread every day." This coded insult implied that Kid Azteca, despite coming from the same poor neighborhood as Casanova, had turned his back on working-class Mexicans.[46]

As Eric Hobsbawm noted, the perception that a popular hero disdained his or her working-class roots after obtaining wealth and fame often served to undermine popular support: "Paradoxically, therefore, the conspicuous expenditure of the bandit, like the gold-plated Cadillac and diamond inlaid teeth of the slum boy who has become world boxing champion, serves to link him to his admirers and not separate them from them; providing always that he does not step too far outside the heroic role in which the people have cast him."[47]

Though Kid Azteca would later win international boxing titles and represent Mexican virility abroad, he showed his lack of mexicanidad by "asking for a godlike salary" when he "should have felt obligated to help his fellow professional's family."[48] On the other hand, fighters such as the first Mexican-born world champion boxer (1934), Alberto "Baby" Arizmendi, could both Anglicize his nom de guerre and wear an oversized Mexican sombrero in the United States. He also provided fodder for US stereotypes that the Mexican nation as a whole craved a boxing championship over a US American: "The day he fights for the championship his Mexico will pray that he wins in a thousand churches."⁴⁹ Though Arizmendi's costume was a theatrical caricature of working-class Mexican clothing, his perceived faithfulness to his background allowed him to retain popular approbation in 1930s Mexico.⁵⁰ Ethnic stereotyping provided an important narrative often embraced by minority boxers as a means to rally supporters in the United States. For example, for his 1934 bout with Italian American Tony Canzoneri, Arizmendi donned the sombrero for publicity shots while Canzoneri played the street-tough Italian immigrant from New York. The *Los Angeles Times* portrayed the bout as a contest of men "From the Land of Blood and Sand" versus "From the Sidewalks of New York."⁵¹ Arizmendi had a relatively long career in the United States, boxing into the 1940s, and was often denigrated by US writers for his "social activity," which meant his carousing.⁵²

As Anne Rubenstein has shown, these portrayals (in this case nonfiction) served as didactic lessons to readers about the roles and responsibilities of working-class Mexicans who gained notoriety in a rapidly modernizing and urbanizing period. Rubenstein further argues for the importance of these vehicles of mass culture as constitutive of the Mexican public sphere in this period: "The interpretive communities gathered around popular culture *were* Mexican civil-society in this era."⁵³ Similar to books on etiquette, popular narratives showed the dangers of success and the permissible public behaviors required of upwardly mobile members of the marginal classes. Athletic contests were universally rule-driven and (ideally) governed by an ethic of fair play. They provided an imagined avenue for personal advancement within and beyond a boxer's local environment. Sports, as Louis Pérez Jr. argued, "are inherently neutral in the sense that they do not form their own social function."⁵⁴ In Mexico by the 1930s, boxing's social function was, partially, as a pressure release for working-class aspirations of social mobility. This advancement, however, was to be governed by behavioral norms if successful individuals were to maintain the public's approbation.

Scholars of the post-Revolutionary period are split over the content and even the existence of a unitary national culture. Recently, Alan Knight has critiqued the "many Mexicos" thesis put forth by anthropologist Guillermo Bonfil Batalla. According to Bonfil and historian Luis González y González, Mexico is best understood as a series of separate entities, be they regions, states, or villages. Historian Steve Stern has argued that examination of various cultural trends reveals deep underlying commonalities in the Mexican experience (since the colonial era), while Alan Knight suggests that national culture is a product of the post-Revolutionary rise in consumer culture that was greatly aided by new forms of mass media. This study finds evidence to support Knight's thesis. Cultural mediators in the popular press drew on extant Mexican tradition to invent new heroes within an increasingly transnational context. This study also supports the ideas put forth by Jorge Larrain: National identity is situated between the two poles of constructivism and essentialism. Larrain calls this in-between area "historical structural." Mexicans transformed these features rather than creating them anew. "Negotiation" is an imprecise term to explain cultural shifts, but it approximates the process wherein the new is grafted onto and digested within the extant.[55]

## Civil Society Versus Government: Boxing and Popular Culture

In the immediate post-Revolutionary era, boxing as blood sport, despite and perhaps because of its popularity, was scorned by the Mexican government as an antisocial behavior to be replaced by team sports such as basketball and baseball. As Mary Kay Vaughan has demonstrated, the Revolutionary Mexican state deployed educational literature and radio programs to discourage cockfighting, bullfighting, and boxing and to encourage other pastimes, such as baseball and basketball. This preference was clearly illustrated by attempts to lead the masses away from violent sport and to instill the values of teamwork and "health and sobriety."[56] The state attempted to mold its citizens, but civil society ignored strict control over cultural preferences.

Spectators, in mass, spent their earnings to view blood sports. The mass media brought them dramatic daily narratives, posing boxing matches as moments of international importance. One such bout occurred on January 1, 1936, between Rodolfo "Chango" Casanova and the US American Freddie Miller. It took place in El Toreo, the largest bullring in Mexico, and was attended by a capacity crowd of thirty thousand people. Newspapers published drawings, pictures, vignettes, and brief biographies of the opponents, and thousands attended their training camps. On New Year's Day, Casanova defeated the US fighter. One observer explained the Mexican's triumph by citing the negative effects of high altitude in Mexico City, but grudgingly lauded Casanova, giving him perhaps the highest compliment for a boxer in this period: "He is game and can give as well as take . . . the world will have to reckon with this rough and tough hombre from Mexico."[57] US journalists in Mexico City had predicted since the early 1930s that Mexican boxers would eventually triumph in the United States because of their "stout hearts" and that prizefighting would displace bullfighting as the "national sport." Promoters had traveled to Mexico since the 1920s in search of a lucrative "talent" who would translate well into US prize rings.[58] The two Mexicans fighting on the undercard also defeated US boxers.

Since the late Porfiriato, Mexican newspapers imported innovations from their counterparts in the United States. English-language newspapers published in Mexico, such as the *Mexican Herald*, began publishing entire "sport" pages. These sheets relayed detailed reports and photographs that localized distant events and athletic celebrities.[59] Hybrid publications, such as *Arte y Sport* (1919), catered to the newly emergent demand for transnational information of sport culture. They printed accounts of boxing matches and paired them with poetry, musical compositions, and essays on politics and art. Such magazines styled themselves as bettering agents for their readers. Their issues carried a broad and eclectic sampling of ideas and images from diverse places from the United States to Japan. Their pages bore such lofty statements as "In the practice of sport lies the salvation of the race."[60] Weekly magazines, responding to increased demand and the frequent enactment of sporting contests in Mexico, shifted from weekly to daily issues. One publication's title illustrates the evolving demand for both traditional and imported pastimes: *Toros y Deportes*.[61]

Post-Revolutionary Mexican spectators embraced this hybrid and modern mix of tradition and innovation, even when their evolving tastes ran counter to the goals of government projects. In some cases, the state sought to replace popular religious practice with a new focus on team sports. Keith Brewster recounts state initiatives to educate and civilize rural Mexicans by encouraging the celebration of national holidays through the secular practice of sport. Athletics figured into local political struggles as villagers communicated directly with President Lázaro Cardenas to plead for the creation and preservation of sport fields for "patriotic activities." Brewster reproduces a choreographed script for Revolution Day in the early 1940s to show the theatrical and highly symbolic use of organized amateur sport as a panacea for a number of perceived social ills in rural Mexico. When tennis is introduced into an inebriated and violent rural milieu via the white-clad teachers of sport, all social disorder is quelled due to cooperative community engagement in the game.[62] Out of the confusion emerges a robust, white-clad couple that represents the end product of cooperation with state goals. The subculture of boxing was a relatively autonomous component of Mexican national identity that rejected or ignored official state rhetoric and, as Carlos Monsivais has argued, in part "made possible and extended that minimal democratic space" of civil society and the public sphere.[63]

In the early 1920s, the checkered legality of boxing was replaced by the first substantial attempts at state regulation. The Mexico City government founded the

Comisión de Box (Boxing Commission) to regulate boxing and to profit through taxation and licensing fees on the sport.[64] By 1930, more than five hundred licenses for professional boxers had been granted, signifying for many the final end to the popularity of bullfighting.[65] The Ayuntamiento turned to journalists to learn international norms that governed boxing and asked for sportswriters' assistance in drafting legislation to cover the "enormously popular" sport. The Mexico City rules governing boxing as public spectacle became an example for provincial cities when they confronted the same conditions.[66]

Social critics, such as Federico Gamboa, pressed the government to ban boxing. His opinion carried political weight when he demanded action in his capacity as director of the Cultural and Artistic Advisory Board of Mexico City. This group, employed by the Ayuntamiento, was a post-Revolutionary censorship board particularly interested in policing morality and preventing displays offensive to their vision of Mexican nationalism.[67] They inveighed against what they labeled the *malas artes* employed by controversial boxers such as Patricio Martínez Arredondo in the early 1920s. Gamboa chastised the Ayuntamiento for granting a boxing license to two children whose fighting names were Baby Dempsey and Baby Carpentier (after the US American and French boxers then making headlines).[68] Gamboa grudgingly admitting that boxing was too popular to effectively repress; the state needed legislation to regulate it and to offset the most depraved aspects of the sport. In extreme cases, he argued, the rules of public diversions against the exploitation of children should be sufficient to prohibit future "shames" of this sort. In the early 1920s, the board employed more than one hundred censors, who were responsible for every entertainment venue. These censors included specialists in foreign films who protected the public from obscene or anti-Mexican content. Under Gamboa's leadership, the advisory board promoted his vision of high culture (the celebration and subsidization of novelists, artists, and sculptors) and sought to repress and regulate mass culture such as boxing and foreign films.[69]

In 1923, police inspector Pedro Gómez complained to the Ayuntamiento. The crowds at boxing matches were dangerous and he was unwilling to risk the safety of his officers at those events.[70] According to Gómez, the matches attracted an "obnoxious" element of the population. Spectators were violent when they felt boxers did not merit the price paid for tickets. Gómez did not ask that boxing matches be stopped, though he found them offensive, but that the government increase oversight to provide the public with "better quality boxers."[71] With daily press coverage and tens of thousands of Mexicans flocking to see local and foreign performers, the city government sought to tame the crowd, not to eliminate the reason for its excitement.

## "Firpo Carries the Hopes of the Race in his Hands": A Boxing Match in New York Becomes a Focal Point to Gauge Mexican Identity

> Our temperament, always conditioned to follow whatever is fashionable, influences progress in the intensification of pugilism in Mexico, and so we have seen that in schools, in shops, in factories, in the home, boxing predominates, and even the newspaper criers in the street, thinking themselves diminutive Firpos and Dempseys, fight their world-wide matches bare knuckled.... Boxing, like bullfighting, will always live in Mexico.[72]

On September 14, 1923, a former miner and hobo from Colorado, Jack Dempsey, met a one-time pharmacy bathroom attendant and stevedore from Buenos Aires, Luis Ángel Firpo, at the Polo Grounds in New York City. Along with the heavyweight championship belt, they competed for racial supremacy in the Western Hemisphere. Or so promoters and journalists around the world claimed. Historian José Speroni argues that this bout, despite Firpo's defeat, was a formative moment for the construction of modern Argentine national identity. Spectators outside of Argentina and the United States also imbued the match with great meaning.[73] In Mexico, newspapers stoked interest in the distant prizefight. Reporters noted the excitement fueled by the racialized framing of the spectacle. Ticket sales alone totaled over one million dollars.

Despite the duration of the international attention focused on Firpo-Dempsey, the match was most remarkable for its brevity. It lasted less than four minutes. Dempsey knocked Firpo to the canvas a brutal nine times in the first round and ended the fight in the first minute of the second round. It was a tenacious but futile showing for Firpo against the US American world champion. The controversial moment of the bout, one still discussed by Argentine and US boxing fans, came when Firpo knocked Dempsey through the ropes and out of the ring.[74] Ringside reporters pushed him back in ring, which was a violation of the rules and should have resulted in Dempsey's disqualification and Firpo's victory.[75]

Tex Rickard, the famous boxing promoter, pitched the match as a racial and nationalist spectacle. He drew on longstanding US disdain for Latin Americans as barbaric racial others.[76] He reputedly coined Firpo's nom de guerre "Wild Bull of the Pampas."[77] Though Firpo lived most of his life in the cosmopolitan port city of Buenos Aires, not in rural hinterland of the pampas, Rickard calculated that the name would conjure ideas of Argentine gauchos and aggressive masculinity, an imagined national type that succeeded in selling tickets. Rickard's framing and production of the fight also influenced self-representations in some of the most exclusively male and working-class venues in Mexico: pulquerías.[78]

Pulquerías were spaces where *pulque*, an alcoholic beverage fermented from the maguey cactus, was sold to a largely working-class clientele. Throughout the colonial and modern eras, they have been sites where the urban poor congregated to imbibe and socialize. In 1923, they were a controversial incarnation of popular sociability, where rural and urban Mexico met. Travelers and journalists often wrote of them as a quintessentially Mexican institution characterized by colorful and picaresque wall paintings and names. Pulquerías were also focal points of legislative attempts to regulate the behavior of lower-class Mexicans. These venues had long been portrayed by the colonial and national elite as an impediment to the modernizing efforts of the Mexican state. Carleton Beals, the radical American journalist, along with others resident in Mexico City at the time, remarked that some pulquerías changed their names to celebrate the legacy of Firpo as a masculine symbol and a challenger to American dominance in the prize ring:

> When Firpo fought Dempsey the first reports gave the Argentinian bruiser the victory. The local crowds were delirious with enthusiasm. At the time, I was teaching in a little school in the poverty-stricken Colonia Vallejo. The owner of the pulque shop there had hastened to repaint the name of his establishment, even before the final returns came in: "Firpo Won," and so it remained defiantly for years.[79]

By the late 1920s, another popular pulquería, "El Campeonato" (The Championship), decorated its exterior wall with portraits of a boxer and bullfighter on either side of the entrance.[80]

In Mexico City, the cigarette company El Buen Tono funded the first commercial radio broadcast in Mexican history, relaying to large crowds the round-by-round details of the bout. Established during the Porfiriato, the company manufactured cigarettes and cigars and was one of Mexico's first mechanized industries.[81] It was also significant for its early role in graphic design and advertising and for publishing one of the first series of popular graphic novels. Some of its advertisements featured local boxers and other performers such as Conde Koma (Yamato Maida), the Japanese jujitsu professor, to show the manly effects of smoking its cigarettes. In 1923, it was run by Senator José J. Reynoso, who maintained his position as senator throughout his tenure at the company's helm.[82] El Bueno Tono later seized on the visit of Jack Dempsey to Mexico in

1925. It invited and likely paid him, as a publicity stunt, to tour one of its factories, where he was photographed examining its machinery.[83]

The pairing of a boxing celebrity alongside Mexico's most advanced mass machines drew on prizefighting's status as both modern and popular. On the day of the bout, radio broadcast news competed with the more traditional telegraph services used by major local newspapers *Excelsiór*, *El Demócrata*, and *El Universal*. These newspapers fought to bring the swiftest updates from New York. Ringside announcers spoke directly to Mexican spectators who hustled to spread the news of Firpo's second-round defeat. Spectators bought extra print editions of newspapers that had gone to press within minutes of the bout with the disenchanting information of the Argentine's defeat. Mexicans from peripheral areas around the metropolis who had come to the city center to celebrate the 113th anniversary of the Grito de Dolores (and Mexican independence from Spain) gathered on street corners, stopping traffic, to watch the radiograms of the bout projected onto improvised outdoor screens. One reporter wrote that "the streets were full of people, everywhere, in theaters, cinemas, cafes, restaurants, cantinas, billiard halls, stores and public meeting places: the point most debated and the topic of conversation was about boxing."[84] An illustrator filled nearly the entire front page of *El Demócrata* with imaginative renderings of Dempsey and Firpo in various pugilistic poses. It would take weeks for photographs from New York to reach Mexico, but readers of *El Demócrata* seemingly could not wait to envision the scene.[85]

The event became an opportunity for Mexican cultural mediators to look outward to discuss the mundane meanings of race in a comparative context. Writers discussed the essential natures of the peoples represented by Firpo and Dempsey. This was the same period when José Vasconcelos wrote his most famous essay, "Mestizaje" (1925).[86] In it, Vasconcelos deployed a variant of racial determinism to argue that Mexicans, and other Latin Americans, through miscegenation, were on the verge of forming a new race, what he deemed a *mestizaje universal* (universal racial mixing). The Cosmic Race, as he called it, would transcend and replace previous racial classifications that assumed that certain races, those derived from Europe in particular, occupied the highest position on a descending scale. Most writers in the press, whether they shared this assumption or not, wrote in a language that presupposed the validity of, or at least the general public's adherence to, these racist assumptions, even when they posed Latin Americans as inferior.[87] Though Vasconcelos's ideas challenged the supremacy of Anglo-Saxons, they were written in a dense and abstract language that presupposed a specialized knowledge of history, literature, and a range of scientific fields. Ideas thus expressed were unlikely to be embraced and deployed by a broad public.

The concepts of race, nation, and gender deployed by writers to explain events such as the Firpo-Dempsey match likely reached more readers and served as a better gauge of how ordinary people understood and digested the meaning of such abstractions in their everyday lives. Writers presupposed consensus on the valences and meanings of the national types represented by the two boxers. As the front-page headline for a Mexico City newspaper formulated it, "The symbols of two opposing races . . . have become the focal point where world attention is converging."[88]

Readers followed daily reports about the temperaments, eating habits, and even the clothing worn by Firpo and Dempsey. They went by the thousands to watch African American journeyman fighters perform at the bullring, El Toreo, in the affluent Colonia La Condesa.[89] Members of the "beautiful sex," if accompanied by a man, were given free tickets to such events. In other venues, amateur boxers from athletic clubs and workers' unions staged public bouts to prove their mastery of modern sport. Impresarios colluded with the Mexican government to lower ticket prices so that Mexican youths, both civilian and military, could witness professional boxers to learn the finer points of the masculine "art."[90] The public rhetoric surrounding boxing had changed enormously since the pre-Revolutionary era.

Firpo's loss was a catalyst for commentaries on US treachery and unfairness.[91] Cheating, or perhaps confusion by the US referee, had robbed a Latin American of one of the most important popular titles of the era. Mexicans debated the legitimacy of sport as vehicle of international fair play in the weeks after the bout as details became available and later when the film of the match played in dozens of theaters in Mexico City. Most concluded that sport itself was not the culprit, but that the rules were unfairly applied. Immediately after the bout, the Mexico City government decided to lower the taxes charged on "that class of spectacles," in order to promote the spread of boxing as an essential form of knowledge and cultural attainment for citizens of Mexico City. *El Demócrata* reported the attendance of the governor of the state of Mexico and the director of the Military College of San Jacinto. They worked with boxing promoter Baldomero Romero, who had labored for nearly two decades with such intellectuals as José Juan Tablada to popularize blood sport and physical culture as public spectacle in the capital:[92]

> The sport of boxing, which has been taken up with so much enthusiasm in Mexico, has in this company that presents this spectacle a great element of encouragement, the great bouts have been so frequent in which true boxers have fought [that it is] developing a labor of physical culture that is appreciated by the municipal and educational authorities such to give, due to its merit and

effects, a lowering of the taxes that this type of shows must pay without any other reason than taking into account its cultural character in favor of the bettering of the race.[93]

These evolving sentiments were expressed in new vocabularies that evoked mundane occurrences. "Dempsey" became synonymous with cheating as far away as Oaxaca, where boxing matches were held to celebrate Mexican Independence Day.[94] Editorialists argued that modern responsibilities of educators were "to develop in youth the same in physical strength as in intellect in order to invigorate the race, which in the current epoch has so many tendencies that make it more and more feeble."[95]

The racial framing of the Dempsey-Firpo bout was also evident in how some US Americans perceived its importance in Latin America. George Trevor, writing for the *Brooklyn Daily Eagle*, reported how he imagined all of "South America" was feeling. His musings were a rare moment of critical reflection on racist assumptions about Latin Americans, but they were also an opportunity to deploy long-held stereotypes:

> An intelligent force, none the less potent because it is unseen, will inspire Luis Angel Firpo as he takes his corner to face Jack Dempsey on the evening of Sept. 14. We refer to the driving power of patriotism. Love of country is a powerful passion. . . . Now, whatever his faults, Firpo is no coward. He has a sort of fatalistic faith in his massive forearms. He fears no man. But Firpo will gain added courage by the knowledge that he is the lone champion of the Latin race in this battle against the representative of the Northland. . . . As Luis flings aside his purple and gold checkered bathrobe he will feel the eyes of all South America upon him. Argentines, Chilians [*sic*], Peruvians, Bolivians will sink their time-honored differences in his common support. He is their champion—by his success or failure, they feel instinctively that their manhood will be judged. . . . Americans do not realize the intense racial hatred for the United States underlying the polite veneer which cloaks the secret thoughts of our Latin neighbors. This hostility is doubtless inspired by our own attitude to South Americans . . . we of the North look down contemptuously upon all the peoples to the south of the Rio Grande. This contemptuous dislike is feverishly reciprocated. The mistrust is mutual . . . we are the despised "Gringos." . . . They chafe under the vaunted physical ascendency of the Anglo-Saxon stock. Always they have passionately yearned for a champion who could fight with his fists in the virile fashion of the North.[96]

The match was an opportunity to register opinions on the racial and national other. It was embedded within a broader range of comparative moments in this period. Mauricio Tenorio-Trillo recognized the tensions in constructing a national identity between the government-supported national traditions and an outwardly oriented "cosmopolitan nationalism." He further argues:

> Cultural, economic, and political nationalism was at odds with both cultural and political cosmopolitanism. Cosmopolitanism was a model of modernity that simultaneously required the homogenization of all human characteristics and desires and recognized and appreciated the exotic and the bizarre. That was an insurmountable existential irony: an organized model of the world, and a fascination with what was not part of the model but which ought to be part of the picture of the modern world. In addition, the very national need to be cosmopolitan seemed to be in conflict with the requirement of being culturally and racially unique and, presumably, superior.[97]

Looking outward to gauge national culture was always an act of subjective translation. Mexican appropriation of boxing was emblematic of this tension between nationalism and cosmopolitanism. Cultural critics engaged this irony, adopting the image of Luis Ángel Firpo as their own and identifying him as a standard bearer for a greater, though ill-defined, pan–Latin American identity. As Tenorio-Trillo identified, sporting events in the age of the "massive appropriation of popular taste and consciousness" became a series of symbolic displays used to express one's place in the world.

The day after the bout, José Juan Tablada recorded his impressions. As a correspondent in New York, he witnessed the environment surrounding the match. In the early twentieth century, his fascination with boxing mirrored his enthusiasm with the culture of Japan and with the transnational world of modern sport. He had boxed and served as a trainer and second for illegal Mexico City bouts when foreigners competed with Mexican athletes. As a young writer, he defied official prohibitions of prizefighting, arguing in favor of its introduction and dissemination among the juventud dorada (golden youth) and as a panacea for national decadence.

Tablada's career spanned the era in which increasingly rapid international communication transformed the dissemination and consumption of knowledge, especially popular culture. By the 1920s, he was offended by the notoriety and wealth attained by athlete-celebrities like Jack Dempsey. He viewed them—individuals almost always from the uneducated working classes—as unintelligent and undeserving of fame. For Tablada, the celebration of Dempsey and Firpo was a triumph of lowbrow culture and proof of the danger of masses choosing, without the guidance of their social betters, their own heroes.

Observing the vitality of popular culture in New York, he feared the spread to Mexico of such spectacles and the celebration of people like Dempsey and Firpo.[98] Firpo's loss provided an opportunity to chastise Mexican society (and Latin American society more broadly) for seeing racial superiority as an aspect of such events. Tablada summarized his position in the article's title: "Dempsey, the Stupidest Man in the World."[99] He attached primary blame, however, to the "ignorant" and brutalized spectators. They craved and consumed these fraudulent narratives. They were brainwashed and didn't realize they were being exploited.

Fundamental to Tablada's reasoning was an appraisal of commercialized sport as an unskilled and "troglodyte" pursuit that was a disfigurement on an otherwise praiseworthy US culture. Though he argued that the terms of racial superiority used to advertise the bout were a trap to ensnare thoughtless observers, he succumbed to the this temptation to describe why US Americans were adept at the practice: "It is because boxing is a sport that is absolutely Saxon, suitable for the qualities of the cold, prudent, and calculating race."[100] US society, he argued, was largely worthy of imitation, but "Neither have the triumphs of Dempsey made me admire this nation that I do admire and envy for the libraries, the museums, certain civic and social virtues and some of its poets who were much less popular than Dempsey."[101] Boxing was a hereditary vice of the Saxon races.

Tablada's musings reached a large audience of Latin American readers. In 1921, his dispatches from New York were serialized in the Costa Rican magazine *Repertorio Americano*.[102] In a previous article on a Dempsey bout, he excoriated the US public as simian, barbaric, and idiotic. Dempsey was an ape, a coward (for not fighting in World War I), and an egotistical buffoon. He juxtaposed US primitiveness with the modernity of the Spanish, French, and the Japanese. They embraced bullfighting, fencing, and jujitsu, sports, Tablada reasoned, that relied on cerebral activity and human dominance over nature. US civilization should not be judged by "the oil men or the Jews on Wall Street," he admonished. The "stone age" Saxons and Africans who excelled at boxing should be degraded as racially backward.

Tablada collaborated with the losing side in the Mexican Revolution after the assassination of Francisco Madero in 1911. He served as the director of the official newspaper of Huerta's government, the *Diario Oficial*. He backed Huerta, the dictator, as a "warrior of the ages" and later went into exile in New York after the fall of the regime.[103] By 1923, Tablada had a peripatetic past, from morphine addiction and treatment to his attempts to meld Japanese and Mexican culture; he was both cosmopolitan and nationalistic.[104] For Tablada, his class-inflected definition of intelligence was the sole criterion when evaluating any social practice—including commercialized sport—which he found dangerously similar to the brutality of the Roman circus. His comparisons were explicit: "There is not in this sport [boxing] any intelligence as there is in Latin fencing or in Japanese jujitsu."[105] The popular appeal of boxing, he argued, was an impediment to elite attempts to guide cultural change. He lamented the representation of this match as a "cosmic catastrophe" similar in scale to recent earthquakes in Japan:[106] "I detest the troglodytic and gregarious spirit because of which the cultural spirit, the true, the artistic and free, fights desperately to improve and be recognized as a social end, and in contrast, the uncivilized and stolid pugilist is acclaimed and idolized to fanaticism, ignominiously."

Despite this forceful rejection of mass cultural spectacle, Tablada took sides on the outcome. He argued that the bout was fundamentally unjust given Firpo's inexperience and lack of knowledge. The US American Rickard had taken advantage of the unsuspecting Argentine, and Firpo's showing he likened to "taking candy from a baby" and "robbing a drunk." Tablada's description of the highly specialized and trained athlete, Dempsey, and his brutal handling of Firpo mirrored the comparison between Latin America and the United States in José Enrique Rodó's famous *Ariel*.[107]

Other Mexican journalists in New York and in Mexico City disagreed with Tablada. Mexico City saw an increase in boxing matches and massive attendance at interracial bouts where black and white Americans were pitted against local fighters. These matches filled bullrings, theaters, and temporary tents (carpas) erected in public plazas. Writing for *Excelsior*, one journalist commented:

> It is undeniable that the fashionable sport is boxing and more undeniable that it is developing each day more and more and that the adepts in Mexico are uncountable. Proof that pugilism has been naturalized among us is that there is not a Saturday and Sunday in which all the tents in the city and the diverse neighborhood theaters do not have fights with their preliminaries, their special events, and their semifinals.[108]

African American boxers Tiger Flowers, Cyclone Turner, and Battling Norfolk, among others, fought weekly in El Toreo in front of enthusiastic crowds.[109] Veteran journeyman fighters "Fireman" Jim Flynn and Canadian "Rough House" Burns, joined them. These men, the Mexico City press assured its readers, were legitimate "artists" because they had proven themselves in the rings of the United

States and because the American press found them to be praiseworthy. Mexican journalists, most of them avid readers of US newspapers, regularly cited the foreign press to legitimize their claims. Looking to the United States for support and legitimacy in matters concerning modern sport continued a pattern that Mexican boxers like Patricio Martínez Arredondo had initiated by traveling to the north to prove themselves.

Don Gaspar, a sportswriter for *El Demócrata*, argued that the "stable" of American boxers brought to Mexico by the Mexican American impresario Julio Montes had much to teach Mexican youth.[110] Raúl Talán touted Julio Montes and his brother, the boxer Mercy Montes, along with Baldomero Romero, as the "saviors" of boxing in Mexico. Along with Jimmy Fitten, they were among the earliest professional promoters. Not only did the nature of the sport suit Mexican temperament, it had already taken root:

> Boxing has pre-eminence among all sports: at least it is one of the most liked and attended practices [in Mexico City]. And this is natural, our people are made for spectacles and diversions of this nature. Boxing, like bullfighting, will always live in Mexico. Now . . . beginning next Sunday, boxing will enter into a new epoch, its modern development, in a period of the progress of yanqui pugilism, which is what is practiced in Mexico. And it is just to say, these movements toward advance, or better said this dawn, is due to the pugilists who just arrived and from whom Mexican boys will learn a lot, [they are] those whose [blood has already] clotted [i.e., have experience as fighters] and that are beautiful hopes that sport will gain the prestige that other [Mexican] sports once had, that are now defunct and unremarkable.[111]

Don Gaspar extended his analysis of the benefits of sport, and boxing especially, to social challenges in Mexico City. Gaspar claimed that pugilistic training was a fundamental component of the US educational process. Mexicans should learn and disseminate the knowledge of how to defend themselves through mastery of the "beautiful and virile sport." In an imagined future, the widespread adoption of the "chivalrous" culture of pugilism would create a peaceful and increasingly stable urban society. "Ruffians" and "louts," who were parasites on the social body, would be elevated by the discipline required to practice such a "noble" pursuit. Disciplining the bodies of these men would also provide a licit way for them to earn a living. In the process, it would diminish the use of pistols and knives in street and bar fights. The cumulative effect of this shift would depopulate prisons and hospitals, saving government expenditures and giving the lower classes a "way to live honorably." In Gaspar's idealized future, Mexico would join in the community of advanced nations to produce "pugilistic seeds."[112]

Pablo Piccato argues that Mexican elites imagined a lurid underworld of violent crime that served to destabilize the long-term civilizing process of both the Porfirian and Revolutionary social mission. According to these prevalent ideas, the Mexican masses were hopelessly backward and biologically predisposed to delinquency. Newspapers and popular broadsheets were the primary means of dissemination for the sensationalized narratives of violence and intrigue in the margins of Mexico City society.[113] Though lurid and ominous reports occupied highly visible spaces in public discourse, they shared room with self-help narratives that ostensibly relayed constructive self-criticism to readers. The appropriation of foreign cultural elements, like those embodied in the self-discipline inherent in modern sport in general and boxing in particular, would serve the patriotic ends of socially concerned Mexicans. The creation of "diminutive Firpos and Dempseys" would help Mexico to obtain modernity.[114]

The intellectual foundations of public sphere debates were embedded in a worldview that transcends traditional periodization into pre- and post-Revolutionary watersheds. In his examination of the rhetoric of José Vasconcelos, Tenorio shows that many of the ideas credited to the "Mexican Ulysses" were little changed from mainstream Porfirian intellectual conceptions of race and nation. Don Gaspar's creative imagining of a Mexican future mediated and molded by influences imported from abroad mirrored the modernizing project of pre-Revolutionary científicos who built railroads, courted foreign investment, and sought to regulate even the traditional clothing and drinking habits of Mexican peasants.[115]

Encouragement of emulation was mirrored in Mexican advertising. The male body was frequently illustrated in athletic poses, running races, or boxing to demonstrate desirable forms of vigorous masculinity. Shirtless boxers furnished some of the only publicly displayed seminude images of the male body. Jack Dempsey, much to the chagrin of José Juan Tablada, spoke directly to Mexican men via advertisements for products touted to increase virility and prepare men for the daily competition and uncertainties of urban life. In the early 1920s, a tonic called Hierro Nuxado was advertised to men throughout Latin America. A common image portrayed Dempsey, in a boxing stance, encouraging men to cultivate and protect their virility. The enfeebling culprit, the ad explained, was iron deficiency: "Lack of iron in the blood makes a man a physical and mental nonentity, it leaches his virile force, mental vivacity, will power etc., possessions of incalculable importance in all spheres of life." Other iterations asked men if they felt "old, tired, and weak." To confirm the positive effects of Hierro Nuxado, Dempsey's image was captioned to explain how he had consumed the product before his most difficult bouts. The advertisement cited the names of his opponents without explaining who they were. It drew on the assumption of an extant reservoir of knowledge about the outside world and transnational popular culture.[116] Half-page images of Jack Dempsey and Luis Ángel Firpo with confident smiles appealed to readers under such headlines as "The Cultivation of Muscle."[117]

The Sociedad de Chauffeurs (Taxi Drivers Society) held public boxing matches between its members in the rooms above the Teatro Ideal in the center of Mexico City. Reporters lauded the taxi drivers for what they deemed a performance of knowledge. Their mastery of these skills, cultural commentators argued, increased their masculinity and proved their cosmopolitan outlook on life and self-improvement.[118] They held charity matches to benefit earthquake victims a world away in Japan. They attended boxing matches between globetrotting African American prizefighters and young Mexican boxers like Carlos Pavón, Miguel "Mike" Febles, "Jimmie" Drieguez, and the Mazatlan-born son of Scottish immigrants, Tommy White.[119] Many of these fighters, African Americans in particular, found greater possibilities for self-advancement in their professions in Latin America, where interracial matches did not stir such controversy as in the United States.[120]

Cultural mediators looked not only to the United States but to other Latin American nations such as Cuba to find proof of the beneficial role of athletics for the social body. In Cuba, readers learned, Representative Ramón Zaydin introduced legislation that would funnel state revenue into the construction of sporting facilities and make *matricula deportiva* mandatory in public schools. *El Demócrata* reprinted Zaydin's proposal in full, including its forceful and nationalistic language that placed responsibility for the cultivation of "vigorous youths" in the hands of the state.[121] The deployment of transnational measures to gauge Mexican progress in forging the masculine national body increased around events like Firpo-Dempsey. This cosmopolitanism existed simultaneously with the intense nationalism of the first post-Revolutionary decade and was reflected daily in mass-produced chronicles of life in Mexico City.

Writers juxtaposed prizefighting to extant forms of entertainment in Mexico that offered a means to understand the theatrical yet utilitarian staging of violence. One anonymous commentator cited the public's ignorance of boxing customs to account for the disorder during matches at El Toreo.[122] The writer posed a rhetorical question to his readers: "Can one believe that a people with our traditions is impassioned by and maintains enthusiasm for such a cruel and trivial spectacle?" Boxing fans argued that knowing how to defend oneself against others represented practical and therefore superior knowledge: "That there is manly necessity and gallantry in knowing how to [enact] violence and avoid with dexterity the punch that could come from around any corner or from any discussion."[123] A modern urban man, these *partidarios* insisted, was a superior specimen of manhood if he knew how to defend against anonymous attackers that populated the city. These opposing sides found a focal point in the bullring in the days leading up the Dempsey-Firpo bout.

On September 9, 1923, journalists, promoters, boxers, and a crowd of thousands inaugurated the boxing season with a "star bout" between two African Americans, Cyclone Turner and Battling Norfolk, with an undercard of Mexicans and Americans.[124]

The journalist covering the event in Mexico City for *El Demócrata* explained that the "scandal" caused by angry fans overrunning the ring was caused by their impassioned ignorance of the intricacies of prizefighting. In the sixth round of the Turner-Norfolk bout, the crowd threatened to overrun the ring because they believed the two heavyweights were not fighting hard enough. Responding to the growing agitation around the ring, the police intervened and convinced the boxers to continue fighting. This was an odd exhibition: a police force that had once raided illegal boxing matches and arrested those involved now promoted prizefighting and demanded it be more violent to satiate the crowd whose violence they feared. After their admonition to increase the ferocity of the bout was apparently not heeded, the police mounted the ring to take the boxers to jail for defrauding the public. The boxing fans in El Toreo then changed their minds and prevented the police from arresting them. Turner was too injured to continue. After the bout, he was taken to the Cruz Verde Hospital, where doctors confirmed his broken hand. The reporter suggested that the public take as "legal faith," endorsed by the Ayuntamiento, that the fight had not been a "fake."[125] The spectators, not the police, determined the order of things in these massive public gatherings.

Local boxing shows, composed of Mexicans and journeyman US American fighters, competed for public attention with the preparations for the New York bout. *El Universal* declared there had never before been such excitement in Mexico as that generated by an athletic contest. The betting was in favor of Firpo, even though the *peritos* (experts) argued that the Argentine had little chance against the superior knowledge and experience of Dempsey.[126]

Diplomatic recognition reflected Firpo's embodiment of Hispanic progress in sport. Consular agents and representatives of the "21 Spanish speaking nations" held a banquet in Firpo's honor at the Unión Benéfica Española in New York. The diplomats presented Firpo with a gold medal and a pair of gilded boxing gloves purchased with funds collected from the Latin community in New York.[127] John Barrey, the former director of the Pan American Union, called upon the American public to treat Firpo with dignity and fairness in the name of good hemispheric relations. He feared that New Yorkers and the myriad other Americans who had traveled to witness the bout in the Polo Grounds would let their love of Dempsey get the better of their good manners and hospitality for the representative of the "sister" republic to the south.[128]

Don Gaspar, writing for *El Demócrata* the day of the bout, distilled what he viewed as the most salient hopes Mexicans and other Latin Americans placed on the performance of the Argentine pugilist. The world's attention was focused on the Polo Grounds for the performance of the "two opposing races."[129] A South American, as Gaspar explained, went "to the New York stage to demonstrate the potency of the race."[130] Firpo would enter the ring with "the infinite hopes that all Latin Americans have placed on him." Firpo represented Mexico and "all the nations that by ideological communion, by religious identity, and through linguistic equality are the same." The mere status of Firpo as a contender struck a blow to US pretensions to superior masculinity.

This hyperbolic rhetoric indicated a cultural climate in which Latin Americans embraced a means of competing with "superior" cultures by engaging them on their own terms. Public sphere intellectuals like Don Gaspar and Aguilar Reyes appropriated the language and symbolism of prizefighting to engage and rebuff US cultural power in a meritocratic field. By the end of the decade, Mexicans seldom debated the status of boxing as a symbolic embodiment of Mexican popular culture. Contributing to and perhaps shaping this nationalist appropriation, mass media and popular culture in the form of cinema, pamphlets, and popular histories enshrined Mexican boxers as paradigmatic of mexicanidad. Shortly after Firpo's attempt to win the heavyweight title, a young Mexican boxer and wrestler rechristened himself: Francisco Segura, from the barrio of Guerrero in Mexico City, would be known for the rest of his life as Firpo Segura.[131]

### Inventing Heroes in the Slums: Making Memories of Boxing in Urban Mexico in the 1930s and 1940s

The 1930s and 1940s were a prolific era in the production and dissemination of mass culture via film, radio, and the popular press in Mexico. This period has been so often cited as the "Golden Age" of Mexican mass culture production that this designation has become a truism.[132] Cultural icons from marginal neighborhoods of the capital rose to national and international fame through media coverage and the literary and cinematic dramatization of their paths to notoriety. The celebration of working-class Mexicans as paragons of national identity signified the post-Revolutionary democratization of culture. The millions of Mexican spectators who consumed these narratives encountered heroic morality plays that drew on metaphors of urban modernity to create aspirational symbols of Mexican manhood. The examination of popular culture via prizefighting offers a vantage point for the dramatization of class antagonism, nationalism, perceptions of Mexican Americans in Mexico, and changing gender norms in rapidly modernizing Mexico City.

By the late 1920s, boxing and wrestling had become "genuinely popular sports."[133] Historian Stephen Niblo argues that by the 1940s, sport had generated some "authentic heroes." By the mid-1920s, boxing had become an emblem of mexicanidad. Before Paco Sotelo's death in 1936, Mexican boxing fans, sounding their *gritos de ranchero*, regularly packed spaces like El Toreo with more than thirty thousand *fanáticos*.[134]

Boxing was also a point of convergence between Mexican popular and elite cultures. Though prizefighting spectacles were one of the most attended public events of the era and the popularly celebrated athletes were predominantly from the working class, elite Mexicans, through their business interests and preferences in personal entertainment, continued to play a role within the sport. As Anne Rubenstein has shown, consumers of popular literature (readers of sports papers being prominent among them) were not limited to the lower classes. She cites several studies conducted in mid-century Mexico on the consumers of this media.[135]

Through film, *historietas* (comic books and graphic novels), and popular literature in the post-Revolutionary era, boxing became a vehicle for the expression of ideal gender and social roles, especially aspirational masculinity and working-class solidarity. In these examples of heroic posturing, the consumer of mass culture glimpses social conflict and insecurity as well as the optimism of working-class Mexicans. Many of these documents are didactic manuals on how to act like men in the modern city. The first full-length Mexican boxing film, *Todo un Hombre* (A Real Man, 1935), was an aptly titled "glorification of boxing in Mexico."[136] Raúl Talán, the film's protagonist, was Mexico's first boxing matinée idol, and he appeared in this film with such well-known Mexican boxers as Baby Arizmendi, the first Mexican pugilist to win a world boxing title. The movie played in Mexican American communities in US border states, as well as in New York City and Chicago and in Europe.[137]

Talán, the author of *En el 3er Round* and *Y . . . Fueron Idolos!* (And . . . They Were Idols!) was a transnational promoter of Mexican popular culture. Over his career he was matched with boxers such as the Cuban Kid Chocolate.[138] He boxed professionally until the mid-1930s, when he took up acting and appeared in several movies, the most successful being *Todo un Hombre*, by the Cuban-born director of Mexican films, Ramón Peón.[139] In this performance, Talán plays a poor orphaned boxer who courts an aristocratic young woman against the wishes of her father. He proves his worth, valor, and moral rectitude by resisting the corrupt forces of the boxing underworld and through his physical prowess in the ring. After his acting career, Talán became the chronicler of what he saw as the Golden Age of Mexican boxing, the 1920s and 1930s.

*En el 3er Round*, along with Raúl Talán's later book *Y Fueron Idolos!*, is part popular memoir, part evocation of collective memory. The firsthand accounts of the culture of boxing and boxers serve several connected purposes. In his first book, Talán narrates his interviews and travels over the breadth of Mexico City to locate individuals whose careers he witnessed from the 1920s to the late 1940s as a boxer and later as a sport journalist for the revista *Mañana*. He creates a micro-geography of a rapidly growing city. He portrays the former boxers inhabiting the range of social class, from destitute drunks to successful businessmen. He comments extensively on the minutiae of their family lives, their memories, and aspirations, and he situates them as heroes of popular culture and mexicanidad. As Talán describes them, these men fill the role of masculine exemplars, not just the stereotyped Mexican boxers as hyper-aggressive alcoholic womanizers and dandies, but as dedicated fathers and husbands and inhabitants of the complex urban milieu of modern Mexico City.[140]

Talán's memoirs were produced and consumed within the context of what Armando Bartra has termed "the first tumultuous moments of mass literacy in post-Revolutionary Mexico."[141] The increased number of literate Mexicans (and massive population growth in general) in the 1930s and 1940s created conditions for an explosion of accessible reading material in the form of popular novels and historietas. The efforts of post-Revolutionary educational programs were not limited to instruction in reading and writing. They also sought to create cultural consumers, who through newspapers, revistas, radio, murals, and film were presented with the dramatization of Mexican national identities.[142]

Bartra poses sport as an embedded and established facet of Mexican culture in this period. During his overview of these mass productions he identifies Mexican affinity for athletic contests as "the Mexican's proverbial affection for the vicarious enjoyment of sports."[143] He poses sport as Manichean entertainment the valence of which is tied to the very fact that it is simple and dualistic. He continues:

> If literary serials, comics, movies and radio dramas capture their readers,

spectators and listeners through conflict and dramatic tension, commercial sports also resort to suspense, except that the drama unfolding before our eyes is not a representation but an actual confrontation. Sporting events, therefore, resemble the narrative genres found in popular culture. And the sports spectacle—collective catharsis and the rite (or cry) of national identity—provides invaluable material for other media.[144]

One vehicle for the Mexicanization of prizefighting as a metaphor for working-class life lies in the enormous reach of popular novels and historietas such as those produced by the García Valseca media conglomerate. This publishing house began as a maker of pocket comic books known as *pepines*. It later expanded to become one of the largest publishing interests in the world. Some of its most popular productions were representations of "fields, mats, and rings, populated by countless heroes."[145] As Bartra argued, "although they did not begin in Mexico, the sports historietas expanded and overflowed here."[146] Beginning in the 1930s, dozens of historietas used prizefighting storylines to illuminate the daily struggles of urban Mexicans, among them: "A batacazo limpio" (Clean Fighting), "A fuerza de puños" (The Force of Fists), "Campeón," "El Campeón," "Kid Azteca," "Pies Planos" (Flat Feet)" and "Relámpago Kid" (Lightning Kid). The use of sport as parable presupposed a familiarity with the language, spaces, rules, and characters that such narratives drew upon to entertain and inform. This genre also reflected a collaboration between Mexican and US illustrators such as Manny Moran, who came to Mexico City to work on popular publications.[147]

In one example, the character "Luis," in the comic book series *El Viejo Nido* (The Old Nest), becomes a boxer as a means to make money and court a local girl, Consuelo. He is constantly surrounded by signifiers of modernity in the boxing ring: bright lights and radio transmission wires that contrast with the poverty of his home life in a small village. Luis is the protagonist. Without the advantage of formal education or a wealthy family, he rises, through natural talent, to obtain middle-class status. He eventually travels to the United States, where he wins a championship bout, enabling him to buy back his family home, the "old nest," which had been foreclosed upon by a villainous banker. Luis overcomes the problems of modern life through his traits of determination and skill funneled into professional sport. As Rubenstein argues, "'El Viejo Nido' was as close to typical as any of the hundreds of serialized narratives published in the daily comic books between 1934 and 1950 . . . it reached out for an audience across age, class and sex."[148]

In the series "A fuerza de puños," Mexican boxer Enrique Ramírez travels to New York where he wins a world championship. He returns to Mexico to marry

"Nora." The narrative is intensified when his trainer commits suicide because he had bet against his pupil; he had lost faith in the underdog. Pepines such as this one were accompanied by overt subtexts that imbued the graphic subject matter with nationalist admonitions. In one issue recounting Ramírez's championship bout, the illustrations are followed by the text: "National Military Service disciplines the body and the character and that will make better citizens who will labor to make a better Mexico . . . being a paladin in the National Military Service is to be a good patriot . . . serving the Fatherland (Patria)."[149]

These nationalist messages were accompanied by more general admonitions to readers. In the biographical pepin that acclaimed the boxer Kid Azteca as a national hero, these lines appeared below the illustrations: "True eloquence consists in only saying what is indispensible. . . . There is no arm that serves better in the struggle for life than knowledge of letters . . . education in the best safeguard of man's liberty . . . a country in which there is little education will be smashed by others." Though these mantras seem out of place alongside melodramatic narratives, they were likely included to appease conservative censors who regularly complained and sought to regulate such "disreputable periodicals." If publishers could reasonably argue they were educational or patriotic, they might enjoy a reprieve from punitive taxes. They might also be able to obtain government-subsidized newsprint.[150]

Raúl Talán's popular histories of Mexican boxing are an example of what Roger Bartra deemed "other media," that which is not easily classifiable. Though extensively illustrated with stylized pictures of boxers and written in accessible and dramatic prose, they fit uneasily into the genre of comic books and pepines. They are hybrid documents directed at a middle- and working-class urban audience. They apprise readers of the degraded status of many of the individuals who entertained them in previous decades when boxing developed into a symbol of working-class identity, and they call on readers to have sympathy for their former heroes. These gritty characters, he implies, are the basis of the popular fictional accounts through which Mexicans read about and celebrate themselves as Mexicans, as an imagined community. These boxers, Talán pleads, should be considered part of the national patrimony. He places their accomplishments in the realm of popular memory, often starting a description with "as you will all remember." Such invocations refer to dramatic moments when a Mexican boxer confronts a foreigner in the ring or wins against seemingly insurmountable odds. These are triumphant moments when nostalgia serves as a cohesive element for the readers. This appeal to collective memory is repeatedly followed by admonitions and soft recriminations: it is now a national responsibility, Talán implies, to take care of these men whose past exploits provide collective meaning.

These appeals to identity and social cohesion, as media scholar Jesus Martín Barbero argues, occur when popular memory is appropriated and portrayed within mass culture.[151] It is an element, to borrow historian Louis Pérez Jr.'s phrase, of the slow and continuous process of "becoming" Mexican through the elaboration and repetition of commonly understood metaphors and symbols.[152] Martín Barbero argues that these mass cultural inventions are "the development of certain potentialities already within the popular itself."[153]

In his interview with Fidel Ortiz, a boxer who represented Mexico in four Olympic Games, Talán explains, "Not only in war have we had heroes, also in other civilian fields and occasions have heroes given great prestige to the patria; one of them is Fidel Ortiz who boxed with no other interest than winning cups, medals, and prestige for our country."[154] Boxers are also portrayed as foundational figures in the transnational drama of Mexican underclass culture fighting for survival against the encroachment of the United States.

Not all his interviewees are impoverished. Those who have achieved middle-class status, conversely, are defined and celebrated by what they consume, not by the details of their decline. In the late 1930s and throughout the 1940s, Mexicans experienced a rapid increase in consumerism that paralleled the growth of Mexico City and the advent of modern industrial capitalism.[155] As he visits his characters in their homes, Talán provides a critical description of each neighborhood, the quality (in terms of "modern" or "American") of the home furnishings, and the degrees of filial piety he observes. Talán celebrates each boxer's fully realized paternalism; he lauds both the respect given to these men by their children and the sacrifices the prizefighters made to support their own elderly parents. In this manner, as well, he creates archetypes for proper mexicanidad.

*En el 3er Round* also illustrates some Mexican critiques of US culture and racial prejudice as the readers accompany these popular heroes on reluctant journeys into the United States. Travel and success in *el norte* become a badge of honor and an affirmation of traditional Mexican values among Talán's informants. Patricio Martínez Arredondo, for example, was the "first boxing idol of Mexico" and began his boxing career in 1911, in the last year of the Porfiriato. When he was interviewed in the late 1940s he ran a one-man watch repair shop on Calle Honduras, north of the zócalo in the working-class neighborhood of Lagunilla. His father had been a watch repairman and Martínez Arredondo started in that business before becoming a prizefighter. Hearing of money to be made volunteering to fight in preliminary bouts, he joined a group of "bootblacks and paper boys," who congregated outside the aristocratic Academia Metropolitana whenever a bout was announced, hoping to be chosen by the Academia's impresario. After his first few bouts he came under the tutelage of the Mexican "boxing professor," Salvador Esperón, himself a migrant from Oaxaca, who taught pugilism and physical culture to the Mexican upper class.[156] Esperón fought illegal matches as early as 1907, hiding from the police and making an illegal living as a prizefighter.[157] His tendency to challenge authority suited Arredondo well.

In Talán's narrative, Martínez Arredondo was an impoverished youth with natural ability. When this talent was paired with the training he received from Esperón, he earned up to a thousand pesos per fight. In addition to his prowess in the ring, he "never backed down to anyone." Talán also portrayed his theatrical and stereotyped virility by citing escapades with expensive prostitutes. In those days, he recalls, there was no lack of women in his life, especially those who would take him for rides in the *carretelas de bandera azul*. The poet López Velarde remembered these carriages as being occupied by *"cortesanas"* (luxury prostitutes) who charged the exorbitant rate of 1.50 pesos per hour.[158] Arredondo recalls one prostitute from Merida who promised to marry him and then made off with another man.

Arredondo's career took him to distant states such as Yucatán, where his Chinese corner man taught him the "American" trick of bandaging his hands with hard tape to defeat a "glingo" [sic] opponent who had used the same trick to beat him on two previous occasions.[159] He sarcastically recalls that he knocked an opponent, Mike Febles, out of the ring but that Jack Dempsey, the American heavyweight champion the 1920s, got all the credit for that move because Martínez Arredondo was only a "little champion of Mexico." The Firpo-Dempsey match he evoked needed no further explanation; it was an event sure to conjure memories for the reader.

These details, relayed decades after the events, provide texture to the few details of Martínez Arredondo's life in the historical record. He was a seminal figure in the popularization of prizefighting in Mexico and one of the first boxers from the working class to successfully challenge foreign prizefighters such as the Afro-Dutch Jim Smith, who had made a successful living by defeating all Mexican comers and by training locals.[160]

A 1919 article on Arredondo appeared in *El Heraldo de Mexico*. It pictured a muscular athlete in boxing stance. The young prizefighter, writes the reporter, challenged the *negro* Jim Smith, who despite being a foreigner was then champion of Mexico.[161] Mexicans should be proud of him, the writer implies, because he is an "able, studious, and dedicated" boxer.[162] In 1919, journalists still referred to boxing as the "Saxon sport," which Mexicans were slowly starting to embrace. Evidence of this was the previous match between Arredondo and Smith, in which the

Mexican ("our countryman") demonstrated his "bravery and knowledge" by taking the offensive during twenty rounds of boxing. The journalist extols the skill, talent, and ability of the Mexican boxer that is evident precisely because he is the first to be able to go the distance with the foreigner and not be completely destroyed by the effort.[163]

One social commentator identified the young boxer as a standard bearer for those who should be emulated by youths. Despite his general disgust with professional boxing as little more than glorified street fighting, the critic Rodolfo Álvarez dedicated an article in the weekly magazine *Arte y Sport* to the championship bout between Cuban/Mexican Mike Febles and Martínez Arredondo.[164] He writes of the crowd in fearful terms; the "profane ones," a euphemism for the boisterous fight fans, threaten disorder and must have the rules of the match explained to them by the referee lest they disrupt the proceedings.[165] Because of its tenuous legal status, the Mexican government did not impose uniform rules on the conduct of prizefighting in the ring until 1922. Decades after prizefighting had begun in Mexico, the rules still had to be translated from English for functionaries working for the city government.[166] This improvisation was becoming unnecessary as the first generation of professional Mexican boxing promoters such as Baldomero Romero, whose professional letterhead by the early 1920s presented him in English as a "Boxing Promoter," were increasingly successful at obtaining permission from the Mexico City government.[167]

Despite this unease with such surroundings, Álvarez praises the Mexican fighter as "valiant and herculean" and a "true marvel." When Arredondo wins the bout, Álvarez wishes him luck in his travels to the United States, where he will "improve and perfect" his skills as a boxer. This journey to the United States as a prerequisite to mastering the imported art would become a leitmotif for Mexican boxers in the years to come.[168] By 1919, spaces such as the Club Ugartechea were insufficient to contain the masses that wanted to attend boxing matches.[169] One reporter for *Excelsior* recounted the scene at the gym during an Arredondo/Jim Smith match as "full of lovers of the virile and daring sport."[170] The reporter rebuked the impresarios of the bout for not separating seats for the press: he had to stand on top of a chair in the back of the gym and still was unable to get a decent view of the match.

The following year on March 12, a rematch between the young Mexican and *negro* Jim Smith caused "scandal" and near bloodbath outside the ring.[171] Toward the end of the match, held at the Frónton Nacional on Iturbide Street near the Alameda (the elite promenade), Arredondo was disqualified by the referee for repeated low blows.[172] Though the observer argued that the Mexican was leading in the bout, the Queensbury Rules stipulated that the victory go to Jim Smith.[173]

Upon this decision, Arredondo immediately assaulted the referee, who happened to be the veteran boxer Fernando Colín. When Colín fought back, the police guard at ringside immediately sprang into action on the command of the police chief, who was a spectator at the match.[174] From this point onward, veteran boxers such as Colín and Esperón were charged by the city government with reining in the malas artes of Arredondo in the prize ring.[175]

Arredondo called the crowd to come to his defense and prevent his arrest. The spectators threw chairs into the ring and threatened the police. Thankfully, the reporter wrote, the spectators had been forced to give up their weapons, a normal prerequisite for entrance, before entering the frontón and a possible "tragedy" was averted. Despite these security precautions, however, several pistols were still seized from members of the crowd who were in the process of mounting the ring to free Arredondo. The writer for Excelsior used the opportunity to comment on the shamefulness of boxing in general and to imply that it did not suit "Latin" temperament. He called the readers' attention a similar situation that had occurred recently in Spain. How could so many propose that such a brutal sport, with its inherent disorder, replace the national pastime of bullfighting? His musings matched hundreds of similar journalistic writings in the preceding decades. That the match took place in an arena dedicated to the practice of a Hispanic-derived sport heightened its incongruity.

A week later, Arredondo sent a letter of public apology to the editor of Excelsior.[176] In it he agrees with the above assessment and blames his striking of the referee on his "Latin temperament." He pleaded that he was "blinded . . . with courage." He begs forgiveness from the public, the authorities, and above all the referee, against whom he claims to hold no rancor. He adds that he is shortly to leave for the United States, where he will perfect his boxing skills and will "put on high the banner (pabellón) of [his] dear patria."[177] On his return, he hopes to make up for his transgression by showing "the advances obtained" from the north.

The media record of Martínez Arredondo's career, complemented by the testimony recorded by the chronicler Raúl Talán, portrays the boxer as an ambiguous symbol of Mexican national pride. He was a transitional figure between elite acceptance and engagement of sport and the popularization of prizefighting.[178] He fought and trained in locales such the Club Ugartechea, a gymnasium founded in the early twentieth century to build the muscles of the capital's gentry. He also fought in theaters and jai alai courts before the massive constructions of the late 1920s and early 1930s capitalized on the Mexican appropriation of combat sport.[179] He was born into a lower-middle-class family and competed for employment with bootblacks and paperboys before earning temporary wealth and elite status, only to return to the profession of his father. He traveled Revolutionary Mexico in the company of Jim Smith, the Afro-Dutch journeyman fighter with whom he maintained a rivalry for over forty years.[180] Newspaper readers in Mexico encountered news of his travels and triumphs alongside explanations of Pancho Villa's latest campaigns; as Talán alluded to above, Mexican civil society was slowly introduced to a new kind of "idol."[181]

Miguel "Mike" Febles was a contemporary and an opponent of Martínez Arredondo. He was a circus performer turned prizefighter who fought under the pseudonym "The Veracruz Lion." Before taking up boxing, Febles was a naval cadet in Veracruz and was stationed in Mexico City at the beginning of the twentieth century. There he began work in the entertainment industry, performing and drawing crowds with such feats as hanging by his teeth from a wire between the city's two tallest buildings. He was an actor/performer for the famous Orrin Circus, which was known for its risqué shows and was a highly visible cultural mainstay of late-Porfirian Mexico.[182]

Febles, like Arredondo, led a peripatetic career that took him all over Mexico, the Caribbean, and the United States.[183] In a given week, his promoters might have him box in Puebla, Pachuca, Guadalajara, and Mexico City. In his interview with Talán, he recounts having been a captain in Obregón's cavalry during the Revolution and later becoming a boxing instructor for government officials in the National Palace.[184] Also like Arredondo, Talán portrays him as a forgotten and forlorn character who in his later years made a meager salary as a masseuse and "professor of physical education."[185] Like so many of the "forgotten idols" encountered by Talán, Febles was a foundational figure in a hybrid Mexican culture.

As archetypal figures in Talán's pantheon of early Mexican athletes, Febles and Arredondo, who both live in relatively impoverished conditions in the narrative, call out for more elevated positions in Mexican popular memory.[186] Even taxi drivers mock Febles, and when Talán finds him, the writer is taken by "a great sadness in finding another fallen idol." He continues, "Febles, the long ago glorious pugilist whom even the chorus girls fought over and had a harmonious and athletic body is now a washed-up man (*un hombre acabado*), with clothes not exactly fresh from the laundry."[187] Febles, who had boxed in front of sold-out crowds into the 1920s to prove to foreigners that "in Mexico there [were] good fighting cocks" (*en México hay buenos gallos*), now suffered a precarious life in a marginal neighborhood of the capital.[188] Despite Febles's poverty, he emerges as a "cultured" and adventurous person who, famous in his time, was an "idol" before mass spectatorship created the enormous wealth and celebrity of athletes in the era when Talán wrote his account.

## Fight Films: The Dramatization of Mexicanness through Boxing in Golden Age Cinema

> The vast increase in channels of communication which flow across cultural boundaries has the effect of dismantling old forms of marginalization and domination and making new forms of democratization and cultural multiplicity possible.[189]

Of the numerous boxing films created in Mexico during the "Golden Age," one in particular enjoyed wide distribution and elicited significant commentary. It illustrates the centrality of boxing in popular representations of urban mexicanidad that followed the period in which the sport was popularized in the 1920s and 1930s. Alejandro Galindo's *Campeón Sin Corona* (Champion Without a Crown, 1946) starred the matinee idol David Silva. The film is a thinly veiled biopic of the most admired Mexican boxer of the 1930s, Rodolfo Casanova.[190] Silva's character is a modest ice cream salesman who becomes the champion boxer Kid Terranova. *Campeón Sin Corona* debuted in 1945 to laudatory reviews that called the film a nationalist triumph of artistic movie making that was the "*cañonazo del año*" (Cannonade of the Year), and it continued to be shown in theaters across the country for more than a year.[191] It also reached audiences in all the US states on the US-Mexico border, playing for Mexican immigrants and Mexican Americans until the early 1950s.[192] The role of Kid Terranova had enthroned David Silva as the Mexican cinematic symbol of "virility."[193] The magazine *El Redondel*, citing the several reviews and "elegies" to the film, counseled its readers: "You will see this Mexican film and intensely live this simple and human story, taken from the lives of men of the barrios of Mexico, of those beings who, tired of fighting against adversity, give themselves up to vice and misery. . . . Alejandro Galindo knows how to impress [into the film] all the soul of the barrios of Mexico."[194]

Other reviews further developed this evaluation, citing the picture as "the most Mexican film . . . the most Mexican labor" and calling on viewers to "celebrate Mexican Independence Day (*las fiestas pátrias*) by seeing the most Mexican of films."[195] One reviewer in Guadalajara viewed the character of Kid Terranova as a mirror of a well-known type: "the Mexican athlete, invincible sometimes, enervated and decadent others, victim of female wiles, like all heroes who come from the dirt (*barro*).[196] Critics portrayed the film as an accurate vignette of life in Mexico City. For his role in the film, Silva won the Ariel award for the best male lead in Latin American cinema. Although this fairly complex and symbolic story warrants extended treatment, a brief overview of the plot gives insights into how boxing was presented as a double-edged sword for poor, urban Mexicans.

Kid Terranova, in the beginning of the film, works in an ice cream parlor on a busy street in Mexico City, likely in the barrio of Tepito. He has boxed a few times for small purses in raucous venues where the crowd is inebriated and vicious. One day on the street, while standing up for a defenseless individual, Terranova is discovered by a local Mexican boxing promoter. Over the course of the next several months, Terranova rises through the ranks in several bouts. His long-suffering mother worries over the violence of the ring and the boxer's newfound wealth that has begun to change his personality. He has now donned the zoot suit, a symbol of Mexican and Mexican American urban identity that has received its due amount of historiographical treatment.[197] As the melodrama unfolds, the boxer turns his back on his previous life. His first love interest, who has long dark braids and works in a local taquería, is replaced by a wealthy Mexican blonde who uses the boxer sexually and as a symbol of her elite pastime of slumming. She speaks English with her friends and uses language to embarrass the boxer while getting him hooked on alcohol. Terranova's inability to speak English becomes a central conflict of the film and a reminder of working-class origins. Meanwhile, the working-class girl in the taquería turns her back on Terranova due to his newfound arrogance and ostentatious displays of wealth.

Language continues to figure prominently in the film as a signifier of class and a point of shame for Terranova, who is frozen by fear when a Chicano boxer, Joe Ronda (a thinly veiled reference to the Scottish Mexican Joe Conde), taunts him in English during a bout.[198] The protagonist is confused and terrified, unable to react. Another scene takes place in the offices of the Boxing Commission. The fighter is angered when English is spoken in front of him. He refuses to smoke "American" cigarettes like Joe Ronda and his arrogant entourage do. Though Terranova is eager to be accepted by the wealthy set, his inability to speak English, his inferiority complex, and his sentimental ideas of romance make him the "mascota" (pet), of the promiscuous blond.[199] As the boxer begins to self-destruct he is ultimately rescued by his renewed esteem for his working-class identity. He returns to his roots, leaving the moneyed blonde, again wearing his previous wardrobe as a uniform of his class. He concludes that the dignity of his class and the importance of his family are his sources of stability and identity. The only way Terranova is able to make sense of the dizzying urban world around him is in a return to mexicanidad. While boxing is an established fact of national life, it represents in Galindo's films what film historian Ernesto Acevedo Muñoz has called a "modernization dilemma" in that it epitomizes both local Mexican culture and the decadent influences of urban life.[200]

The choice of boxing as the medium to express working-class Mexican identity and the transnational challenges to tradition in this era was an apt one. The movie drew on personalities and ideas that were imagined as typical of the rapidly evolving challenges to traditional, rural Mexican identities in the period. The characters and situations were accessible and understandable to popular audiences. Boxing had moved, in the period of a few decades, from elite spaces and exotic foreign culture into a trope for the Mexican engagement with modernity.[201] As Mexican film historian Charles Ramiréz Berg demonstrated, the genre of boxing films poses the question "of whether a poor urban youth can rise above poverty and hold on to his birthright of mexicanidad."[202] Boxing, in this genre of popular culture, is a powerful symbol of the post-Revolutionary challenges of Mexican urban identity.

## Conclusion

As this chapter demonstrates, the appropriation of boxing after the Revolution was a means to express working-class identity, masculinity, and the Mexicanization of a transnational cultural form. These samplings of foreign practices were first a means to raise the cultural level of elite Mexicans. Following the Revolution, this process continued and was taken up by poor, urban men who used boxing as an aspirational instrument to gain upward mobility and a way to leave the barrio. By 1930, boxing had moved into a cultural space shared with bullfighting and was expressed as a threat to Mexican tradition. Though both boxing and bullfighting continued to exert influence on Mexican masculine identity, the Mexican appropriation of prizefighting as a narrative trope mirrors the hybrid, transnational society of the post-Revolutionary cultural terrain.

CHAPTER SIX

# Marching at the Head of Civilization

THIS CHAPTER EXAMINES the Cuban transformation of prizefighting into a mass spectacle and vehicle for the celebration of Afro-Cuban athletes as national symbols in the 1920s and 1930s. Boxers such as Kid Chocolate and Eladio "Black Bill" Valdés became transnational idols, notable for their skill in the ring, and were embraced by the public as paragons of masculinity. This variant of modern manhood, as embodied by these prizefighters, was an obtainable characteristic reachable through the embrace of athletics and the subculture of international knowledge that made fans into *sportsmen*. This approbation in the public sphere, serial reproduction of their images, and the commercialization of Afro-Cuban bodies were anomalies in this period. The chapter also demonstrates how boxing was legalized in the early 1920s through the sustained efforts of a cross-class and interracial group of activists, journalists, and athletes. As occurred in Mexico, they represented prizefighting culture as a eugenic solution to urban social ills and as a means to represent Cuban modernity to the broader world.

When the nineteen-year-old Afro-Cuban Eligio "Kid Chocolate" Sardiñas arrived on a hydroplane in the Havana harbor from New York in September of 1929, he was greeted as a national hero, a welcome few Afro-Cubans had experienced. Members of the city government and thousands of habaneros thronged the docks and the seafront drive (malecón) to escort him to the temporary City Hall, where he was awarded a medal as a national treasure.[1] He had defeated the Jewish American Al Singer in front of forty-five thousand boxing fans at the Polo Grounds in New York and in the process was hailed by the Cuban (and American) press as an exceptional example of national accomplishment abroad. He excelled in a highly symbolic medium that for more than a century was dominated by US Americans and Europeans. Boxing in Cuba was now largely dominated by Afro-Cubans from the working class.[2] The public celebration of foreign and national athletes as paragons of "racial" excellence (be they of the "Latin," Afro-Cuban, Mexican, or Argentine "races") was not new. But the international press coverage and popularity resulting from Kid Chocolate's dominance made him the most celebrated Afro-Cuban since War of Independence general Antonio Maceo.[3] The image of Maceo, the "Bronze Titan," had been widely adopted in Republican Cuba as a symbol of Afro-Cuban contributions to the thirty-year struggle for Cuban independence from Spain (1868–98). Cuban politicians and scientists after independence subjected the general's memory to a "whitening process," through which they declared that his fighting ability on the battlefield was due to his African heritage. His capacity for military strategy and abstract thought, however, they attributed to his white ("Parisian") cranial capacity. His physicality was African; his brain was European. His inclusion in the nationalist pantheon was, therefore, explicitly tied to a favorable mix of genetics. His celebrity resulted from a racial synthesis in which the Cuban elite located the possibility of national and racial progress. This was a biological expression of Cuban scholar Fernando Ortiz's idea of transculturation. Cuban society, according to Ortiz, was the outcome of racial and cultural mixtures that had created a unique synthesis and a distinctively Cuban national identity.[4] Kid Chocolate was explicitly and favorably compared to that lionized symbol of Afro-Cuban bravery and selfless cubanidad.[5] His success was also, ironically, linked in the public sphere to the brainpower of his white manager.

Despite attempts by legislators and influential sectors of civil society like the National Association of Veterans of the Wars for Independence to prevent the implantation of the "yankee passion," Cubans appropriated the transnational practice that, for many writers, defined modern cosmopolitan masculinity.[6] The news of "El Kid's" triumph was daily fodder for the Cuban press. He was celebrated by poets and playwrights and posed for nude photographs for avant-garde artists in Havana and sculptors in the United States. His face and shirtless form was featured in dozens of advertisements for products ranging from upscale men's clothing to alcoholic beverages. He received "hundreds of letters daily from adoring fans."[7] His life was dramatized in artistic, intellectual, and popular mediums. The rise of Chocolate is only the most visible part of the process that began with Cubans looking outward to define their competitive national identity.[8]

Surveying the city of Havana in the early 1930s, the physician and writer Mariano Aramburu lauded the visible changes evident in the bodies of his fellow citizens that the mania for "physical culture" had shaped over the preceding years:

> Today one no longer sees in Havana that lamentable specimen of weak flaccid

homunculus, standing ridiculously small, nervous, and gesticulating, that the Spanish left us ... like the silly bird in our backlands. The habanero has gained much in size, in amplitude of chest, in biceps and in muscular fortitude.[9]

Cubans were no longer the backward and effeminate men that their Spanish heritage had inculcated. They had transformed their bodies into modern and masculine forms. Aramburu worried that this process was taken to the extreme, to the point that the writer was alarmed at the importance placed on developing robust physiques at the expense of a cultured intellect.[10] In the space of a generation, Cubans had embraced modern sport as a remedy for backward ideas of the male body. They trained themselves into new and improved forms that were proof of their manliness and cultural attainment.

Whether this appraisal of changes in Cuban men's bodies was accurate or not, Aramburu reacted to the expansive transformations in Cuban body culture of the 1920s. These novel ideas of proper masculinity centered around the growing fascination with athletics, boxing in particular, and the perception that national greatness was connected to the cultivation of imported notions of public spectacle and physicality.[11] Many influential Cubans rejected what they perceived as the backward and effeminate colonial legacy for the much-vaunted standards of male beauty emanating from the United States with its mass cultures of sport.[12] The US opinions that Cuban men were "like a woman ... weak and vacillating, flaccid and without fiber ... wanting in appreciation for manliness for its own sake" and characterized by an "effeminate spirit" had a long pedigree in American denigration of Cuban men.[13] The concern with the relationship between "effeminate" men and the health of society in general was not new in Cuba and Latin America (or elsewhere for that matter), but the use of athletics as a curative agent was a distinctly modern means of addressing long-standing negative perceptions.[14]

The process that Aramburu cited took place in the hectic racial climate of the 1920s, when the avenues of social advancement for Afro-Cubans were markedly decreasing amid the economic downturn resulting from falling sugar prices and the advent of worldwide depression.[15] The idolization of rare Afro-Cuban celebrities like Kid Chocolate as masculine role models served as a pressure release for mounting social tensions that increasingly brought into question the promise of a "raceless" Cuban nationalism that celebrated the bloodshed of the cross-racial alliance during the wars for independence.[16] If a poor Afro-Cuban from a peripheral neighborhood of Havana could excel by international standards of masculinity to gain prominence and wealth, wasn't this type of bootstrapping available to all? The answer, clearly, was no, but the print media, theater, and radio had long waged a campaign to sanctify the images of talented athletes as exemplars of cross-racial cohesion and national solidarity.[17]

Print media, political and civic-social groups, and pamphleteers interpreted and enshrined the novel popularity of prizefighting in the 1920s and 1930s as a harbinger of national progress and virility and as a focal point for Cuban prestige. This clear impulse in the Cuban public sphere melded cosmopolitan admiration for foreign athlete-celebrities with a didactic language of national regeneration and the desire to emulate international symbols of modern masculinity such as celebrity athletes Jack Dempsey, Babe Ruth, George Carpentier, and Luis Ángel Firpo.[18]

The expansion of the national pantheon of heroic individuals to include Afro-Cuban athletes at the end of the 1920s was only possible after the success of this project. The most salient example of efforts in the public sphere to appropriate physical culture was the 1922 publication of *El Arte de los Puños*. This popular history, examined in depth in this chapter, explicitly linked the growing Cuban embrace of boxing with outward-looking currents in Cuban nationalism and cosmopolitanism. The language of this appropriation located virile, masculine, and worldly men alongside affinity for sport as a eugenic solution to a variety of perceived urban social problems. Afro-Cuban boxers, the vehicles for this strain of nationalism, challenged racial norms while becoming the accidental standard bearers of Cuban modernity abroad. As this book has shown, these trends were not unique to Cuba but formed part of the increasingly global cultural industries that were an integral part of Latin American daily life by this period.

As Alejandro de la Fuente has argued, the official rhetoric of Cuban racelessness opened many (if not all) social spaces to Afro-Cubans. Many of these avenues for participation in the nation were denied to their African American counterparts; sport was one of these.[19] To build more broadly on these claims and to explore a novel sector of public sphere dialogue, this chapter examines three related case studies from the 1920s: The first is the concerted efforts of the press and civil society for the legalization of prizefighting, a project that culminated in the publication of the 1922 pamphlet *El Arte de los Puños*. Second is the accompanying work by newspaper editorials, letters to the editor, and radio broadcasts of transnational events like the 1923 match between Argentine Luis Ángel Firpo and American Jack Dempsey. The third is the late 1920s rise of Kid Chocolate and Eladio Valdés as controversial symbols of Afro-Cuban participation in the imagination of a more inclusive nation. These case studies focus on transnational events and their significance as interpreted by journalists, Cubans from around the island, poets, and politicians as they strove to implant in the Cuban public the conviction that modern manliness lay in the pursuit of international prizefighting titles and the celebrity that accompanied them. Through these three examples, Cuban social critics further constructed prizefighting as an essentially and necessarily Cuban *and* "Latin" pursuit that would grant entrance into competitive modernity.[20]

In the 1920s, Cuban racial nationalism and masculinity were increasingly mediated through the novel public appropriation of transnational modern sport.[21] *Carteles*, the popular weekly magazine, along with other newspapers and pamphlets, regularly expressed this idea in direct and didactic language that exhorted readers to buy the flags of the patria along with the flags of their athletic clubs.[22] As a range of scholars such as Rosalie Schwartz, Frank Guridy, and Louis A. Pérez Jr. have shown, nationalist Afro-Cuban intellectuals such as Gustavo Urrutia and Nicolás Guillén forged transnational ties with African American thinkers such as Langston Hughes and the Afro–Puerto Rican Arthur Schomberg in an attempt to broaden the scope of Afro-Cuban political and social engagement with African American struggles for social equality.[23] Though most of the scholarship on these deepening intercultural relationships focuses on discriminatory practices that prevented collective action, both groups of intellectuals were intensely interested in the celebration and encouragement of Afro-Cuban and African American achievements in a broad array of pursuits, including the democratic and potent public sphere created by sport. Afro-Cuban celebrity complicates our understanding of how race, identity, and masculinity functioned in the interstices between institutional practices of racism and the lived experience of race. The Cuban state, in its celebration of Afro-Cuban achievements, mimicked trends in the popular culture of civil society that were beyond the government's ability to regulate.[24]

In addition to their critiques of structural racism in Cuba and the United States, Guillén and Uruttía argued that the athletic accomplishments of Afro-Cubans should be used as tools to increase race consciousness and give weight to calls for social equality. The nearly universal acclaim for Cuban athletes, they argued, was an opportunity to collaborate with white Cubans on the common ground of national pride. For these Afro-Cuban activists, transnational athletes became vaunted representatives of Afro-Cuban *and* Cuban achievements within and beyond Cuba. More importantly, their notoriety was a focal point for broader debates about the Cubanness of Afro-Cubans. These writers debated the divergent strategies of how to use the triumphs of Kid Chocolate to further their goals of racial integration and social equality.

As in the United States, race played a central and problematic role in the popular cultures surrounding sport in general and boxing in particular.[25] Cuban appropriation of imported cultural practices, from musical forms to foreign cinema to athletics, increased the array of publicly acknowledged Afro-Cuban cultural contributions to Cuban national identity and molded public discussions on the nature of Cuban modernity. Through the concerted efforts of reformers aided by improvisation and epoch-defining changes in the speed and availability of both written and aural information, Cubans experienced the dramatic personalities and encounters of modern sport as representatives of the broadening of cubanidad.[26] These novel representations mirrored the mainstream sampling of Afro-Cuban folk culture, known collectively as afrocubanismo and popularized through the works of Fernando Ortíz.

The saturation of 1920s Cuba with foreign standards for masculine behavior illustrates both the conscious and improvisational emulation of *lo extranjero* that forms key aspects of modern Cuban identity.[27] Sport was a new forum in which to show how Cubans were able to learn, train their bodies, and manage the complexities of celebrity; the result was an expansion of the public sphere.[28]

Across the class spectrum, Cuban men reveled in self-applying the honorific title of "sportman" and sought to cultivate the values self-reliance, fairness, and meritocracy through the training of bodies and knowledge of the world through sport. *Knowing* the American boxer Jack Dempsey through reading his biometrics and his biography and emulating his appearance was a way to show one's manliness and dedication to a transnational worldview. Cuban entrepreneurs, politicians, and public intellectuals alike prescribed and encouraged the conditions in which lower-class Cuban athletes could pursue international titles for the explicit construction of national honor. In the process, they assured themselves that Cuba was free of racial prejudice, was democratic, and, above all, was modern.

The practice of sport had, since the late nineteenth century, been identified and recommended by Cuban social critics as means to teach masculine values that, among other boons to the social body, would help to stem effeminacy and homosexuality.[29] The image and culture of the modern, robust male athlete was praised by these social commentators as both a eugenic solution to perceived social ills and a contrast between "backward" Hispanic cultural traditions and the development of "modern" cultural forms.[30] The qualitative changes and quantitative increase of new media, from the stand-alone sports page and dedicated sports magazines to radio broadcasts of boxing matches, facilitated these flows of information. Following the Cuban Wars for independence, athletics became arguably the most salient public venue for Cuban men to display their masculinity. Cubans, the state and the media stressed, were athletes on par with international standards of masculinity. They were no longer the effeminate and decadent victims of backward Spanish colonialism. From Paris to Buenos Aires to New York, Cuban athletes represented the patria as a masculine and modern actor in an increasingly global culture.[31]

Looking beyond what was traditionally Cuban to enliven and enrich domestic life was also a problematic solution to perceived Cuban insularity and backwardness. The Cuban "tendency" toward emulation was often said to detract from the process of modernization through sport. Social critics like Jorge Mañach mocked those who touted such ridiculous foreign innovations as a panacea for Cuban social ills. He spoke for many observers when he defined the outwardly looking sport fan as a servile copier of foreign forms who displayed novel behaviors and fashions in a comical attempt to exhibit masculinity and cosmopolitan status. Sportmen who "showed their biceps" and preferred American cigarettes were braggarts and tools of American economic and cultural imperialism.[32] Other observers, like journalists and authors Vicente Cubillas and Bernardino San Martín, wrote extensively on Cuban boxing to counter those who sought to repress further engagement with transnational sport.[33] José Sixto de Sola, one of the most important public intellectuals of the era, posed the issue in clear terms:

> In this century [twentieth] ... those nations marching at the head of civilization pay ever more attention to every class of sport, as much as to intelligence ... and their publications, even the most cerebral and serious, dedicate [to sport] a preferential space, and their educators, sociologists and governors earnestly study the considerable social forces that sport develops ... along with other social factors, toward collective betterment.[34]

Intellectuals such as Sixto de Sola praised and acted on these ideas by founding gyms, importing foreign athletes, and funding Cubans who showed promise in sport. Sixto de Sola, for example, became president of the middle-class Club Atlético de Cuba.[35] Such writers encouraged Cuban women, in their ascribed role as the domestic molders of men, to encourage boxing to teach men the most essential characteristics of manliness. Occasionally, Cuban women appeared as boxers and wrestlers, as in one undercard bout when "Miss Luisa" from Spain wrestled "Miss White Luz" in a charity match to benefit the boxer Bernardo San Martín in 1916.[36] The purpose of the benefit was not printed, but it was likely to pay the legal fees that San Martín accrued after one of his arrests for staging illegal prizefights of "the virile sport ... behind closed doors for fear that the police would take us again to the precinct, accused of a street brawl (*reyerta*).[37] Writers in specialized sport magazines, such as *El Heraldo Deportivo*, seconded Sixto de Sola's ideas. One observer of a boxing match in 1918 applauded the attendance of women among the thousands of spectators of a match at the Recreo de Belascoaín. "Fans" of the "noble art of the Marquis of Queensbury," as he called the "fanáticos cubanos," were finally appreciating the values of prizefighting. The attendance of women proved that Cuban women, "equally as the North American [women]," were partisans for sport and its "intense emotions." Those critics who believed that boxing was too brutal for women were puritanical moralists. They should, the writer admonished, concern themselves with pornographic theaters in Havana, where men debased themselves and women lured them to houses of prostitution. This reflection on comparative vice in Havana ended with an exhortation: "Is there any more moral entertainment for women than sport?"[38]

In the first decades of the twentieth century, sport was inextricably tied to "national" attributes and racial proclivities and was often portrayed as an integral part of European-derived cultural traditions. Cubans, Mexicans, Argentines, Panamanians, Puerto Ricans, and other Latin Americans discerned within sport a novel and positive force for social change that could be detached from its origins and implanted in rapidly growing urban areas. In Cuba, more so than in other Latin American nations, this process of cultural appropriation was accelerated by the presence of foreign athletes and entrepreneurs who trained, taught, and performed in front of curious Cuban spectators.[39] Cubans depicted sport as an ideal democratic space wherein class mobility, especially tied to the lucrative possibilities of professional athletics, was possible based solely on individual merit disconnected from class and previous social status.[40]

As Nancy Stepan and Alejandra Bronfman have suggested, the pseudoscience of eugenics received widespread intellectual dissemination and problematic acceptance among the Latin American elite during this period. Latin American social engineers such as José Vasconcelos in Mexico molded these relatively static ideas of racial hierarchies and social progress to the diverse ethnic and racial mixtures that characterized Latin American nations. Within the culture of the everyday, journalists reflected and disseminated these "scientific" ideas and translated these macro-social prescriptions into the public sphere.[41] Despite these abstractions, the lived perceptions of race constantly undermined the proscriptive admonitions on racial superiority espoused by Spencerian-influenced social scientists.[42] If sport was not just brute force, as influential Latin American cultural mediators argued, how were the supposedly inferior and culturally backward Afro-Cubans able to appropriate the forms of knowledge and skill that made them successful athletes? Why were they the most salient examples of the Cuban appropriation of a body culture whose transnational idols were not only white Americans, African Americans, and Africans like Harry Wills and Amadou M'Barick Fall (aka Battling Siki)?[43]

Even marginal politico-ideological groups (such as the Communist Youth) reproduced imagery of the Afro-Cuban male body in the pursuit of honorific and lucrative titles (e.g., heavyweight "throne" or "champion"). This imagery, and the accompanying rhetoric, were self-examinations that celebrated the accomplishments of mostly lower-class athletes in their competition against foreign professionals. Having little basis in the long tradition of the Cuban media, such representation of Afro-Cuban celebrity was subject to improvisation as Cuban newspapers and revistas both reacted to and molded the public perceptions of a cross-racial group of international celebrities. The images of African American, Afro-Cuban, and European athletes saturated the visual experience of life in Havana and entered into popular memory. By 1923, even illiterate Cubans gathered to hear, via the new technology of radio broadcasts, the blow-by-blow racial dramas of boxing matches between Latin Americans, Americans, Africans, and Europeans.

From the weekly column "Ideales de una Raza," a number of Afro-Cubans and African Americans praised athletes as paradigmatic embodiments of cubanidad.[44] These narratives were highly manipulated to increase the earning potential of such spectacles. But in that process, it was the oft-enunciated perceptions of these events and their impact on the Cuban public sphere that signaled a shift in the public sphere.

### El Arte de los Puños (The Fistic Art) and the Search for the New Cuban Man: Boxing Legality and Illegality in the early 1920s

The 1920s' boom in the popularity of prizefighting in Cuba corresponded to the sport's widespread international legalization. These international events were mirrored by the efforts of Cuban promoters and politicians to domesticate boxing. Daily coverage of virile foreign celebrities was not enough; two journalists published a lengthy pamphlet as a plea to the Cuban public and government to support their efforts.

In the first lines of their promotional history of boxing in Cuba, *El Arte de los Puños* (The Fistic Art, 1922), Cuban authors Bernardino San Martín and Vicente Cubillas proposed to create culture in order to "make the nation."[45] Both authors claimed more than a decade's experience in the (often illegal) promotion of Cuban boxing and had organized illicit prizefights behind closed doors in the patio of the building that housed the newspaper *Cuba*.[46] The authors praised the owner and director of the newspaper, the elderly, Spanish-born political agitator José María Villaverde, for allowing them to hold the clandestine matches on his property. There they hid from the police in a ring located on the inner patio of the building.[47]

Cubillas and San Martín lauded the recent legalization of prizefighting under the newly elected mayor of Havana. Boxing had been outlawed (once again) since 1919 following the ring death of an Afro-Cuban sailor from the Cuban navy, José "Joe" Marroquín, in the Recreo de Belascoín stadium on the outskirts of Central Havana.[48] The authors pass over this tragic event, citing medical findings and creatively arguing that his death had not been due to any trauma suffered during the bout but had happened because he had eaten moments before entering the ring. There was no danger in boxing, they explained, and the benefits for Cuban virility were so numerous that the exclusion of the sport was an antipatriotic act. A review of the major newspapers published during the time of Marroquín's death shows them to be conspicuously lacking in coverage of that tragic event.[49] Given the connections of major newspaper figures to the movement to popularize and legalize prizefighting, this lack of coverage suggests that this information was suppressed, or at least downplayed, by the Havana press. In comparison, the death during a basketball game of one of the city's elite youth in this period received wide press coverage.[50]

Despite these attempts to soften the tragic death of Marroquín, Havana mayor Varona Suárez raged against boxing promoters in a letter to the authors in 1919:

> Boxing is savage, it is barbarous. Don't imagine that you will receive a single permit to celebrate these sordid fiestas. While I'm mayor of Havana, and while I can deny permits for this barbarous sport, I will do so. Don't encourage Cubans to box; this is for foreigners, for North Americans, they are "made" for such things.[51]

Cubillas and San Martín, despite resistance from the Havana government, posit that boxing is an ancient and venerable practice:

> Politicians beginning with Plato and Aristotle, admitted that it was a necessity. This demonstrates the extraordinary importance it was given in ancient times for the physical constitution of men. It evinces the extant necessity that we make some sacrifice, for our own and our children's good, that we take time from our work and our pleasures to fortify our muscles, in order to obtain the appearance and the constitution of real men.[52]

They celebrated masculinity, both on the individual and national level, as a characteristic to be achieved, and boxing was a vehicle for the realization of manly status. It also, they held, would diminish the "hateful" use of revolvers and cutting weapons (*armas blancas*) that had for so long reigned among "the People" and terrorized public life.⁵³ San Martín and Cubillas promoted themselves as socially concerned proponents of this modernizing process. They had been instrumental in forming civic social associations, such as the "El Habana Boxing Club" (1915), the goal of which was the "cultivation of all sports, in general, with preference to those of personal defense: boxing, jujitsu, catch-as-catch-can and Greco-Roman [wrestling]."⁵⁴ Though public boxing matches remained illegal in the two years after Johnson-Willard (1915), athletes such as Mike Febles gained permits to fight jujitsu matches in venues such as Santiago's Oriente Theater but had to venture to Mexico or the United States to box legally.⁵⁵

In December of 1917, following their activism and social agitation, San Martín and Cubillas were granted the first official license to hold boxing matches as public events since the infamous Jack Johnson bout of 1915.⁵⁶ Their use of the public sphere was central to their success, as was their promise of tax revenues for the city. Though in this instance they succeeded as lobbyists, Cubillas and San Martín were primarily journalists. From their columns they impugned Cuban society as lacking in the "manliness" and will power that characterized healthy, forward-thinking nations.⁵⁷ These social conundrums had a solution: If only the government would allow the incipient process of cultural change. Civil society, they implied, had overtaken government policy in its progressive appropriation of modern behaviors. The intransigence of powerful members of the political class was an impediment to healthy change and autonomy of the public sphere.⁵⁸

Modern sport culture, which such authors justified as a normative system, provided even mundane guidance for one's daily routines, a rhythm for life amid urban modernity. The values associated with being an athlete, proponents insisted, were useful tools capable of stemming even atavistic criminal impulses. Social critics and scientists such as Fernando Ortiz and Israel Castellanos argued in this period that Cuba's mixture of races and ethnicities, complicated by a tropical climate, created endemic criminality.⁵⁹ As Alejandra Bronfman has shown, elite Cubans worried that the accident of progress had placed delinquent races, Afro-Cubans in particular, in a dangerous position.⁶⁰ Unable to navigate complex and competitive urban life, Afro-Cubans, they argued, were prone to acts of violence and superstition. Soft eugenics, or neo-Lamarckian eugenic ideas, stressed that races could be improved through public health programs and hygiene, along with the promotion of sports and physical fitness.⁶¹

It is difficult to gauge the spread of these ideas from academic texts like those produced by Fernando Ortiz (i.e., *Los negros brujos*) to the broader public. The evidence through popular media representations and works like *El Arte de los*

*Puños* suggests that by the early 1920s Cubans involved in transnational sport had come to reject the idea of fixed moral/racial degeneracy among Afro-Cubans. The education and training that were key elements of modern sport cultivated moral beings, even among supposedly atavistic Afro-Cubans.

Studies by Ortiz and Castellanos posited that racial division and miscegenation (illustrated by phrenology, biometrics, and craniology) accounted for the relative backwardness of Cuban culture. Cubillas and San Martín, conversely, portrayed a cross-racial class of Cubans equally endowed with intelligence paired with physical traits that made them internationally competitive athletes. Their depiction of this racially mixed subculture fighting for social legitimacy and legal status was a quotidian counterpoint to contemporary scientific understandings of racial determinism. Those abstractions, painstakingly applied by Cuban social scientists, have been overrepresented as an explanation of how race functioned in Republican Cuba, yet they have yielded much of the historiographical understanding of race in this period.

A survey of newspapers (among them *Diario de la Marina*, *Heraldo de Cuba*, *El Mundo*, and the *Havana Post*), revistas, and other media of public discourse suggests that the most visual and written portrayals of Afro-Cuban men were as criminals, servants, and other socially marginalized members of Cuban society.[62] The increasing notoriety of athletes from ostracized racial and ethnic groups—not only Afro-Cuban, but Chinese Cuban (Víctor Achán) and Filipino Cuban (Chau Aranguren)—accompanied laudatory pictures and drawings of their seminude bodies. Such images of the cultivated modern body in triumphant pose were striking deviations from the degrading portrayals of nonwhite Cubans so common in this period. Less than a decade after the massacre of the Partido Independiente de Color, the Cuban press portrayed Afro-Cuban men, once again, as violent. In this case, though, they were practitioners of a regulated, scientific, and modern practice. They deployed violence in a field that promised the elevation of all Cuban manhood.

In the 1910s, racially diverse Cuban boxers such as Achán, Aranguren, and Mike Febles gained international fame. When boxing was officially outlawed in Cuba between 1915 and 1917, they were contracted by the Mexican Yucatán Theater Circus to make a boxing and wrestling tour of the city of Merida.[63] San Martín reported to readers of *El Mundo* in 1916 that a young habanero, Herculano Caula, wanted to travel from his temporary residence in New York to hold a boxing match in Havana. Though Caula was a successful boxer in the United States, he was unable to travel to his native city to hold a bout:

> It is shameful that our compatriot would arrive to his patria and not be able to

hold his fight with Haley. As we all know, the municipal government of Havana denies permission to hold boxing matches, unless they are held by a foreign company with deep pockets.... Despite this we congratulate our criollo Caula for his success in the ring... and we, the Cuban amateurs and fans, will find funds so that the match may happen here... even in a private home or perhaps in some sport club.... This point is to demonstrate to Caula and his adversary that boxing is prohibited in Cuba... against the will and the desire of the sovereign people, who are nothing less than the Cuban fans.[64]

The writer Gabriel Lersundi marveled after meeting the Chinese Cuban boxer Víctor Achán as if it were his first time to encounter a Cuban of Chinese descent: "Wide forehead, very oblique eyes that affirm his descent from the yellow race, straight and smooth black hair, short of stature, flexible with a feline gait." Lersundi described meeting him in Havana's Central Park and was impressed by his physical presence and demeanor. He used the opportunity to mock Cubans who opposed boxing as barbaric, citing Achán as an exemplar youth. Jack Johnson had recently fought in Paris, where men and women, Lersundi reminded, embraced prizefighting. Cuban youths such as Achán were a salubrious example for "the majority of young Cubans who are weak and sickly because their parents don't allow them to practice these healthy sports that give life and physically educate men instead of brutalizing them, as is erroneously believed."[65]

In the early 1920s Cubans hailed a "rebirth" of boxing as positive step toward the regulation of violent impulses and, ultimately, nearer to modernity.[66] Writers spoke of the "seed of boxing" that had "germinated" in Cuba and praised the "fearlessness" of those Cubans who took up the challenge.[67] At issue, these writers hoped, was the civilized channeling of aggression and conflict. Cubans published commentaries by foreigners, especially US Americans, that lauded their "advances" in the realm of sport as proof that "other nations should take note."[68] San Martín and Cubillas agreed, hailing the "sporting betterment that will be realized within [their] young and glorious republic."[69]

Imported sport, especially baseball, had been a common feature of life in Havana since the 1860s. By the early 1920s, sport clubs were one of the most visible civic social organizations in the city. Such voluntary organizations served several interconnected purposes as points of socialization, a locus of social prestige, and as focal points for regulated competition.[70] As fundamental elements of civil society, they reflected the social divisions prevalent in Cuban culture, but they also served to undermine them. In addition to interracial groups like those who held boxing "fiestas" in old Havana, other clubs organized around racial, ethnic, and historical themes. Such suggestive names included Agrupación Hombres de Mañana, Aponte Sport Club (an Afro-Cuban Club named after the leader of the Aponte Rebellion), All American Baseball Club, Boxer Club de Cuba, Antillano Sport, Bohemia Sport Club, Asociación Cubana Clean and Jerk (a bodybuilding club), Asociación Deportista Cubana Indian, Asturias Sporting Club, Canarias Sport Club, the Cerro Atlético Club, the Cuba Base Ball Club de Personas de Color, the Lindbergh Sport Club, and the Amigos de Maceo (Sporting).[71] The National Association of Cuban Boxing, though founded shortly after this period, explained its purpose in a language similar to many of these clubs:

> Since sport is the fecund source where pueblos are nurtured and made vigorous, and in accordance with the valued maxim of our Apostle Martí who preached that We must make men in order to make pueblos . . . we search for unified front . . . for those who practice the most virile of sports . . . collectively rejecting all forms of religious, racial, or political sectarianism.[72]

Civic associations organized around race and sport also included the Asociación Nacional de la Raza Trigueña o Mestiza (National Association of the Olive Skinned or Mestizo Race). This club's members explained their goals to foment, extend, and promote sport among those who shared their racial identity.[73]

Knowledge of the cosmopolitan practices and the attitudes associated with being an aficionado were a designator of social distinction; being a "sportman" (the English term almost universally used) went hand in hand with the attainment of masculinity and social deference. Public figures like former mayor Varona Suárez and brothers Gonzalo and Eduaro López de la Torre organized competitions "to develop to the best of their abilities the sport of boxing in the youth of our sporting societies, the National University, and High Schools of Havana."[74] Athletic venues also served to differentiate Cuban race relations from their US counterpart.

Cuban social critics argued that professional boxing and baseball were exemplary democratic spaces. The lack of segregation, in the ring or in the crowd, proved that Cubans enjoyed a greater degree of racial equality than Americans. Conservative House of Representatives candidate and attorney Dr. Manuel Castellanos Mena reasoned the practice of boxing in Cuba was proof of racial and social equality:

> In Cuba, luckily for us, no other differences have existed than those that are imparted by the different weight [classes]. In this field [boxing], we have given conclusive proof that our sentiments are more democratic and more liberal

than those of the great American people, who disallowed the exhibition of the film of the fight between Johnson and Willard, and who desire that [Jack] Dempsey not dispute his championship with [African American] Harry Wills.[75]

Cubillas and San Martín portrayed Jack Dempsey, despite his drawing the color line, as the paragon of modern manhood. Other writers described Dempsey's body as a "perfect and marvelous machine," in "the flower of life" with an "excellent physical and scientific preparation."[76] In the span of four years, Cuban readers learned, he had risen from the social status of a "vagabond" to the heights of celebrity. The US American world champion came from the working-class margins of yanqui society. He ascended the social ladder through dedication and individual talent. The writers stressed Dempsey's unwillingness to remain within the boundaries of a class-based society. He was also an epitome of complex American (in the hemispheric sense) racial identity: he refused to risk his title to the African American contender Harry Wills, yet Dempsey admitted that he was of mixed racial heritage; "in his veins [ran] mixed together Scottish and Indian blood."[77] Cuban writers cited this unwillingness to face an African American challenger as a blemish on his otherwise laudable image.[78] Dempsey was, for other Cuban critics, an antihero. They commented negatively on his character, labeling him deficient in patriotic values for avoiding military service in the World War.[79]

Narratives of transnational athletes like Jack Dempsey and the famed French war hero and boxer George Carpentier filled pages of Cuban newspapers and intellectual reviews. They were symbols that Cuban boxers, and members of the broader public, sought to emulate. Some athletes used pseudonyms in the ring. An Afro-Cuban boxer from the province of Matanzas fought under the name of "Black Dempsey" in the early 1920s alongside other Afro-Cubans like "Cuban Jack Johnson."[80] From 1921 onward, they fought regularly in front of the "thousands of fanáticos of Havana . . . the contingents of fans from the interior of the Republic . . . [who attend] the virile sport . . . on Zulueta Street."[81] Cuban consumers purchased serialized images and boxing cards.[82] Books, magazines, and newspapers printed and reprinted the boxers' biometrics, their photographic images, and laudatory drawings of their faces and bodies. Cuban tobacco companies published images and brief biographies of Cuban and American athletes on boxing cards that were included in cigarette packs as incentives to buy their products.

A normal program in 1921 for a given night of boxing included a multinational array of performers. On March 9, spectators attended a series of prizefights during which the latest Cuban boxing star, Ponce de León, fought against the African

American "Young Kid Norfolk." The lesser bouts that evening included a contest between Battling Hoyte (Colombia) and Kid Howel (Panama) and another match between Roger Hernández (Havana) and Andrés Martínez (champion featherweight of Costa Rica). These spectacles took place at the Parque Santos y Artigas, which had replaced the previous boxing venue, Arena Colón, on the border between Old and Central Havana.[83] These bouts competed for spectators with a program announced for the Nuevo Frontón by the nascent Havana Boxing Committee (the title always written in English). The committee sold tickets for the bout between US Americans and Cubans at venues all over the city. They promised "emotional" bouts between *boxeadores criollos* and Cuban soldiers. The referees and timekeepers were to be drawn from the most distinguished "sportmen" of the city. The committee advertised its improved lighting and seat arrangement that would surround the press box. Interracial prizefighting also took place at another venue in the same period, Palisades Park. The promoters of that series of bouts promised the crowd US American, Afro-Cuban, and Panamanian boxers.[84]

In bouts such as these, Afro-Cubans who had previously been employed cutting sugar cane or as stevedores, tailors, or soldiers entered Cuban popular consciousness as minor celebrities, worthy of admiration and imitation. Increasingly, Cuban entrepreneurs and the press represented them as both elegant and masculine, their accomplishments in the ring revered alongside the expensive clothing that characterized their highly public lives outside of sport.[85] A writer for *El Mundo* proudly reflected upon boxer Eladio "Black Bill" Valdés, writing that "all the Americans that have visited us have given him great elegies."[86] Writers attended training sessions at the Arena Colón, where Afro-Cuban boxers Black Bill, Kid Charol, Santiago Esparraguera, Kid Campillo, and others trained. Images of these boxers as masculine symbols were ubiquitous on the streets of Havana. Advertisements of their sculpted bodies greeted passersby in advertisements pasted to walls and arcades. The spectacles that took place in the public sphere in Havana on a regular basis taught lessons to Cuban men on how to be men. Dr. Manuel Castellanos Mena wrote:

> The man who boxes is ennobled. Can you imagine a more noble action that demonstrates more pure thoughts than those that we see in the ring every day when a defeated and sometimes bloodied man stretches out his hand without rancor or mental reserve to he who just produced that damage to his person and who is his defeater?[87]

Sportsmen paired interest and participation in prizefighting with other honorific titles and associated themselves with men of the lower classes who entered the ring in pursuit of opportunity. Though by the 1920s boxers in Cuba were almost uniformly drawn from the working class, an association with their professional culture was emblematic for young Cuban men from the middle and upper classes.[88] Mena, for example, advertised his political candidacy by citing his decades-long engagement with Cuban athletics. He joined other lawyers and doctors, along with newspaper publishers such as José María Villaverde, who were often at odds with the Cuban government over social policy.[89] Castellanos Mena distinguished himself as a baseball player in 1909 and had since worked alongside Cubillas and San Martín for the legalization and proliferation of prizefighting. He was an "assiduous devotee" of physical culture, and his efforts to legalize prizefighting purportedly made him worthy of Cuban votes in the upcoming elections for House of Representatives.[90] His *aficiones* established him as a proponent of new Cuban manhood, engaged with international sporting trends, an athlete himself, and one who encouraged prizefighting. The knowledge of this history of boxing, embodied in *El Arte de los Puños* and other popular culture sources, became essential for a man who wanted be fashionable and modern or, in the case of Mena, electable.[91]

For Castellanos Mena, sport in general and boxing in particular were the most modern examples of democratic and gender-inclusive spaces and practices, reaching across race and class. "Modern" women, he reasoned, were attracted to athletics and the men who practiced them. In the United States, female boxers appeared in public matches; he hoped Cuban women would soon follow suit. The embrace of boxing by women was proof of its universal appeal. They saw elegant fighters like George Carpentier, as he received thunderous applause "greater than kings and emperors," as symbols of prodigious sexual powers. Carpentier's wife, Castellanos Mena imagined, could not fault other women who threw themselves at him: "Wherever he disembarks the most beautiful women . . . they have fought over him . . . for that man's kiss . . . even chaste ones, who have only sympathy and admiration for the fighter . . . even Carpentier's wife does not feel by those kisses the dart of jealousy nailed into her heart."[92] The sex appeal of boxers like Carpentier, accordingly, was powerful enough to transcend the boundaries of social decency.

Carpentier's masculinity, in such articles, read as both cultured and violent. If properly imitated, the combination of these seemingly antithetical qualities supposedly made a man irresistible to women. This explicit pairing of sport and the attainment of masculinity spoke to another aspiration: sexual attractiveness.[93] Men could become more appealing to women. Mastery of boxing could also enhance one's honor. It would help relieve "shame before foreigners." Cubans, in this vision, would increasingly control and discipline their bodies, change their national customs, and define the use of weapons as "cowardly," the opposite of virile modern manhood. The mimesis of transnational hero-athletes—especially the forging of healthy bodies and dedication to a craft—would ameliorate the conditions that created pernicious social types in Cuba: "It will remove from our political scene that repugnant type [who carries] the fearsome revolver."[94] Effeminate men had underdeveloped bodies and they relied on weapons to settle disputes, and in the process continued the "hateful" backwardness of Cuban society. He implied that the adversaries of boxing clung to an outdated understanding of middle-class masculinity. Due to ignorance and fear they disdained the "noble" labor of Cuban sport promoters. Boxers, especially Afro-Cubans, were the owners of "admirable physiques"; they were "crafty and intelligent," never "lost poise," and helped "conquer fame" for Cuba.[95] Mena and like-minded writers wrapped boxers in the Cuban flag. Cubillas and San Martín, along with Mena, argued that Cuban manhood was under attack. They impugned Cubans with a language of "manliness" (varonil), while "relating truths like the Gospel." Like Raúl Talán's histories of the Mexican prize ring, *El Arte de los Puños* was a popular manual on how to attain modernity and masculinity.

Echoing Cuban intellectuals like José Sixto de Sola, they posited that Cubans who refused to accept modern athletics as a positive social force and continued to disdain prizefighting were "short of intelligence and willfully blind."[96] The preface of *El Arte de los Puños*, written for a supposedly more intelligent audience, is directed to the "Distinguished Sportsmen" of the recently established Comisión Nacional de Boxeo, an influential group of upper- and middle-class Cubans whose favor San Martín and Cubillas had cultivated over the preceding years. They call for the benevolence of this commission while stating their goal as "the regeneration of the manly art of the Marquis of Queensbury in our Republic." The use of terms such as "regeneration" evoked a progressive understanding of social maladies that drew on the language and ideas of positive eugenics. The repositioning of prizefighting from a marginal and detestable social position into one widely portrayed as a nationalist effort to regenerate the Cuban people did not convince all critics.

A few months after the 1921 formation of the National Boxing Commission, President Zayas directed the prestigious Academy of Sciences of Havana to report to the government on the "dangers of boxing."[97] In March of 1922, Dr. Julio F. Arteaga, an obstetrician who had published work on infectious disease, eugenics, and public health, read the academy's findings to the House of Representative in Havana. Arteaga presented a brief history of boxing from antiquity to the present. He argued that though it was a "Saxon" pursuit, embraced by individuals such as Lord Byron and the Marquis of Queensbury, other Europeans such as Alexander

Dumas had also worked to create humane rules and propagate their practice among the public. Arteaga argued that from a medical and hygienic standpoint, boxing was "not advisable for the health of the individual." Though dangerous, he posited that if it were practiced among "civilized" individuals and regulated by modern rules, the risk of serious and permanent injury was relatively low. His report, when opened for comment by the members of the House of Representatives, was met with ancillary proof that prizefighting was a dangerous and even anti-Christian pursuit. Arteaga's report was accepted by the House, but no further action was taken. Boxing, though dangerous and philosophically suspect, was to remain legal in Cuba. Activists like San Martín and Cubillas had succeeded in swaying public opinion. Political and scientific resistance could not reverse their years-long project to legalize boxing.[98]

The foundation and growth of the Comisión Nacional de Boxeo was the result of continuous pressure emanating from Cuban civil society.[99] The government moved to regulate the sport and tax it heavily. The new legislation required prodigious sums from sport clubs and promoters (five thousand pesos), referees (five hundred pesos), and "managers" (three hundred pesos) that, the legislation suggested, could be obtained from certain finance companies. It also required up to three hundred pesos to issue licenses in the form of cards (*carnets*) to be carried by anyone involved in a boxing match, from timekeepers and club owners to "seconds" and announcers. In keeping with the idea that boxing was a path to social advancement, boxers were only required to pay ten pesos and to prove their "moral condition" before the commission.[100] These cards were to carry their fingerprints, biometrics, biographical information, and photographs.[101] The commission went on to regulate every aspect of the public spectacle, from the pay given to referees and timekeepers, the number of free tickets that could be distributed to the press (two for every hundred people the arena could hold), how often a boxer could fight, where and when he could fight, and the minimum age of a professional boxer: eighteen.[102]

Though the government had reversed its previous legal position and sought to impose its rule over civil society through precise regulations, it had no control over the growing public taste for prizefighting.

### The "Virile and Energetic Reality of our Race": How Luis Ángel Firpo Embodied the Transnational "Manly Ideal" in Cuba

In the months leading up to the September 1923 championship between Argentine Luis Ángel Firpo and American Jack Dempsey, Cubans writers published thousands of words of prose and poetry, pictures and illustrations, predictions and prayers. They conveyed for their readers the importance of the international racial drama unfolding a thousand miles away in New York. Cubans from around the island wrote to newspapers expressing their racial solidarity with the Argentine. They articulated their emotions and cited the match as a historic moment in the Latin American encounter with global culture. The public sphere, where opinions were voiced and debated, sprang into life in the months before the bout.

On the evening of September 14, 1923, one newspaper writer estimated that fifty thousand Cubans in Havana alone gathered on street corners and in parks to hear the radio broadcast of the bout.[103] Advertisements for patent medicines seized on the popularity of boxing to extol the effects of their product: to make vigorous men capable of surviving in the allegoric struggle for national and racial supremacy. They also promised to remedy the effects of the "mal del siglo": neurasthenia.[104] Racial struggle, the enervating effects of modern life, and the ways to cultivate "virility," were entangled with this distant and highly theatrical "crisis." In Argentina, thousands more miles away, the rise of Firpo fomented congressional debates on how best to incorporate boxing into Argentine culture in order to close the gap between Argentine masculinity and "Anglo Saxon" martial prowess.[105] Similar ideas, circulating in Cuba, materialized as thousands gathered in hope that Firpo, and "Latins" in general, would show their manhood and modernity in the New York ring.

Cuban writers, broadcasters, and theater/cinema owners mirrored and enhanced the popular acclaim created by the match by stressing regional identity and the growing racial solidarity with the Argentine boxer, not only across Latin America, but with Latin countries of Europe. Firpo, Cuban readers learned, was an innocent and powerful practitioner of the yankee pastime. Yet he also possessed a keen business acumen that allowed him to strategically turn his financial windfall into further business opportunities for himself and the Argentine public. In 1923, for example, with limited English speaking ability, Firpo negotiated the exclusive distributorship for Stutz automobiles for all of Argentina and Uruguay.[106] His lack of language skills in English, usually cited as a prerequisite for success in el norte, were overcome by the force of his personality and the notoriety of his profession. Educated and upper-class Latin Americans were no longer the only ones who could compete for financial success abroad. Firpo, given these multiple pursuits, was presented to readers as simultaneously *salvaje* (savage) and refined, successfully wielding both violence and commerce as aids in his self-advancement: a self-made man.

One dramatic Cuban commentator petitioned God to assist Firpo in defeating the famous American and his shadowy supporters.[107] Cuban sympathies, journalists argued, lay with the Argentine as a "racial brother" and a symbol of "Latin" virility in combat with the hegemonic power to the north. The 1923 bout was the first time a Latin American challenged a representative of the United States for the designation of "world heavyweight champion." The boxers served as archetypal characters, shorthand for larger national and racial identities. They represented the aspirations of Cuban writers—and, they argued, large segments of the public—to vicariously excel at regulated and highly theatrical violence.[108]

The Cuban poets Manuel Giz and José F. de la Peña recorded the significance of the distant event and the sentiments of many writers in their two odes to the Argentine boxer on the eve of the bout:

> "To Luis Ángel Firpo"
> The ideal laurels of smiling
> August victory will crown your head . . .
> demonstrating in the contest that you are
> a descendant of this race of invincible immortals.
>
> Raise your imperturbable right hand, challenge,
> Struggling you will win, this is your destiny;
> On you is pinned our Latin honor,
> most perfect and formidable athlete.
> Continue your wrathful, triumphant career.
> Hercules, Hispano-American Goliath;
> you come from the most warrior-like lineage
> That here was able to found a fraternal people.
> Thus Cuba, joyful and elevated,
> offers her arm, and grips your hand.[109]
>
> "The Victor"
> Shining star on which a Race fixes
> Its honor and hope:
> Inspired by faith in his strength.
> Without concern for whom destiny may chose!
> . . . . . . . . .
> Remember that this is the "chance" of your life
> to acquire unimaginable glory
> Offering your race what it loves.[110]

Manuel Giz, José de la Peña, and other amateur poets wrote these lines to express their solidarity with a man they had never met but who they felt furthered the standing of their race. The poets characterize Cubans as part of a regionally and racially defined group. Racial identity, accordingly, should be experienced in that context as a pan-Latin American constant formed by common Spanish racial heritage and history (and excluding indigenous or Afro-descended Latin Americans).

Luis Ángel Firpo served as a pivotal figure in the contemporary Cuban understanding of race and sport. Imagined as a racially pure Argentine of European stock, he was the first Latin American in a long line of increasingly darker-skinned athletic idols that came to represent regional and national symbols of vigorous manhood. Many editorials published in the weeks leading up to the bout focused on Firpo's mixed yet completely Spanish heritage and his embodiment of aspirational manhood.[111] Others claimed he was the son of an Argentine woman (of Spanish heritage) and an Italian immigrant father.[112] Amid these different constructions of Firpo's race and ethnicity, the honor of Latin America manhood as a whole was "pinned" on the boxer as a "perfect" athlete. Writers simultaneously defined Firpo as a representative of the "Latin," "Hispanic-American," "Indo-American," or "Latin American" races.[113] A writer for *La Prensa*, a Spanish-language daily published in New York City, took issue with an editorial from the *Evening Telegram* that characterized Firpo as part of the "rising tide of color." Firpo, *La Prensa* argued, was "of pure Caucasian blood, Argentine, son of an Italian from Genoa and a Spanish mother from Asturias."[114] The editorialist took this pairing of Firpo with African American boxer Harry Wills, "of pure African race," as a deliberate affront: "He who wrote that which we have translated above fails knowingly in telling the truth and demonstrates that the feeling of true sportsmanship is often lacking among those charged with shaping public opinion."[115]

In describing Firpo, the deployment of racial ideas was sometimes confused and confusing, often fluid and contingent upon context and motive. Firpo became a representative of the national virilities of several nations. Official representatives of the Argentine, Italian, and Spanish governments voiced their support of him and appropriated his image as emblematic of the most masculine and modern characteristics of their respective peoples. His popularity stimulated Latin Americans in the United States to show their solidarity with the boxer through the purchase of an honorific medal and ceremonial pair of boxing gloves that were awarded him in a public ceremony.[116] According to US writers, he was "lionized ... by the Latin American colony in New York." The readers of *La Prensa* each mailed ten cents to the editorial offices, subscribing to purchase a gold medal in his honor. He was entertained at the New York headquarters of the Spanish Society, where crowds gathered to see him.[117] On the evening of the bout, the consul general of Argentina, Ernest Pérez, delivered a stirring speech on behalf of the Argentine people. Cubans read of these events in detailed coverage in daily newspapers. Hundreds of Cubans could not wait to receive news of the fight's outcome.

Hundreds traveled to New York to witness the bout, investing time and sometimes hundreds of dollars in bets, travel fare, and lodging fees.[118] Cuban sport fans were keenly aware of the racial injustice perpetrated by American athletes who refused to give African Americans their due chance. Despite this general knowledge, many reveled in the knowledge that a Latin man might become champion. Jack Dempsey refused to risk his title to worthy boxers of African descent, but the Argentine was seemingly less of a risk to the white races' protection of the title.[119] Two weeks before the Firpo-Dempsey bout, *Diario de la Marina* reported that the mayor of Key West, Florida, had intervened to stop a scheduled bout between the Cuban Eladio "Black Bill" Valdés and a white American boxer, "Kid Shakey." Such bouts, Cubans read, violated "the law of the race line." The editorialist commented that the color line would benefit Cuban promoters Santos y Artigas by displacing the lucrative bout to Havana. Black Bill had defeated other "white Americans" before, in a "manner that astonished all the experts."[120]

By the time of the Dempsey-Firpo match in 1923, the relationship between race, sport, and wider identities were common topics in Cuba.[121] It is clear that, as in the United States, many Latin American observers subscribed to the idea that success in competitive sport was a badge of achievement that indicated the vigorous masculinity espoused by many proponents of manliness in the United States, most famous among them Theodore Roosevelt.[122] US historians of gender, among them Gail Bederman and Kristin Hoganson, have explained the importance to middle- and upper-class US men of displaying manhood through athletics. The significance of athletic performances like boxing resulted partly from the widespread assumption that urban life was undermining older normative notions of masculinity. Men had to cultivate manliness and protect it from the degenerating effects of overcivilization. The need to prove national virility, in part, explained why the United States invaded Cuba in 1898.

These ideas were celebrated in popular culture, as illustrated by the voluminous coverage of Firpo-Dempsey in Cuba and across Latin America. Beyond the success of individual racial and national groups in combating the dangers of urban life, victory in boxing was portrayed as a border-crossing "democratic" achievement. Individual and racial merit, such reasoning held, was decided fairly and dramatically in the boxing ring. Cuban commentators presented transnational athletic events to their readers in these terms, strikingly similar to those deployed in the United States. They made explicit comparisons of events in distant New York with the rapid development and legalization of boxing on the island.[123]

Cuban advertisers seized on the popularity of boxing in the early 1920s to appeal to deep-seated fears that urban life was sapping the vital energies of Cuban men. In thousands of advertisements, Cubans were promised tonics and patent medicines to shield them from the "evil of the century," neurasthenia. A nervous condition that supposedly attacked urban men in particular, neurasthenia was a condition of weakness, effeminacy, and lack of decisiveness that stemmed from "alterations in the nervous system resulting from the vegetative life." In extreme cases, neurasthenia threatened to disrupt normal sexuality.[124] Physicians attributed the condition to the loss of primal energies that had previously been cultivated by vigorous, healthy, and rural living.[125] Cuban intellectuals imported the idea and applied it to the men who, they feared, were also undergoing these debilitating transformations from life in the modern city. These same ideas appeared, with increasing frequency, into the 1920s.[126] One locus for the transfer of these intellectual ideas into public life was through newspapers and the advertisements for products to reverse this dreaded condition. Transnational advertisements for patent medicines, such as a tonic called Globeól, portrayed a bottle of the substance anthropomorphized into a white boxer delivering a knockout blow to a black fighter.[127] Such visual keys promised regeneration and strengthening of the primal instincts of man through a combination of medication and affinity for virile sports such as boxing.

As advertisers focused visually on the threatened masculinity and the racial divide between black and white men, Cuban writers reported that the gifted African American heavyweight, the "candidate of the colored race," would never be allowed to fight for Jack Dempsey's title.[128] Young Sam McVea, an African American boxer from New Orleans, arrived in Havana after a barnstorming tour of Jamaica and Panama. He carried newspaper clippings to prove his success in the ring and his bona fides as a challenger. He praised Cuban racial tolerance, where "boxers of the colored race can fight with white fighters and win the money they deserve."[129] Cuban journalists reproduced detailed accounts of the legal battles of the African American boxer Harry Wills for a chance to meet the champion Jack Dempsey in the ring. Race alone, Cuban readers were informed over and again, was the only factor that prevented Wills from reaping the fruits of his long career.[130] Once again, Cubans celebrated the civic nationalism that, social commentators stressed, was more democratic than that of the United States, and they decried racial segregation that limited the upward mobility for Cubans of African descent.[131] The great American champion, in risking his title to a member of the Latin race, would continue to deny his African American countrymen a shot at the heavyweight crown.

In the weeks leading up to Dempsey-Firpo, habaneros attended a variety of boxing matches in virtually all parts of the city. In the beach suburb of Marianao, entrepreneurs held "Battle Royale" boxing matches in conjunction with social outings to the beach, where they invited Cubans to take part in such traditional games "played by [their] ancestors" as catching a greased duck.[132] These entertainments were augmented by prizefights in a ring erected on the beach, where "all those who feel themselves to be manly" were encouraged to mount the ring. No limits on "weight, age, or [skin] color" were established to segregate Cubans in the manner that was common practice in the rings of the north.[133] The promoters of these events portrayed these entertainments as a quintessentially Cuban form of recreation and relaxation: "You will have an agreeable day in the open air, swimming, listening to music, dancing, watching boxing [matches], walking on the beach . . . it will take away your bad mood and the worries of business."[134] Watching men pummel each other in the ring was as Cuban as dancing and walking on the beach. The social seat of aristocratic habanero society, the Cuba Lawn Tennis club, opened its facilities for the amateur boxing championship, where a cross-racial group of dozens of young men from the YMCA, the town of Regla, Police, Customs Agents,' Sporting, Clerks,' and La Salle athletic clubs competed for honorary titles.[135]

In the suburbs and in the working-class heart of the city, Cubans attended, wagered scarce pesos, and were entertained by prizefighting. In the professional and amateur stadiums of Central Havana, boxers from the furthest reaches of the island fought in front of crowds of self-styled Cuban sportsmen. Afro-Cuban fighters from Cienfuegos (Gustavo "Sparring" Caballero), Cárdenas (Kid Cárdenas), and Sagua la Grande (Ramón "Releaux Saguero" Cabrera) joined white Cubans like Enrique "The Topaz of Cienfuegos" Ponce de León and other Latin Americans like the Uruguayan Juan Carlos Casala to compete for increasingly lucrative purses. They engaged in highly publicized grudge matches, published defaming letters in the press, and engaged in other theatrical behavior to boost revenues.[136] Local businesses backed fighters like Antonio Valdes, "the Creole Marvel" and "Pride of the Harris Brothers."[137] Juan Garzón squared off against the "Cuban [George] Carpentier." In one bout, a police escort led Ponce de León to the ring. He was not under arrest, the writer stressed, but had the honor guard to pay homage to him as the boxing trainer for the Third Police Station gym. Customs agent Alberto Dumois represented his fellow workers in a match held in the Stadium of the

Marina. An amateur tournament took place "to foment the sport of boxing in Cuba as one of the means of physical and moral betterment for Cuban youths."[138] All these events took place in the first weeks of September 1923.

These local matches were juxtaposed with the transnational event of the prizefight between Firpo and Dempsey. Accounts of the bout dominated news from abroad in Havana newspapers for weeks surrounding the match, and men were challenged "to show their manliness" by taking part in boxing matches.[139] "Experts," both Cuban and foreign, predicted the outcome of the racialized battle between North and South in lengthy diatribes in the Havana press. Former champions Jim Corbett and Jess Willard and the African American heavyweight Harry Wills's opinions were published in lengthy articles translated into Spanish for Cuban readers.[140] When the day of the fight finally arrived, it had been dissected, predicted, argued, and justified in public discourse by dozens of individuals from countries on every inhabited continent.

A Havana law student, José Luis Sandoval, boarded a steamship bound for New York in order to witness the match between "the colossus of the Anglo Saxon race and that of the Latin." Presented as the paragon of Cuban youth, Sandoval had proven his status by exhibiting a thorough grasp of prizefighting.[141] Hundreds of Cubans, *El Mundo* reported, had "invaded New York," traveling on trains and steamships to witness the bout. Among them was Celso Cuellar del Rio, son-in-law of the president, who traveled to see the bout in the company of his family.[142] Joe Massaguer, writing an account of one such voyage on the steamship *Governor Cobb*, suggested they rename the ship the "Dempsey-Firpo Special." Ninety percent of the passengers, he mused, were headed to New York to witness the bout.[143] To represent the "Firpista Party," one Sr. Martín took it upon himself to purchase a ringside seat and travel to New York.[144]

Guillermo Pi, writing for *Diario de la Marina*, informed his readers of the daily events taking place in the training camps of the two boxers. He called upon his readers to imagine urban and rural scenes in the United States where the careful preparations were taking place. Even the training camps, Massaguer explained to his readers, were cosmopolitan sites. In Firpo's camp one could hear conversations in Italian, Spanish, German, English, and French.[145] Italian and Argentine laborers, one Cuban wrote, avoided work in New York City in order to watch Firpo hit the punching bag and skip rope.[146] The Cuban Boxing Commission (CBC), juxtaposing itself with the New York Boxing Commission, published its weekly proceedings for public consumption and transparency. The CBC listed boxers, promoters, trainers, ring doctors, and seconds along with their assigned license number. The commission printed elaborate reasons for denying certain fighters eligibility to enter the ring. One boxer, Ponce de León, was prevented from engaging in a bout because the Cuban Boxing Commission's doctors, after a thorough examination, deemed him physically unfit to fight. This type of bureaucratic ostentation mirrored that of the sister commission in the United States.[147]

Firpo, to the joy of Cuban observers, received foreign dignitaries in his training camp outside of New York. One of them was the Italian consul, who presented him with a coat of arms from his mother's Italian-descended family and assured him that his ancestors were warriors and conquerors, "soldiers of Christ," and that the "race was admirably incarnated in him."[148] Firpo carried great responsibility on his shoulders: "A tree that has these roots—that has been fed from generation to generation with such powerful sap, can only continue the tradition. He is obligated to do it." Playing on the moniker associated with the defeat of Jack Johnson, one journalist proclaimed that Firpo was "the Latin Hope (la esperanza latina)."[149] Firpo as the Latin Hope became a common phrase in Cuba. Writing from Matanzas, the "Athens of Cuba," Manuel Fernández had predicted in February of 1923 that Firpo would become the world champion: "A toast, to Luis Ángel Firpo, a toast! Wild Bull of the Pampas. A toast to your noble lineage. A toast to the tenacity you personify . . . a toast from Matanzas, you are an emblem that sublimates our strong and indomitable Latin race . . . for the immense glory that you bring to the race for beautiful Italy, for Spain, and for all of the nations that speak Spanish and are Latin."[150]

José Massaguer, the cosmopolitan sports editor for the Havana newspaper *El Mundo*, reacted to the voluminous mail he received about the bout from even the smallest towns on the island. He opened a section of the newspaper to publish these letters that expressed the hopes that Cubans placed in the victory of the Argentine.[151] Antolín Gómez, from Cárdenas, wrote that his "heart [was] with Firpo." Gómez proclaimed that he was a "100% boxing fan" and that he devoured the daily press about the sport that he received in his provincial town. Firpo, he reasoned, was in "perfect physical condition" and embodied the "Greatest of Latin Hopes." His intellect told him, however, that Dempsey stood a better chance to win.[152] Rolando Casas, writing from Matanzas, expressed his hopes in messianic terms: Firpo, for Casas was "a figure who will defeat the Saxon race once and for all, a figure to represent the Latin Race, [who] will know how to carry proudly the paladin of Championship of the World." Furthermore, he flattered the editor, Massaguer, for his genius in giving common Cubans a platform from which to express their racial solidarity.[153]

Several Cubans agreed with Casas that the fight was to decide more than just supremacy in the boxing ring. Trying to avoid the "Latin passion" of other writers, Ricardo de la Torre wrote that he believed that brute force always wins, and since Firpo was brutishness incarnate, he would certainly prevail.[154] One writer, who identified himself only as S.Q., differed from most. He reasoned that thousands of people awaited with true anxiety the result of the fight, what some have called a *"Pelea de raza,"* not for the determination of supremacy in boxing, but the supremacy of the Saxon race over the Latin, or vice versa.

> It is an absurd danger to see in Firpo or Dempsey the representative of a race; races should never be represented by brute force, but in how advanced they are in Art, Science, Industry, etc. In our century, the force of intellect is more important, and Dempsey and Firpo have little of that.... We, as Latins, should hope for the triumph of Firpo, but we should not blind ourselves and hope for the defeat of the world champion."[155]

It was true that the Argentine had a good "chance," but "Dempsey [had] better science, and Firpo was already morally defeated because he wanted more time to learn before the fight."

Aurelio Baldoz, writing from Havana, appointed himself to speak on the pettiness of Americans in regard to fair competition: "We all know that the Americans cannot tolerate a Latin besting them in anything, much less will they look kindly upon the world's crown passing to the Latin race."[156] Arroyo Ruz, also writing from Havana, denounced those Cubans whom he saw as traitors to national identity. Those who hoped Dempsey would win did so because they had "spent their month" in the United States and fancied themselves "Franks" instead of "Franciscos." They deluded themselves into thinking that they had a connection with the American champion.[157] R. G. Tilla concurred but also impugned Cubans for talking out of turn about an "art" they knew little about. It made Cubans look ridiculous, as would an American who pretended knowledge that was not a product of his culture:

> The immense majority of those of us who speak about Firpo and Dempsey are not authorized to do so.... Either we don't know the first word on boxing, or because we don't know the current conditions of the boxers. Some of us think that because we have seen ten or twelve bad local fights we know what boxing is, and the truth is that whichever authentic Frank or Peter, not these false ones that Senor Arroyo alluded to, know possibly more than whichever of us about the art that currently enriches Firpo, the powerful Argentine, and the reason is

very simple; perhaps presenting the opposite would be more clear: "Can you all imagine the ridiculous role Mr. Runyan, the great North American chronicler, would play writing about a cock fight?"[158]

J. Martínez shared the admiration many felt for Dempsey as an emblematic physical specimen. Dozens of Cuban men voiced similar opinions: "Dempsey is one of the most perfect human examples that exists, all of his body is in proper proportion." Despite this, Firpo was still the best Latin hope.[159] Ramos Izquierdo, writing from an unstated location in Cuba, evoked his experience living in the United States immediately after Cuban independence and his years as an assiduous boxing fan to reason that Firpo, without doubt, would win.[160] It was not a question of races for Izquierdo, but of Firpo being hungry and the champion being worn out.[161]

Rafael Román from his home in the rural town of San José de los Ramos (Matanzas province, population eight thousand), supported his idea that Dempsey would win through "reading the opinions of sport critics the world over."[162] Even in farming communities, the distant events in New York fascinated readers who felt themselves integral parts of a battle for racial supremacy on the small stage. From Guanajay, in Havana Province, one J. R. H. worked out mathematical equations contingent on his measurement of the comparative endurance, strength, and "chins" of Firpo and Dempsey. He concluded with "scientific certainty" that Firpo would triumph.[163] On the day of the bout, amid a flurry of letters stating carefully reasoned predictions and bold hopes, one man expressed his determination to "pawn" his underwear, pants, and even his wife in order to bet on Firpo's victory.[164]

The widespread engagement of public opinion, as expressed in these dozens of letters, reveals the importance of vicarious identification and the power of received ideas about manhood and identity, even in the remotest corners of Cuba. The sometimes bizarre arguments may strike some modern readers as false consciousness or as a naïve attachment to a novel and manipulative transnational moneymaking machine, but it is obvious that heartfelt emotion and racial pride and were at stake for these writers. Knowledge, the consumption of transnational information, was the key factor in most of these letters as they explained their bona fides as critics and sportmen. Given the recent history of American military and economic domination of Cuba, this fervent admiration of Firpo is reasonable. They placed hope in Firpo as a representative Latin and Cuban and as a challenger to American cultural pretensions. By 1923, their reading of days-old newspapers was no longer the only avenue to stay informed of such events.

In Havana, owning a radio in these early days of broadcasting was a symbol of social status and wealth.¹⁶⁵ The evening of the bout, however, individuals, soap factories, mattress companies, theaters, and "radio clubs" shared their prized possessions with the masses of Cubans who gathered in parks, on street corners, and in front of hotels to hear the live broadcast of the fight. *El Mundo*'s radio editor stopped counting the public locations where these radios were placed at twenty, but he estimated the perhaps twice that amount would be deployed.¹⁶⁶ For many Cubans, this was likely the first radio transmission they had ever heard. Afro-Cubans, white Cubans, men, women, and children gathered to listen to the bout, an estimated fifty thousand people in the city of Havana alone. Little else in this period had such a powerful hold over the public imagination. For one radio enthusiast, such excitement showed "the culture of our people."¹⁶⁷

Despite the frenetic energy surrounding the fight, most Cuban writers took Dempsey's second round knockout of Firpo in stride. They took pride in Firpo's courageous attempt and called it a "moral victory" for Latin America.¹⁶⁸ There were a number of people to blame, but the Wild Bull of the Pampas was not one of them. Most newspapers in the United States fulminated against the victor, Jack Dempsey, for repeatedly fouling Firpo while the referee stood by and did nothing. The hundreds of Latin Americans who attended the fight increased their dedication to the Argentine and held high hopes for his future.

Cubans readily adopted new technologies and aficiones that, cultural commentators argued, marked them as a cultured and modern people. They utilized the public sphere, where they wrote passionate defenses of their "racial" preferences in a boxing match that seemingly determined little about their daily lives. Nowhere was the transnational public sphere more energized in the early 1920s than in the appropriation of transnational sport idols. Expressing affinity became a way to align oneself and one's place amid transnational cultures, a means of identifying beyond the local or the national. Before the close of the decade, Afro-Cuban boxers reached those heights of international celebrity that had been reserved for foreigners.

## "Kid Chocolate," the Communist Youth, and the Rise of Afro-Cuban Celebrity

In August of 1929, the Afro-Cuban boxer Kid Chocolate defeated the Jewish American Al Singer in front of fifty thousand fans at the Polo Grounds in New York.¹⁶⁹ In Havana, the Cuban public gathered in the streets, in front of newspaper offices, in cafes, and in bars to listen to the blow-by-blow wireless broadcast of the bout. Amateur radio stations set up receivers on street corners and in windows to accommodate the public excitement over the match. "Chocolate," or "El Kid" as he was affectionately known, was transformed into a popular culture hero in Cuba, particularly for Afro-Cubans. His unique style in the ring became a model for African American prizefighters such as Harlem's Cyril Josephs.[170] Advertisers in Cuba contracted him to endorse local champagne and beer. Advertisers for "Champan Sport" reproduced his autograph alongside his image in a boxing stance on product labels seeking to channel Kid Chocolate's cross-class popularity.[171] In the months following his return to Cuba, he toured the island with his entourage and the film of his bout to show in local theaters. In Camagüey, the mayor led a special session of the town council to celebrate the boxer as among those patriots who had "put the Cuban flag on high."[172] In Havana, clothing stores in the most elite shopping center, the Manzana de Gómez on Central Park, passed out handbills with the "Kid's" picture to advertise their expensive suits.[173]

Eligio Sardiñas Montalvo was an unlikely national hero. He had begun boxing around the age of twelve while working as a newspaper crier for the evening paper *La Noche*. Unbeaten in Cuba, Sardiñas headed for the United States at the age of seventeen. As historian Enver Casimir wrote, Kid Chocolate "boosted the image of Cuba in the United States," and in an era when athletic achievement was viewed across the globe as a proxy for the overall capacity of a nation or race, Kid Chocolate's success loomed large for a nation seeking to establish its capacity for self-governance in the face of North American political tutelage and the racist ideology used to justify it.[174]

Though Eligio Sardiñas was became the best-known Cuban boxer in the United States during this period, he was not the first Afro-Cuban prizefighter to move to Harlem and try his hand at athletic celebrity. The trajectory of Eladio "Black Bill" Valdes was shorter, more tragic, and perhaps more common for Afro-Cubans who challenged the color line in the United States. In February 1925, the Cuban manager and boxing promoter Luis "Pincho" Gutiérrez announced he would take two Afro-Cuban fighters, Cirilín Olano and Black Bill, to New York to arrange matches.[175] Newspapers recalled that Black Bill had easily defeated seasoned US boxers in Havana, but that despite the touting of Olano and Valdes by Cuban sport journalists, "you can never tell about these Latins."[176] In his first US bout, Black Bill impressed sportswriters. He exhibited the speed, precision, and evasiveness that would make him a favorite in New York rings over the next few years.[177] Within a few months of his arrival, Black Bill was considered by boxing critics to be a contender for the flyweight boxing championship. In the short time after his arrival, he boxed in eight matches—all victories—and often embarrassed his opponents by making them look slow and inept.[178]

*Diario de la Marina*'s special correspondent, who traveled with Kid Chocolate and sent daily cables to apprise the Cuban public of his every move, attributed the victory to the union of white Cuban intelligence in the form of manager Luis "Pincho" Gutiérrez and Afro-Cuban athletic ability in the body of Kid Chocolate.[179] The white manager's strategy, the correspondent argued, had proven to be the decisive factor in the fighter's victory. The Cuban manager had outthought US American experts. Cuba, in the form of the 125-pound Afro-Cuban boxer, had defeated the hero of Jewish America.[180] In this case, the triumph over the North was dramatic and complete. Intelligence and wit on the part of Gutiérrez had guided his Afro-Cuban "Bon Bon" to victory.[181]

The boxer's triumphant return to Havana a week later was one of the most anticipated public events in recent memory. After a tumultuous reception by the Cuban consul and enormous crowds of Cuban Americans and African Americans in Miami, Chocolate and his manager "Pincho" landed in the harbor in Havana on September 8. They made their entrance on a special hydroplane, to the music of the municipal band, with thousands of fanáticos lining the shores. Nearly every boat in the harbor was packed with people waiting for a glimpse of the small, dark-skinned boxer from the shantytown of Cerro, on the margins of Havana.[182] Reporters gushed over Chocolate's fame; the negrito, in addition to being a "perfect" boxer, had a friendly smile and was an "ebony statue, perfectly symmetrical and exquisitely modeled."[183] He was hailed as the "chosen son" of Cuba.[184]

From the lighthouse tower of the sixteenth century fort El Morro, constructed by slave labor, the signal to close the Havana harbor was given as the hydroplane approached from the north. The thousands of spectators stumbled over themselves, causing numerous injuries and nearly sinking one of the harbor's docks.[185] The entire malecón was filled with people as the special car sent by the mayor's office drove the boxer and his manager to the town hall, where Kid Chocolate's mother and girlfriend waited with the mayor. Several writers evoked Cuban nationalism to describe the valor, patriotism, and national honor that were intricately connected to the boxer's triumph in New York. Comandante Enrique Recio compared Chocolate, the "Bronze Hero," with General Antonio Maceo, the "Bronze Titan" martyred in 1896 during the Cuban wars for independence. While Recio spoke in the patio of the colonial-era prison on the Prado (which was temporarily housing the Ayuntamiento), the crowd grew impatient and the boxer and the government functionaries took the balcony overlooking the crowd. The Kid and his manager Pincho Gutierrez received medals from the government to the thunderous applause of the gathered public.[186]

In anticipation of the Kid's return, in early September of 1929 Havana mayor Miguel Mariano Gómez, along with representatives from the most elite

Afro-Cuban social club, the Club Atenas, held a special session of the Ayuntamiento to pay homage to the ascendant career of Eligio Sardiñas Montalvo, the "beloved Kid Chocolate," upon his victorious return from the United States.[187] Afro-Cuban civil society, even the less elite fraternal organizations like the Unión Fraternal, the Club Jóvenes del Vals, and the Magnetic Club, along with the aristocratic scions of white, elite Cubans (Mayor Gómez was the son of former president José Miguel Gómez) voted to award medals to the boxer and his white "irreplaceable" manager as heroes of the nation. Florentino Pedroso, the director of the Afro-Cuban revista *Renacimiento* and an "enthusiastic admirer" of the boxer, served as the director of the commission to receive him. They engaged the municipal band to greet the boxer.[188]

As Robin Moore has shown, the Club Atenas was highly selective in its valorization of the cultural achievements of Afro-Cubans. Into the 1950s, popular Afro-Cuban music and dance traditions such as *son* and *mambo* were repressed by public representatives of black Cubans in favor of more European, "smooth" forms of expression. While upper-class whites in the 1920s and 1930s encouraged and emulated Afro-Cuban popular culture and appropriated music and dance as emblematic of Cuban national identity, many elite Afro-Cubans disdained them as remnants of lower-class, even atavistic black culture.[189] The Club Atenas's official support and admiration for the class-ascendant Cuban boxer suggests the ambiguity of certain cultural practices as symbols of high cultural attainment among Afro-Cubans. Normally, their primary goal was to integrate and educate their fellow black Cubans into mainstream ideas of propriety and sociability. Fame, it seems, was enough to impel members of Club Atenas to put their stamp of approval on the athletic endeavors of the former shoe shiner and newspaper crier.[190]

Though Afro-Cubans and white Cubans almost universally praised Kid Chocolate as a symbol of national pride and achievement in the competitive arenas of the north, Afro-Cubans debated the form and semantics of this valorization. From Havana to Camagüey to Santiago de Cuba, Afro-Cuban writers wrestled with the significance of Kid Chocolate's rise to fame and the example it provided for Cuban youth. For Nemesio Lavié, an author and journalist from Oriente, Afro-Cuban acknowledgment of the Cuban athlete *as an Afro-Cuban* was a self-defeating symbol of racial inferiority.[191] He argued that the language used in the praise lavished on Chocolate in the weekly newspaper section "Ideales de Una Raza" increased the racial divisions between Cubans by acknowledging that the boxer was of African descent and therefore not entirely and primarily Cuban. Though Kid Chocolate had risen to "the plane of consecration" and deserved public acknowledgment of his achievements, to list him as an Afro-Cuban implied an inherent sense of surprise at the success of those with black skin. Lavié used the opportunity to impugn the entire Afro-Cuban intellectual team that published the weekly Afro-Cuban perspective column in *Diario de la Marina*.[192]

The young writer and poet Nicolás Guillén, who closely followed Cuban boxing and paid homage to Kid Chocolate in his 1929 poem "Pequeña Oda a un Negro Boxeador," reacted with surprise and indignation to Lavié's chastisement. He defended the main target of these attacks, the section's bilingual editor Gustavo Urrútia, against the accusation that he sowed racial division by maintaining the inferiority of black Cubans through the very existence of "Ideales de Una Raza." For Guillén, Lavié misunderstood the mission of the writers who collaborated on the weekly examination of Afro-Cuban society. Lavié was "blind" to the fact that these intellectuals and poets enjoyed the esteem of their white colleagues. The writers attempted to unify the races through a critical examination of the numerous "exes on the chalkboard" placed against the advancement of Afro-Cubans. To gloss over these realities and to pretend that key differences did not exist in the social position of Afro-Cubans only exacerbated the problems. The de facto barriers experienced by Afro-Cubans would be overcome by an honest examination that highlighted such hypocrisy. Afro-Cuban public figures should learn from foreign examples of race relations and celebrate the achievements of those black Cubans who excelled in any field, be it art or athletics. Furthermore, with the understanding and support of white Cuban intellectuals and journalists, "Ideales de Una Raza" sought to bridge the racial divides inherent in modern Cuba by celebrating Afro-Cubans *as* Cubans. They sought contributions from African Americans in an attempt to forge transnational intellectual ties that would widen cultural engagement and raise the level of comparative discourse among Afro-Cubans and African Americans. Kid Chocolate served as a conduit for Afro-Cuban–African American discourse. The important issue, Guillén argued, was to celebrate cubanidad in the form of Kid Chocolate. Lavié, and those like him who had "already arrived" at elite status, were part of the problem. They prevented a straightforward acknowledgment of Cuban racial divides. Guillén further argued that to solve these national issues, writers must speak both in the "language of Cuba" and "in the Negro language, which is the language of justice." Boxing, and Kid Chocolate, were fodder for divisive ideas on how Afro-Cubans should seek advancement within a racially unequal society.[193]

In a less critical and vehemently positive vein, one writer from Camagüey expressed the national sentiment demonstrated by the enormous public affection that was codified by the governmental decree of congratulation to Kid Chocolate:

Eligio Sardiñas y Montalvo, a nineteen-year-old negrito, who was born in a miserable house in the shantytown of Cerro, in the capital of the Republic, has become a great citizen in this historic moment, admired and revered by all of his compatriots and is surrounded by the aura of an authentic national hero.[194]

In hyperbolic prose, the editorialist argued that Kid Chocolate was the greatest boxer of all time and that his celebrity rivaled that of US aviator Charles Lindbergh. The boxer was even more worthy of admiration because he was from the poorest class and claimed no exalted lineage. Yet through his dedication and natural ability he had risen to the heights of fame. He had "made a magnificent affirmation of the sporting capacity of Cubans for great undertakings and placed the name of the patria at an immeasurable height." Kid Chocolate was the paragon of a modern, democratic Cuba, where all citizens, regardless of race or class, had opportunities to ennoble the nation. He was comparable to Alexander the Great, but unlike him had earned fame through his honestly and individually attained merits, not through inheritance. Perhaps most importantly, "Kid Chocolate represents a most beautiful, edifying, educative, transcendent example for all of his compatriots and especially for his kind, the negro Cubans!" It was thanks to democracy, the same forces that transformed Abraham Lincoln from "woodcutter to statesman," that the boxer rose "from an unhappy and needy child into an idol of his people and the glory of world sport."[195]

Though the language of these tributes seems hyperbolic, it captures the national sentiment surrounding the most famous Afro-Cuban of his generation. As political and social tensions mounted and the nation was on the brink of civil war to end the dictatorship of President Gerardo Machado, the celebration of Kid Chocolate as hero-athlete was widely accepted as a point of national cohesion. Like José Martí, the young black athlete was transformed into an image deployed by opposing sides of the political spectrum. From black nationalists to the white conservative social and economic elite to the activists in the League of Communist Youth, a Cuban champion rose as a symbol of national achievement and fair play. The public embrace of Kid Chocolate's success was expressed in the language of both civic and racial nationalism: For Afro-Cubans, the boxer was the foremost example of black Cuban success; for others, his rise was proof of the opportunities for advancement that were a product of Cuban democracy.

Unlikely political groups appropriated Kid Chocolate. The dramatic language and symbolism of sport and the popular appraisal of Cuban athletes as "bulwarks" of lower-class masculinity were malleable concepts. Though Cuban sport idols, boxers in particular, achieved enormous public notoriety and rapid financial success, they were portrayed by some political activists as victims of transnational capitalism and domestic classism. An undated pamphlet from the late 1920s or early 1930s, published by the Communist Youth League of Havana, celebrated Kid Chocolate as a class hero worthy of emulation by poor Cuban youths in their struggle against the "traps" set for them by the international capitalist system in Cuba.[196] While labeling the Cuban boxer a "negrito," a racist term of paternalistic endearment often assigned to Afro-Cubans and a stock character played in blackface by white Cubans in popular theater, the Communist Youth repeatedly called for popular emulation of the athlete due to his representation of Cuban "manliness" and "self-discipline" as a "sublime example" of the perseverance of the Cuban poor.[197] Though Kid Chocolate was an example of the possibilities of lower-class Cubans, he was still unable to transcend the mocking and racist portrayals of even those who celebrated his success.

Despite losing some important matches in the United States and having his talent and potential leached by shadowy capitalist figures who sought to destroy his "crown and prestige," Chocolate represented for the Communist Youth the "prestige of [their] country." The boxer had been pushed, the league argued, into a "corrupt and disordered" lifestyle by a malevolent capitalism that used lower-class Cuban talent for its own ends before closing the door on upward mobility. Chocolate, the league implied, was further handicapped by his childlike intelligence: the credulity of the "negrito." While living in Harlem, Kid Chocolate had imbibed the Bohemian atmosphere of the late 1920s and, many writers observed, had damaged his career potential by leading a dissolute lifestyle. The Kid, according to the propagandists, had fought through this adversity and risen to "definitive and grandiose" triumph by taking control of his life to lift himself out of the "quagmire" of the class system.

The pamphleteers insisted on the worthiness of the Kid for the imitation of all Cuban youth and rhetorically asked their readers:

> How many youths don't dream of becoming a Kid in other sports and in other activities? How many don't dream of honors and laurels from his people? But their dreams are truncated when they crash against sad reality: a regime of pain and injustices that closes the doors of the future; that destroys all of their dreams and pushes them each day toward dishonor and obscurity. The Cuban youth suffers the same as Chocolate, the same disgraces of a youth who are shut out from all possibility of greatness, success and triumph.[198]

Kid Chocolate was a problematic representative of communist aspirations for a more just and equitable society. He embodied the extremes of capitalist consumption. He was popularly understood to own more than three hundred suits, nearly one for each day of the year. He drove new and expensive cars and purchased a home in the all-white suburb of Marianao. His portrayal by the Communist Youth League indicates the appropriation of his image as shorthand for larger economic and cultural issues, yet he remained firmly embedded in traditional stereotypes of black Cubans. The pamphleteers draw on recent popular memory of the Kid, self-assured that their readers would all be aware of the events that led to the athletes' defeats and interpreting them as symbolic, indeed the foremost symbol, of the plight of the Cuban poor.

As a professional athlete, Kid Chocolate utilized one of the few venues open to lower-class Afro-Cubans in challenging the "traps" laid for them by the dominant socioeconomic system that created both opportunities and limitations on social ascent. The medium of his celebrity was central to the argument of his representative cubanidad. Sport as a quintessential democratic space contingent on little more than individual merit and not upon race or class had become a tool of first resort for class mobility and the showcase of Afro-Cuban achievement in an emblematically, yet controversially modern endeavor.

## Conclusion

By the end of the 1920s, amid growing popular discontent that would culminate in the overthrow of the Machado dictatorship a few years later, sportswriters in the Cuban public sphere operated tangentially to and often at odds with broader political discourses. Civil society continued to evince a fascination with modern forms of masculine display that opened new spaces and forms of social organization. In a broader sense, these cultural shifts survived and intensified amid or even despite the tumultuous political shifts that have accounted for much of the historiographical understanding of this period.

This novel orientation of the public sphere, taking place simultaneously in many Latin American nations, has proven to be more long lasting than even the many political systems that have come and gone in the ensuing decades. Cuba, in particular, is a prime case study in the tenacity with which popular culture outlasts even the most dramatic political changes and attempts at cultural reorientation. While the Castro government disdained professional athletics as the product of capitalist cultural decadence and class exploitation, the underlying ideas about manhood, the body, and the competitive engagement of modernity have remained. Kid Chocolate's face still stares out with a confident smile, greeting passersby on the sidewalk in front of the massive Capitolio building in the most central area of Havana.[199] Félix Savón, the three-time Olympic boxing champion, advertises the local Havana television station, where he is portrayed as the most masculine of Cuban patriots.

# Conclusion

*Legacies of Domesticating the Exotic in Cuba and Mexico*

THIS BOOK EXAMINES pugilism from its controversial beginnings through its popularization in Mexico and Cuba over a period of nearly one hundred years. Boxing served as a narrative thread and a means to show processes that are connected to, but go far beyond, the confines of sport history. Prizefighting has served as a way to relate broader ideas of cultural change and the Mexican and Cuban engagement with modern transnational ideas of masculinity, national identity, and race. There are many terms used to describe the process whereby something once exotic becomes nationalized to the extent that it is a pillar of popular culture, a point of pride across the class spectrum, and an important signifier of national identity and masculinity. Whether this process is called negotiation, syncretism, or appropriation, the ever-evolving outcome is highly visible today. Modern sport is one of the few, at least perceived, legal means of upward mobility in Mexico and among economically disadvantaged Chicanos and Cubanos in the United States. As of 2019, professional sport remains illegal in Cuba.

From the 1840s to the 1940s, the popularization of boxing paralleled a broadening of the boundaries of lo cubano and lo mexicano. In the first period, elite commentators in the public sphere were split over the meanings of this cultural import. For most, the highly symbolic practice was paired with such degrading American cultural practices as lynching. Taken together, boxing, lynching, and racial discrimination were posed as a mirror and counternarrative to widespread supposition that Anglo-Saxons operated within a superior and more modern culture and were, under the dictates of a twisted Social Darwinism, superior genetic specimens. The science of eugenics and the dissemination of Spencerian cultural and racial hierarchies caused many observers across the region to search for methods through which Latin Americans could change national bodies and other elements of collective identity they deemed central to the positive evolution of their cultures.

As US influence in the form of capital, politics, and popular culture extended through Latin America in the early twentieth century, lower-class black, white, and Asian practitioners of commercialized body culture traveled and worked throughout the region. As members of the marginal classes in the United States and beyond, these boxers and wrestlers and their culture enjoyed a highly visible presence and broad influence in Mexico and Cuba. Their representation of American popular culture often ran counter to the refined ways in which the more established and conservative "American colonies" sought to present themselves.

The American victory over the Spanish in 1898 and the Japanese defeat of Russia in 1905 gave "physical cultures" (boxing, jujitsu, bodybuilding, and even sumo wrestling) from these two emergent powers the force of revealed truth: nations that cultivated and celebrated "manly arts" ascended to the apex of the Social Darwinist hierarchy. No longer tied to Victorian ideals of masculinity that celebrated refinement, reflection, and a sedate manhood, Latin Americans from across the class spectrum increasingly celebrated vigorous and muscular virility. Sports such as boxing became a salient feature of civic social organization and cultural engagement outside of traditional means of masculine self-representation. Where once the military or dueling provided proving grounds for aristocratic honor, sport now provided a cross-class interest where once marginal Cubans and Mexicans became national symbols of excellence.

The newly popular practice of imported blood sport challenged government regulation of public entertainments. With no regulatory infrastructure for combat sport in place, the police and government officials played a game of catch-up with the evolving tastes of the populace. The vacillating and decades-long process that culminated in the legalization of prizefighting across Latin America by the early 1920s showed political and cultural resistance and later accommodation to what was, from the early nineteenth century, deemed "Anglo-Saxon barbarism." Cultural critics, mainly in the growing press, argued in the early years of the twentieth century that the appropriation of modern sport would have regenerative effects for the masculine nation as a whole. Among other factors, the cultural spread of muscular masculinity would make good soldiers and brace Cubans and Mexicans for the challenges of modern, urban life. These justifications often appeared as apologies, seeking to elevate popular passions to the level of national honor.

The often theoretical debate among the elite was largely overridden by the more immediate and widespread celebration of local *boxers del patio* (local boxers) who rose to fame and wealth in the 1920s. The cultural elite, men such as Federico

Gamboa and, had he lived longer, José Martí had or would have had to stomach a grudging acceptance of imported blood sport as a feature of working-class culture. This inclusion of boxing as Mexican and Cuban public spectacle was a thoroughly transnational process, and the sites where these dramatic narratives unfolded were largely made possible by new media, especially radio and the popular press. The availability of cheap written sources, such as *El Imparcial* in Mexico and *El Mundo* in Cuba, reacted to and helped constitute the lucrative market of new consumers of athletic news from abroad. They guided governments in the first tentative steps toward making new regulations, and they fueled public engagement with local and international events and celebrities, often citing men such as Luis Ángel Firpo (Argentina), Rodolfo Casanova (Mexico), Eladio Valdéz (Cuba), Jack Johnson, Jack Dempsey, and Georges Carpentier as archetypes of modern manhood worthy of imitation.

Government was most often an actor of secondary importance. It provided the resistance against which civil society molded the meaning of prizefighting. The enormous affective power of these public spectacles alone makes them worthy of study, explanation, and an attempt to understand the meanings they held for the millions who shared in the creation of that broader social and cultural meaning. Attempts to prohibit the implantation of boxing failed as practitioners and fans took boxing underground or to areas of uncertain jurisdiction. Temporary legalizations and the first steps toward regulation followed. By the 1920s, governments facilitated the culture of boxing as a site where national heroes were created and translated, first in the public sphere and only later valorized by official recognition. Sport became one of the few avenues through which members of the lower classes—Afro-Cuban laborers and newspaper criers, Mexican shop workers and miners—came to symbolize mexicanidad and cubanidad in the transnational public sphere. Ideally, at least, Mexicans and Cubans challenged cultural and physical dominance of US Americans and other foreigners on the leveling plane of a meritocratic, rule-driven, and popular pursuit.

Central in this evolution from foreign barbarism into nationalism was the broadening of social spaces for participation embodied in new social clubs and qualitative shifts in media coverage that privileged commentary on foreign and local transnational cultures. In the 1890s, thousands of Mexicans voted with their feet, boarding trains to view a prizefight between foreigners in a neighboring state where it was tenuously legal. By the 1920s, millions had spent hard-earned pesos to attend bouts where Mexicans, literally wrapped in the flag, challenged foreign boxers who had claimed the title "Champion of Mexico."

In early twentieth-century Cuba, one of the few examples of Afro-Cuban achievement celebrated by the national elite was Antonio Maceo, the martyred hero of the hero of the wars for independence. By the 1920s, writers and politicians paired him with Afro-Cuban boxers who became *"champions de la patria."* In Mexico, lower-class boxers were among the first working-class individuals to be touted as evidence of Mexican accomplishment abroad in a medium dominated by foreigners.

By the late 1920s, Cubans and Mexicans from around the national territories expressed themselves as members of transnational public, aficionados, or the "fancy" that consumed highly theatrical images of virile masculinity. The rise of Mexican and Cuban boxers in this period served as a mechanism through which these aficionados were further drawn into international events, often expressing their allegiances in forceful language that evoked racial solidarity and regional and national identities. New publications such as *Nocaut* in Cuba and *Afición* in Mexico catered to the enormous popularity of what once had been an exotic and raffish sampling of lower-class American culture. These specialized media sources provided outlets for the expression of what had become "national passions."

By de-centering the state and working in the interstices between elite and popular cultures, this narrative complicates our understanding of how Mexican and Cuban cultures evolved against the backdrop of the upheavals of the early twentieth century. The popular cultures of sport have been deployed by and have outlasted political regimes. In the case of Revolutionary Cuba, boxing serves as a point of legitimacy for the regime. For a sugar cane cutter from the rural interior of Cuba to name himself "Black Dempsey" and take up a marginal sport as a means of self-advancement illustrates an early strain of globalization absent from most historiography of Latin America during this period.

This study has also complicated generalizations of Cuban and Mexican culture in this period that focus on the imitative elite that appropriated transnational ideas in a mimetic and unreflective fashion. By showing the resistance, debates, and transformations cast upon ideological and even corporeal levels, it demonstrates the need to re-evaluate the metrics used to determine abstractions such as tradition and authenticity. The diversity of cultural factors that constituted lo cubano and lo mexicano in the public sphere looked very different in 1930 than they had in 1890. The affective power of celebrity, the cult of virile masculinity, and suppositions about the innate valences of the racialized body and sport, as Hobsbawm argued, constituted one of the most important new social factors at the end of the nineteenth century. It is now problematic to approach the cultural history of Latin America without understanding the cross-class, interracial, and transnational significance of sport as a rallying point and bearer of meaning for millions across the region.

# Notes

## Preface

1. Román Vidal Tamayo, "Tepito: impulsor del boxeo en México," *Casa del Tiempo* 99 (2007), 30.

## Chapter One

1. See figure 14.
2. Helg, *Our Rightful Share*, chap. 5.
3. See figure 12.
4. Habermas, *The Structural Transformation of the Public Sphere*.
5. For similar arguments, see Elias and Dunning, *Quest for Excitement*; Christesen, *Sport and Democracy in the Ancient and Modern Worlds*; Elsey, *Citizens and Sportsmen*.
6. Moore, *Nationalizing Blackness*, 1–12; Tarica, *The Inner Life of Mestizo Nationalism*, 1–30.
7. The creation of the "athlete-hero-star-celebrity" followed a similar chronology in US popular culture. See Tudor, *Hollywood's Vision of Team Sports*, 3–32.
8. R. W. Connell and James W. Messerschmidt, "Hegemonic Masculinity: Rethinking the Concept," in *Gender and Society* 19, no. 6 (Dec. 2005): 832.
9. Hoganson, *Fighting for American Manhood*, 17, 1–14.
10. Justo Sierra, "En tierra yankee: notas a todo vapor," *El Mundo Ilustrado*, August 21, 1898. See also Rubén Darío's poem "A Roosevelt" (1904), in Darío, *Antología poética*, 144–46. They are among many Latin American portrayals of the United States as a muscular behemoth devoid of intellectual or spiritual depth.
11. Hart, *Empire and Revolution*, 7–46; Beezley, *Judas at the Jockey Club*.
12. Beezley, *Judas at the Jockey Club*, 3–13.
13. José Martí, "Una pelea de premio," *La Opinión Nacional* (Caracas), March 4, 1882.
14. "Correspondencia del Diario de la Marina," *Diario de la Marina*, February 22, 1882.
15. *La Lucha*, December 29, 1906; January 14, 1907; *Diario de la Marina*, May 4, 1907.
16. Iglesias Utset, *A Cultural History of Cuba During the U.S. Occupation*, 1–10, 88–100.
17. Bartra, *Blood, Ink, and Culture*; Schelling, *Through the Kaleidoscope*; Canclini, *Hybrid*

*Cultures*; Joseph, LeGrand, and Salvatore, *Close Encounters of Empire*; and Larraín, *Modernity and Identity in Latin America*.

18. Salvador Esperón, "El boxeo científico" (unpublished manuscript), Archivo General de la Nación (Mexico, hereafter AGN), Propiedad Artística y Literaria, Caja 684, exp. 8.

19. Helg, *Our Rightful Share*. The Partido Independiente de Color (Independent Party of Color) was outlawed and persecuted and its members and other Afro-Cubans were massacred in 1912.

20. Iglesias Utset, *A Cultural History of Cuba During the U.S. Occupation*, 52.

21. Ferrer, *Insurgent Cuba*, 7.

22. "Charla pugilística," *Diario de la Marina*, November 18, 1922; "Un beneficio para uno que lo merece," *El Mundo*, July 1, 1924.

23. Menéndez and Ortega, *Kid Chocolate*.

24. Enver M. Casimir, "Contours of Transnational Contact: Kid Chocolate, Cuba, and the United States in the 1920s and 1930s." *Journal of Sport History* 39, no. 3 (2012): 487–506.

25. Vianna, *O mistério do samba*.

26. *Cuba News*, February 27, 1915.

27. Beattie, *The Tribute of Blood*.

28. Elsey, *Citizens and Sportsmen*, 1–16, 42, 45, 59.

29. Pérez, "Between Baseball and Bullfighting," 493–517.

30. Clifford Geertz, *The Interpretation of Cultures* (New York: Basic Books, 1973), 5.

31. In particular his study of the impact of North American popular culture in Pérez, *On Becoming Cuban*. On sport and the forging of an anticolonial Cuban national identity see Pérez, "Between Baseball and Bullfighting," 493–517.

32. Buffington, *A Sentimental Education for the Working Man*, intro.

33. Anderson, *Imagined Communities*.

34. Two works that distill the connections between prizefighting and nationalism, for an earlier and later period, respectively, are Ronald Schechter and Liz Clarke, *Mendoza the Jew: Boxing, Manliness, and Nationalism* (New York: Oxford University Press, 2014); and Allen, *A History of Boxing in Mexico*.

35. For studies on the process of urbanization in Mexico City under the dictatorship of Porfirio Díaz, see Piccato, *City of Suspects*; Bliss, *Compromised Positions*; Johns, *The City of Mexico in the Age of Díaz*; and Schell, *Integral Outsiders*. For Cuba, see Iglesias Utset, *Las metáforas del cambio en la vida cotidiana*; Sippial, *Prostitution, Modernity, and the Making of the Cuban Republic*; García, *Beyond the Walled City*.

36. *El Mundo*, March 23, 1910.

37. See figures in the photo gallery.

38. Aladar Hajdu was Hungarian Jewish photographer who operated the Rembrandt Studio in Havana. His nude image of Kid Chocolate occupied a full page in the September 1931 issue of *Social*.

39. Mora, *Mexican Cinema: Reflections of a Society*, 80.

40. Allen, *A History of Boxing in Mexico*, 57.

41. The Mexican consulate in Los Angeles hosted a public exhibition of the film

*Campeon Sin Corona* to celebrate the bicentennial of independence in 2010. http://mexico2010encalifornia.org/boletinenero2010z.htm, accessed September 19, 2010.

42. The 1923 bout in which the Argentine Luis Ángel Firpo, "The Wild Bull of the Pampas," fought the American "Half Breed" Jack Dempsey captured the imagination of thousands of Mexicans and Cubans. This will be examined in depth in chapters 3 and 4. Firpo, who in reality was an attendant in a drugstore in Buenos Aires before taking up boxing, was portrayed to a transnational audience as the quintessential Argentine cowboy of the pampas.

43. Runstedtler, *Jack Johnson, Rebel Sojourner*, 1.

44. This is examined further in chapter 4.

45. *Diario de la Marina*, April 7, 1848; April 2, 1857.

46. Huesca, *Diccionario hípico y del sport*, 609.

47. A word search on the tool Google Ngram gives precise numerical registers for printed material.

48. This attempt by the city bureaucracies to change basic rules is examined in chapter 2.

49. Warshaw, *The New Latin America*, vii, 209.

50. Stepan, *The Hour of Eugenics*.

51. Hobsbawm, *The Invention of Tradition*, 299–300.

52. A paper read at the annual meeting of the American Historical Association, held in Cincinnati, December 28, 1988. Published in *American Historical Review* 94, no. 1. (Feb. 1989): 1–10.

53. Guy Debord, *Society of the Spectacle*, cited in Markowitz, *Racial Spectacles*, 4.

54. Schwarz, *Spectacular Realities*, 2.

55. Runstedtler, *Jack Johnson, Rebel Sojourner*, 6–7.

56. Matthew C. Gutmann, "Discarding Manly Dichotomies in Latin America," in Gutmann, *Changing Men and Masculinities in Latin America*, 1–26.

57. Víctor Macías-Gonzalez and Anne Rubenstein, "Masculinity and History in Modern Mexico," in *Masculinity and Sexuality in Modern Mexico*, ed. Víctor Macías-Gonzales and Anne Rubenstein (Albuquerque: University of New Mexico Press, 2012), 2.

58. Mosse, *The Image of Man*.

59. Bederman, *Manliness and Civilization*, 8.

60. President Donald Trump recently granted Jack Johnson a posthumous pardon for his conviction of violating the Mann Act, also known as the White Slave Traffic Act. "Trump Pardons Jack Johnson," *New York Times*, May 24, 2018.

61. Many of these journeyman boxers and "professors of sport," such as the African American Kid Mitchell and the Afro-Dutch islander Jim Smith, will be examined in the following chapters.

62. The best among these are J. A. Mangan, "The Early Evolution of Modern Sport in Latin America: A Mainly Middle English Middle-Class Inspiration," and Joseph Arbena, "The Later Evolution of Modern Sport in Latin America: The North American Influence," in Mangan and Dacosta, *Sport in Latin American Society*, 9–42, 43–58.

63. This need was most recently recognized by Laura Podalsky in her introduction to Sheinin, *Sports Culture in Latin American History*, 1–15.

64. On boxing in Colombia, see David M. K. Sheinin, "Boxing in the Making of a Colombian *Costeño* Identity," in Sheinin, *Sports Culture in Latin American History*, 137–58.

65. I borrow the definition of modern sport from Huggins, *The Victorians and Sport*.

66. *Diario de México*, March 10, 1806; "Pugilato, Londres," *Diario de México*, April 9, 1810.

67. Gorn, *The Manly Art*. Other helpful works include Riess, *Sport in Industrial America, 1850–1920*. For a study of boxing and its wider implications for race and masculinity, see Early, *The Culture of Bruising*. The literature on boxing and culture in Latin America is much more limited. Two important exceptions are Stephen D. Allen's *A History of Boxing in Mexico* and David M. K. Sheinin's "Boxing in the Making of a Colombian *Costeño* Identity," in Sheinin, *Sports Culture in Latin American History*, 137–58. Both of those studies focus on periods subsequent to the focus of this book. For popular sources, see, for Cuba, Encinoso, *Azúcar y chocolate*; Encinoso, *Hard Leather*; and Menéndez and Ortega, *Kid Chocolate*; for Mexico see Maldonado and Zámora, *Historia del box mexicano*.

68. Beezley, *Judas at the Jockey Club*. For an account of a select few civil social organizations see Pérez, *On Becoming Cuban*; and Guridy, *Forging Diaspora*.

69. Piccato, "Politics and the Technology of Honor."

70. Campos, *Home Grown*, 84.

71. Ricardo, *La imprenta en Cuba*.

72. Quoted in Piccato, "Public Sphere in Latin America," 165.

73. Anderson, *Imagined Communities*.

74. Piccato, "Public Sphere in Latin America," 167–68.

75. See Norton, *Norton's Complete Handbook of Havana and Cuba*, 142–44.

76. Figures cited in Beezley and Meyer, *The Oxford History of Mexico*, 409; and Lear, *Workers, Neighbors, and Citizens*, 52–54.

77. Consejo Nacional de Población, *México Demográfico* (México DF, 1978), 78. Ricardo Urioste, *Annuario Mexicano, 1982* (México DF, 1982), 72–73; cited in Hayes-Bautista, Schink, and Chapa, *The Burden of Support*.

78. Dominguez, *Cuba: Order and Revolution*, 71–72.

79. Ibid.

80. Rama, *The Lettered City*, 112.

## Chapter Two

1. My understanding of the public sphere follows Jürgen Habermas and Pablo Piccato as it applied to Mexico in this period. The public sphere is the conglomeration of social spaces, from voluntary clubs to newspapers to venues of public spectacle, where opinions and preferences are formed, debated, and challenged. The public sphere was where many of these cultural debates took place in Porfirian Mexico: newspapers, clubs, bullrings, and theaters. See Piccato, *The Tyranny of Opinion*.

2. The disruptive presence of new "modern" behaviors such as bicycle riding and the Porfirian reactions to it have been detailed by Beezley in *Judas at the Jockey Club*.

3. Buffington, *Criminal and Citizen in Modern Mexico*, 53.

4. Throughout the colonial era and after Mexican independence, risqué theater performances were censured and prohibited by local authorities. Boxing as public spectacle, however, was largely unknown and it created confusions of jurisdiction. All censorship of public spectacle was under the control of local authorities until 1917, when the new the Mexican constitution federalized the censorship of moving pictures.

5. See figure 22.

6. On the enforcement of Article 33, see Pablo Yankelovich, "Extranjeros indeseables en México (1911–1940): Una aproximación cuantitiva a la aplicación del artículo 33 constitucional" *Historia Mexicana* LIII, núm. 3 (2004), 693–744.

7. Piccato, *The Tyranny of Opinion*, 1–26.

8. Buffington, *A Sentimental Education for the Working Man*.

9. Schell, *Integral Outsiders*, 65–67.

10. Matthews, *The Civilizing Machine*.

11. See Schell, *Integral Outsiders*; and Ruiz, *Americans in the Treasure House*.

12. Bunker, *Creating Mexican Consumer Culture*; and Buffington, *A Sentimental Education for the Working Man*.

13. Piccato, *Tyranny of Opinion*; Bunker, *Creating Mexican Consumer Culture*; Sanders, *The Vanguard of the Atlantic World*.

14. Gorn, *The Manly Art*, 69–81.

15. Rudolfo Palma Rojo, Gabriela Pulido Llano, and Emma Yanes Rizo, *Rumberas, boxeadores, y mártires: el ocio en el siglo XX* (México, DF: Instituto Nacional de Antropología, 2013), 69–87.

16. "Adelantos de la civilización," *El Popular*, June 21, 1900.

17. *Gaceta de México*, August 13, 1806; *Diario de México*, March 10, 1806; "Pugilato, Londres," *Diario de México*, April 9, 1810.

18. "Filadelfia," *Gazeta de México*, April 16, 1852, April 7, 1825, December 18, 1825; "Estados Unidos: Ensayos del pugilato en el Senado," *El Universal*, November 25, 1850. Manuel Larrainzar equated British boxing with barbarism and Hispanic traditions of cockfighting and bullfighting as the "favorite pastimes of a *certain part* of society." Larrainzar, *Estudios Sobre La Historia de América*, 230–31. E. Harris and another fighter identified as "A. Champion" petitioned the Cabildo to approve a wrestling exhibition, stressing that no pugilism would be involved. Mexico City and Ignacio Bejarano, *Actas de Cabildo del Ayuntamiento Constitucional de México* (México: Impr. del "Socialista," 1884).

19. The search tool Google Ngram shows a dramatic increase in the instances of the term "pugilato" in Spanish in printed material from the 1860s to the end of the nineteenth century.

20. Navarro, *Calendario de Juan R. Navarro*, 62–65. María José Esparza Liberal, "Los calendarios mexicanos en el siglo XIX, una publicación popular," *Boletín de Monumentos Históricos*, Tercera Época, Núm. 18, Enero-Abril, 2010, 132–46.

21. See Buffington, *A Sentimental Education for the Working Man*. On social segregation in this period as an extension of Social Darwinism, see Alicia Castellanos Guerrero, Aída Isela González, Cristina Oemichen, and María Dolores París Pombo, *Imágenes del racismo en México* (México, DF: Palza & Valdes, 2003).

22. Juvenal, "Charla de Domingos," *El Monitor Republicano*, May 29, 1887. Duclós Salinas, *The Riches of Mexico and Its Institutions*, 423; Cabrera Acevedo, *La Suprema Corte de Justicia durante el fortalecimiento del Porfirismo*.

23. Francisco González, "Boletín del Monitor," *El Monitor Republicano*, May 31, 1887.

24. Ibid.

25. *La Voz de México*, June 12, 1892.

26. Olavarría y Ferrari, *Reseña histórica del teatro en México*, 605.

27. E. P. Gaston, "La Asociación Cristiana," *El Partido Liberal*, December 4, 1894. Santibáñez, *Mexico; revista de sociedad, arte y letras*.

28. The YMCA, by the late nineteenth century, was a global organization that sought to expand the ideas of "muscular Christianity" that were prevalent in Protestant American thinking in this era. See Putney, *Muscular Christianity*, 1–11.

29. Lobato and Escudero were put forth as superb physical specimens and were included in an 1893 study by the Mexican biologist Alfonso L. Herrera of the effects of environment on the development of physique. Herrera and Escobar, *La vie sur les hauts plateaux*, 285, 400.

30. *El Partido Liberal*, December 4, 1894; *El Mundo*, December 9, 1894.

31. *El Tiempo*, January 17, 1910.

32. Eugene Sandow was a well-known figure in Mexico. His name was used to market bodybuilding equipment to transform men into a "modern Hercules." "Sandow: El Hercules Moderno," *La Voz de Mexico*, August 16, 1899; *El Siglo Diez y Nueve*, August 16, 1894; "Alrededor del Mundo," *El Siglo Diez y Nueve*, August 16, 1894.

33. Figueroa Domenech, *Guía general descriptiva de la República Mexicana*, 622.

34. "Circulo de Gimnásia Mexicana," *El Monitor Republicano*, April 19, 1890; Lobato also gave speeches on physical education and Mexican youth to Mexican Society of Pedagogic Studies.

35. José María Alvarez, *Añoranzas*, 7.

36. Ernesto Lobato, "Gimnástica," in *Conferencias científicas de los alumnus de la Escuela Nacional Preparatoria* (México: Imprenta de "La Voz de Oriente," 1891), 185–94. For an overview of the impact of Lombrosian and Spencerian ideas of positive eugenics in Latin America, see Stepan, *The Hour of Eugenics*, chaps. 2 and 5.

37. Stepan, *The Hour of Eugenics*; Lobato, "Gimnástica."

38. Lobato, "Gimnástica," 193. Emphasis added.

39. "Mexico. Secretaria de instrucción pública," *Boletín de instrucción pública* 19, no. 4, (1912): 499.

40. "To the Public," *The Mexican Sportsman*, September 5, 1896.

41. Though I have not been able to consult the document, there is a card listing for William A. Clark requesting permission to hold a boxing match in the bullring of

Guatemala City in late 1894. Archivo General de Centro America, Juegos y Diversiones, Leg. 3602 Exp. 83051. Clarke was listed as an "engineer" in a civil registry document in Mexico City.

42. *The Mexican Sportsman*, September 12, 1895; September 19, 1895; September 26, 1895. The early Mexican boxer Policarpo Santa Maria remembered following Billy Clarke on the streets of Mexico City as a child. Clarke ate regularly at the lunch counter run by Santa Maria's mother and encouraged the young man to box. See Talán, *Y . . . Fueron Idolos!*

43. Nicholson, *Hitters, Dancers and Ring Magicians*; Beezley, *Judas at the Jockey Club*; Fields, *James J. Corbett*.

44. Archivo Histórico del Distrito Federal, *Diversiones Públicas*, Tomo 804, Numero 840.

45. *Mexican Herald*, January 28, 1896.

46. *El Siglo Diez y Nueve*, November 31 1895; "Sparring Exhibition," *Mexican Herald*, October 9, 1895.

47. *El Globo*, December 4, 1895. Also see Beezley, *Judas at the Jockey Club*, 32.

48. *Mexican Herald*, November 24, 1894; Olavarría y Ferrari, *Reseña histórica del teatro en México*, 605–6.

49. *Mexican Herald*, October 9, 1895, October 25, 1895; *La Voz de México*, November 19, 1895.

50. *El Mundo*, December 1, 1895.

51. Gorn, *The Manly Art*, 222.

52. "Athletic Battle in Pachuca," *El Demócrata*, November 26, 1895.

53. "Love at First Sight: A Hidalgo Damsel to Wed Billy A. Clark [sic]," *The Two Republics*, January 22, 1896.

54. "Matrimonio con un pugilista" (Matrimony with a pugilist), *El Demócrata*, July 23, 1896.

55. "Los pugilistas quieren balazos," *El Siglo Diez y Nueve*, November 29, 1895.

56. *El Globo*, December 4, 1895.

57. Ibid. This episode is also recounted in Valadés, *El porfirismo: historia de un régimen*, and Juan Felipe Leal, Carlos Arturo Flores Villela, and Eduardo Barraza, *Anales del cine en Mexico, 1895–1911* (México: Voyeur, 2007).

58. Flores, *Telegramas en el Archivo Historicó*, 140–42. Díaz also dispatched "agents" to the border to report on the bout. *La Voz de México* (Mexico City), February 16, 1896. This order was enacted in Ciudad Juárez. Ciudad Juárez Municipal Archive (CJMA), MF 513, part 1, roll 8.

59. See figure 22.

60. "Me moro" is likely a depiction of an incorrect conjugation of the verb *morir* (to die); *me muero* would mean "I'm dying."

61. *El Mundo*, December 1, 1895. Lilly Clay was a British-born American burlesque actress who toured Mexico in the 1890s. Her shows caused scandals in México. O'Neill, *How He Does It*.

62. Ibid.

63. *El Mundo*, December 1, 1895.
64. "El match de Pachuca y la amnistia á las duelistas," *El Mundo*, December 1, 1895.
65. *El Mundo*, December 1, 1895.
66. "Billy Clarke's Mishap," *Mexican Herald*, May 15, 1896; "Los que se casan," *Diario del Hogar*, January 22, 1896.
67. See multiple case files for Billy A. Clarke: Archivo General de la Nación, Tribunal Superior de Justícia del Distrito Federal (TSJDF); Caja C-1475.
68. Ibid.; "Billy Clarke's Mishap," *Mexican Herald*, May 15, 1896.
69. Lic. D. Rafael Rebollar, *Álbum conmemorativo de la construcción e inauguración de la penitenciaría de México* (México DF: Compañía Litográfica y Tipográfica, 1900), 9–10; "The Troubles of Billy Clarke," *Mexican Herald*, October 8, 1896.
70. *El Contemporaneo*, January 15, 1898.
71. *El Demócrata*, January 11, 1896.
72. "Clarke in Effigy," *Mexican Herald*, September 9, 1897.
73. "Libertad del pugilista Clarke," *El Mundo*, November 4, 1896.
74. "Charla de domingos," *El Monitor Republicano*, October 11, 1896.
75. "El combate pugilistico: merecida sentencia, carcel y multas," *El Monitor Republicano*, October 14, 1896.
76. Braniff owned massive haciendas and wielded political influence in Mexico City. He would later serve as a mediator between Porfirio Díaz and Francisco Madero.
77. "At Billy Clarke's," *Mexican Herald*, July 5, 1897.
78. "Sabe Vivir," *El Popular*, September 2, 1897.
79. "Chamusquinas," *El País*, August 25, 1897.
80. "Las costumbres y las leyes: problema social," *La Patria de México*, July 29, 1897.
81. *El Mundo*, December 1, 1895.
82. Ibid.
83. "Progresamos: hacia el salvajismo (We are progressing toward savagery)," article from *El Tiempo*, quoted in *La Voz de México*, November 29, 1895.
84. Gamboa, *Mi diario*, 258.
85. Ireneo Paz, "Las costumbres y las leyes," *La Patria*, July 29, 1897.
86. "La civilización al servicio del salvajismo," *El Mundo*, March 20, 1898.
87. Archivo Estatal del Distrito Federal, Libro de Actas de Nacimientos, entry for "Ana Clarke y Barrón," January 15, 1897.
88. Archivo Estatal del Distrito Federal, Registro Civil del Distrito Federal, courtesy of the Academia Mexicana de Genealogia y Heraldica.
89. *Mexican Herald*, September 24, 1897.
90. "Fragments," *The Evening Telegram*, August 23, 1897.
91. "The Showmen Were Mobbed," *El Paso Herald*, August 6, 1900.
92. "Exhibition of Strength," *El Paso Daily Herald*, July 16, 1900.
93. Talán, *Y . . . Fueron Idolos!*
94. Clarke was the first foreign athlete often referred to as "champion of Mexico." "Los campeones luchadores," *El Continente Americano*, June 21, 1899.

95. "Notable Pugilistic 'Match,'" *El Imparcial*, September 15, 1905; "In the Cosmopolitan Club," *El Tiempo*, September 23, 1905.
96. "On Sport," *Gaceta de Policía*, November 19, 1905.
97. Luis G. Urbina (writing under pseudonym "x.y.z"), "Mexico in the Open Air: Games and Diversions," *El Siglo Diez y Nueve*, August 10, 1892; Olea Franco, *Literatura mexicana del otro fin de siglo*, 375.
98. "De Sport," *El Imparcial*, November 8, 1905.
99. "Escuela de pugilato," *La Voz de México*, August 8, 1908.
100. Similar arguments are explored in the Chilean case in Elsey, *Citizens and Sportsmen*, 1–17.
101. "Mexico Bars Prizefight," *Atlanta Constitution*, November 17, 1895; "Big Fellows Sign Articles," *Courier Journal* (Louisville), November 17, 1905.
102. "General Chronicle," *El Mundo*, November 21, 1905; "The Colín-Esperón Match," *El Mundo Ilustrado*, November 26, 1905.
103. "Neoyorkinas" (Things from York), *Diario del Hogar*, January 14, 1905.
104. The poet Carpio refers to is José Juan Tablada. Tablada was angered by this insult and recorded part of the article in his diary. Sandow refers to Eugene Sandow, then the most famous bodybuilder in the world. *El Tiempo*, September 21, 1905; Tablada and Sheridan, *Diario*, 59–60.
105. See figures 2, 3, 15, and 16.
106. "A Buddhist Sermon," *El Mundo Ilustrado*, April 23, 1905.
107. "On Society," *La Patria*, January 20, 1905; "In the Capital," *El Correo Español*, January 28, 1905.
108. "Exhibición Atlética," *El Tiempo*, July 29, 1905.
109. "Notas de la semana," *El Tiempo*, July 30, 1905.
110. As noted previously, the term "científico" was broadly used to describe Porfirian positivists.
111. "Ugartechea: Científico," *México Industrial*, June 15, 1905.
112. "The 'Olimpic' Club [sic]," *El Mundo Ilustrado*, July 23, 1905.
113. Manuel Flores, "Which Is the Best Sport?," *El Mundo Ilustrado*, July 23, 1905.
114. Manuel Flores, "The Moral 'Sport,'" *El Mundo Ilustrado*, September 24, 1905.
115. "El Club Atlético 'Ugartechea,'" *El Mundo Ilustrado*, August 13, 1905.
116. "De Sport," *El País*, October 22, 1905.
117. Esperón birth record: Archivo General del Gobierno del Estado de Oaxaca, Civil Registration Births, 1861–1930, 1879, vol. 22.
118. "Colín-Esperón Match," *El Imparcial*, November 19, 1905.
119. "Sport in Mexico: Notable Progress: The Olimpic Club," *El Mundo*, July 24, 1905.
120. *El Mundo*, February 23, 1906.
121. *El Imparcial*, February 25, 1906.
122. Burgos, *Playing America's Game*, 103–4; Peter C. Bjarkman, *Baseball With a Latin Beat* (London: McFarland, 1994), 198.
123. "At the Olympic Club," *El Mundo*, November 5, 1905.

124. "On Sport: Today's Exhibition" *El Imparcial*, November 15, 1905.
125. "Energetic Stance Taken by the Governor of the District," *Diario del Hogar*, November 26, 1905.
126. Katz, *The Life and Times of Pancho Villa*, 186. Mexico, *Memoria de la Secretaría de Gobernación* (México: Imprenta del gobierno federal, 1906), 442.
127. "Prohibits Boxing Match: Governor of the District Refuses Permission," *Mexican Herald*, November 16, 1905.
128. "On Sport: The Great Boxing Match at the Cosmopolitan Club," *El País*, November 16, 1905.
129. "On Sport . . .," *Gaceta de Policía*, November 19, 1905.
130. Jack London, "English Race Likes a Fight," *Indianapolis News*, June 29, 1910.
131. This Pablo Escandón is likely the same who was later appointed governor of Morelos by Porfirio Díaz in 1908. According to historian F. Katz, Escandón did more than any other person to create the intolerable conditions that led to the uprising of Emiliano Zapata. See Katz, *The Life and Times of Pancho Villa*, 186.
132. "De Sport," *El Imparcial*, November 18, 1905.
133. Schell, *Integral Outsiders*, 160.
134. "Notas de la Semana," *El Tiempo*, November 26, 1905.
135. Arenas Guzmán, *El periodismo en la Revolución Mexicana*, 158.
136. Buffington, *A Sentimental Education for the Working Man*.
137. "El campeonato de box," *El Mundo*, November 21, 1905.
138. "Crónica General," *El Mundo*, November 21, 1905.
139. "On Sport," *Gaceta de Policia*, November 19, 1905.
140. "Crónica General," *El Mundo*, November 21, 1905.
141. "He Trained in Belem," *Mexican Herald*, November 24, 1905.
142. "Out After Eight Days," *Mexican Herald*, November 22, 1905.
143. "Big Banquet for Colín," *Mexican Herald*, November 22, 1905; "Feasts and Ovations," *Mexican Herald*, November 21, 1905.
144. Among them were Kid Mitchell (El Paso), Kid Levigne (African American "Champion of Acapulco," origin unknown), "The Original Hicks" (African American from Pennsylvania), "Black Satin" (Chicago), Joe Maljoy (African American or Cuban American from Kentucky), "Battling Kid Mulligan" (Brooklyn, NY).
145. "Mitchell Draws Color Line," *Mexican Herald*, September 13, 1905.
146. Archivo General de la Nació, TSJDF, Caja 0374, Exp. 065562; Caja 0413, Exp. 074052.
147. José B. Velasco, "A Pleasant Fiesta: Our Youth," and "The National Apprehension," *La Gaceta de Guadalajara*, January 7, 1906.
148. "Championship Fight Exhibition Today," *Mexican Herald*, April 20, 1909.
149. "For Fifteen Rounds," *Mexican Herald*, October 17, 1905.
150. "Young Woman Drinks Acid from Goblet," *El Paso Herald*, December 19, 1905.
151. "Kid Mitchilla [sic]," Acervo Histórico de la Secretaría de Relaciones Exteriores (Mexico City), 17-27-305.

152. His landlord was the future women's rights activist Refugio de Goribar de Cortina. AGN, Tribunal Supremo de Justícia del D.F., Caja 0504, exp. 088506.
153. "Will Not Fight Negro ... Kid Mitchell Is Willing," *Mexican Herald*, November 11, 1905.
154. "Davis and Lavigne Quit Ring with Good Records," *Mexican Herald*, August 25, 1908.
155. *Mexican Herald*, July 7, 1907.
156. For a detailed study of the Cananea massacre see Eugenia Meyer, Cynthia Rading, Martha Rocha, and Guadalupe Villa, *La Lucha obrera en Cananea, 1906* (México, DF: Secretaría del Trabajo y Previsión Social, 1980); and Vanderwood, *Disorder and Progress Bandits*.
157. *The Mexican Herald*, August 26, 1907; August 27, 1907; November 29, 1907.
158. Archivo General de la Nación, Registro de Extranjeros, Holandeses, No. 9518.
159. This period saw the rise of border cities like Ciudad Juárez and Tijuana as permissive zones where border-crossing Americans could enjoy disreputable and often illegal pursuits like boxing and horse racing, even before the advent of prohibition increased the appeal of these neighboring vice havens. Ciudad Juárez became known by a series of sordid nicknames such as "New Sodom," "Black City of Mexico," and "Swamp of Immorality." Katz, *The Life and Times of Pancho Villa*, 268; Martínez, *Border Boom Town*, 30, 103.
160. *Bisbee Daily Review*, May 5, 1903. On Ennis as an inventor and miner see the *Mexican Mining Journal* 6 (August 1908): 28; and "Claimant Adrew Ennis," United States, *Arbitration Series* [State Department] (Washington: US Government Printing Office, 1940), 132–33.
161. Division of Passport Control: Passport Applications for Declarants, 1907–1911 and 1914–1920. NARA Microfilm Publication ARC 1244178: A1 538. US National Archives, Washington, DC, General Records of the Department of State, Record Group 59.
162. Though Kid Mitchell received laudatory press coverage in this period, he was later remembered by the boxer Policarpo Santa Maria as an arrogant, tobacco-chewing, dirty fighter who spit alcohol in the eyes of his opponents. Talán, *Y ... Fueron Idolos!*
163. One writer for the newspaper *Excelsior* remembered Kid Mitchell and Kid Levigne as "those two darkies" who drew huge crowds in the years immediately prior to the Mexican Revolution. *Excelsior*, October 3, 1922; "Kid Levigne Pays a Visit to Mexico," *Mexican Herald*, March 26, 1910; *El Paso Herald*, April 20, 1910; *El Imparcial*, February 27, 1910; *Mexican Herald*, March 3, 1910; March 15, 1910; *El Diario*, August 2, 1909; *El Diario*, July 25, 1910.
164. Appadurai, *Modernity at Large*, 110.
165. Mauricio Tenorio-Trillo, "1910 Mexico City: Space and Nation in the City of the Centerario," in Beezley and Lorey, *¡Viva Mexico!*, 167–90. Tenorio-Trillo shows convincingly that the elaborate centennial celebrations marked both the high-water mark and the beginning of the end of the Porfirian ideals of modernity and cosmopolitanism in the Mexican capital. As John Mraz and Pablo Piccato have shown, the media played a central and highly regulated role in the representation of Mexico City as a paragon of modernity. See Mraz, *Looking for Mexico* and Piccato, *The Tyranny of Opinion*.

166. This transition forms much of the substance of chapter 3.

167. Salvador Esperón was an interpreter of Nahuatl poetry who became a boxing instructor for the Mexican military. Patricio Martínez Arredondo was a working-class repairman who became one of the earliest and most controversial boxers in Mexico.

168. Ceballos and Anaya, *Panorama mexicano 1890–1910*, 256. Nervo, Guerrero, and Plancarte, *Obras completas* (Madrid: Aguilar, 1962), 616. Tablada and Villaseñor served as seconds in the Colín-Esperón match in 1905.

169. As Stephen Riess has noted, the growth of sport in the United States was tied to urbanization and movements to counter the perceived debilitating effects of urban life. This process took place in Mexico at roughly the same moment. Riess, *City Games*.

170. Tenorio-Trillo, "1910 Mexico City," 189.

171. Piccato, *The Tyranny of Opinion*, 11.

172. Ibid., 13–17.

173. Palti, *La invención de una legitimidad razón y retórica*, 52–53.

174. Piccato, *The Tyranny of Opinion*; and Connell, *Masculinities*, 37.

175. Beezley, *Judas at the Jockey Club*.

176. Eric Hobsbawm's ideas on the oppositional nature of the "invention of tradition" are particularly helpful here. He argues that the imagination of the nation often is a product of defining the national self in terms what it is not. Sport, in particular, in this period gives a useful window onto both "national" identities and traditions and the construction of class identities. Hobsbawm characterizes sport as "one of the most significant of the new social practices of our period." See Hobsbawm, *The Invention of Tradition*, 298. Beezley, for example, grossly oversimplifies this process when he claims (writing about boxing) that "During the Porfirian years it demonstrated only the influence of foreigners, the imitative quality of the Mexican elite, and the desire for excitement in a comfortable, secure society." Beezley, *Judas at the Jockey Club*, 35.

177. Tenorio-Trillo, *Mexico at the World's Fairs*.

178. For a more in-depth account of the sensitivity of the Porfirian government to external and internal criticism, see David C. LaFevor, "Assassination, Race, Extradition, and the Public Sphere: The Cabrera-Barillas Affair in Porfirian Mexico," forthcoming in Kenyon Zimmer and Cristina Salinas, ed. *Deportation in the Americas* (College Station: Texas A&M Press); and Mraz, *Looking for Mexico*, 13–59.

179. AHDF, Ayuntamiento, Secretaría General: Espectáculos Públicos, vol. 1396, exp. 1096.

180. AHDF, Ayuntamiento: Justícia, licencias en general, vol. 2990, exp. 25; vol. 2990, exp. 520; vol. 3039, exp. 5017.

181. AHDF, Fondo Ayuntamiento, Secretaria General Espectaculos Publicos, vol. 1393, exp. 888.

182. "Spinner Is Defeated in Twenty Round Go," *Mexican Herald*, August 10, 1908.

183. AHDF, Fondo Ayuntamiento, Secretaria General Espectaculos Publicos, "Acuerdo del Gobernador," vol. 1393, exp. 872.

184. AHDF, Fondo Ayuntamiento: Licencias para cantinas no concedidas, vol. 1361, exp. 65.

185. AHDF, Gobernación: Asuntos Varios, vol. 812, exp. 1690.
186. AHDF, Juegos Permitidos, tomo 14, exp. 888, July 12, 1911.
187. An exhaustive search of numerous Mexican newspaper repositories found no remaining copies of this magazine.
188. "Notas de la Semana," *El Tiempo Ilustrado*, May 15, 1910.
189. Ibid.
190. *El País*, November 5, 1909.
191. "Gran entusiasmo reina para el festival deportivo," *El Díario*, June 20, 1910; *El País*, August 9, 1909.
192. "Se forma una club atletico en la escuela de agricultura," *El Imparcial*, July 18, 1910.
193. *El País*, April 16, 1910.
194. "Iniciativa del Club Atletico Internacional," *El Díario*, July 24, 1910; "Reina Gran entusiasmo por el festival deportivo," *El Díario*, June 20, 1910.
195. "Las carerras organizadas por el Club Atlético," *El Imparcial*, June 24, 1910; "Grandes pruebas pedestres," *El Díario*, June 24, 1910.
196. AHDF, Juegos Permitidos, tomo 14, exp. 888.
197. This match, which received wide newspaper coverage in Mexico, took place on July 4, 1910, between "Bad Nigger" Jack Johnson and the "Great White Hope" Jim Jeffries, in Reno, Nevada. The term "bad nigger" is borrowed from Al-Tony Gilmore's biography of Johnson and his representation by the contemporary media. See Gilmore, *Bad Nigger!*
198. "Championship Fight Exhibition Today," *Mexican Herald*, April 20, 1909.
199. Gerald Early, cited in Ward, *Unforgivable Blackness*, 18.
200. "The Hope of the Whites," *El Imparcial*, July 6, 1910. El Imparcial was among the first Mexican newspapers, along with the American-edited *Mexican Herald*, to receive extensive telegraphic cables of news from abroad. See García, *El imparcial*.
201. As a journalist, Jack London had followed Jack Johnson's career, making the trip in 1908 to Australia, where Johnson became the first black heavyweight boxing champion in his bout against a white Canadian. "Critica de la lucha Jefferies Johnson," *El Dictámen*, July 23, 1910; "American Fighters Enjoying Long Sea Trip to Australia," *Mexican Herald*, October 30, 1910.
202. "El gran Campeónato de box Jefferies-Johnson," *El Díario*, April 7, 1910.
203. "Casos y Cosas," *El Correo Español*, July 6, 1910.
204. "Casos y Cosas: Dudas norteamericans," *El Correo Español*, July 7, 1910.
205. "El Regreso de Johnson a Chicago," *La Patria*, July 8, 1910; "Aprehensión de Johnson," *El Imparcial*, November 27, 1910.
206. "El Contrincante de Johnson," *El Dictamen*, September 22, 1910.
207. Jack Johnson Dará la Vuelta al Mundo," *El Díario*, July 16, 1911.
208. "La Lucha Jeffries-Johnson," *El Tiempo Ilustrado*, July 7, 1910.
209. "Nuestro gobernador y la lucha Jeffries-Johnson," *El Abogado Cristiano*, July 28, 1910. *El Abogado Cristiano* was the official newspaper of the Methodist Church in Mexico.
210. "La vista cinematografica de la lucha Jeffries-Johnson," *La Opinión*, July 23, 1910.
211. "La veradera razón del encuentro Jeffries y Jhonson [sic]," *La Opinión*, August 15, 1910.

212. "Las películas de la lucha Jeffries-Johnson," *El Tiempo*, August 5, 1910.
213. "La pelicula Jeffries-Johnson," *El Diario*, September 30, 1910.
214. Carlos González Peña, "La fuerza brutal," *El Mundo Ilustrado*, July 17, 1910.
215. "Naderías: La Mano Negra en acción," *La Iberia*, August 17, 1910.
216. "Honra y provecho," *Diario del Hogar*, August 20, 1910.
217. See figure 21.
218. *El País*, August 9, 1910.
219. Ibid.
220. "Se concertó un match de Box," *El Imparcial*, May 6, 1911; "La Tournee [*sic*] Cuauhtemoc Aguilar," *El Imparcial*, May 10, 1911.
221. "El Match Johnson Aguilar," *El Imparcial*, May 19, 1911. This news appeared with the announcement that the previously reported news, that the town of Salina Cruz had been taken by rebels, was false and that Felix Díaz was taking over the city. The boxing show then moved to Puebla, within easy traveling distance of Mexico City and to which "an infinite" number of Mexico City fans planned to travel for the bout. The boxers challenged each other through the columns of newspapers like "Asalto entre C. Aguilar y J. Johnson," *El Díario*, July 5, 1911; "Reto al Campeón Tijera," *El Imparcial*, July 25, 1911; "Un desafío a Carlos de la Tijera," *El Díario*, July 26, 1911.
222. Gómez Carrillo, *Antología de Enrique Gómez Carrillo*.
223. "El Culto de la Fuerza: Francia ha triunfado en el boxeo," *El Imparcial*, March 12, 1911. Gómez Carrillo, born in Guatemala City in 1873, was the "most widely read [Latin American] chronicler of his day." He was the official representative of several Latin American countries in various European capitals, and he published more than eighty books and more than three thousand articles.

## Chapter Three

1. The most salient exceptions to this generalization are the establishment of monarchical empires in Brazil (1822–1889) and two relatively brief instances of imperial government in Mexico (1821–1824; 1863–1867).
2. Karp, *The Vast Southern Empire*, 67.
3. Julio Le Riverend, *Historia económica de Cuba* (La Habana: Editorial Nacional de Cuba, 1965); Jacobo de la Pezuela, *Ensayo histórico de la isla de* Cuba (New York: Imprenta de R. Rafael, 1842), 465–66; Murray, *Odious Commerce*, 208–9.
4. See the classic accounts of the Cuban economy in the nineteenth century, Moreno Fraginals, *El Ingenio*; and Fernando Ortiz, *Contrapunteo cubano del tabaco y el azúcar* (La Habana, Jesús Montero Editor, 1940).
5. Louis Pérez Jr., *Intimations of Modernity: Civil Culture in Nineteenth Century Cuba* (Chapel Hill: University of North Carolina Press, 2017), 103–7; Kate Ferris, "Modelos de abolición: Estados Unidos en la política cultural española y la abolición de la esclavitud en Cuba, 1868–1874," in *Visiones del Liberalismo: Política, identidad y cultura en la España del siglo XIX*, ed. Alda Blanco and Guy Thomson (Valencia: Universitat de Valencia, 2008), 195–219.

6. Sartorious, *Ever Faithful*, 5.
7. Ferrer, *Freedom's Mirror*, 38.
8. On these social freedoms as markers of modern democratic culture, see Habermas, *The Structural Transformation of the Public Sphere*.
9. Beatriz Calvo Peña, "Prensa, política y prostitución en La Habana finisecular: El caso de *La Cebolla* y la 'polémica de las meretrices,'" *Cuban Studies* 36 (2005): 24.
10. Pérez, *Intimations of Modernity*, 46.
11. For example, "Censura de prensa," Archivo Histórico Nacional (Madrid, Spain, hereafter AHN), Ultramar 4684, exp. 25.
12. Spain, *Ley de imprenta para la isla de Cuba* (Madrid: Imprenta Nacional, 1881).
13. Pérez, *Intimations of Modernity*, 17–54.
14. Spain, *Ley para el ejercicio del derecho de asociacion en las islas de Cuba y Puerto Rico y ley de reuniones públicas para la isla de Cuba* (Habana: Imprenta del gobierno y capitanía general, 1891), 3–11. See also Roldán de Montaud, *La Restauración en Cuba*, 257–59.
15. José Maria Zamora y Coronado, *Biblioteca de legislación ultramarina*, vol. 3 (Madrid: Imprenta de J. Martin Alegría, 1845), 73–74.
16. Francisco García Morales, *Guia de gobierno y policia de la isla de cuba* (La Habana: La Propaganda literaria, 1881), 85.
17. Pérez, "Between Baseball and Bullfighting," 493–517.
18. AHN, Ultramar, leg. 14, exp. 7.
19. Roca, *Ni con Lima ni con Buenos Aires*, 543.
20. Arthur Corwin, *Spain and the Abolition of Slavery in Cuba, 1817–1886* (Austin: University of Texas Press, 1967).
21. See the dozens of restrictions enforced by the Valdés administration. These laws of vigilance and oversight were intended to govern public life, public spectacles, and any civic social association. Geronimo Valdes, *Bando de gobernación y policia de la isla de Cuba expedido por el Exco. Sr. D. Geronimo Valdes* (Habana: Imprenta del Gobierno por S.M, 1844).
22. AHN, Ultramar, leg. 14, exp. 7.
23. Corwin, *Spain and the Abolition of Slavery in Cuba*, xv.
24. García, *Beyond the Walled City*.
25. The Aponte Rebellion (1812) began in these neighborhoods. By the 1840s, there were at least two regiments of regular cavalry stationed there. See Childs, *The 1812 Aponte Rebellion in Cuba*.
26. The Spanish Cortéz did not pass a comprehensive freedom of association law until 1887. See Casanovas, *Bread or Bullets*, 178–79.
27. The files containing these petitions for civic social organization have been lost.
28. AHN, Ultramar, leg. 14, exp. 7.
29. Jose de la Luz y Caballero to José L. Alfonso, March 31, 1839, reprinted in *Revista de la Biblioteca Nacional José Martí*, vol. I (1909), 104–5.
30. Ibid.; Domingo del Monte to José de la Luz y Caballero, December 2, 1839.
31. Vicente Antonio de Castro, "Gimnástica," *La Cartera Cubana* (Havana), September 1838, 193–200.

32. Corwin, *Spain and the Abolition of Slavery in Cuba*, 76.
33. This pedigree, however uncomfortable for the Spanish authorities, impressed the members of the Sociedad Economica in Havana. See Domingo del Monte to José de la Luz y Caballero, December 2, 1839.
34. V. Boix, "Apuntes para la biografía del coronel D. Francisco Amorós, marqués de Sotelo," *El Fénix*, March 15, 1846.
35. De Castro, "Gimnástica," 195.
36. On the liberal press and censorship in the nineteenth century see *AHN*, Ultramar, leg. 4612, exp. 33; leg. 4684, exp. 22; leg. 4684, exp. 20.
37. *AHN*, Ultramar, leg. 4608, exp. 2.
38. *AHN*, Ultramar, leg. 4603, exp. 47.
39. *AHN*, Ultramar, leg. 4610, exp. 20.
40. See for example the case of Federico Pérez Calzadilla, who worked for years without pay as an "honorary theater censor" and was later rewarded with a land grant. *ANC*, Ultramar, leg. 4707, exp. 47.
41. De Castro, "Gimnástica," 194.
42. Pérez, *Intimations of Modernity*, 4.
43. Ibid., 3.
44. "New Spectacle," *Diario de la Marina*, April 7, 1848.
45. Garcia, *Beyond the Walled City*.
46. See "Plano Pintoresco de la Habana con los numerous de las casas," David Rumsey Map Collection (www.davidrumsey.com).
47. Cuba, *Resumen del censo de la población de la isla de Cuba, 1841* (Habana: Imprenta del Gobierno, 1842), 25–27.
48. "New Spectacle," *Diario de la Marina*, April 7, 1848.
49. "Boxing," *Diario de la Marina*, April 7, 1848.
50. Ibid.
51. Dueling in nineteenth-century Cuba was tied to defense of masculine honor. See Cervantes, *Los duelos en Cuba*, xv, xii, 30, 84.
52. "Second Function of Boxing and Wrestling," *Diario de la Marina*, April 20, 1848.
53. "At the Circus: Wrestling and Boxing," *Diario de la Marina*, April 25, 1848.
54. "Theater of the *Circo Habanero*," *Diario de la Marina*, April 29, 1848.
55. "A Boxing-Bullfighting Dream," *Diario de la Marina*, May 3, 1848.
56. "Bouts," *Diario de la Marina*, May 9, 1848. Bernardo Gaviño was a Spanish-born bullfighter who lived and fought in Cuba and Mexico and is credited with revolutionizing bullfighting in Latin America.
57. Ibid.
58. "Circo: los dos gladiadores," *Diario de la Marina*, April 27, 1848.
59. "Boxeo," *Diario de la Marina*, April 28, 1848.
60. "Otro campeón," *Diario de la Marina*, May 10, 1848; May 16, 1848.
61. "Circo Lucha," *Diario de la Marina*, May 23, 1848.
62. *La aurora* (Matanzas), June 14, 1848.

63. Chambers, *No God But Gain*, introduction.
64. The Circo Habanero later became known as the Teatro Villanueva and was near the Colón Gate within the city walls. Serafin Ramirez, *La Habana artística: apuntes históricos* (Havana: Impresa del E. M. de la Capitanía General), 351.
65. Sippial, *Prostitution, Modernity, and the Making of the Cuban Republic*, 22, 32.
66. "Gran Circo Habanero," *Diario de la Marina*, May 28, 1847.
67. "Circo Habanero," *Advisador del Comercio*, January 11, 1848, cited in *Diario de la Marina*, January 12, 1848.
68. *Diario de la Marina*, May 16, 1848.
69. *Diario de la Marina*, May 20, 1848.
70. "Nuevo Café," *Diario de la Marina*, July 7, 1848.
71. "Luchas en el circo," *Diario de la Marina*, May 5, 1849; "Luchas," *Diario de la Marina*, July 23, 1852.
72. *Diario de la Marina*, August 18, 1853.
73. *Diario de la Marina*, December 17, 1850.
74. "Escuela Gimnastica Normal," *Diario de la Marina*, July 26, 1855.
75. Ibid.
76. "Escuela normal gimnastica," *Diario de la Marina*, December 22, 1855.
77. "Escuela normal gimnastica," *Diario de la Marina*, March 16, 1856.
78. Amadeo Chaumont, "Gimnástica," *Revista de la Habana*, 1855, 59–60.
79. Public ordinances in Havana (1855) prohibited any female nudity, especially in the public baths. Franklin, *Women and Slavery in Nineteenth Century Colonial Cuba*, 56–57.
80. Amadeo Chaumont, "Gimnastica," *Revista de la Habana*, 1855, 59–60.
81. *Diario de la Marina*, April 25, 1856.
82. *Diario de la Marina*, June 4, 1856.
83. *Diario de la Marina*, August 27, 1861.
84. *El Siglo*, November 11, 1861, quoted in *Diario de la Marina*, November 12, 1861.
85. *El Moro Muza*, December 13, 1863.
86. Lorenzo Lopez y Muñiz, *Flores de alma* (Habana: El Iris, 1865), 86.
87. Mariano Dumá Chancel, *Guía del profesorado Cuban para 1868* (Mantanzas: Imprenta el Ferrocarril, 1868).
88. Jean-Michel Desvois, *Prensa, impresos, lectura en el mundo hispánico contemporáneo* (Pessac (France): Institut d'études ibériques & ibéro-américaines, Université Michel de Montaigne-Bordeaux, 2005), 378.
89. Anonymous, *History of the Great International Contest Between Heenan and Sayers . . .* (London: George Newbold, 1860).
90. *Diario de la Marina*, November 4, 1858.
91. Ibid.
92. *Diario de la Marina*, May 15, 1860; May 18, 1860; May 20, 1860.
93. Slout, *Olympians of the Sawdust Circle*, 221. The Nixon circus troupe died in a shipwreck shortly after leaving Havana on April 19, 1861.
94. *El Siglo*, January 13, 1861.

95. *La Gaceta*, January 13, 1861; reprinted in *Diario de la Marina*, January 13, 1861.
96. *Diario de la Marina*, January 17, 1861.
97. *El Siglo*, November 27, 1866.
98. "Barbarous Spectacle," *Diario de la Marina*, August 11, 1874.
99. "Importancia Higienica de Base-Ball," *El Sport*, July 1, 1886; Pérez, "Between Baseball and Bullfighting."
100. "Bulls or Base Ball," *El Sport*, September 9, 1886; "No More Bulls!," *El Sport*, November 25, 1886; "Notas de año Nuevo," *El Sport*, December 28, 1886.
101. "Not So Much English!," *El Sport*, September 9, 1886; Dalia Antonia Muller, "Cuban Émigres, Mexican Politics and the Cuban Question, 1895–99" (PhD Dissertation, University of California Berkeley, 2007), 71–72.
102. Antonio Prieto, "Ni gallos, ni toros, ni pugilato (Neither cocks, nor bulls, nor pugilism)," *El Base-Ball*, March 12, 1882.
103. Felipe Pérez y González, "Oh, qué gran nación" in *Filibusterías y yankee al hombre* (Madrid: Hijos de E. Hidalgo, 1898), 164–66.
104. Diocletiano Ramos García, "Hipocresia Social," in *Cuadros Yankees* (Caracas: Imprenta Caraqueña, 1898), 23–24.
105. "Especáculos inhumanos," *La Patria*, November 2, 1899. For boxing prohibitions under the occupation, see Puerto Rico, Cuba, United States, *Translation of the Penal Code in Force in Cuba and Porto Rico* (Washington: Government Printing Office, 1900), 148.
106. "Pugilato," *Diario de la Marina*, April 2, 1903.
107. "The Mote in Our Neighbor's Eye," *Puck*, July 12, 1899. See figure 23.
108. *Diario de la Marina*, December 28, 1899.
109. *Diario de la Marina*, February 27, 1900.
110. "Ser celebre es lo importante," *La Lucha*, October 2, 1903.
111. "Sesión Municipal," *Diario de la Marina*, April 12, 1904.
112. A. Rivero, "Habaneras," *Diario de la Marina*, February 3, 1905.
113. "Actualidades," *Diario de la Marina*, February 6, 1905.
114. G. A. de Caillavet, "Un Cuento Diario," *La Lucha*, January 2, 1906.
115. "La edad de oro," *Diario de la Marina*, February 16, 1906.
116. "Una víctima del boxeo," *La Lucha*, March 2, 1906.
117. "A bordo del 'Louisiana,'" *La Lucha*, October 11, 1906.
118. "La Prensa," *Diario de la Marina*, October 12, 1906.
119. Ibid. *Agiaco*, or *ajiaco*, is a stew made of legumes and root vegetables with many variations throughout the island. It also serves as a metaphor for the cultural and racial mixtures—a stew—that make Cuba unique. Ajiaco was a central metaphor for Fernando Ortiz. Fernando Ortiz and João Felipe Gonçalves, "The Ajiaco in Cuba and Beyond: Preface to 'The Human Factors of Cubanidad'" *HAU: Journal of Ethnographic Theory* 4 (2014), 445–80.
120. Raúl Mareñas, *El Mundo*, October 11, 1906; Enrique Fontanills, *Diario de la Marina*, October 12, 1906.
121. Enrique Fontanills, *Diario de la Marina*, October 12, 1906. Two months later,

Fontanills reported seeing an announcement for a boxing match at the Eden Garden in Havana. *Diario de la Marina*, December 29, 1906. American marines also held a bout in the Teatro Payret on New Year's Day 1906. *Diario de la Marina*, December 30, 1906; January 1, 1907.

122. "Eden Garden," *La Lucha*, December 29, 1906; "Boxeo," *Diario de la Marina*, December 30, 1906.

123. "De Sport," *Diario de la Marina*, January 1, 1907.

124. Abel Du Breuil, "Boxeo," *La Lucha*, January 14, 1907.

125. "Baturillo," *Diario de la Marina*, January 28, 1907.

126. Gabriel Camps, "Los Gallos," *La Lucha*, January 30, 1907.

127. Alfredo Zayas, Letter to the Editor, *La Lucha*, February 9, 1907.

128. "Boxeo en Matanzas," *La Lucha*, January 29, 1907.

129. Hernández, "Un 'Match' de boxeo causa terrible impresion en el public," *La Lucha*, February 11, 1907.

130. One pamphlet from 1892 deals specifically with lynching in the United States: González y Lanuza, *La ley de lynch en los Estados Unidos*. See also Urbano de Sotomayor, *Isla de Cuba*, 48–49.

131. Joaquín Aramburu, "Baturillo," *Diario de la Marina*, December 29, 1909.

132. Bederman, *Manliness and Civilization*; Rotundo, *American Manhood*; Sachsman, Rushing, and Morris, *Seeking a Voice*.

133. The best public reaction study of Johnson's impact across the United States is Gilmore, *Bad Nigger!* Johnson was also covered avidly in the African American press, with hundreds of articles appearing in the *Chicago Defender* that vacillated between support and celebration of the boxer and criticism of his handling of celebrity.

134. Helg, *Our Rightful Share*, 19.

135. Pérez, *On Becoming Cuban*.

136. "Vida Deportiva: El combate Jefferies-Johnson: detalles interesantes sobre la actitud del Gobernador de California," *Diario de la Marina*, June 17, 1910; Manuel de Linares, "El Gobernador de California y los boxeadores Jefferies y Johnson," *Diario de la Marina*, June 16, 1910; "La Contienda de los Campeónes," *Diario de la Marina*, June 17, 1910; "Vida Deportiva," *Diario de la Marina*, June 28, 1910.

137. "Vida Deportiva," *Diario de la Marina*, October 9, 1909.

138. *La Lucha*, July 5, 1910. Mathews, Musser, and Braun, *Moving Pictures: American Art and Early Film*, 111. For a study on the business of boxing through moving pictures in this period, see Streible, *Fight Pictures*.

139. Pérez, *On Becoming Cuban*.

140. The construction of national identity in oppositional terms has been developed by a number of scholars: Hobsbawm, *The Invention of Tradition*; Gouldner, *The Future of Intellectuals*.

141. Pérez, *On Becoming Cuban*.

142. See chapter 1 for a discussion of Jack Johnson in Mexico.

143. "Santiago Agramonte acepta el reto de Ryan," *Diario de la Marina*, June 28, 1910.

144. The image of "Tío Sam" in Cuba was highly ambiguous in this period. While visual reproductions in the era after independence reflected both the Cuban "debt of gratitude" and the anti-imperialism embodied in the writings of the Cuban patriot José Martí, this particular rendering shows a feeble and helpless America cowering from a confident, muscular Jack Johnson. The varying visual images of Tío Sam throughout Latin America after the defeat of the Spanish and the occupation of Cuba and Puerto Rico would make for a revealing case study in the reactions of Latin Americans to expanding US influence in the region. For discussions on Tío Sam, see Font, *The Cuban Republic and José Martí*; Terry, *Terry's Guide to Cuba*.

145. "The Man of the Week," *La Lucha*, July 10, 1910.

146. The best account of the expansion of American capital in Cuba during this period remains Pérez, *Cuba Under the Platt Amendment*.

147. Pérez, *Cuba Under the Platt Amendment*. Pérez's work on the reciprocal cultural influences between the two countries gives further context. Pérez, *On Becoming Cuban*.

148. "La Lucha Jeffries Johnson," *El Triunfo*, July 4, 1910.

149. *La Lucha*, July 4, 1910. This article reviewed what had become familiar in the Havana press, that the legal battles to prevent prizefighting were unable to stem the enthusiasm for boxing, but that it was likely that this would be the last major prizefight to be allowed in the United States. Presciently, the writer mused that with illegality in the north, the only place left to stage such bouts would be in Mexico or Cuba.

150. Roberts, *Papa Jack*, 103.

151. *La Lucha*, July 6, 1910.

152. "The Disorder Continues," *La Lucha*, July 6, 1910.

153. *El Triunfo*, July 8, 1910; "El Negocio del cine en peligro," *La Lucha*, July 6, 1910.

154. "Even in South Africa," *La Lucha*, July 7, 1910.

155. *El Triunfo*, July 8, 1910.

156. "El negocio del cine en peligro: Temese el Enardecimiento del Pueblo," *La Lucha*, July 6, 1910.

157. "Prohibits the Pictures: Secretary of the Interior Orders Prevention," *La Lucha*, July 8, 1910.

158. For an account of the use of this myth in the early years of the Republic, see Lillian Guerra, "From Revolution to Involution in the Early Cuban Republic," in Appelbaum et al., *Race and Nation in Modern Latin America*, 132–62. There are several studies on the massacre of the Partido Independiente de Color that focus on the elite (both black and white) Cuban interpretation of the political mobilization of Afro-Cubans as a treasonous violation of Martí's vision of a republic where race was subsumed into national identity. The most recent and comprehensive is Helg, *Our Rightful Share*.

159. A. E. Amenabar, "Notas de Sports," *El Triúnfo*, July 18, 1910.

160. Ignacio Rivero, "Pisto Manchego," *Diario de la Marina*, March 8, 1907. Similar to the match earlier witnessed by José Martí, boxing matches were held in rural areas, on farms, and, in the United States, on river barges or ocean vessels.

161. See chapter 5.

162. *American Physical Education Review* 14, no. 56 (1909): 48.
163. "Actualidades," *Diario de la Marina*, September 15, 1909; Budinich is advertised as the "notable South American pugilist," and he likely earned a portion of the gate receipts for the theater. Cuban theaters charged the audience by "tandas," or acts. Budinich would sometimes box two times per night, appearing between acts of Turkish dancers and Spanish vaudeville acts. See also *Diario de la Marina*, September 23, 1909. Budinich remains an enigmatic figure and is still celebrated in Chile as a sport pioneer of the early twentieth century. In an interview with a surviving nephew in 2008, more of the details around Budinich's travels came to light. After sailing from Chile he landed in San Francisco and left just before the massive earthquake of 1906. He traveled by rail across the country and later enrolled at Columbia University to study physical education. Leaving Colombia in 1907, he traveled to the Panama Canal Zone, where he engaged in several prizefights, most famously with the African American (or Panamanian) Sam Odon. Budinich claims to have won US$5,000 for this fight. The earnings enabled him to take a steamship to Havana, where he opened a boxing gym and entered the Cuban narrative. He returned to Chile by 1917, where he continued boxing and became a sports journalist, helping to promote Chilean boxing. See Rodrigo Fluxa, "La incredible historia de Juan Budinich, el primer boxeador chileno," *El Mercurio*, December 7, 2008. The details of this story, told by an aging relative of Budinich, have been verified through immigration documents and newspapers, with only a few errors on dates.
164. San Martín, *El Arte de los Puños*; Jorge Alfonso, "Centenario del boxeo cubano," *Bohemia*, September 28, 2010. Alfonso's article (he has long written on the history of Cuban boxing) continues the mistake of dating the first boxing match on the island, between Budinich and Ryan, in 1912. This error has been repeated dozens of times since San Martín's original mistake in dating that bout after the massacre of the Partido Independiente de Color in 1912.
165. Chanan, *Cuban Cinema*, 53–54.
166. Abel, *Encyclopedia of Early Cinema*, 815–16. Santos y Artigas, who would become most well-known for their traveling circus that circulated in Latin America and the United States, would make an interesting case study in Cuban appropriation and transformation of popular cultures from abroad. Santos y Artigas have been cited as forces in the popularization of rumba, and their park in Old Havana served as the site for important transnational events such as the speeches of Marcus Garvey. See Guridy, *Forging Diaspora*, 84. For an account of the circus in Costa Rica, for example, see Fumero Vargas, *Teatro, público y estado en San José 1880–1914*. The enormously popular circus remained a feature of Cuban life until the Revolution. The term *mambí* was used to describe Cuba's largely Afro-Cuban guerrilla army on the eve of independence.
167. Gabriel Camps, "La estación de Invierno: foment de turismo," *Diario de la Marina*, November 1908.
168. Ibid.
169. Gabriel Caruso, "Discurso Inaugural del Cúrso Académico," Universidad de La Habana, *Revista de la Facultad de Letras y Ciencias* 7 (1908–1909): 209–17.
170. Ibid.

171. Ibid.
172. Aramburu y Torres, "A otras epocas...," 184–87.
173. Ibid.
174. Aramburu, "Baturillo," *Diario de la Marina*, December 29, 1909.
175. *Diario de la Marina*, February 17, 1906.
176. Ibid.
177. Ironically, Fontanills was reacting to another attempt at importing barbarism, an American football match that had taken place in Havana in 1905. Proof of the stupidity of football was that Cuban women, so efficient at determining new "fashions," were repulsed by it and boxing. Enrique Fontanills, "Habaneras," *Diario de la Marina*, March 2, 1905; *El Mundo*, June 2, 1905.
178. *Diario de la Marina*, May 6, 1910.
179. See chapter 1.
180. Darío's poem "To Roosevelt" is a well-known denunciation of American cultural imperialism in the early twentieth century.
181. *Caras y Caretas* (Buenos Aires), 1909.
182. Budinich staged several performances in the Teatro Actualidades in late 1909.

## Chapter Four

1. Pérez, *On Becoming Cuban*, 219–79.
2. Anderson, *Imagined Communities*, 35.
3. For example, colonial African newspapers: "Jack Johnson Knocked Out," *The Nyasaland Times* (Blantyre, Malawi), April 8, 1915; "Boxing," *The Rhodesia Herald* (Harare, Zimbabwe), April 9, 1915; "Jack Johnson Beaten," *Colony and Provincial Reporter*, April 10, 1915. Colonial Asian newspapers: "Jack Johnson Beaten," *The Tribune* (Lahore, Pakistan), April 8, 1915. South American newspapers: "Notas Sportivas," *Mercurio* (Santiago, Chile), April 7, 1915; "La victoria del pugil Willard," *El Universal* (Caracas, Venezuela), April 22, 1915. Australian newspapers: "Jack Johnson's Defeat," *Dubbo Dispatch and Wellington Independent*, April 9, 1915; "Heavyweight Championship," *Truth* (Perth), April 10, 1915.
4. "Los aliados y Johson [sic]," *La Crítica* (Buenos Aires), April 9, 1915.
5. See figure 11.
6. "Sesión municipal," *Diario de la Marina*, April 12, 1904.
7. Leonard Wood, *Report of the Military Governor of Cuba on Civil Affairs*, vol. 1 (Washington, DC: Government Printing Office, 1901), 312–13.
8. Schwartz, *Pleasure Island*, 23–27.
9. One example of this was Johnson's chartering of the ship *Henry Krager* to travel from Barbados to Cuba. "Johnson to Cienfuegos," *El Mundo*, February 12, 1915.
10. Katz, *The Life and Times of Pancho Villa*, 500.
11. "Carranza Make Take Hand in Juarez Prizefight," *Waco Morning News*, January 14, 1915. "Will Arrest Johnson: General Carranza Says...," *Harrisburg Daily Independent*; "Todavía puede luchar Johnson el la Habana," *El Mundo* (Havana), January 19, 1915.

12. "Todavía puede luchar Johnson en la Habana," *El Mundo* (Havana), January 19, 1915; "Johnson, Villa, Willard, Carranza," *The Houston Post*, January 24, 1915; "Carranza Tells Johnson to Stay out of Mexico," *Pittson* (PA) *Gazette*, January 14, 1915.

13. *Chicago Tribune*, February 23, 1915. This was widely reported in the United States and Latin America but is strikingly absent from newspapers in Mexico. Whether Carranza gave this order or not is impossible to say. Johnson claimed to be in contact with promoters in Mexico and to have obtained this warning via telegram.

14. Reynaldo González, *Coordenadas del cine cubano*, vol. 2 (Santiago de Cuba: Editorial Oriente, 2001), 37–38, 85.

15. Bob Edgren, "What Happened Before the Men Went into the Ring," *The Evening World*, April 5, 1915.

16. See figure 13.

17. "Teatro Victoria," *El Mercurio* (Santiago, Chile), October 30, 1915; "Espectáculos públicos," *El Universal* (Caracas, Venezuela), October 2, 1915; "The Johnson-Willard Film," *Daily Post* (Hobart, Tasmania), February 16, 1916. The film was still submitted to censors in Zimbabwe almost three years after the bout and was allowed to play to a "well attended" crowd. "Que Que," *The Bulawayo Chronicle*, December 12, 1918. It was shown "for the first time in Southern Africa" in Mozambique in 1917. "Film sensacional," *O Africano* (Maputo, Mozambique), October 17, 1917.

18. "Johnson-Willard Films Aren't Within the Law," *The Evening World* (New York), April 11, 1916; "Guarding the Ports: Customs Officials Determined to Keep Johnson-Willard Films Out," *Topeka State Journal*, April 16, 1915; Melvyn Stokes, *D. W. Griffith: A History of the Most Controversial Motion Picture of All Time* (Oxford: Oxford University Press, 2007), 132–33.

19. James Weldon Johnson, "Perverted History," *New York Age*, April 22, 1915.

20. "Jack Johnson en Cuba," *El Mundo*, February 10, 1915.

21. See figures 12 and 14.

22. Helg, *Our Rightful Share*, 98.

23. Roberts, *Papa Jack*; Ward, *Unforgivable Blackness*; Bederman, *Manliness and Civilization*.

24. Cuban newspapers regularly printed news of his matches, legal battles, and the racial politics of his self-exile. Theaters showed films of his mundane life in Paris. "Politeama: Jack Jhonson [sic] en Paris," *Diario de la Marina*, November 2, 1913.

25. "Campeáo mundial de box," *Estado de São Paulo*, December 17, 1914.

26. "Jack Johnson," *Estado de Sao Paulo*, January 16, 1915.

27. "Theatro Carlos Gomes," *Jornal do Commercio* (Rio de Janeiro), March 23, 1916; "Força e nobreza," *Estado de São Paulo*, December 1, 1919.

28. "Jack London Describes the Fight and Jack Johnson's Golden Smile," *The San Francisco Call*, December 27, 1908. Campbell Reesman, *Jack London's Racial Lives*, 184–92.

29. Roberts, *Papa Jack*, 144–53.

30. Ibid., 176–77.

31. United States National Archives, College Park, General Records of the Department

of Justice, File 164211, Record Group 60. These records show an unnamed agent tailing Johnson in Havana.

32. Edgren, "What Happened Before the Men Went into the Ring."
33. Victor Muñoz, "Johnson," *El Mundo*, February 23, 1915.
34. As the writer "Left Hook" mused for the *Tacoma Times*, the prospects for Willard to take back the title from the "ebony battleship" were not promising: "Is Big Jess a Big Enough Man to Capture the World's Title?" *Tacoma Times*, November 24, 1914.
35. One visual illustration of this was printed in the *Nashville Tennessean*. It shows Johnson prostrate, knocked out by a bottle of whisky.
36. James J. Corbett, "Johnson and Willard Signed; May Fight at Juarez [sic] Track," *El Paso Herald*, December 23, 1914.
37. Lucien E. White, "Status of the Negro Boxer," *The New York Age. The Freeman*, November 28, 1914.
38. Johnson, *In the Ring and Out*, 103.
39. "Jack Jhonson" [sic], *La Crítica*, December 21, 1914.
40. Ibid.
41. *Caras y Caretas: Almanaque*, 1915.
42. See figure 5.
43. "Jack Johnson," *Caras y Caretas*, January 9, 1915.
44. "Jack Johnson en el ring," *Fray Mocho*, January 15, 1915.
45. "Cuestiones Educacionales," *Nosotros*, January 1915.
46. *PBT: Seminario Ilustrado*, January 1, 1916.
47. "El Viejito Ortiz y el negro Johnson: una Aventura nocturna," *La Crítica*, December 23, 1914.
48. The Casino Theater was one of the largest and most modern in the city. It had staged a few boxing matches, on the margins of legality, by 1914.
49. "Carta abierta al negro Johnson," *La Crítica*, December 27, 1914; Shohat and Stam, *Multiculturalism, Postcoloniality, and Transnational Media*, 113.
50. "Carta abierta al negro Johnson," *La Crítica*, December 27, 1914.
51. "Local Events," *The Standard* (Buenos Aires), January 31, 1864; Rodríguez, *Regulation of Boxing*, 163–90.
52. "El Augue de la barbarie," *La Vanguardia*, January 10, 1915.
53. Ibid.
54. "Johnson to Cienfuegos," *El Mundo*, February 12, 1915.
55. "Declaraciónes de Menocal," *El Mundo*, March 29, 1915; "El Match Willard-Johnson," *Diario de la Marina*, March 29, 1915; "Cuban President Sees Negro," *The Morning Oregonian*, March 16, 1915.
56. *El Día* (Havana), April 2 1915; *El Día*, April 6, 1915.
57. *El Día*, April 3, 1915.
58. "Miss Cecilia Wright en el campamento de Willard," *El Mundo*, March 26, 1915.
59. "Jess Willard," *El Heraldo de Cuba*, March 17, 1915; *El Paso Herald*, April 6, 1915; *Washington Herald*, April 6, 1915; "Life and Career of Our New Champion," *Tacoma Times*, April 6, 1906.

60. Message from "Hermano Juan [sic] Ryan" *El Día*, April 4, 1915.
61. La nota del día," *El Día*, April 5, 1915.
62. See figure 7.
63. "Battling Nelson triunfó a los Venticinco rounds," *El Mundo*, March 26, 1915.
64. There were dozens of athletic clubs, the most visible of which was the Club Atlético de Cuba (opened in 1909), that competed in an array of athletics and also served as social clubs for a cross-class group of Cubans. The records can be found in the Archivo Nacional de Cuba, Fondo Clubes y Asociaciones. Hereafter cited as "ANC, Fondo Asociaciones."
65. "Johnson y Mc Vea [sic] se preparan para el sabado," *El Mundo*, February 17, 1915.
66. "El Club Atlético de Cuba en plena actividad deportiva," *El Mundo*, February 17, 1915.
67. Santovenia y Echaide, *Libro conmemorativo de la inauguración*. See figure 7.
68. "The American Amuk," *The Crisis*, April 1918.
69. On Esténoz, see Helg, *Our Rightful Share*, 142–46, 167–68.
70. "The American Amuk," *The Crisis*, April 18, 1918.
71. *The Cuba Review: All About Cuba*, December 1911.
72. "El Match Ahearn Lewis," *El Mundo*, February 10, 1915.
73. Abel Linares, "Deportivas," *Diario de la Marina*, February 11, 1915.
74. "Asa Daniel Roberds," Reports of the Deaths of American Citizens, compiled 01/1835–12/1974. US National Archives at College Park, Maryland, USA, Publication A1 5166, Record Group 59.
75. "Tourists Do not Chase Around After Nigger Pugs," *The Cuba News*, October 24, 1914.
76. Asa D. Roberds, "Jack Johnson in Town," *The Cuba News*, February 27, 1915.
77. Ibid.
78. "Johnson Barred at Havana Hotel," *Chicago Tribune*, February 23, 1915. "Johnson Refused All Accommodation," *Washington Times*, February 22, 1915.
79. Victor Muñoz, "Johnson," *El Mundo*, February 23, 1915.
80. See figure 12.
81. Victor Muñoz, "Johnson," *El Mundo*, February 23, 1915.
82. "Estadio, el sabado," *El Mundo*, February 11, 1915; "Johnson a Cienfuegos," *El Mundo*, February 12, 1915.
83. San Martín, *El Arte de los Puños*.
84. "Del municipio habanero," *El Mundo*, January 9, 1915; "La session de ayer en al ayuntamiento," *El Mundo*, January 12, 1915; "Champion, Thought to Be in Mexico, Shows Up in Cuba, Will Push Ahead," *Freeman* (Indianapolis), February 27, 1915.
85. *New York Times*, February 3, 1915, 12. Fights "to a finish" were those in which a set number of rounds did not determine the end of a match. Finish fights could be extended indefinitely to the point where one boxer was definitively the winner.
86. "Atractivos para los turistas," *El Mundo*, January 8, 1915.
87. "Habrá luchas de boxeo," *El Mundo*, January 22, 1915.
88. *Havana Post*, January 8, 1915.
89. "La sesion municipal de ayer," *El Mundo*, February 6, 1915.

90. *Havana Post*, January 13, 1915.
91. "Battle Royale," *El Mundo*, April 7, 1915.
92. Fermin de Iruña (Enrique Ruiz de la Serna), "Boxeo en el Estadio," *El Mundo*, April 1, 1915.
93. "En el Estadium," April 4, 1915.
94. "Willard Wins in Great Fight," *Elmira Star-Gazette*, April 5, 1915.
95. *El Día*, April 6, 1915.
96. Ibid.
97. Ibid.
98. *El Mundo*, March 4, 1915 (italics added).
99. *El Mundo*, March 19, 1915.
100. Ibid.
101. *El Mundo*, March 6, 1915.
102. Ibid.
103. Ibid.
104. *El Día*, April 5, 1915.
105. *El Heraldo de Cuba*, February 23, 1915.
106. "Jack Johnson no encuentra donde hospedarse," *El Heraldo de Cuba*, February 23, 1915. Madán was the focus of many headlines generated by his stances for Afro-Cuban "honor," such as when he dueled with swords against a white member of the Ayuntamiento later in 1915. See Primelles, *Cronica Cubana*, 51; Néstor Carbonell and Emeterio S. Santovenia, *El Ayuntamiento de la Habana: Noviembre 16 de 1519 -Noviembre 16 de 1919: Reseña Histórica* (Habana: Seoane y Fernández, 1919).
107. *El Heraldo de Cuba*, February 25, 1915.
108. *El Heraldo de Cuba*, March 17, 1915.
109. Madán, *Tratado de los Odu de Ifa*; Casa del Caribe, *Del Caribe* (Santiago de Cuba: Casa del Caribe, 1983). For the public campaigns against Afro-Cuban religion in this period, see Bronfman, *Measures of Equality*, 24–25. Personal communication with Marcelo Madán (grandson of Eligio Madán), May 20, 2016.
110. "Special Box for Menocal," *New York Tribune*, April 2, 1915.
111. Primelles, *Crónica Cubana*, 102. This group of senators was the same seeking to legalize bullfighting.
112. "Asociacíon Nacional de Veteranos de la Independencia to President Major General Mario Mencoal," Archivo General de Cuba, Fondo Secretaría de la Presidencia, leg. 19, no. 8.
113. Ibid.; Albert Doogan to President of the Republic, Menocal, April 6, 1915. There is no record of Doogan having any association with the University of Michigan.
114. Ibid. Convención Bautísta de Cuba Oriental to Secretaría, s/f.
115. President Menocal went several times to watch Johnson train while preparing for the fight in Havana. Johnson remembered giving Menocal's son, Mario Jr., a pair of the gloves he had trained with. Johnson, *In the Ring and Out*; *El Mundo*, March 16, 1915; *Washington Times*, March 16, 1915.

116. "Holiday Crowds See Johnson and Willard," *Elmira Star Gazette*, March 29, 1915.

117. "De juzgado de guardia," *El Mundo*, April 8, 1915; *El Mundo*, March 23, 1915; "Johnson Victim of 'Mañana,'" *Havana Post*, April 8, 1915.

118. Luchas entre blancos y negros," *El Mundo*, April 8, 1915.

119. "Johnson Victim of 'Mañana,'" *Havana Post*, April 8, 1915.

120. "No American Passport for Johnson," *The Atlanta Constitution*, April 10, 1915. This story is supported by the aforementioned Bureau of Investigation files and was a major embarrassment for the American legation in Cuba.

121. Methodist Episcopal Church, South, *Missionary Voice* (Nashville: Methodist Episcopal Church, South, Board of Missions, 1911).

122. "Contra el boxeo," *El Mundo*, April 8, 1915; *Havana Post*, April 9, 1915.

123. "Anti-Boxing Bill Is Approved by Senate," *Havana Post*, April 9, 1915. Pushing his impunity in the face of Cuban resistance, Bradt published a list of upcoming boxing matches at his stadium next to the announcement of the new prohibition.

124. Mario Muñoz Bustamante, *Ideas y Colores* (Havana: Imprenta Avisador Comercial, 1907), 3.

125. Mario Muñoz Bustamante, "De lunes a lunes," *El Mundo*, April 12, 1915. Jeannette Ryder waged a decades-long crusade against animal cruelty and in defense of Cuban children. "Jeannette Ryder, the Humane Heroine of Cuba," *Our Dumb Animals* 53, no. 3 (Aug. 1920): 43.

126. "Peñalver sube al ring," *El Mundo*, March 27, 1915; "Esta noche dubtará el Johnson Cubano," *El Mundo*, March 31, 1915.

127. "La lucha de los boxeadores," *El Mundo*, March 31, 1915.

128. Cecilia Wright, "Hermoso gesto de Johnson," *El Mundo*, April 6, 1915.

129. "Perdido del Champion," *El Mundo*, April 7, 1915.

130. "En la casa de Johnson," *El Mundo*, April 6, 1915.

131. "Waking Up with a Big Head," *Cuba News*, April 12, 1915.

132. Attaché (Victor Muñoz), "Junto al Capitolio: El Campeon," April 15, 1915.

133. "Club Estradense," *El Mundo*, April 17, 1915. This song was copyrighted by on March 27, 1915, by the Enrique Peña Orchestra. Cuba, *Boletín oficial de la Propiedad Industrial* (Havana: Imprenta Avisador Comercial, 1915), 783. The original composition has been lost.

134. "Perdido el Champion," *El Mundo*, April 7, 1915; San Martín, *El Arte de los Punos*, 16–18.

135. The best scholarly account of this relationship remains Pérez, *Cuba Under the Platt Amendment*, 108–82.

## Chapter Five

1. "Nocaut," *La Afición*, July 18, 1932.

2. Mexico, *Diario de debates de la Cámara de Diputados*, año II, período XXXIII, Legislatura, tomo V., numero 30.

3. Florescano, *Historia gráfica de México*, 103; Allen, *A History of Boxing in Mexico*, 32, 62.

4. On the connection between sport and antialcohol campaigns, see Gretchen Kristine Pierce, "Sobering the Revolution: Mexico's Anti-Alcohol Campaigns and the Process of State Building" (PhD diss., University of Arizona, 2008).

5. On anti-blood-sport advocates see Sluis, *Deco Body, Deco City*, and on public spectacles, Paulina Suárez-Hesketh, "The Frivolous Scene: Cosmopolitan Amusements in Mexico City's 1920s," *The Global South* 9, no. 2 (2015): 103–30.

6. "Viríl y pintoresco?," *El Abogado Cristiano*, December 5, 1929.

7. "Propone que se prohiban las corridas de toros," *El informador* (Guadalajara), November 20, 1929, and November 23, 1929; *Acron Beacon Journal*, November 26, 1929.

8. "Bill to Eliminate Bull, Cock-Fighting Arouses 'Mexicanos,'" *Green Bay Press-Gazette*, November 26, 1929.

9. *El Universal*, quoted in "Would Purge Mexico of Bull Throwing, Cock Fighting, Boxing," *Akron Beacon Journal*, November 26, 1929; "Movement Launched to Ban Fights in Mexico," *The Vernon* (Texas) *Daily Record*, November 25, 1929.

10. "Pide que se prohiban en México," *El Imparcial* (Madrid, Spain), November 21, 1929; "Would Purge Mexico of Bull Throwing, Cock Fighting, Boxing," *Akron Beacon Journal*, November 26, 1929.

11. Alejandro Aguilar Reyes, "Sótelo esta gravisimo," *Afición*, June 7, 1936; *El Nacional*, June 9, 1936; *El Porvenir*, June 8, 1936.

12. Dr. Gilberto Bolaños Cacho was the chief medical doctor of the Boxing Commission of Mexico City beginning 1926. He was known as "the best friend of all prizefighters."

13. Martínez, *La vieja guardia*, 82.

14. Samuel León and Ignacio Marván, *En el cardenismo: 1934–1940* (México: Siglo Veintiuno, 1985), 141.

15. On controversial comics in post-Revolutionary Mexico, see Rubenstein, *Bad Language*.

16. Hugo Arroyo, "Designan a ganadores de premios Fray Nano y Ángel Fernández," *NTR: Periodismo Crítico* (Zacatecas), September 13, 2017.

17. Kevin Brewster, "Patriotic Pastimes: The Role of Sport in Post-Revolutionary Mexico," in Wood and Johnson, *Sporting Cultures*, 1–20.

18. "Murio Paco Sotelo cuatro horas despúes de la pelea," *Afición*, June 8, 1936.

19. Definitive figures are difficult to establish. *Afición* places the number at twenty thousand and is backed up by Talán, who was present at the funeral, while newspaper reports from *El Universal* and *Excelsior* place the number at "many thousands."

20. "Punetazo trágico: murio el boxeador Sotelo," *El Universal*, June 8, 1936.

21. Aguilar, "Murio Paco Sotelo cuatro horas despúes de la pelea," *Afición*, June 8, 1936.

22. Archivo General de la Nación, Fondo Migración, exp. 162744, Luis James Fitten y Sarmiento file. Fitten was an ideal candidate to promote boxing in Mexico. His mother was Mexican, he was Catholic, and he spoke fluent Spanish and was bicultural. He managed some of the first Mexican international champions such as Juan Zurita and Baby Casanova in the 1930s.

23. Talán, *En el 3er Round*, 59–64.

24. Aguilar, "Murio Paco Sotelo cuatro horas despúes de la pelea," *Afición*, June 8, 1936.
25. Carlos Vera, "20,000 personas desfilaron ante el cadáver de Sótelo," *Afición*, June 9, 1936.
26. "Millionaire Toreador Fears Boxing Will End His Sport in Mexico," *New York Times*, February 22, 1928.
27. Ibid.
28. As Gregory Rodríguez has shown, Mexican American boxers from the 1910s onward also fought in Mexico, aided by promoters such as Fitten. Rodríguez, "Palaces of Pain."
29. Overmeyer-Velazquez, *Visions of the Emerald City*, 31–33, 89.
30. Archivo Histórico Muncipal de Xalapa (AHMX), Secretaría de Comercio y Mercados, vol. P-8, exp. 142.
31. AHMX, Comisión Oficial de Box, Programas, no. 2–7.
32. As will be examined below, in 1923, for example, boxing matches like Firpo-Dempsey garnered hundreds of inches of newspaper coverage and spurred the first national radio broadcast. Films of the bout were shown in every major theater in Mexico City, and Jack Dempsey's image was used as an advertisement to sell elixirs to increase male potency.
33. *Afición*, June 15–20, 1936, advertisement: "Reconstruction, blow by blow and round by round," June 18, 1936. This bout and its racial and political implications on the eve of World War II is the subject of Margolick, *Beyond Glory*.
34. Benjamin, *La Revolución*. Stephen Allen makes a similar argument for the correlation between boxing and nationalism in Mexico for a later period. Allen, *A History of Boxing in Mexico*.
35. Eric J. Hobsbawm, *Nations and Nationalism Since 1780: Programme, Myth, Reality*, 2nd edition (Cambridge: Cambridge University Press, 1992), 143. This statement by Hobsbawm paraphrases the ideas of George Orwell.
36. See image in Manuel Alvarez Bravo, Henri Cartier-Bresson, and Walker Evans, *Documentary and Anti-Graphic Photographs* (Steidl: Göttingen, Germany, 2005), 87.
37. Fototeca Nacional del INAH, Catálogo. http://fototeca.inah.gob.mx/fototeca/, retrieved September 25, 2017.
38. "Varios aficionados, El público dice," *Afición*, January 7, 1932.
39. For a discussion of modern sport as product of urban industrial society, see Giulianotti, *Sport: A Critical Sociology*.
40. Jorge Larraín, "The Concept of Identity," in *National Identities and Sociopolitical Changes in Latin America*, ed. Mercedes Durán-Cogan and Antonio Gomez-Moriana (London: Routledge, 2001), 23; Thompson, *The Media and Modernity*, 207.
41. "Comentarios de Fray Nano," *Afición*, June 17, 1936.
42. Paranaguá, *Mexican Cinema*, 125; Ernesto R. Acevedo-Muñoz, *Buñuel and Mexico*; and Mora, *Mexican Cinema*.
43. Boxing places emphasis on individual merit and perseverance fused with primal violence, and this has made it a vehicle for narratives of national and class identities. Clifford Geertz provides a theoretical model for treating boxing as a cultural ritual. See Geertz, "Deep Play: Notes on a Balinese Cock Fight," 1–37.

44. "Hoy es la velada de box pro monument a Sotelo," *Afición*, June 20, 1936.

45. Tepito, a marginal neighborhood in the north of Mexico City, has often been portrayed as a locus of lower-class Mexican urban identity. See Bertaccini, *Ficción y realidad del héroe popular*. Casanova and other boxers still form a central place in Mexican popular memory of this era; they are held up as exemplars of Mexican perseverance and masculine behavior. See, for example, the hagiographic treatment of Casanova in Páez, *A solas en el altar*.

46. "Temas del Día," *Excelsior*, June 16, 1935.

47. See Aguilar Rodríguez, "Cooking Modernity: Nutrition Policies, Class, and Gender in 1940s and 1950s Mexico," 177–205; and Pilcher, *¡Que Vivan Los Tamales!*. Eric Hobsbawm in his work on social banditry has argued that boxers and other popular heroes who come from the slums, like Kid Azteca, can be flashy and arrogant only so far and maintain their credibility in their community of origin. Hobsbawm, *Primitive Rebels*, 22–23.

48. "Temas del Día," *Excelsior*. Mexican popular memory has, however, been kind to the legacy of Kid Azteca.

49. Kay Owe, "Mexicans Hope for Champion," *Los Angeles Times*, February 26, 1933.

50. Arizmendi, like other Mexican boxers, had problems with alcohol and was arrested in the United States for driving while intoxicated. These incidents helped to implant the image of the raffish, working-class Mexican fighter. "Arizmendi, fue acusado en Los Angeles, Calif.," *El Informador* (Guadalajara), November 15, 1936.

51. "Canzoneri Fights Baby Tonight," *Los Angeles Times*, March 13, 1934.

52. Dick Hyland, "Arizmendi Too Soft," *Los Angeles Times*, June 24, 1940.

53. Rubenstein, *Bad Language*, 3.

54. Pérez, "Between Baseball and Bullfighting," 494.

55. See Bonfil Batalla, *México profundo*; González y González, *Invitación a la microhistoria*; Knight, "Revolutionary Project, Recalcitrant People; and Larrain, *Identity and Modernity in Latin America*, 34–42.

56. Mary K. Vaughan, "Nationalizing the Countryside: Schools and Rural Communities in the 1930s," in Vaughan and Lewis, *The Eagle and the Virgin*, 160–61.

57. John E. Wray, "Casanova Punishes Miller in the Last Four Rounds to Win Fight," *St. Louis Post-Dispatch*, January 2, 1936.

58. William E. Loftus, "Evening Chatter," *Evening News* (Wilkes-Barre, PA), January 26, 1932.

59. The pioneer of modern journalism in Mexico, *El Imparcial*, had a sport section beginning in 1908. For more on *El Imparcial*, see García, *El Imparcial*, and Bunker, *Creating Mexican Consumer Culture in the Age of Porfirio Díaz*.

60. *Afición*, July 22, 1942.

61. This dual coverage of traditional Mexican pastimes, bullfighting, and the novel import of modern competitive sport made it an arbiter of both established culture and emergent Mexican association with both domestic and international trends in popular athletics.

62. Brewster and Brewster, *Representing the Nation*.

63. Monsivais, *Mexican Postcards*, 23.
64. These records, which likely would have provided a robust documentary source, have been lost or destroyed.
65. *Revista Pan-Americana*, vol. 43 [1930], 206; Franco, *Glosa del período de gobierno*.
66. Mexico City Ayuntamiento to Fernando Manuel Campos, Offices of the Newspaper *El Universal*, March 2, 1922, AHDF: Fondo Secretaría General Licencias, vol. 3960, exp. 34.
67. Francisco Peredo Castro, "Catholicism and Mexican Cinema," in Daniel Biltereyst and Daniela Treveri Gennari, *Moralizing Cinema* (New York: Routledge, 2015), 69.
68. F. Gamboa to Ayuntamiento, August 5, 1922; AHDF: Fondo Secretara General, Licencias, vol. 3961, exp. 101.
69. AHDF, Fondo Secretaría General, Diversiones, vol. 3924, exp. 64.
70. Ibid.
71. Ibid.
72. *El Demócrata*, September 9, 1923.
73. Speroni, "Firpo-Dempsey," 26–32.
74. Maxi Salgado, "Firpo vs. Dempsey: más que una pelea," *Los Andes* (Mendoza, Argentina), August 28, 2017.
75. The film of the bout, which was exported and shown all over Latin America, shows a number of fouls committed by Dempsey that, most commentators agreed, should have resulted in the victory being awarded to Firpo. See Boxing Hall of Fame Las Vegas, "Jack Dempsey KOs Luis Firpo This Day September 14, 1923," YouTube video, 3:58, Posted September 2016, https://www.youtube.com/watch?v=wciZKMMW7Xc.
76. The two best general studies of these views are Pike, *The United States and Latin America*, 193–215; and John Johnson, *Latin America in Caricature* (Austin: University of Texas Press, 1980).
77. Sheldon Anderson, *The Politics and Culture of Modern Sports* (Lanham, MD: Lexington, 2015), 48.
78. On pulquerias during the Porfirian era see María Áurea Toxqui Garay, "'El Recreo de los Amigos,' Mexico City's Pulquerías During the Liberal Regime," (PhD diss., Arizona State University, 2008); Moats and Lord, *Thunder in Their Veins*; Lauderdale Harrison, *México simpático, tierra de encantos*; and Beals, *Glass Houses, Ten Years of Free-Lancing*.
79. Carleton Beals, "The Magic that Won the Realm," *Scribner's* 100, no. 4 (October, 1936): 90.
80. "El Campeonato," photographer unknown, ca. 1937; author's private collection.
81. Bunker, *Creating Mexican Consumer Culture in the Age of Porfirio Díaz*, 49–56.
82. Romero, Valdez, and Reyes, *Poder público y poder privado*; Camacho Morfin, *Imágenes de México*; and Bunker, *Creating Mexican Consumer Culture in the Age of Porfirio Díaz*, 12–57.
83. "Jack Dempsey, Flavio Aguirre Cárdenas, José Reynosa, en la fábrica El Buen Tono," photographer unknown, 1925, Fototeca Nacional de México.
84. *El Demócrata*, September 15, 1923.

85. *El Demócrata*, September 10, 1923.

86. Stavans, *Jose Vasconcelos: The Prophet of Race*; José Vasconcelos and Didier Tisdel Jaén, *The Cosmic Race: A Bilingual Edition* (Baltimore, MD: Johns Hopkins University Press, 1997).

87. For a broader discussion of race in Mexico, especially elite attempts to "improve" the racial stock of Mexicans, see Suárez y López Guazo, *Eugenesia y racismo en México*, 85–167.

88. "Nueva York sera hoy la capital del mundo deportivo," *El Demócrata*, September 14, 1923.

89. "Cyclone Turner," *El Demócrata*, September 2, 1923.

90. Ibid.

91. "Tarde o Temprano Firpo Será Campeón Mundial," *El Informador*, September 17, 1923; *El Excelsior*, September 12, 1923; *El Universal*, September 11, 1923; "La Verdad Sobre la Lucha Firpo-Dempsey," *El Informador*, September 21, 1923.

92. "Inaguración de una escuela japonesa de jiu-jitsu," *El tiempo*, August 9, 1908; *El popular*, August 5, 1908.

93. *El Demócrata*, September 25, 1923.

94. Ibid. In this account of a boxing match in the Juarez Theater of Oaxaca on September 16, the writer used the pen name "Periquín Rascarabias."

95. *El Demócrata*, September 20, 1923.

96. George Trevor, "Firpo Fulfills Dream of Latin Race for Champion Who Fights With His Fists," *Brooklyn Daily Eagle*, September 5, 1923.

97. Tenorio-Trillo, *Mexico at the World's Fair*, 9.

98. José Juan Tablada, "Dempsey, el hombre más bruto del mundo," *Excelsior*, September 14, 1923.

99. Ibid.

100. Ibid.

101. Ibid.

102. José Juan Tablada, "Dempsey-Carpentier," *Excelsior*, July 3, 1921, reproduced in *Repertorio Americano*, August 20, 1921.

103. Lozano Herrera, *José Juan Tablada en Nueva York*.

104. "Un poeta en San Hipólito," *La voz de México*, September 11, 1895.

105. José Juan Tablada, "Dempsey, el hombre más bruto del mundo," *Excelsior*, September 14, 1923.

106. This refers to the Great Kantō earthquake and tsunami that struck Japan on September 1, 1923, killing between 100,000 and 140,000 people.

107. Rodo warned that unchecked democracy—that not guided by supposedly nobler sentiments—would inevitably lead to barbarism and utilitarianism. Tablada viewed Dempsey as the embodiment of these. José Enrique Rodó and Belén Castro, *Ariel* (Madrid: Cátedra, 2007).

108. *El Demócrata*, September 9, 1923.

109. For more on Tiger Flowers, though his time in Mexico receives little attention, see Kaye, *The Pussycat of Prizefighting*.

110. See Talán, *En el 3er Round*.
111. Don Gaspar, *El demócrata*, September 9, 1923.
112. Ibid.
113. There is significant analysis of the artist José Guadalupe Posada's work and its role in disseminating cultural messages to semiliterate Mexicans during and before this period. See Frank and Posada, *Posada's Broadsheets*; Berdecio, *Posada's Popular Mexican Prints*.
114. *El Porvenir* (Monterrey), May 19, 1923.
115. For an overview of several of these diverse attempts to bring Mexico into line with European and American forms and ideas during the Porfiriato, see Daniel Cosío Villegas et al., *Historia moderna de México. 4, La vida social: el porfiriato (1877–1911)*.
116. *El Informador*, February 9, 1923; *El Demócrata*, August 26, 1923; *La Prensa* (Buenos Aires), October 19, 1919; *El Mundo* (Havana), June 1, 1921; *Star and Herald* (Panama City), August 26, 1921; *Excelsior*, October 12, 1922.
117. *El Demócrata*, August 26, 1923; September 23, 1923.
118. *El Demócrata*, August 25, 1923.
119. There is scant documentation on the identity of most of these fighters. The "negrito," who fought under the name "Battling Duce" in Mexico City, seems to have worked in the capital for several months. Casasola, *Seis siglos de historia gráfica de México*, 2217.
120. Runstedtler, *Jack Johnson, Rebel Sojourner*.
121. *El Universal*, September 8, 1923; *El Demócrata*, September 2, 1923.
122. "La Inauguracion de la temporada de box en 'El Toreo,'" *El Demócrata*, September 10, 1923.
123. Ibid.
124. Ibid. Unfortunately, as with most transnational journeymen fighters in this period, little is known about the background of Battling Norfolk or Cyclone Turner.
125. *El Demócrata*, September 3, 1923.
126. *El Universal*, September 13, 1923.
127. *El Demócrata*, September 14, 1923.
128. Ibid.
129. Ibid.
130. Ibid.
131. *El Nacional*, April 23, 1932; Manuel López de la Parra, "Lucha libre professional en México y su filosofía," *El Informador* (Guadalajara), May 18, 1991.
132. Joseph, *Fragments of a Golden Age*; Rubenstein, *Bad Language*; Garcia Riera, *Historia del cine mexicano*; and Mora, *Cinemachismo*.
133. Niblo, *Mexico in the 1940s*, 64.
134. El Toreo was built as a bullfighting venue but became a popular space for boxing matches in the 1920s and 1930s.
135. Rubenstein, *Bad Language*, 1–40.
136. "The Screen: At the Campoamor," *New York Times*, January 6, 1936.
137. *Mi Revista* (Barcelona), November 15, 1937; "Notas de La Produccion Mejicana," *La Vanguardia* (Barcelona), October 23, 1936; "Royal Theater," *Tampa Times*, December 11, 1935.

138. *El Informador*, September 5, 1929.

139. Ramón Peón was a pioneering director of Cuban and Mexican cinema. He made the last Cuban silent films in the late 1920s and after a stint in Hollywood made several films in Mexico. He was ultimately unable to compete with Hollywood films of the era that "poached" much of the Latin popular music talent that was increasingly shown on film. See Chanan, *Cuban Cinema*, 83–87.

140. The population of Mexico more than doubled between 1940 and 1970. See Francisco Alba and Joseph E. Potter, "Population and Development in Mexico since 1940: An Interpretation," Population and Development Review 12, no. 1 (March 1986): 47–75. For a detailed analysis of comic books and Mexican culture from the 1930s through the 1970s, see Rubenstein, *Bad Language*.

141. Bartra, "The Seduction of the Innocents," 301–26.

142. For an account of these efforts in Mexico City under the Cardenas administration (1934–1940), see Olsen, *Artifacts of Revolution*, 169–99.

143. Bartra, "The Seduction of the Innocents," 308.

144. Ibid.

145. Ibid.

146. Ibid., 314.

147. Ibid., 320.

148. Ibid., 50, 52.

149. "A fuerza de puños," undated clipping from Pepin #72, Biblioteca Nacional de México.

150. Rubenstein, *Bad Language*, 133.

151. Martín-Barbero, *De los medios a las mediaciones*, xxix, 114–22.

152. Pérez, *On Becoming Cuban*.

153. This view on the co-constitutive relationship between popular and mass cultures has been put forth by many scholars of modern Latin America. The idea is a critique of Adorno and Horkheimer's characterization of "cultural industries" as pernicious influences on the masses that stifle creativity and individuality and destroy traditional culture.

154. Talán, *En el 3er Round*, 135. Fidel Ortiz, after his retirement from the amateur ring, continued on the Mexican national team as a boxing coach. He attended the games in Amsterdam (1928), Los Angeles (1932), Berlin (1936), and London (1948).

155. See Moreno, *Yankee Don't Go Home!*, 207–29.

156. Recalling this era, Esperón states that boxing was a preserve of the elite but that after the Porfirato, "the Revolution came and they passed out gloves to everyone." AGN, Propiedad Artistica, caja 684, exp. 8: Salvador Esperón de la Flor, unpublished manuscript "El boxeo científico."

157. *Mexican Herald*, August 14, 1907.

158. López Velarde and Luis Martínez, *Obra poética*, 252.

159. Similar to the character "Luis" in the pepin series *El Viejo Nido*, Martínez Arredondo was a working-class Mexican who through his boxing career was able to travel the country, knowing distant regions of Mexico and the United States that he would have been unlikely to experience given his class status.

160. There is fragmentary documentation on the identity of Jim Smith, who arrived in Mexico City sometime toward the end of the Porfiriato. He was variously cited as American, Jamaican, and Australian. He was an enormously prolific prizefighter and traveled virtually all of Mexico, fighting from Oaxaca to Ciudad Juárez. His rivalry with Martínez Arredondo provided constant fodder for newspaper columns toward the end of the military phase of the Mexican Revolution.

161. In 1928, after a series of foreigners held the title of "Mexican champion" throughout the years of the Revolution and the 1920s, the Boxing Commission decreed that to hold such a distinction a fighter would have to be Mexican-born.

162. *El Heraldo de Mexico*, September 10, 1919.

163. There are several pictures of his trip to Mexico housed in the photographic collection of the Archivo Casasola in the Archivo General de la Nación.

164. *Arte y Sport*, February 28, 1920.

165. Ibid.

166. AHDF, Fondo Ayuntamiento, Diversiones Publicas, Vol. 811, Exp. 1637.

167. Ibid.

168. *Arte y sport*, February 28, 1920.

169. Enrique Ugartechea, though little information on him survives, should be seen as one of the first Mexicans to introduce modern physical culture to the Mexican elite in the early twentieth century. He was a bodybuilder and wrestler who made a living through his "Centro de Cultura Física Ugartechea," the first of its kind in Mexico. He began his career by trying to incorporate the methods of the famous German body builder Eugene Sandow. See chapter 1.

170. *Arte y sport*, February 28, 1920.

171. *Excelsior*, March 13, 1920.

172. A frontón is a space dedicated to the Basque-derived sport of jai alai. Along with bullrings, these were symbolic spaces that recalled Hispanic culture, and they were often used to stage modern boxing matches in both Mexico and Cuba.

173. The Queensbury Rules, codified in 1867 in London, replaced the London Prize Ring Rules that had guided boxing matches since 1743. Their adoption in Mexico was important to elite observers like the journalist for *Excelsior*, who hoped that by narrowing the possibilities for disagreements over boxing matches, disorder could be avoided.

174. *Excelsior*, March 13, 1920.

175. AHDF, Diversiones, vol. 811, exp. 188, "Comision nombrada para los asaltos de box."

176. *Excelsior*, March 22, 1920.

177. Ibid.

178. As Allen Guttmann and Alan Klein have shown, modern sport culture in general first entered Latin American societies through the transnational contacts and travels of elite society and through the presence of foreign residents, especially British and Americans. Guttmann argues, citing Klein, that modern sport "was first the province of the elite and then taken over by other sectors of society only underscores the fact that culture is competed for." Guttmann, *Games and Empires*, 70; and Klein, "Sport and Colonialism in Latin America and the Caribbean," 257–71.

179. On the career of Enrique Ugartechea, see chapter 1.

180. Looking back on this rivalry, Arredondo claimed that Smith had once bit him in the forehead during a fight. Despite their supposed dislike for each other, they engaged in several bouts, including taking part in carnival festivities. See Talán, *En el 3er Round*.

181. *Excelsior*, September 26, 1917.

182. The circus in Porfirian Mexico employed athletes. For an overview of the Circo Orrín as an important site in the cultural life of Mexico City, see Revolledo Cárdenas, *La fabulosa historia del circo en México*, 160–65.

183. Febles also figures in the early history of boxing in Cuba, and there is some debate as to whether he was born in Cuba or Mexico. It is likely that he was born in Veracruz, as he himself stated in his interview with Raúl Talán. His origins may have been kept purposely vague and contingent on the necessity to stir controversy when advertising a boxing match. The Mexico City press was often contradictory, sometimes citing him as "South American," sometimes as "Mexican," and often as simply "Southeastern." In 1913, he lived in Havana, where he held boxing matches in his home. See Encinosa, *Azúcar y Chocolate*; and Alonso, *Puños dorados*, 21.

184. This claim is supported by an article in *Revista de policía*, December 30, 1925.

185. Talán, *En el 3er Round*, 26–28.

186. Febles, according to Talán, lived in an impoverished neighborhood of Tacuba with a "humble" seventy-year-old woman. Even the taxi driver has a difficult time finding the house and has to ask a couple of local drunks for assistance.

187. Talán, *En el 3er Round*, 24.

188. *Excelsior*, October 10, 1922. Jimmie Dundee took up residence in Mexico City, married a Mexican woman, and later became a naturalized citizen.

189. Rowe and Schelling, *Memory and Modernity*, 1.

190. Alejandro Galindo (dir.), *Campeón Sin Corona* (Excaliber Media Group, 1946). Galindo was the most outspoken Mexican director in this period. He was the first to use, in *Campeón Sin Corona*, what Carl Mora describes as authentic street dialogue from the slums of Mexico City. Similar to the films of his contemporary Elia Kazan, Galindo's work used Marxian critiques to represent the struggles of working-class Mexicans in the face of immobile socioeconomic difficulties. The Mexican relationship with the United States also figures prominently in Galindo's critique of transnational capitalism, as in his overtly political films *Wetbacks* (1952), in which his explicit purpose was "to convince Mexicans not to go to the United States." Mora, *Mexican Cinema*, 88.

191. Aviña, *David Silva*, 71; *El Informador* (Guadalajára), August 27, 1946; April 28, 1947; February 13, 1949.

192. *Bakersfield Californian*, December 16, 1947; *Arizona Daily Star* (Tucson), December 23, 1949; *Brownwood* (Texas) *Bulletin*, February 5, 1956; *Albuquerque Journal*, December 20, 1949.

193. The most famous actor of the period, Pedro Infante, would also play the role of the Mexican boxer in *Pepe el Toro* (1953).

194. *El Redondel*, June 16, 1946.

195. Aviña, *David Silva*, 73.
196. "Cinematográficas," *El Informador*, September 3, 1946.
197. Ramírez, *The Woman in the Zoot Suit*; Obregón Pagán, *Murder at the Sleepy Lagoon*.
198. Maldonado, *Pasión por los guantes*; Talán, *En el 3er round*. Conde was born in Mazatlán to Scottish parents and was a successful but unpopular boxer in the late 1920s and early 1930s.
199. The film historian Carlos Mora has identified the "inferiority complex" of the Mexican men as one of the most salient ideas in Galindo's films. Mora, *Mexican Cinema*, 71.
200. Acevedo-Muñoz, *Buñuel and Mexico*, 169.
201. Other films that drew on boxing as an established medium of expressing working-class mexicanidad are *El Gran Campeón* (1949); *Kid Tabaco* (1954); *Pepe el Toro* (1953); *Guantes de Oro* (1961); *Barrio de Campeónes* (1977); *Ángel del Barrio* (1980); *Nocaut* (1984).
202. Ramírez Berg, *Cinema of Solitude*, 169.

## Chapter Six

1. "Homenaje a Kid Chocolate" (Homage to Kid Chocolate), *El Diario de la Marina*, September 1, 1929.
2. José "Joe" Massaguer, *New York Times*, August 30, 1929; John Kieran, "Sports of the Times," *New York Times*, October 24, 1929.
3. See Bronfman, *Measures of Equality*; and Foner, *Antonio Maceo*.
4. "I have chosen the word transculturation to express the highly varied phenomenon that have come about in Cuba as a result of the highly complex transmutations of culture that have taken place here ... in the economic ... institutional, legal, ethical, religious, artistic, linguistic, psychological, sexual, or other aspects of life.... The real history of Cuba is the history of its intermeshed transculturations." Ortiz, *Cuban Counterpoint*.
5. "Ideales de una Raza," *Diario de la Marina*, October 29, 1929.
6. Association of Veterans to President Mario Menocal, ANC, Secretaría de la Presidencia, caja 19, numero 8.
7. Kanellos, *Hispanic Literature of the United States*. Chocolate was photographed nude by the Cuban Hungarian photographer Aladar Hajdu in his Havana studio, "Rembrandt," located on the Paseo del Prado. Alonso, Contreras, and Fagiuoli, *Havana Deco*, 156–57; Díaz Burgos et al., *Cuba—100 años de fotografía*, 111.
8. As shown in chapter 2, this tendency to gauge Cuban culture through the lens of American norms was a defining characteristic of Cuban life in this period. See Pérez, *On Becoming Cuban*.
9. M. Aramburu had been a proponent of the Cuban appropriation of physical culture since the early twentieth century. Mario Aramburu, "La Cultura Física y la Cultura Intelectual," *Diario de la Marina Numero Centenario, La Habana, Cuba* (La Habana: Úcar, García y Cía, 1932), 58–59. This idea of Cuban culture as vacillating between the Hispanic legacy and the onslaught of American culture, broadly defined, is echoed by Cuban intellectual Fernando Ortiz: "The attraction to Spain each day weaker across the Atlantic, and the

attraction to North America every day stronger and closer." Ortiz, *Pueblo Cubano*, quoted in Botín, *Los funerales de Castro*, 24.

10. Botín, *Los funerales de Castro*.

11. There remains much research to be done on Cuban perceptions of the body in a comparative context. There is no similar shortage of historical explorations of American perceptions of Cubans as effeminate and passive. See Kaplan, *Cultures of United States Imperialism*. As will be shown in this chapter, the extent of the Cuban appropriation of American-style sport is cited as a measuring stick by various American observers the first decades of the twentieth century to describe perceptions of positive, American-style changes in Cuban culture.

12. The popular magazine *Carteles*, for example, carried regular accounts of athletes like Jack Dempsey and Babe Ruth as "supermen," who embodied normative masculine prowess. This will be examined in greater depth later in this chapter.

13. Quoted in Pérez, *Cuba in the American Imagination*, 85–86.

14. Sigal, *Infamous Desire*. For modern accounts of the state and attempts to suppress homosexuality and effeminacy as damaging to the social body, see Green, *Beyond Carnival*; Bejel, *Gay Cuban Nation*; Irwin, *Mexican Masculinities*; and Vera and Caruso, *Imported Modernity in Post-Colonial State Formation*.

15. Rosalie Schwartz, "Cuba's Roaring Twenties: Race Consciousness and the Column 'Ideales de Una Raza'"; Keith Ellis, "Nicolás Guillén and Langston Hughes: Convergences and Divergences"; and Lisa Brock and Bijan Bayne, "Not Just Black: African-Americans, Cubans, and Baseball," in Brock and Fuertes, *Between Race and Empire*, 104–20, 129–68, and 168–205, respectively.

16. Helg, *Our Rightful Share*; Fuente, *A Nation for All*; Belnap and Fernández, *José Martí's "Our America"*; Guerra, *The Myth of José Martí*.

17. Joeś Raùl Capablanca and Fred Reinfeld, *The Immortal Games of Capablanca*; Linder and Linder, *José Raúl Capablanca*. As Kid Chocolate remembered in a 1987 documentary about his life, "My fixation, ever since I was a boy, was to get to Madison Square Garden." Cited in Pérez, *On Becoming Cuban*, 413.

18. McGehee, "The Dandy and the Mauler in Mexico. This study gives basic information on the amount of press coverage generated by these two boxers, but gives little analysis of the nature of their reception and does not place them in a broader context.

19. Fuente argues that the official rhetoric of racelessness was a powerful tool for Afro-Cubans to press their claims for social equality. Though the most elite social clubs, for example, were generally closed to them, the type of official public segregation experienced in the American South was unknown in Cuba. Fuente, *A Nation for All*.

20. Cahoone, *Cultural Revolutions*; James, Plaice, and Toren, *Culture Wars*.

21. Aside from hagiographical histories of Cuban boxers like *Azúcar and Chocolate*, and *Kid Chocolate, El boxeo soy yo*, the only scholarly treatment of sport in twentieth-century Cuba, Pettavino and Pye, *Sport in Cuba*, has little analysis of the central role of Cuban sport in the public sphere in the 1920s. "Compre la bandera de su patria o de su club," *Carteles*, December 1921, 16.

22. "Compre la bandera de su patria o de su club," *Carteles*, December 1921, 16.
23. Kellner, *The Harlem Renaissance*; and Antón and Hernández, *Cubans in America*.
24. Moore, *Nationalizing Blackness*. Moore has since extended his analysis of music and cultural change in *Music and Revolution*. Vera Kutzinki examines race and the eroticization of Cubans of color in Kutzinski, *Sugar's Secrets*. Another important study, examining similar issues of popular music in Brazil, is Hermano Vianna, *The Mystery of Samba: Popular Music & National Identity in Brazil*, trans. John Charles Chasteen (Chapel Hill: University of North Carolina Press, 1999).
25. Bederman, *Manliness and Civilization*; Gilmore, *Bad Nigger!*; Kaye, *The Pussycat of Prizefighting*.
26. Carter, "Baseball Arguments," 117–39. Schwartz, *Pleasure Island*.
27. Pérez, *On Becoming Cuban*; López, *La Radio en Cuba*; and Salwen, *Radio and Television in Cuba*.
28. Pettavino and Pye, *Sport in Cuba*.
29. Bejel, *Gay Cuban Nation*, 32–35.
30. The counterpoint to this argument, which failed to stem the Cuban appropriation of boxing, was voiced by conservatives groups like the above-mentioned Association of Veterans, which focused on boxing and bullfighting as threats to the sacrifices they had made to the nation. Boxing was, they argued, simply barbaric, while bullfighting was both barbaric and linked to the colonial past they had sought to sever.
31. Smith, *The Sundowners*, vol. II, part 1.
32. Mañach, *Glosas*. "All those spectacles that offer attraction for the tourist: the races, boxing, cabarets. They are a disgrace. The foreigner comes here to find what is not permitted in his own country." Francisco José Castellanos, *Poca Cosa*, 1915, cited in Pérez, *On Becoming Cuban*, 165.
33. José Sixto de Sola, "El Deporte Como Factor Patriótico y Sociológico," *Cuba Contemporánea* 5 (June 1914): 121–29.
34. Ibid.
35. ANC, Fondo Asociaciones, Exp. Club Atlético de Cuba. San Martín, *El Arte de los Puños*; see chapter 2.
36. "El Beneficio de San Martín," *El Mundo*, March 12, 1916.
37. "Quienes son los champions," *El Mundo*, November 12, 1915.
38. "Charlas Pugilisticas," *El Heraldo Deportivo*, May 12, 1918, 4.
39. Jason, "Algo de Boxeo y de Nuestros Boxeadores," *Carteles*, December 1921, 24.
40. *Outing and the Wheelman* (Boston: Wheelman Co, 1884), 222; Hughson, Free, and Inglis, *The Uses of Sport*; Smith, *Latin American Democratic Transformations*.
41. Piccato, "Politics and the Technology of Honor," 331–54; and Piccato, *The Tyranny of Opinion*.
42. Stepan, *The Hour of Eugenics*.
43. Benson, *Battling Siki*.
44. Guillén, "Ideales de una Raza."
45. Biblioteca Nacional José Martí, *El Arte de los Puños*.

46. For example, they recount a trip to the town of Aguacate (a Hershey sugar mill town in Havana Province), where they chided the local residents for their fascination with baseball and relative lack of interest in boxing. This, Cubillas and San Martín implied, was proof of their backwardness and quaint small-town insularity. The baseball players, they mocked, wore their uniforms in public twenty-four hours before the game and they imagine they "even slept in them." See Kahn and Weatherby, *Sugar*, 70; and *El Arte de los Puños*, 218–19. There are few extant copies of this daily newspaper, too few to gain more than an impressionistic picture of the public discourse it created or sought to mold.

47. Photographer and date unknown; author's private collection,.

48. Cubillas and San Martín, *El Arte de los puños*, 10.

49. *El Diario de la Marina*, *El Mundo*, and *El Día* have no mention of Marroquín's death.

50. Andrés Diago y Guell was a young basketball player and member of the aristocratic Vedado Tennis Club (VTC). He died after an accident on the court and was treated to a public funeral and procession, where his remains were carried on the shoulders of representatives of the VTC, the Club de Dependientes, and the Club Atlético de Cuba. He was buried wrapped in the flag of the VTC. *Carteles*, December 1921, 6. See also the account in León Primelles, *Crónica cubana, 1919–1922: Menocal y la Liga Nacional* (Habana: Editorial Lex, 1957).

51. Unión Panamericana, *Boletín*, vol. 44 (1917), 247; and Primelles, *Crónica cubana, 1915–1918*.

52. Cubillas and San Martín, *El Arte de los puños*, 12–13.

53. Ibid., 10.

54. "El Habana Boxing Club," *El Mundo*, November 15, 1915.

55. San Martín, "Mike Febles contra Andres Duarte," "Notas de ring," *El Mundo*, November 26, 1915.

56. Cubillas and San Martín, *El Arte de los puños*, 10.

57. Ibid., 10–11.

58. Ibid.

59. See Ortiz, *Los negros brujos*, and Castellanos, *Contribución al estudio craneométrico*; Castellanos, *La brujería y el ñañiguismo en Cuba*.

60. Bronfman, *Measures of Equality*, 49, 112, 149.

61. Stepan, *The Hour of Eugenics*.

62. A study to quantify and qualify these ubiquitous visual representations of Afro-Cubans as a comically rendered servant class remains to be done.

63. San Martín, "Notas del ring," *El Mundo*, November 24, 1915; San Martín, "Mike Febles contra Andres Duarte," "Notas de ring," *El Mundo*, November 26, 1915.

64. "Un Cubano pugilistica en los Estados Unidos," *El Mundo*, April 8, 1916; "Saint John's College, Fordham, Eighteenth Annual Commencement," July 8, 1863, 6, 10, 22.

65. Gabriel B. Lersundi, "Comentarios," *El Mundo*, July 13, 1914. Achán would later train the first generation of Cuban boxers to win titles abroad.

66. "El Renacimiento del Boxeo," *Carteles*, November 1921.

67. Jasón, "Algo de boxeo y de nuestros boxeadores," *Carteles*, December 1921, 24.
68. Dr. C. H. Mac Donald, "Cuba se esta hacienda una nación de atlética," *Carteles*, November 1921. As mentioned above, Cubans were well aware of the negative stereotypes held by Americans about the effeminacy of Cubans.
69. Cubillas and San Martín, *El Arte de los puños*.
70. *The Rotarian*, September 1918. There are well over one thousand social and athletic clubs whose charters are preserved in the Cuban National Archives.
71. The thousands of clubs dedicated to physical culture constitute an unstudied sector of the Cuban public sphere. Their records are housed in the ANC, Registro Asociaciones. For example, there are more than thirty clubs listed alone whose title contains "Deportista."
72. ANC, Registro de Asociaciónes, Expediente Asociación Nacional de Boxeo Cubana.
73. ANC, Registro de Asociaciónes, leg. 366, exp. 11152.
74. Oscar Massaguer, "De interes para los amantes de boxeo," *Carteles*, August 1921.
75. Miller and Wiggins, *Sport and the Color Line*.
76. "Cronica de Mexico: Es Dempsey el Campeón del Mundo?," *Carteles*, October 1921.
77. Roberts, *Jack Dempsey, the Manassa Mauler*, 118, 268.
78. Ibid. "Cronica de Mexico: Es Dempsey el Campeón del Mundo?,"*Carteles*, October 1921; and José Albuerne, "Babe Ruth, el famoso beisbolista, es un Superhombre," *Carteles*, November 1921.
79. "Cronica de Mexico: Es Dempsey el Campeón del Mundo?,"*Carteles*, October 1921.
80. In a 1921 bout, "Black Dempsey" fought and defeated the Chinese Cuban Chani Chano at Santos y Artigas Park. "Dempsey knock-out en el Segundo," *El Mundo*, February 21, 1921.
81. "Boxeo: La fiesta pugilística de esta noche," *Diario de la Marina*, February 24, 1921.
82. *Carteles*, December 1921.
83. See chapter 3 and "Boxeo," *Diario de la Marina*, January 3, 1921.
84. "Breenan [sic], peleará el dia 14," *El Mundo*, March 9, 1921.
85. Menéndez and Ortega, *Kid Chocolate, "el boxeo soy yo—."*
86. "Black Bill peleará contra Molinet," *El Mundo*, June 13, 1923.
87. Cubillas and San Martín, *El Arte de los puños*, 3–6.
88. Though there are no statistical figures on the races of the hundreds of Cuban boxers in this period, those who gained international prominence were almost uniformly Afro-Cubans. This association of sport with Afro-Cuban participation remains today. Though before the Revolution, most aristocratic sporting clubs were, de facto, closed to Afro-Cubans, they excelled nonetheless in the most visible forms of physical culture on the island.
89. *New York Times*, August 21, 22, 1911.
90. Partido Conservador, "Plataforma Electoral para las elecciones de 1932," in Biblioteca Nacional José Martí, Colección Cubana, 1932. Cited in Rosell, *Luchas obreras contra Machado*, 205.
91. See, for example, Jacques Montane, "Sport in the World By Way of Great Boxing Championship: The First Days of Boxing," *Carteles*, December 1921.

92. Cubillas and San Martín, *El Arte de los puños*, 7.
93. Lewis, *The Culture of Gender and Sexuality in the Caribbean*.
94. Thomas, *Cuba, or, The Pursuit of Freedom*; Fowler and Lambert, *Political Violence and the Construction of National Identity*.
95. Fowler and Lambert, *Political Violence and the Construction of National Identity*; Jason, "Algo de Boxeo y de Nuestros Boxeadores," *Carteles*, December 1921, 24.
96. Cubillas and San Martín, *El Arte de los puños*, 14.
97. *Anales de la Academia de Ciencias Medicas, Físicas, y Naturales de la Habana*, vol. 58 (1921–22): 291.
98. Ibid., 322–29.
99. ANC: Reglamento de la Comisión Nacional de Boxeo, *Gaceta Oficial*, July 19, 1922, 1587.
100. Ibid.
101. Unfortunately, none of these records remain. They would have been a rich source and a social profile for the perhaps thousands of Cubans who registered as professional boxers before the Revolution.
102. *Gaceta Oficial*, July 25, 1923, 13997; García, *Legislación social de Cuba*, 406.
103. *El Mundo*, September 15, 1923.
104. "Globetol," artist and date unkown; author's private collection.
105. *Diario de sesiones de la Cámara de Diputados* (Buenos Aires, Argentina, Congreso de la Nación. Cámara de Diputados de la Nación, issues 129–205, 1922), 271.
106. *La Nación* (Buenos Aires), November 11, 1923; *El Mundo*, September 11, 1923.
107. Lears, *Fables of Abundance*, 151. See also Leach, *Land of Desire*.
108. Boddy, *Boxing: A Cultural History*; "Jack Johnson" file at the National Museum of Immigration (Buenos Aires, Argentina).
109. Manuel Giz, "To Luis Ángel Firpo," *Diario de la Marina*, September 1, 1923
110. José F. de la Peña, "The Victor," *El Mundo*, August 28, 1923.
111. "Tratemos de Algo . . . ," *Diario de la Marina*, September 11, 1923.
112. "Firpo Looks on Lodge Bout as Set-Up," *Brooklyn Daily Eagle*, February 12, 1924.
113. "Hoy," *El Mundo*, September 15, 1923; Luis Ángel Firpo, "Firpo's Experience in America," *Pittston Gazette*, March 19, 1924. See chapter 4.
114. *La Prensa*, July 14, 1923, reprinted as Grantland Rice, "The Latin Viewpoint," *Nashville Tennessean*, July 29, 1923; *Ogden Standard-Examiner*, July 21, 1929; *Bridgeport Telegram*, July 20, 1923.
115. *La Prensa*, July 14, 1923.
116. See chapter 4 for an account of this meeting of the Spanish Beneficent Society of New York in which Luis Ángel Firpo was awarded these tokens of admiration. *El Mundo*, September 11, 1923.
117. "Firpo's Friends Present Medal," *Harrisburg Telegraph*, September 14, 1923.
118. *El Mundo*, September 12, 17, 1923.
119. "Warrant for Firpo Denied as Artifice," *New York Times*, September 12, 1924; "Reformers Now Seek Mann Act Warrant for Wayward Firpo," *Chicago Daily Tribune*,

September 11, 1924; Brian D. Bunk, "A 'Suspiciously Swarthy' Boxer: Luis Firpo and the Ambiguities of the Latin Race," *Radical History Review* 125 (2016); Sann, *The Lawless Decade*.

120. "Magnífico programa presentan los Sres. Santos y Artigas a los fanáticos, hoy," *Diario de la Marina*, September 1, 1923.

121. "El Verdadero Valor de los boxeadores de color." *Carteles*, May 1922.

122. Roosevelt, *The Strenuous Life*; Bederman, *Manliness and Civilization*; Hoganson, *Fighting for American Manhood*; Gerstner, *Manly Arts*.

123. Benítez Veguillas, *Cuba ante la historia y el sentido común*.

124. Baudilio Danes, "Las glándulas endocrinas y la neurasthenia," *Revista médica cubana* 32 (1921): 826.

125. Lears, *Rebirth of a Nation*.

126. Alejandro Andrade Coello, "El Ecuador Intelectual," *Cuba Contemporanea* 12 (1916): 179–91.

127. See Image in *El Mundo*, September 21, 1923.

128. "Wills No Podra Nunca Disputar a Firpo El Titulo Mundial," *Diario de la Marina*, September 7, 1923; "Harry Wills Dice Que El Argentino No Ataja a Nadie," *El Mundo*, September 24, 1923.

129. *El Mundo*, August 22 and 23, 1923.

130. "El Manager de Harry Wills Trata de Impedir la Pelea Desmpey-Firpo," *El Mundo*, September 6, 1923; "Dempsey Dice que Jamas le Dara un Chance a H. Wills," *El Mundo*, September 7, 1923.

131. "Dempsey Dice que Jamas le Dara un Chance a H. Wills," *El Mundo*, September 7, 1923.

132. *El Mundo*, August 29 and 31, 1923; *Diario de la Marina*, August 29, 1923.

133. *Diario de la Marina*, August 29, 1923.

134. Ibid.

135. "Boxeo Amateur," *El Mundo*, August 22, 1923; "Union Atletico de Amateurs," *El Mundo*, September 3, 1923.

136. Massaguer, "Topicos de *El Día*," *El Mundo*, August 28, 1923.

137. Harris Brothers was one of the first department stores in Cuba. It still exists (2010) as a store for tourist and Cubans with access to outside currency.

138. "Convocation of the Amateur Boxing Championship of Cuba," *Diario de la Marina*, September 2, 1923.

139. *El Mundo*, August 28, 1923.

140. *Diario de la Marina*, September 8, 1923.

141. "Un firpista más (Another Firpo Supporter)," *Diario de la Marina*, September 6, 1923.

142. E. N. Robaina "Un gran número de cubanos ha invadido la ciudad de N. York," *El Mundo*, September 13, 1923.

143. Joe Massaguer, "Tópicos de *El Día*," September 12, 1923.

144. Joe Massaguer, "Tópicos de *El Día*," September 7, 1923.

145. "Joe" Massaguer, "Topicos de El Día," *El Mundo*, August 25, 1923.
146. *Diario de la Marina*, September 10, 1923.
147. Ibid.
148. *Diario de la Marina*, September 11, 1923.
149. Ibid.
150. Manuel Fernández, "Cachorro de León," *El Mundo*, July 6, 1923.
151. *El Mundo*, September 3, 1923.
152. "Gana Dempsey Mr. Gallagher! . . . Gana Firpo, Mr. Shean . . . !," *El Mundo*, September 13, 1923.
153. Ibid.
154. "Un Firpista 'verdá,'" *El Mundo*, September 5, 1923.
155. Ibid.
156. Ibid.
157. *El Mundo*, September 3, 1923.
158. *El Mundo*, September 6, 1923.
159. Ibid.
160. *El Mundo*, September 12, 1923.
161. Ibid.
162. *El Mundo*, September 13, 1923; Ángel C. Betancourt y Miranda, *Census of the Republic of Cuba 1919* (Havana: Maza, Arroyo y Caso Printers, 1920), 392.
163. Bentancourt y Miranda, *Census*, 392.
164. *El Mundo*, September 14, 1923.
165. López, *La radio en Cuba*.
166. *El Mundo*, September 14, 1923.
167. "Radiotelefonia," *Diario de la Marina*, September 12, 1923. Pictures published the following day in *El Mundo* show four locations where a racial, gender, and age mix of people listened to the match.
168. Ibid.
169. The racial/ethnic overtones of the fight generated dramatic media coverage that played on ethnic stereotypes. One writer expressed the victory of the Afro-Cuban fighter over the Jewish American in comedic terms: "Without even being Arab, Kid Chocolate imposed a terrible punishment on the Hebrew." "La gran estregia de Pincho fue factor principal en el triunfo de Kid Chocoalte," *Diario de la Marina*, September 7, 1929.
170. "Meet Cyril Josephs," *The New York Age*, January 9, 1932.
171. "Kid Chocolate en Guanabacoa," *Diario de la Marina*, September 30, 1929.
172. "Recibe y agasaja el ayuntamiento Camagueyano a 'Kid' Chocolate y su manager Pincho Gutierrez," *Diario de la Marina*, September 29, 1929; *Diario de la Marina*, September 12, 1929.
173. Advertisement for "El Sol: Trajes," circa 1929; author's private collection.
174. Enver Casimir, "Contours of Transnational Contact: Kid Chocolate, Cuba, and the United States in the 1920s and 1930s," *Journal of Sport History* 39, no. 3 (2012): 494.

175. "Cuban Boxers Are on the Way to New York Arena," *Fort Lauderdale News*, February 28, 1925; "Cuban Lightweight Boxer on Way to New York," *Brooklyn Daily Eagle*, March 1, 1925.

176. Readers as far from New York as Racine, Wisconsin, and Billings, Montana, read coverage of the shadowy Cubans entering the US boxing circuit. "Among the Battlers," *Racine Journal-Times*, March 7, 1925; "Cubans Seeking Leonard Crown," *Billings Gazette*, March 10, 1925.

177. "Black Bill Wins His First Bout in U.S. at the Commonwealth Club," *New York Age*, April 11, 1925.

178. "The Death of Pancho Villa," *Pittsburgh Courier*, July 25, 1925. The Pancho Villa referred to in the title of this article was a Filipino flyweight boxer.

179. Ibid.

180. Ibid.

181. The Cuban Bon-Bon was how Chocolate was often referred to in the United States. "Chocolate to Bid for Three Crowns," *Evening News* (Wilkes-Barre, PA), April 6, 1929; "Chocolate Gets Chance at Featherweight Title," *Tallahassee Democrat*, January 19, 1930; "La Baraba Wins from Graham," *Los Angeles Times*, May 29, 1930.

182. *Diario de la Marina*, September 8, 1923.

183. Edward J. Neil, "Cuba cuenta con una estrella en el reino de Pugilism (Cuba has a star in the realm of pugilism)," *Diario de la Marina*, September 8, 1929.

184. Ibid.

185. Ibid.

186. Ibid.

187. The Club Atenas was the most elite Afro-Cuban social club. ANC, Fondo Secretaria de la Presidencia, caja 39, numero 19. For a detailed account of the public outrage and protest generated by this event, see Guridy, *Forging Diaspora*, 171–75; Guillermo Pi, "Homenaje a Eligio Sardiñas 'Chocolate,'" *Díario de la Marina*, September 1, 1929.

188. "Bibliografia de autores de la raza de color, de Cuba," *Cuba Contemporanea*, January 1, 1927, 69.

189. The Club Atenas regarded itself as the representative of the "high life de color" in Cuba. "El Banquete del Club Atenas," in *Ideales de Una Raz*, September 30, 1929.

190. Kid Chocolate's background is explored in Menéndez and Ortega, *Kid Chocolate*.

191. Nemesio Lavié, "Blanco y Negro," *Diario de Cuba*, September 4, 1929.

192. Ibid.

193. Nicolás Guillén, "La Humilidad, Kid Chocolate, y El Senor Lavié,'" "Ideales de una Raza," *Díario de la Marina*, September 15, 1929.

194. "La Lección que enseña Chocolate," *El Camagueyano*, date unknown, reprinted in "Ideales de una Raza," September 15, 1929.

195. Ibid.

196. Archivo Nacional de Cuba, Fondo Especial, caja/legajo 4, no. nuevo 675; L. Vizcaíno, *Apuntes para la historia del movimiento juvenil comunista y pioneril cubano* (La

Habana: Editora Política, 1987); Donald F. Busky, *Communism in History and Theory: Asia, Africa, and the Americas* (Westport, CT: Praeger, 2002).

197. Moore, *Nationalizing Blackness*, 46, and Rine Leal, *Breve historia del teatro cubano*.
198. ANC Fondo Especial, caja/legajo 4, no. nuevo 675.
199. Image by the author; author's private collection.

# Bibliography

## Archives

Acervo Histórico de la Secretaria de Relaciones Exteriores (Mexico)
Archivo Casasola (Mexico)
Archivo Histórico del Distrito Federal (Mexico)
Archivo General de la Nación (Mexico)
Archivo Nacional de la Nación (Argentina)
Archivo Nacional de Cuba
Archivo del Museo del Deporte (Cuba)
General Records of the Department of State, Record Group 59, National Archives, Washington, DC
Records of the Immigration and Naturalization Service, Record Group 85, National Archives, Washington, DC
Museo Nacional de Inmigración (Argentina)

## Newspapers and Periodicals

### ARGENTINE PERIODICALS

*Caras y Caretas*
*El Monitor de la educación común*

### ARGENTINE NEWSPAPERS

*La Critica*
*La Vanguardia*
*La Nación*

### CHILEAN NEWSPAPER

*El Mercurio*

## CUBAN NEWSPAPERS

*El Dia*
*Diario de la Marina*
*Havana Post*
*Heraldo de Cuba*
*La Lucha*
*Minerva*
*El Mundo*
*La Noche*
*La Patria*
*El Triunfo*

## CUBAN PERIODICALS

*El Base-Ball*
*Bohemia*
*Carteles*
*Cuba Contemporanea*
*Cuba y América*
*Gaceta Internacional*
*Gaceta Oficial*
*La Insutrucción Primaria*
*Revista de la Facultad de Letras y Ciencias*
*Sport*

## ITALIAN PERIODICAL

*Cineteca*

## MEXICAN NEWSPAPERS

*Afición* (daily)
*Daily Anglo-American*
*El Díario*
*El Dictámen*
*El Espectador de México*
*Excelsior*
*Gazeta de México*
*El Globo*
*El Imparcial*
*El Informador*
*La Patria*

*La Voz de México*
*Mexican Herald*
*El Monitor Republicano*
*El Mundo*
*El Nacional*
*Nueva Era*
*El Partido Liberal*
*El Popular*
*El Redondel*
*El Siglo Diez y Nueve*
*El Tiempo*
*El Universal*

MEXICAN PERIODICALS

*Afición* (weekly)
*Annuario Mexicano*
*Arte y Sport*
*Boletín de instrucción pública*
*Consejo Nacional de Población, México Demográfico*
*Cosmos*
*La Enseñanza normal*
*Futból*
*Memorias y revista de la Academia Nacional de Ciencias Antonio Alzate*
*Mexico; revista de sociedad, arte y letras*
*Mexican Sportsman*
*El Mundo Ilustrado*
*Revista Pan-Americana*
*Ring Mundial*

PANAMANIAN NEWSPAPERS

*Estrella de Panama*

UK PERIODICALS

*The Statist: A Journal of Practical Finance and Trade*

US NEWSPAPERS

*Bisbee Daily Review*
*Daily Herald*
*Freeman*

*Gazette*
*Houston Post*
*The New York Herald*
*New York Times*
*Ogden Morning Examiner*
*El Paso Herald*
*Salt Lake Herald Republican*
*San Francisco Call*
*Tacoma Times*
*Washington Post*
*Washington Tribune*

US PERIODICALS

*Arbitration Series*
*Bulletin of the United States Geographical Survey*
*Cuba Review and Bulletin*
*Dun's International Trade Review*
*The Crisis*
*The Friend*
*Mexican Mining Journal*
*Missionary Voice*
*Outing*
*The Rotarian*
*Ring*
*Scribner's*

BRITISH GUYANA

*Daily Chronicle*

## Documentary Films

Burns, Ken. *Unforgivable Blackness* (2008).

## Books and Articles / Primary and Secondary

Abel, Richard. *Encyclopedia of Early Cinema*. New York: Routledge, 2005.
Acereda, Alberto, and Rigoberto Guevara. *Modernism, Rubén Darío, and the Poetics of Despair*. Lanham, MD: University Press of America, 2004.
Acevedo-Muñoz, Ernesto R. *Buñuel and Mexico: The Crisis of National Cinema*. Berkeley: University of California Press, 2003.

Aguilar Rodríguez, Sandra. "Cooking Modernity: Nutrition Policies, Class, and Gender in 1940s and 1950s Mexico." *The Americas* 64, no. 2 (2007): 177–205.
Aguirre, Beltrán G. *La población negra de México*. México: Fondo de Cultura Económica, 1972.
Alec-Tweedie. *Porfirio Díaz, Seven Times President of Mexico*. London: Hurst and Blackett, 1906.
Allen, Stephen D. *A History of Boxing in Mexico: Masculinity, Modernity, and Nationalism*. Albuquerque: University of New Mexico Press, 2017.
Alonso, Alejandro G., Pedro Contreras, and Martíno Fagiuoli. *Havana Deco*. New York: W. W. Norton, 2007.
Alonso, Jorge. *Puños dorados: apuntes para la historia del boxeo en Cuba*. Santiago de Cuba: Editorial Oriente, 1988.
Álvarez, José María. *Añoranzas; el México que fue, mi Colegio Militar*. México: Imprenta Ocampo, 1949.
Anderson, Benedict. *Imagined Communities*. London: Verso, 1993 (1984).
Ángel, Nicolás R. *Historia Del Toreo En México: Epoca Colonial 1529–1821*. México: Imp. M. L. Sánchez, 1924.
Antón, Alex, and Roger E. Hernández. *Cubans in America: A Vibrant History of a People in Exile*. New York: Kensington Books, 2003.
Appadurai, Arjun. *Modernity at Large: Cultural Dimensions of Globalization*. Minneapolis: University of Minnesota Press, 1996.
Appelbaum, Nancy P., Thomas C. Holt, Anne S. Macpherson, Karin Alejandra Rosemblatt, and Peter Wade, eds. *Race and Nation in Modern Latin America*. Chapel Hill: University of North Carolina Press, 2003.
Aramburu y Torres, Joaquín Nicolás. "A otras epocas . . .," in *Paginas, colección de trabajos en prosa y verso*. Habana: Imprenta Avisador Commercial, 1907.
Arbena, Joseph L., and David G. LaFrance. *Sport in Latin America and the Caribbean*. Wilmington, DE: Scholarly Resources, 2002.
Arenas Guzmán, Diego. *El periodismo en la Revolución Mexicana*, vol. 2. México: Patronato del Instituto Nacional de Estudios Históricos de la Revolución Mexicana, 1967.
Argudín, Yolanda, and María Luna Argudín. *Historia del periodismo en México: desde el Virreinato hasta nuestros días*. México, DF: Panorama Editorial, 1987.
Ashley, David. *History Without a Subject: The Postmodern Condition*. Boulder, CO: Westview Press, 1997.
Aviña, Rafael. *David Silva: un campeón de mil rostros*. México, DF: Universidad Nacional Autónoma de México, 2007.
Bacardí Moreau, Emilio. *Crónicas de Santiago de Cuba*. Madrid: Gráf. Breogán, 1972.
Barr, Alwyn. *Black Texans: A History of African-Americans in Texas, 1528–1995*. Norman: University of Oklahoma Press, 1996.
Bartra, Armando. "The Seduction of the Innocents: The First Tumultuous Moments of Mass Literacy in Post-Revolutionary Mexico." In *Everyday Forms of State Formation: Revolution and the Negotiation of Rule in Modern Mexico*, edited by Gilbert M. Joseph and Daniel Nugent, 301–26. Durham, NC: Duke University Press, 1994.

Bartra, Roger. *Blood, Ink, and Culture: Miseries and Splendors of the Post-Mexican Condition.* Durham, NC: Duke University Press, 2002.

Bass, Amy. *In the Game: Race, Identity, and Sports in the Twentieth Century.* New York: Palgrave Macmillan, 2005.

Beals, Carleton. *Glass Houses, Ten Years of Free-Lancing.* Philadelphia: J. B. Lippincott Company, 1938.

Beattie, Peter M. *The Tribute of Blood: Army, Honor, Race, and Nation in Brazil, 1864–1945.* Durham, NC: Duke University Press, 2001.

Bederman, Gail, *Manliness and Civilization: A Cultural History of Gender and Race in the United States, 1880–1917.* Chicago: University of Chicago Press, 1995.

Beezley, William H. *Judas at the Jockey Club and Other Episodes of Porfirian Mexico.* Lincoln: University of Nebraska Press, 2004.

Beezley, William H., and Linda Ann Curcio. *Latin American Popular Culture: An Introduction.* Wilmington, DE: Scholarly Resources, 2000.

Beezley, William H., and David E. Lorey, *¡Viva Mexico!, ¡Viva La Independencia!: Celebrations of September 16.* Wilmington, DE: Scholarly Resources, 2001.

Beezley, William H., and Michael C. Meyer. *The Oxford History of Mexico.* Oxford: Oxford University Press, 2000.

Bejel, Emilio. *Gay Cuban Nation.* Chicago: University of Chicago Press, 2001.

Benítez Veguillas, Mariano. *Cuba ante la historia y el sentido común.* Habana: Imprenta "El Figaro," 1897.

Benjamin, Thomas. *La Revolución: Mexico's Great Revolution As Memory, Myth & History.* Austin: University of Texas Press, 2010.

Belnap, Jeffrey Grant, and Raúl A. Fernández. *José Martí's "Our America:" From National to Hemispheric Cultural Studies.* Durham, NC: Duke University Press, 1999.

Bennett, Herman Lee. *Africans in Colonial Mexico: Absolutism, Christianity, and Afro-Creole Consciousness, 1570–1640.* Bloomington: Indiana University Press, 2005.

Benson, Peter. *Battling Siki: A Tale of Ring Fixes, Race, and Murder in the 1920s.* Fayetteville: University of Arkansas Press, 2006.

Berdecio, Roberto. *Posada's Popular Mexican Prints.* Chemsford, MA: Courier Dover Publications, 1972.

Bertaccini, Tiziana. *Ficción y realidad del héroe popular.* México, DF: Consejo Nacional para la Cultura y las Artes, 2001.

Bjarkman, Peter. *A History of Cuban Baseball, 1864–2006.* Jefferson, NC: McFarland & Co, 2007.

Blanco Abarca, Amalio, Elisa Larrañaga Rubio, and Santiago Yubero Jimé. *Convivir con la violencia.* Navarra: Universidad Pública de Navarra, 2007.

Bliss, Katherine Elaine. *Compromised Positions: Prostitution, Public Health and Gender Politics in Revolutionary Mexico City.* University Park: Pennsylvania State University Press, 2001.

Boddy, Kasia. *Boxing: A Cultural History.* London: Reaktion, 2009.

Bonfil Batalla, Guillermo. *México profundo.* México: Secretaría de Educación Pública, 1987.

Bortz, Jeffrey L., and Stephen Haber. *The Mexican Economy, 1870–1930: Essays on the Economic History of Institutions, Revolution, and Growth.* Stanford, CA: Stanford University Press, 2002.
Botín, Vicente. *Los funerales de Castro.* Barcelona: Ariel, 2009.
Brewster, Clair, and Keith Brewster. *Representing the Nation: Sport and Spectacle in Post-Revolutionary Mexico.* New York: Routledge, 2010.
Bristol, Joan Cameron. *Christians, Blasphemers, and Witches: Afro-Mexican Ritual Practice in the Seventeenth Century.* Albuquerque: University of New Mexico Press, 2007.
Brock, Lisa, and Digna Castañeda Fuertes, eds. *Between Race and Empire: African-Americans and Cubans before the Cuban Revolution.* Philadelphia: Temple University Press, 1998.
Bronfman, Alejandra. *Measures of Equality: Social Science, Citizenship, and Race in Cuba, 1902–1940.* Chapel Hill: University of North Carolina Press, 2005.
Brunk, Samuel. *The Posthumous Career of Emiliano Zapata: Myth, Memory, and Mexico's Twentieth Century.* Austin: University of Texas Press, 2008.
Buffington, Robert. *Criminal and Citizen in Modern Mexico.* Lincoln: University of Nebraska Press, 2000.
———. *A Sentimental Education for the Working Man: The Mexico City Penny Press, 1900–1910.* Durham, NC: Duke University Press, 2015.
Bunker, Steven. *Creating Mexican Consumer Culture in the Age of Porfirio Díaz.* Albuquerque: University of New Mexico Press, 2012.
Burgos, Adrian. *Playing America's Game: Baseball, Latinos, and the Color Line.* Berkeley: University of California Press, 2007.
Burns, E. Bradford. *The Poverty of Progress: Latin America in the Nineteenth Century.* Berkeley: University of California Press, 1980.
Cabalé Ruiz, Manolo. *Teófilo Stevenson: Grande entre los grandes.* Habana: Editorial Científico Técnica, 1985.
Cabrera Acevedo, Lucio. *La Suprema Corte de Justicia durante el fortalecimiento del Porfirismo, 1882–1888.* México, DF: Suprema Corte de Justicia de la Nación, 1991.
Cahoone, Lawrence E. *Cultural Revolutions: Reason Versus Culture in Philosophy, Politics, and Jihad.* University Park: Pennsylvania State University Press, 2005.
Calhoun, Craig J. *Habermas and the Public Sphere.* Cambridge, MA: MIT Press, 1992.
Camacho Morfin, Thelma. *Imágenes de México: las historietas de el Buen Tono de Juan B. Urrutia, 1909–1912.* México, DF: Instituto Mora, 2002.
Campbell, Reau. *Campbell's New Revised Complete Guide and Descriptive Book of Mexico.* Chicago: Rogers & Smith Co, 1909.
Campbell Reesman, Jeanne. *Jack London's Racial Lives: A Critical Biography.* Athens: University of Georgia Press, 2009.
Campos, Isaac. *Home Grown: Marijuana and the Origins of Mexico's War on Drugs.* Chapel Hill: University of North Carolina Press, 2012.
Canclini, Néstor García. *Hybrid Cultures: Strategies for Entering and Leaving Modernity.* Translated by Christopher L. Chiappari. Minneapolis: University of Minnesota Press, 1997.

Capablanca, Joeś Raùl, and Fred Reinfeld. *The Immortal Games of Capablanca.* New York: Dover, 1990.
Carroll, Patrick James. *Blacks in Colonial Veracruz: Race, Ethnicity, and Regional Development.* Austin: University of Texas Press, 2001.
Carter, Thomas. "Baseball Arguments: *Aficionismo* and Masculinity at the Core of Cubanidad." In *Sport in Latin American Society: Past and Present,* edited by J. A. Mangan and Lamartine P. DaCosta, 117–38. London: Frank Cass, 2002.
Casanovas, Joan. *Bread or Bullets: Urban Labor and Spanish Colonialism in Cuba, 1850–1898.* Pittsburgh: University of Pittsburgh Press, 1998.
Casasola, Gustavo. *Seis siglos de historia gráfica de México, 1325–1900.* México: Ediciones G. Casasola, 1966.
Casimir, Enver Michael. "Champion of the Patria: Kid Chocolate, Athletic Achievement, and the Significance of Race for Cuban National Aspiration." PhD dissertation, University of North Carolina, 2009.
Castellanos, Israel. *La brujería y el ñañiguismo en Cuba, desde el punto de vista médico-legal.* Habana: Lloredo, 1916.
———. *Contribución al estudio craneométrico del hombre negro delincuente.* Habana: (s.n.), 1916.
Ceballos, Ciro B., and Luz América Viveros Anaya. *Panorama mexicano 1890–1910: (memorias); Al siglo XIX, ida y regreso.* México: Universidad Nacional Autónoma de México, Coordinación de Humanidades, 2006.
Cervantes, Agustín. *Los duelos en Cuba.* Havana: A. Miranda, 1894.
Chambers, Stephen. *No God But Gain: The Untold Story of Cuban Slavery, the Monroe Doctrine, and the Making of the United States.* London: Verso, 2015.
Chanan, Michael. *Cuban Cinema.* Minneapolis: University of Minnesota Press, 2003.
Charyn, Jerome. *Gangsters and Gold Diggers: Old New York, the Jazz Age, and the Birth of Broadway.* New York: Thunder's Mouth Press, 2005.
Childs, Matt. *The 1812 Aponte Rebellion in Cuba and the Struggle against Atlantic Slavery.* Chapel Hill: University of North Carolina Press, 2006.
Chomsky, Aviva. "'Barbados or Canada?' Race, Immigration, and Nation in Early-Twentieth-Century Cuba." *The Hispanic American Historical Review* 80, no. 3 (August 2000).
Christesen, Paul, *Sport and Democracy in the Ancient and Modern Worlds.* Cambridge: Cambridge University Press, 2012.
Connell, R. W. *Masculinities.* Berkeley: University of California Press, 2005.
Cope, R. Douglas. *The Limits of Racial Domination: Plebeian Society in Colonial Mexico City; 1660–1720.* Madison: University of Wisconsin Press, 1994.
Cortés, Eladio. *Dictionary of Mexican Literature.* Westport, CT: Greenwood Press, 1992.
Corwin, Arthur. *Spain and the Abolition of Slavery in Cuba, 1817–1886.* Austin: University of Texas Press, 1967.
Cory, Steve, and Ray Webb. *Daily Life in Ancient and Modern Mexico City.* Minneapolis: Runestone Press, 1999.
Cosío Villegas, Daniel, Francisco R. Calderón, Luis González y González, Emma Cosío

Villegas, and Moisés González Navarro. *Historia moderna de México*. México: Editorial Hermes, 1955.
Crafton, Donald, and Charles Harpole. *The Talkies: American Cinema's Transition to Sound, 1926—1931*. Berkeley: University of California Press, 1999.
Craik, George L., and Charles MacFarlane. *The Pictorial History of England During the Reign of George the Third: Being a History of the People, As Well As a History of the Kingdom. Illustrated with Several Hundred Woodcuts*. London: C. Knight, 1841.
Crehan, Kate. *Gramsci, Culture, and Anthropology*. Berkeley: University of California Press, 2002.
Crossley, Nick, and John Michael Roberts. *After Habermas: New Perspectives on the Public Sphere*. Oxford: Blackwell, 2004.
Cullen, Countee, and Gerald Lyn Early. *My Soul's High Song: The Collected Writings of Countee Cullen, Voice of the Harlem Renaissance*. New York: Doubleday, 1991.
Dalton, Kathleen M. *Theodore Roosevelt: A Strenuous Life*. New York: Vintage Books, 2004.
Daniel, Walter M. *The American Club of Havana, Cuba, 1932: History, Constitution, by-Laws, Officers and Members*. Havana: Times of Cuba, 1932.
Dario, Rubén. *Antología poética*. Madrid: Editorial EDAF, 1979.
Dávila, Jerry. *Diploma of Whiteness: Race and Social Policy in Brazil, 1917–1945*. Durham, NC: Duke University Press, 2003.
Davis, Diane E. *Urban Leviathan: Mexico City in the Twentieth Century*. Philadelphia: Temple University Press, 1994.
Debs, Eugene V., and J. Robert Constantine. *Letters of Eugene V. Debs*. Urbana: University of Illinois Press, 1990.
Deocampo, Nick. *Cine: Spanish Influences on Early Cinema in the Philippines*. Manila: Cinema Values Reorientation Program, National Commission for Culture and the Arts, 2003.
Diacon, Todd A. *Stringing Together a Nation: Candido Mariano Da Silva Rondon and the Construction of a Modern Brazil, 1906–1930*. Durham, NC: Duke University Press, 2004.
Díaz Burgos, Juan Manuel, Mario Díaz Leyva, and Paco Salinas. *Cuba—100 años de fotografía: antología de la fotografía cubana 1898–1998 : [exposición]*. Murcia: Mestizo, 1998.
Díaz Zermeño, Héctor. *Aureliano Blanquet, 1848–1919: ¿cancerbero del traidor Victoriano Huerta o militar leal?* México: Universidad Autónoma de México, 2004.
Didapp, Juan Pedro. *Explotadores políticos de México; Bulnes y el Partido científico ante el derecho ajeno*. Mexico: Tip. de F. Diáz de León, 1904.
Doezema, Marianne. *George Bellows and Urban America*. New Haven, CT: Yale University Press, 1992.
Dominguez, Jorge. *Cuba: Order and Revolution*. Cambridge, MA: Belknap Press, 1978.
Domínguez Ruvalcaba, Héctor. *Modernity and the Nation in Mexican Representations of Masculinity: From Sensuality to Bloodshed*. New York: Palgrave Macmillan, 2007.

Donovan, Brian. *White Slave Crusades: Race, Gender, and Anti-Vice Activism, 1887–1917.* Urbana: University of Illinois Press, 2006.
Duclós Salinas, Adolfo. *The Riches of Mexico and Its Institutions.* St. Louis, MO: Nixon-Jones Printing, 1893.
Duke, Dawn. *Literary Passion, Ideological Commitment: Toward a Legacy of Afro-Cuban and Afro-Brazilian Women Writers.* Lewisburg, PA: Bucknell University Press, 2008.
Duncan, John. *In the Red Corner: A Journey into Cuban Boxing.* London: Yellow Jersey, 2001.
Dunning, Eric, Joseph A. Maguire, and Robert E. Pearton. *The Sports Process: A Comparative and Developmental Approach.* Champaign, IL: Human Kinetics Publishers, 1993.
Eakin, Marshall C. *The History of Latin America: Collision of Cultures.* New York: Palgrave Macmillan, 2007.
Early, Gerald. *The Culture of Bruising: Essays on Prizefighting, Literature and Modern American Culture.* New York: Ecco Press, 1992.
Elías, Norbert, and Eric Dunning. *Quest for Excitement: Sport and Leisure in the Civilizing Process.* Dublin: University College Dublin Press, 2008.
Elías, Robert. *The Empire Strikes Out: How Baseball Sold U.S. Foreign Policy and Promoted the American Way Abroad.* New York: The New Press, 2010.
Elsey, Brenda. *Citizens and Sportsmen: Fútbol and Politics in Twentieth Century Chile.* Austin: University of Texas Press, 2011.
Encinoso, Enrique. *Azúcar y chocolate: historia del boxeo cubano.* Miami: Ediciones Universal, 2004.
———. *Hard Leather: A History of Cuban Boxing.* Editorial Printed Fine Arts, 2016.
Estrada, Alfredo José. *Havana: Autobiography of a City.* New York: Palgrave Macmillan, 2008.
Fajardo Estrada, Ramón. *Rita Montaner: testimonio de una época.* La Habana: Fondo Editorial Casa de las Américas, 1997.
Farr, Finis. *Black Champion: The Life and Times of Jack Johnson.* Greenwich, CT: Fawcett Publications, 1969.
Farred, Grant. *What's My Name? Black Vernacular Intellectuals.* Minneapolis: University of Minnesota Press, 2003.
Featherstone, Mike. *Consumer Culture and Postmodernism.* Los Angeles: SAGE Publications, 2007.
Ferreiro Mora, Julio. *Historia del boxeo cubano.* Miami: Selecta Enterprises, 1983.
Ferrer, Ada. *Freedom's Mirror: Cuba and Haiti in the Age of Revolution.* Cambridge: Cambridge University Press, 2014.
———. *Insurgent Cuba: Race, Nation, and Revolution, 1868–98.* Chapel Hill: University of North Carolina Press, 1999.
Fields, Armond. *James J. Corbett: A Biography of the Heavyweight Boxing Champion and Popular Theater Headliner.* Jefferson, NC: McFarland & Co., 2001.
Figueroa Domenech, J. *Guía general descriptiva de la República Mexicana; história, geografía, estadística, etc., etc., con triple directorio del comercio y la industria, autoridades, oficinas públicas, abogados, médicos, hacendados, correos, telégrafos y ferrocarriles, etc.* México: R. de Araluce, 1899.

Flores, Josefina Miguel. *Telegramas en el Archivo Historicó, 1859–1912*. México: Centro de Estudios de Historia de Mexico CONDUMEX, 1988.
Florescano, Enrique. *Historia gráfica de México: Siglo viente*. México: Editorial Patria, 1992.
Foner, Philip Sheldon. *Antonio Maceo: The "Bronze Titan" of Cuba's Struggle for Independence*. New York: Monthly Review Press, 1977.
———. *U.S. Labor Movement and Latin America: A History of Workers' Response to Intervention*. South Hadley, MA: Bergin & Garvey, 1988.
Font, Mauricio Augusto. *The Cuban Republic and José Martí: Reception and Use of a National Symbol*. Lanham, MD: Lexington Books, 2006.
Fowler, Will, and Peter Lambert. *Political Violence and the Construction of National Identity in Latin America*. New York: Palgrave Macmillan, 2006.
Franco, Luis G. *Glosa del período de gobierno del C. Gral. e Ing. Pascual Ortiz Rubio, 1930–1932*. México, 1948.
Frank, Patrick, and José Guadalupe Posada. *Posada's Broadsheets: Mexican Popular Imagery: 1890–1910*. Albuquerque: University of New Mexico Press, 1998.
Franklin, Sarah. *Women and Slavery in Nineteenth Century Colonial Cuba*. Rochester: University of Rochester Press, 2012.
Frick, Marie-Luisa, and Andreas Oberprantacher. *Power and Justice in International Relations: Interdisciplinary Approaches to Global Challenges*. Farnham, Surrey: Ashgate, 2009.
Fuente, Alejandro de la. *A Nation for All: Race, Inequality, and Politics in Twentieth-Century Cuba*. Chapel Hill: University of North Carolina Press, 2001.
Fumero Vargas, Patricia. *Teatro, público y estado en San José 1880–1914: una aproximación desde la historia social*. Colección Nueva historia, San José, C.R.: Editorial de la Universidad de Costa Rica, 1996.
Gamble, Richard M. *The War for Righteousness: Progressive Christianity, the Great War, and the Rise of the Messianic Nation*. Wilmington, DE: ISI Books, 2003.
Gamboa, Federico. *Mi diario*. México and Guadalajara: Imprenta de "La Gaceta de Guadalajara," 1906.
Gamboa, Federico, and José Emilio Pacheco. *Memorias mexicanas*. México: Consejo Nacional para la Cultura y las Artes, 1996.
García, Clara Guadalupe. *El Imparcial: primer periódico moderno de México*. México: Centro de Estudios Históricos del Porfiriato, 2003.
García, Guadalupe. *Beyond the Walled City: Colonial Exclusion in Havana*. Berkeley: University of California Press, 2016.
García, José R. *Legislación social de Cuba*. Vol. 1. Habana: La Moderna Poesia, 1936.
García Krinsky, Emma Cecilia, Rosa Casanova, and Claudia Canales. *Imaginarios y fotografía en México: 1839–1970*. Barcelona: Lunweg, 2005.
García Riera, Emilio. *Historia del cine mexicano*. México: Secretaría de Educación Pública, 1986.
García Rivas, Heriberto. *Historia de la literatura mexicana*. México: Textos Universitarios, S.A., 1971.

Geertz, Clifford. "Deep Play: Notes on a Balinese Cock Fight." In *Myth, Symbol, and Culture*, ed. Clifford Geertz, 1–37. New York: Norton, 1971.
Gems, Gerald R. *The Athletic Crusade: Sport and American Cultural Imperialism*. Lincoln: University of Nebraska Press, 2006.
Gerstle, Gary. *American Crucible: Race and Nation in the Twentieth Century*. Princeton, NJ: Princeton University Press, 2001.
Gerstner, David A. *Manly Arts: Masculinity and Nation in Early American Cinema*. Durham, NC: Duke University Press, 2006.
Gilmore, Al-Tony. *Bad Nigger!: The National Impact of Jack Johnson*. Port Washington, NY: Kennikat Press, 1975.
Gilmore, David D. *Manhood in the Making: Cultural Concepts of Masculinity*. New Haven, CT: Yale University Press, 1990.
Giulianotti, Richard. *Sport: A Critical Sociology*. Cambridge, UK: Polity Press, 2005.
Glick, Thomas F. "Science in Twentieth Century Latin America." In *Ideas and Ideologies in Twentieth Century Latin America*, edited by Leslie Bethell, 287–361. Cambridge: Cambridge University Press, 1996.
Gómez Carrillo, Enrique. *Antología de Enrique Gómez Carrillo*. Guatemala: Artemis Edinter, 2004.
González, Gilbert G. *Culture of Empire: American Writers, Mexico, and Mexican Immigrants, 1880–1930*. Austin: University of Texas Press, 2004.
Gonzales, Michael J. *The Mexican Revolution, 1910–1940*. Albuquerque: University of New Mexico Press, 2002.
González Echevarría, Roberto. *The Pride of Havana: A History of Cuban Baseball*. New York: Oxford University Press, 1999.
González y González, Luis. *Invitación a la microhistoria*. Mexico City: Secretaría de Educación Pública, 1973.
González y Lanuza, José A. *La ley de lynch en los Estados Unidos; disertacion leida en la apertura de la Academia de Derecho*. Habana: La Universal, Ruiz y Hermano, 1892.
Gorn, Elliot J. *The Manly Art: Bare-Knuckle Prize Fighting in America*. Ithaca, NY: Cornell University Press, 1986.
Gouldner, Alvin Ward. *The Future of Intellectuals and the Rise of the New Class*. New York: Seabury Press, 1979.
Graham, Richard, ed. *The Idea of Race in Latin America*. Austin: University of Texas Press, 1990.
Green, James N. *Beyond Carnival: Male Homosexuality in Twentieth-Century Brazil*. Chicago: University of Chicago Press, 2003.
Grosó, José L. *La ciudad de México, novísima guía universal de la capital de la República Mexicana*. México: J. Buxó, 1901.
Guerra, Lillian. *The Myth of José Martí: Conflicting Nationalisms in Early Twentieth-Century Cuba*. Chapel Hill: University of North Carolina Press, 2005.
———. "Tracing the Origins of Divergent Interpretations of Race and Nation in Cuba." In *Race and Nation in Modern Latin America*. Chapel Hill: University of North Carolina Press, 2003.

Guillén, Nicolás. *Las grandes elegías y otros poemas.* Ayacucho, Peru: Biblioteca Ayacucho, 1984.

Guillén, Nicolás, Roberto Márquez, and David Arthur McMurray. *Man-Making Words: Selected Poems of Nicolas Guillen.* Boston: University of Massachusetts Press, 2003.

Guridy, Frank. *Forging Diaspora: Afro-Cubans and African-Americans in a World of Empire and Jim Crow.* Chapel Hill: University of North Carolina Press, 2010.

Gutiérrez Nájera, Manuel, and Elvira López Aparicio. *Crónicas y artículos sobre teatro IV: 1885–1889.* México: Universidad Nacional Autónoma de México, 1985.

Gutmann, Matthew C., ed. *Changing Men and Masculinities in Latin America.* Durham, NC: Duke University Press, 2003.

Guttmann, Allen. *Games and Empires: Modern Sports and Cultural Imperialism.* New York: Columbia University Press, 1994.

Habermas, Jürgen. *The Structural Transformation of the Public Sphere: An Inquiry into a Category of Bourgeois Society.* Cambridge, MA: MIT Press, 1989.

Hardison Londré, Felicia, and Daniel J. Watermeier. *The History of North American Theater: The United States, Canada, and Mexico: From Pre-Columbian Times to the Present.* New York: Continuum, 1998.

Hart, John M. *Empire and Revolution.* Berkeley: University of California Press, 2002.

———. *Revolutionary Mexico: The Coming and Process of the Mexican Revolution.* Berkeley: University of California Press, 1987.

Haviser, Jay B., and Kevin C. MacDonald. *African Re-Genesis: Confronting Social Issues in the Diaspora.* Abingdon, UK: Taylor & Francis, 2006.

Hayes-Bautista, David E., Werner O. Schink, and Jorge Chapa. *The Burden of Support: Young Latinos in an Aging Society.* Stanford, CA: Stanford University Press, 1988.

Hazard, Samuel. *Cuba with Pen and Pencil.* Hartford, CT: Hartford Pub. Co, 1871.

Helg, Aline. "Black Men, Racial Stereotyping, and Violence in the U.S. South and Cuba at the Turn of the Century," *Comparative Studies in Society and History* 42, no. 3 (July 2000): 576–604.

———. *Our Rightful Share: The Afro-Cuban Struggle for Equality, 1886–1912.* Chapel Hill: University of North Carolina Press, 1995.

Herbert, Thomas Walter. *Sexual Violence and American Manhood.* Cambridge, MA: Harvard University Press, 2002.

Herrera, Alfonso Luis, and Daniel Vergara-Lope Escobar. *La vie sur les hauts plateaux. Influence de la pression barométrique sur la constitution et le développement des êtres organisés. Traitement climatérique de la tuberculose.* México: Imprimerie de I. Escalante, 1899.

Hoberman, John M. *Darwin's Athletes: How Sport Has Damaged Black America and Preserved the Myth of Race.* Boston: Houghton Mifflin, 1997.

Hobsbawm, Eric J. *The Invention of Tradition.* New York: Cambridge University Press, 1983.

———. *Primitive Rebels: Studies in Archaic Forms of Social Movement in the 19th and 20th Centuries.* Manchester: Manchester University Press, 1971.

Hodge, Derrick. "Colonization of the Cuban Body: Nationalism, Economy, and

Masculinity of Male Sex Work in Havana." PhD dissertation, City University of New York, 2006.

Hoerder, Dirk. *Cultures in Contact: World Migrations in the Second Millennium.* Durham, NC: Duke University Press, 2002.

Hogan, Lawrence D. *Shades of Glory: The Negro Leagues and the Story of African-American Baseball.* National Geographic Society, 2007.

Hoganson, Kristin L. *Fighting for American Manhood: How Gender Politics Provoked the Spanish-American and Philippine-American Wars.* New Haven, CT: Yale University Press, 1998.

Horne, Gerald. *White Supremacy and the Japanese Attack on the British Empire.* New York: New York University Press, 2003.

Huesca, Federico. *Diccionario hípico y del sport, compuesto por D. Federico Huesca.* Madrid: Imprenta. de J. M. Pérez, 1881.

Huggins, Mike. *The Victorians and Sport.* London: Hambledon and London, 2004.

Hughson, John, Marcus Free, and David Inglis. *The Uses of Sport: A Critical Study.* London: Routledge, 2005.

Hulme, Peter. *Rescuing Cuba: Adventure and Masculinity in the 1890s,* College Park, MD: Latin American Studies Center, University of Maryland at College Park, 1996.

Iber, Jorge, and Samuel O. Regalado. *Mexican Americans and Sports: A Reader on Athletics and Barrio Life.* College Station: Texas A&M University Press, 2007.

Iglesias Utset, Marial. *A Cultural History of Cuba During the U.S. Occupation.* Chapel Hill: University of North Carolina Press, 2011.

———. *Las metáforas del cambio en la vida cotidiana: Cuba, 1898–1902.* Ciudad de La Habana: Ediciones Unión, 2003.

Ingalls, John J. *America's War for Humanity . . . A Complete History of Cuba's Struggle for Liberty.* New York: N. D. Thompson, 1898.

Inglis, David. *The Uses of Sport: A Critical Study.* London: Routledge, 2005.

Irwin, Robert McKee. *Mexican Masculinities.* Minneapolis: University of Minnesota Press, 2003.

Isenberg, Michael T. *John L. Sullivan and His America.* Urbana: University of Illinois Press, 1994.

Jaén, Didier Tisdel. *The Cosmic Race: A Bilingual Edition.* Baltimore: Johns Hopkins University Press, 1997.

James, Deborah Evelyn, Mary Plaice, and Christina Toren. *Culture Wars: Context, Models and Anthropologists' Accounts.* New York: Berghahn Books, 2010.

Johns, Michael. *The City of Mexico in the Age of Díaz.* Austin: University of Texas Press, 1997.

Johnson, Jack. *In the Ring and Out.* New York: National Sports Publishing Company, 1927.

Johnson, Willis Fletcher. *The History of Cuba.* New York: B. F. Buck & Co, 1920.

Joseph, Gilbert M., Catherine LeGrand, and Ricardo Donato Salvatore. *Close Encounters of Empire: Writing the Cultural History of U.S.-Latin American Relations.* Durham, NC: Duke University Press, 1998.

Joseph, Gilbert M., Anne Rubenstein, and Eric Zolov. *Fragments of a Golden Age: The Politics of Culture in Mexico Since 1940*. Durham, NC: Duke University Press, 2001.
Kahn, Allen Ray, and Le Roy Samuel Weatherby. *Sugar: A Simple Treatise on Beet Sugar Manufacture*. Los Angeles: U.S. Sugar Publications Co, 1921.
Kahn, Roger. *A Flame of Pure Fire: Jack Dempsey and the Roaring '20s*. San Diego: Harcourt, Inc., 2000.
Kandell, Jonathan. *La Capital: The Biography of Mexico City*. New York: Random House, 1988.
Kanellos, Nicolás. *Hispanic Literature of the United States: A Comprehensive Reference*. Westport, CT: Greenwood Press, 2003.
Kaplan, Amy. *The Anarchy of Empire in the Making of U.S. Culture: Convergences: Inventories of the Present*. Cambridge, MA: Harvard University Press, 2002.
———. *Cultures of United States Imperialism*. Durham, NC: Duke University Press, 1993.
Karp, Matthew. *The Vast Southern Empire: Slaveholders at the Helm of American Foreign Policy*. Cambridge, MA: Harvard University Press, 2016.
Kasson, John F. *Houdini, Tarzan, and The Perfect Man: The White Male Body and the Challenge of Modernity in America*. New York: Hill and Wang, 2002.
Katz, Friedrich. *The Life and Times of Pancho Villa*. Stanford, CA: Stanford University Press, 1998.
Kaye, Andrew M. *The Pussycat of Prizefighting: Tiger Flowers and the Politics of Black Celebrity*. Athens: University of Georgia Press, 2004.
Kellner, Bruce. *The Harlem Renaissance: A Historical Dictionary for the Era*. Westport, CT: Greenwood Press, 1984.
King, John. *Magical Reels: A History of Cinema in Latin America*. New York: Verso, 2000.
Klein, Alan M. "Sport and Colonialism in Latin America and the Caribbean." *Studies in Latin American Popular Culture* 10 (1991): 257–71.
Knight, Alan. *The Mexican Revolution*. Lincoln: University of Nebraska Press, 1990.
———. "Revolutionary Project, Recalcitrant People: 1910–1940." In *The Revolutionary Process in Mexico*, edited by Jaimie Rodríguez O. Berkeley: University of California Press, 1990.
Kuntz, Jerry. *Baseball Fiends and Flying Machines: The Many Lives and Outrageous Times of George and Alfred Lawson*. Jefferson, NC: McFarland & Co., 2009.
Kurtz, Charles M. *The Saint Louis World's Fair of 1904, In Commemoration of the Acquisition of the Louisiana Territory; a Handbook of General Information, Profusely Illustrated*. Saint Louis: Gottschalk Printing Company, 1904.
Kutzinski, Vera M. *Sugar's Secrets: Race and the Erotics of Cuban Nationalism*. Charlottesville: University Press of Virginia, 1993.
LaFeber, Walter. *Inevitable Revolutions: The United States in Central America*. New York: W. W. Norton, 1993.
LaFevor, David C. "Atavism, Watermelons, and the Bronze Titan: Attitudes Towards Race in the Early Cuban Republic." MA thesis, Vanderbilt University, 2006.

Langum, David J. *Crossing Over the Line: Legislating Morality and the Mann Act.* Chicago: University of Chicago Press, 2006.
Lane, Jill. *Blackface Cuba: 1840–1895.* Philadelphia: University of Pennsylvania Press, 2005.
Larraín, Jorge. *Identity and Modernity in Latin America.* Malden, MA: Blackwell Publishers, 2000.
Larrainzar, Manuel. *Estudios Sobre La Historia De América, Sus Ruinas Y Antigüedades, Etc.* México: Imprenta de M. Villanueva Francisconi y Hijos, 1875.
Lauderdale Harrison, Salomay. *México simpático, tierra de encantos.* Boston: D. C. Heath and Co., 1929.
Leach, William. *Land of Desire: Merchants, Power, and the Rise of a New American Culture.* New York: Vintage Books, 1994.
Leal, Rine. *Breve historia del teatro cubano.* La Habana: Editorial Letras Cubanas, 1980.
Lear, John. *Workers, Neighbors, and Citizens: The Revolution in Mexico City.* Lincoln: University of Nebraska Press, 2001.
Lears, Jackson. *Fables of Abundance: A Cultural History of Advertising in America.* New York: Basic Books, 1994.
———. *Rebirth of a Nation: The Making of Modern America, 1877–1920.* New York: Harper Perennial, 2010.
Lesser, Jeffrey. *Negotiating National Identity: Immigrants, Minorities, and the Struggle for Ethnicity in Brazil.* Durham, NC: Duke University Press, 1999.
Levi, Heather. *The World of Lucha Libre: Secrets, Revelations, and Mexican National Identity.* Durham, NC: Duke University Press, 2008.
Lewis, David L. *W. E. B. Du Bois.* New York: H. Holt, 1993.
Lewis, Linden. *The Culture of Gender and Sexuality in the Caribbean.* Gainesville: University Press of Florida, 2003.
Linder, Isaak Maksovich, and V. I. Linder. *José Raúl Capablanca: Third World Chess Champion.* Milford, CT: Russell Enterprises, Inc., 2010.
Lomax, Michael L. *Sports and the Racial Divide: African-American and Latino Experience in an Era of Change.* Jackson: University Press of Mississippi, 2008.
Lomnitz-Adler, Claudio. *Deep Mexico, Silent Mexico: An Anthropology of Nationalism.* Minneapolis: University of Minnesota Press, 2001.
López, Jesús F. *Pot pourri. Colección de artículos literarios y humorísticos; morales, filosóficos, críticos, biográficos, discursos, peroraciones, viajes, costumbres, revistas, novelas, dramas, comedias, soliloquios teatrales.* Aguascalientes: Imprenta de El Aguila, 1897.
López, Oscar. *La Radio en Cuba: estudio de su desarrollo en la sociedad neocolonial.* La Habana: Editorial Letras Cubanas, 2002.
López Velarde, Ramón, and José Luis Martínez. *Obra poética.* Colección Archivos, 36. Madrid: Allca XX, Ediciones Unesco, 1998.
Lozano Herrera, Rubén. *José Juan Tablada en Nueva York: búsqueda y hallazgos en la crónica.* México: Universidad Iberoamericana, 2000.
———. *Las veras y las burlas de José Juan Tablada.* México, DF: Universidad Iberoamericana, Departamento de Historia, 1995.

Lugo-Ocando, Jairo. *The Media in Latin America*. Berkshire, England: McGraw Hill/Open University Press, 2008.
Luz Torres Hernández, María de la. "La educación física en el proyecto de cultura nacional posrevolucionaria: vasconcelismo y cardenismo." In *Reencuentro*. México DF: Universidad Nacional Autónoma Metropolitana, 1993.
Lynch, Jack. *The Age of Elizabeth in the Age of Johnson*. Cambridge, UK: Cambridge University Press, 2003.
Madán, Marcelo. *Tratado de los Odu de Ifa*. Caracas: Inversiones Orunmila, 2000.
Maldonado, Marco A. *Pasión por los guantes: historia del box mexicano*. México: Clío, 2000.
Maldonado, Marco A., and Ruben A. Zámora. *Historia del box mexicano*. México: Editorial Clio, 2000.
Mañach, Jorge. *Glosas*. Habana, 1924.
Managan, J. A., and Lamartine P. Dacosta. *Sport in Latin American Society Past and Present*. London: Frank Cass Publishers, 2002.
Margolick, David, *Beyond Glory: Joe Louis vs. Max Schmeling and a World on the Brink*. New York: Vintage Books, 2006.
Marichal, Carlos. *Bankruptcy of Empire: Mexican Silver and the Wars between Spain, Britain, and France, 1760–1810*. New York: Cambridge University Press, 2007.
Markowitz, Jonathan. *Racial Spectacles: Explorations in Media, Race, and Justice*. New York: Routledge, 2011.
Martí, José, and Philip Sheldon Foner. *Our America: Writings on Latin America and the Struggle for Cuban Independence*. New York: Monthly Review Press, 1977.
Martí, José, Esther Louise Allen, and Roberto González Echevarría. *José Martí: Selected Writings*. New York: Penguin Books, 2002.
Martin, Percy F. *Mexico of the Twentieth Century*. London: E. Arnold, 1907.
Martín-Barbero, Jesús. *De los medios a las mediaciones: comunicación, cultura y hegemonía*. Santa Fé de Bogotá: Convenio Andrés Bello, 1998.
Martínez, José Luis. *La vieja guardia: protagonistas del periodismo mexicano*. México, DF: Plaza Janés, 2005.
Martínez, Oscar J. *Border Boom Town: Ciudad Juárez Since 1848*. Austin: University of Texas Press, 1978.
Mathews, Nancy Mowell, Charles Musser, and Marta Braun. *Moving Pictures: American Art and Early Film, 1880–1910*. Manchester, VT: Hudson Hills Press in association with the Williams College Museum of Art, 2005.
Matthews, Michael. *The Civilizing Machine: A Cultural History of Mexican Railroads, 1876–1910*. Lincoln: University of Nebraska Press, 2014.
McGehee, Richard V. "The Dandy and the Mauler in Mexico: Johnson, Dempsey, et al., and the Mexico City Press, 1919–1927." *Journal of Sport History* 23, no. 1 (1996): 20.
Menéndez, Elio, and Víctor Joaquín Ortega. *Kid Chocolate, "el boxeo soy yo—."* Ciudad de La Habana: Editorial ORBE, 1980.
Miletich, Leon. *Dan Stuart's Fistic Carnival*. College Station: Texas A&M University Press, 1994.

Miller, J. Martin, and Henry Ford. *The Amazing Story of Henry Ford, the Ideal American and the World's Most Famous Private Citizen*. Chicago: M. A. Donohue & Co., 1922.
Miller, Patrick, and David Wiggins. *Sport and the Color Line*. New York: Routledge, 2004.
Mitchell, Tim. *Intoxicated Identities*. New York: Routledge, 2004.
Moats, Leone Blakemore, and Russell Lord. *Thunder in Their Veins; A Memoir of Mexico*. New York: The Century Co., 1932.
Monsivais, Carlos. *Mexican Postcards*. London: Verso, 1997.
Moore, Robin. *Music and Revolution: Cultural Change in Socialist Cuba*. Berkeley: University of California Press, 2006.
——. *Nationalizing Blackness: Afrocubanismo and Artistic Revolution in Havana, 1920–1940*. Pittsburgh: University of Pittsburgh Press, 1997.
Mora, Carl J. *Mexican Cinema: Reflections of a Society, 1896–2004*. Jefferson, NC: McFarland & Co., 2005.
Mora, Sergio de la. *Cinemachismo: Masculinities and Sexuality in Mexican Film*. Austin: University of Texas Press, 2006.
Moreno, Julio. *Yankee Don't Go Home!: Mexican Nationalism, American Business Culture, and the Shaping of Modern Mexico, 1920–1950*. Chapel Hill: University of North Carolina Press, 2003.
Moreno-Brid, Juan Carlos, and Jaime Ros. *Development and Growth in the Mexican Economy: A Historical Perspective*. Oxford: Oxford University Press, 2009.
Moreno Fraginals, Manuel. *El Ingenio: complejo económico social cubano del azúcar*. La Habana: Editorial de Ciencias Sociales, 1978.
Mosse, George L. *The Image of Man: The Creation of Modern Masculinity*. New York: Oxford University Press, 1996.
Mraz, John. *Looking for Mexico: Modern Visual Culture and National Identity*. Durham, NC: Duke University Press, 2009.
Musacchio, Humberto. *Milenios de México*. México: Hoja Casa Editorial, 1999.
Murray, David. *Odious Commerce: Britain, Spain, and the Abolition of the Cuban Slave Trade*. Cambridge: University of Cambridge Press, 2002.
Mustelier, Evelio. *Mis veinte años en el ring*. La Habana: Impresora Siglo Moderno, 1958.
Naremore, James, and Patrick Brantlinger. *Modernity and Mass Culture*. Bloomington: Indiana University Press, 1991.
Naughton, W. W. *Kings of the Queensberry Realm*. Chicago: Continental Publishing Company, 1902.
Navarro, Juan R. *Calendario de Juan R. Navarro, para el bisiesto*. Mexico City, 1848.
Nervo, Amado, Francisco González Guerrero, and Alfonso Méndez Plancarte. *Obras completas*. Madrid: Aguilar, 1962.
Niblo, Stephen R. *Mexico in the 1940s: Modernity, Politics, and Corruption*. Wilmington, DE: Scholarly Resources, 1999.
Nicholson, Kelly Richard. *Hitters, Dancers and Ring Magicians: Seven Boxers of the Golden Age*. Jefferson, NC: McFarland and Co., 2010.
Norton, Albert James. *Norton's Complete Handbook of Havana and Cuba*. Chicago: Rand, McNally & Co., 1900.

Obregón Pagán, Eduardo. *Murder at the Sleepy Lagoon: Zoot Suits, Race, and Riot in Wartime Los Angeles*. Chapel Hill: University of North Carolina Press, 2003.

O'Brien, Jack. *Boxing*. New York: Charles Scribner's Sons, 1928.

Olavarría y Ferrari, Enrique de. *Reseña histórica del teatro en México*. Segunda edición. México: La Europea, 1895.

Olea Franco, Rafael. *Literatura mexicana del otro fin de siglo*. México, DF: El Colegio de México, Centro de Estudios Lingüísticos y Literarios, 2001.

Olsen, Patrice Elizabeth. *Artifacts of Revolution: Architecture, Society, and Politics in Mexico City, 1920–1940*. Latin American Silhouettes. Lanham, MD: Rowman & Littlefield, 2008.

O'Neill, M. J. *How He Does It: Sam T Jack, Twenty Years a King in the Realm of Burlesque*. Chicago: M. J. O'Neill, 1895.

O'Rourke, Kevin H., and Jeffrey G. Williamson. *Globalization and History: The Evolution of a Nineteenth-Century Atlantic Economy*. Cambridge, MA: MIT Press, 1999.

Ortiz, Fernando. *Cuban Counterpoint; Tobacco and Sugar*. Translated by Harriet De Onis. New York: Alfred A. Knopf, 1947.

———. *Los negros brujos*. Editorial de Ciencias Sociales, 1995.

Overmeyer-Velazquez, Mark. *Visions of the Emerald City: Modernity, Tradition, and the Formation of Porfirian Oaxaca*. Durham, NC: Duke University Press, 2006.

Páez, Pino. *A solas en el altar: vida de Rodolfo Casanova, "El Chango."* México, DF: Edamex, 1997.

Palti, Elías José. *La invención de una legitimidad razón y retórica en el pensamiento mexicano del siglo XIX*. Ciudad de Mexico: Fondo de Cultura Económica, 2006.

Paranaguá, Paulo Antonio. *Mexican Cinema*. London: British Film Institute, 1995.

Pérez, Louis, Jr. "Between Baseball and Bullfighting: The Quest for Nationality in Cuba, 1868-1898." *Journal of American History* 81, no. 2 (September 1994): 493–517.

———. *Cuba in the American Imagination: Metaphor and the Imperial Ethos*. Chapel Hill: University of North Carolina Press, 2008.

———. *Cuba Under the Platt Amendment, 1902–1934*. Pittsburgh: University of Pittsburgh Press, 1984.

———. *On Becoming Cuban: Identity, Nationality, and Culture*. Chapel Hill: University of North Carolina Press, 1999.

Pérez Montfort, Ricardo. *Estampas de nacionalismo popular mexicano: ensayos sobre cultura popular y nacionalismo*. México: CIESAS, 1994.

Pérez-Stable, Marifeli. *Cuban Women and the Struggle for "Conciencia." Cuban Studies* 17 (1987): 53.

Pettavino, Paula J., and Geralyn Pye. *Sport in Cuba: The Diamond in the Rough*. Pittsburgh: University of Pittsburgh Press, 1994.

Piccato, Pablo. *City of Suspects: Crime in Mexico City, 1900–1931*. Durham, NC: Duke University Press, 2001.

———. "Politics and the Technology of Honor: Dueling in Turn-of-the-Century Mexico." *Journal of Social History* 33, no. 2 (1999): 331–54.

———. "Public Sphere in Latin America: A Map of the Historiography." *Social History* 35, no. 2 (2010): 165–92.

———. *The Tyranny of Opinion: Honor in the Construction of the Mexican Public Sphere.* Durham, NC: Duke University Press, 2010.
Philalethes, Demoticus, and Ignacio Franchi Alfaro. *Yankee Travels Through the Island of Cuba; or, The Men and Government, the Laws and Customs of Cuba, As Seen by American Eyes.* New York: D. Appleton & Co, 1856.
Pike, Fredrick B. *The United States and Latin America: Myths and Stereotypes of Civilization.* Austin: University of Texas Press, 1992.
Pilcher, Jeffrey M. *¡Que Vivan Los Tamales!: Food and the Making of Mexican Identity.* Albuquerque: University of New Mexico Press, 1998.
Pino, Willy del. *Enciclopedia del boxeo cubano: con los acontecimientos boxisticos más destacados desde 1910 a 1960.* Miami: Continental Printing, 1988.
Plimpton, George. *The Best of Plimpton.* New York: Atlantic Monthly Press, 1990.
Porter, Robert P. *Report on the Commercial and Industrial Condition of the Island of Cuba.* Washington, DC: Government Printing Office, 1898.
Primelles, Leon. *Crónica Cubana, 1915–1918: la reelección de Menocal y la Revolución de 1917; la danza de los millones; la primera Guerra Mundial.* Habana: Editorial Lex, 1955.
Putney, Clifford. *Muscular Christianity: Manhood and Sports in Protestant America, 1880–1920.* Cambridge, MA: Harvard University Press, 2003.
Rama, Ángel. *The Lettered City.* Durham, NC: Duke University Press, 1996.
Ramírez, Máximo Evia. *México en la historia de los juegos olímpicos.* México, DF: Plaza y Valdés, 2000.
Ramírez, Catherine Sue. *The Woman in the Zoot Suit: Gender, Nationalism, and the Cultural Politics of Memory.* Durham, NC: Duke University Press, 2009.
Ramírez Berg, Charles. *Cinema of Solitude: A Critical Study of Mexican Film, 1967–1983.* Austin: University of Texas Press, 1992.
Ramos Mederos, Omelio, ed. *Cuentos de boxeo.* 2 vol. La Habana: Editorial Arte y Literatura, 1981.
Reejhsinghani, Anju Nandlal. "For Blood or for Glory: A History of Cuban Boxing, 1898–1962." PhD dissertation, University of Texas, 2009.
Reig Romero, Carlos. *YMCA de la Habana: memorias deportivas (1905–1910).* Quito, Ecuador: Departamento de Comunicaciones, Consejo Lationamericano de Iglesias, 2003.
Revolledo Cárdenas, Julio. *La fabulosa historia del circo en México.* México: Consejo Nacional para la Cultura y las Artes, 2004.
Ricardo, José G. *La imprenta en Cuba.* La Habana: Editorial Letras Cubanas, 1989.
Rickard, "Tex," and Arch Oboler. *Everything Happened to Him: The Story of Tex Rickard.* New York: Stokes, 1936.
Riess, Steven. *City Games: The Evolution of American Urban Society and the Rise of Sports.* Urbana: University of Illinois Press, 1991.
———. *Sport in Industrial America, 1850–1920.* Wheeling, IL: Harland Davidson, 1995.
Reyes, Aurelio de los. *Cine y sociedad en México, 1896–1930.* México: Universidad Nacional Autónoma de México, 1983.

Roberts, Randy. *Papa Jack: Jack Johnson and the Era of the White Hopes*. New York: Free Press, 1983.
———. *Jack Dempsey, the Manassa Mauler*. Urbana: University of Illinois Press, 2003.
Roca, José Luis. *Ni con Lima ni con Buenos Aires: La formación de un Estado Nacional en Charcas*. Lima: Instituto Francés de Estudios Andinos, 2007.
Rodríguez, Gregory S. "Palaces of Pain—Arenas of Mexican-American Dreams: Boxing and the Formation of Ethnic Mexican Identities in Twentieth-Century Los Angeles." PhD dissertation, University of California, San Diego, 1999.
Rodríguez, Robert G., and George Kimball. *The Regulation of Boxing: A History and Comparative Analysis of Policies among American States*. Jefferson, NC: McFarland and Co., 2009.
Rodríguez Bustillo, A. *Peligros Americanos: Crítica de "Ciencia Politica."* Córdoba (Argentina): Imprenta La Velocidad, 1899.
Roldán de Montaud, Inés. *La Restauración en Cuba: El fracaso de un proceso reformista*. Madrid: Consejo superior de investigaciones científicas, 2000.
Romero, María Eugenia, José Mario Contreras Valdez, and Jesús Méndez Reyes. *Poder público y poder privado: gobierno, empresarios y empresas, 1880–1980*. México, DF: UNAM, Facultad de Economía, 2006.
Roosevelt, Theodore. *The Strenuous Life: Essays and Addresses*. New York: Century, 1904.
Rosell, Mirta. *Luchas obreras contra Machado*. La Habana: Editorial Ciencias Sociales, 1973.
Rossen, Susan F. *African-Americans in Art: Selections from the Art Institute of Chicago*. Chicago: Institute in Association with University of Washington Press, 1999.
Rotundo, Anthony. *American Manhood: Transformations in Masculinity from the Revolution to the Modern Era*. New York: Basic Books, 1993.
Rowe, William, and Vivian Schelling. *Memory and Modernity: Popular Culture in Latin America*. London: Verso, 1991.
Rubenstein, Anne. *Bad Language, Naked Ladies, and Other Threats to the Nation*. Durham, NC: Duke University Press, 1998.
Ruiz, Jason. *Americans in the Treasure House*. Austin: University of Texas Press, 2014.
Runstedtler, Theresa. *Jack Johnson, Rebel Sojourner: Boxing in the Shadow of the Color Line*. Berkeley: University of California Press, 2013.
Rutherford, John. *Mexican Society During the Revolution*. Oxford: Clarendon Press, 1971.
Sachsman, David, B. S. Kittrell Rushing, and Roy Morris. *Seeking a Voice: Images of Race and Gender in the 19th Century Press*. West Lafayette, IN: Purdue University Press, 2009.
Salwen, Michael B. *Radio and Television in Cuba: The Pre-Castro Era*. Ames: University of Iowa Press, 1994.
Samuels, Charles. *The Magnificent Rube: The Life and Gaudy Times of Tex Rickard*. New York: McGraw-Hill, 1957.
San Martín, Bernardino, *El Arte de los Puños*. Havana: 1922.
Sanders, James. *The Vanguard of the Atlantic World: Creating Modernity, Nation and Democracy in Nineteenth Century Latin America*. Durham, NC: Duke University Press, 2014.

Sann, Paul. *The Lawless Decade: A Pictorial History of a Great American Transition: from the World War I Armistice and Prohibition to Repeal and the New Deal.* New York: Crown Publishers, 1957.
Santibáñez, Enrique. *Mexico; revista de sociedad, arte y letras.* México: Imprenta de "El Nacional," 1892.
Santovenia y Echaide, Emeterio Santiago. *Libro conmemorativo de la inauguración de la Plaza del Maine en la Habana.* La Habana: Secretaría de Obras Públicas, 1928.
Sartorious, David. *Ever Faithful: Race, Loyalty, and the Ends of Empire in Spanish Cuba.* Durham, NC: Duke University Press, 2014.
Schell, William, Jr. *Integral Outsiders: The American Colony in Mexico City, 1876–1911.* Wilmington, DE: Scholarly Resources, 2001.
Schelling, Vivian. *Through the Kaleidoscope: The Experience of Modernity in Latin America.* London: Verso, 2001.
Schmidt, Henry Conrad. *The Roots of "Lo Mexicano": Self and Society in Mexican Thought, 1900–1934.* College Station: Texas A&M University Press, 1978.
Schoonover, Thomas David. *The United States in Central America, 1860–1911: Episodes of Social Imperialism and Imperial Rivalry in the World System.* Durham, NC: Duke University Press, 1991.
Schubert, Adrian. *Death and Money in the Afternoon: A History of the Spanish Bullfight.* New York: Oxford University Press, 1999.
Schwartz, Rosalie. *Pleasure Island: Tourism and Temptation in Cuba.* Lincoln: University of Nebraska Press, 1997.
Schwarz, Vanessa R. *Spectacular Realities: Early Mass Culture in Fin-de-Siècle Paris.* Berkeley: University of California Press, 1998.
Scott, H. T. David. *The Art and Aesthetics of Boxing.* Lincoln: University of Nebraska Press, 2008.
Scott, Rebecca. *Degrees of Freedom: Louisiana and Cuba After Slavery.* Cambridge, MA: Belknap Press of Harvard University Press, 2005.
Sheinin, David M. K. *Sports Culture in Latin American History.* Pittsburgh: University of Pittsburgh Press, 2015.
Shimazu, Naoko. *Japan, Race, and Equality.* London: Routledge, 1998.
Shohat, Ella, and Robert Stam. *Multiculturalism, Postcoloniality, and Transnational Media.* New Brunswick, NJ: Rutgers University Press, 2003.
Sigal, Peter Herman, ed. *Infamous Desire: Male Homosexuality in Colonial Latin America.* Chicago: University of Chicago Press, 2003.
Sippial, Tiffany A. *Prostitution, Modernity, and the Making of the Cuban Republic.* Chapel Hill: University of North Carolina Press, 2013.
Skidmore, Thomas E. *Black Into White: Race and Nationality in Brazilian Thought.* New York: Oxford University Press, 1974.
Skidmore, Thomas E., Peter H. Smith, and James Naylor Green. *Modern Latin America.* New York: Oxford University Press, 2010.
Slout, William L. *Olympians of the Sawdust Circle.* San Bernardino, CA: Borgo Press, 1998.

Sluis, Ageeth. *Deco Body, Deco City: Female Spectacle and Modernity in Mexico City: 1900–1939*. Lincoln: University of Nebraska Press, 2016.
Smart, Barry. *The Sport Star: Modern Sport and the Cultural Economy of Sporting Celebrity*. London: Sage, 2005.
Smith, Kevin. *The Sundowners: The History of the Black Prizefighter, 1870–1930*. Vol. II. New York: CCK Publications, 2006.
Smith, William C. *Latin American Democratic Transformations: Institutions, Actors, and Processes*. Chichester, UK: Wiley-Blackwell, 2009.
Smith Bryan, William, and Walter B. Townsend. *Our Islands and Their People, As Seen with Camera and Pencil: Embracing Perfect Photographic and Descriptive Representations of the People and the Islands Lately Acquired from Spain, Including Hawaii, [Cuba] and the Philippines*. St. Louis: N. D. Thompson, 1899.
Solow, Barbara L. *Slavery and the Rise of the Atlantic System*. Cambridge: Cambridge University Press, 1991.
Speroni, José. "Firpo-Dempsey: el combate del siglo." *Todo Es Historia* 1, no. 6 (October 1967).
Starr, Frederick. *Readings from Mexican Authors*. Chicago: Open Court Publishing, 1904.
Stavans, Ilan. *Jose Vasconcelos: The Prophet of Race*. New Brunswick, NJ: Rutgers University Press, 2011.
Stepan, Nancy. *The Hour of Eugenics: Race, Gender, and Nation in Latin America*. Ithaca, NY: Cornell University Press, 1991.
Streible, Dan. *Fight Pictures: A History of Boxing and Early Cinema*. Berkeley: University of California Press, 2008.
Studlar, Gaylyn. *This Mad Masquerade: Stardom and Masculinity in the Jazz Age*. New York: Columbia University Press, 1996.
Suárez y López Guazo, Laura Luz. *Eugenesia y racismo en México*. México: Universidad Nacional Autónoma, 2005.
Tablada, José Juan, and Guillermo Sheridan. *Diario: (1900–1944)*. Nueva biblioteca mexicana, 117. México, DF: Univ. Nacional Autónoma de México, Centro de Estudios Literarios, 1992.
Talán, Raúl. *En el 3er Round*. México: Raúl Talán, 1953.
———. *Y . . . Fueron Idolos!* México DF, 1954.
Tamayo Vargas, Augusto. *Puerto pobre*. Lima: Editorial Galaxia, 1979.
Tarica, Estrella. *The Inner Life of Mestizo Nationalism*. Minneapolis: University of Minnesota Press, 2008.
Tenorio-Trillo, Mauricio. *Mexico at the World's Fairs: Crafting a Modern Nation*. Berkeley: University of California Press, 1996.
Tenorio-Trillo, Mauricio, and Aurora Gómez Galvarriato. *El porfiriato*. México, DF: Fondo de Cultura Económica, 2006.
Terry, Phillip. *Terry's Guide to Cuba*. Boston: Houghton Mifflin Company, 1926.
Thomas, Hugh. *Cuba, or, The Pursuit of Freedom*. New York: Da Capo Press, 1998.
Thomas, Susan. *Cuban Zarzuela: Performing Race and Gender on Havana's Lyric Stage*. Urbana: University of Illinois Press, 2009.

Thompson, Craig Friend. *Southern Masculinity: Perspectives on Manhood in the South Since Reconstruction.* Athens: University of Georgia Press, 2009.
Thompson, John B. *The Media and Modernity: A Social Theory of the Media.* Cambridge: Polity Press, 1995.
Topik, Steven, Carlos Marichal, and Zephyr L. Frank, eds. *From Silver to Cocaine: Latin American Commodity Chains and the Building of the World Economy, 1500–2000.* Durham, NC: Duke University Press, 2006.
Tudor, Deborah V. *Hollywood's Vision of Team Sports: Heroes, Race, and Gender.* New York: Garland Publishing, 1997.
Urbano de Sotomayor, Feyjoo de. *Isla de Cuba.* Paris: Impr. de A. Blondeau, 1852.
Valadés, José C. *El porfirismo: historia de un régimen.* México: Universidad Nacional Autónoma de México, 1987.
Vanderwood, Paul J. *Disorder and Progress Bandits, Police and Mexican Development.* Wilmington, DE: SR Books, 1992.
———. *Juan Soldado: Rapist, Murderer, Martyr, Saint.* Durham, NC: Duke University Press, 2004.
Van Hoy, Teresa Miriam. *A Social History of Mexico's Railroads: Peons, Prisoners, and Priests.* Lanham, MD: Rowman & Littlefield, 2008.
Vasconcelos, José, and Alicia Molina. *Antología de textos sobre educación.* México: Fondo de Cultura Económica, 1981.
Vaughan, Mary K., and Stephen E. Lewis. *The Eagle and the Virgin: Nation and Cultural Revolution in Mexico, 1920–1940.* Durham, NC: Duke University Press, 2006.
Velasco, Carlos de. *José Sixto de Sola.* Habana: Imprenta."El Siglo XX," 1916.
Vendryes, Margaret Rose. *Barthé: A Life in Sculpture.* Jackson: University Press of Mississippi, 2008.
Vera, Eugenia Roldán, and Marcelo Caruso. *Imported Modernity in Post-Colonial State Formation: The Appropriation of Political, Educational, and Cultural Models in Nineteenth-Century Latin America.* Frankfurt: Peter Lang, 2007.
Verrill, A. Hyatt. *Cuba Past and Present.* New York: Dodd, Mead and Co., 1920.
Vianna, Hermano. *O mistério do samba.* Rio de Janeiro: Universidade Federal do Rio de Janeiro, 1995.
Villaseñor, Victor Manuel *Memorias de un hombre de izquierda.* México: Biografías Gandesa, 1976.
Virgílio, Stanlei. *Conde Koma: o invencivel yondan da história.* Campinas: Editora Átomo, 2002.
Ward, Geoffrey C. *Unforgivable Blackness: The Rise and Fall of Jack Johnson.* New York: Vintage Books, 2006.
Warshaw, Jacob. *The New Latin America.* New York: Thomas Y. Crowell Co., 1922.
Whannel, Garry. *Media Sport Stars: Masculinities and Moralities.* London: Routledge, 2002.
Wiarda, Howard J., and Harvey F. Kline. *Latin American Politics and Development.* Boulder, CO: Westview Press, 2011.

Wood, David, and P. Louise Johnson, eds. *Sporting Cultures: Hispanic Perspectives on Sport, Text, and the Body*. New York: Routledge, 2008.
*The World Today*. Chicago: Current Encyclopedia Co., 1902.
Wright, Ann. "Intellectuals of an Unheroic Period of Cuban History, 1913–1923. The '*Cuba Contemporanea*' Group." *Bulletin of Latin American Research* 7, no. 1 (1988): 109–22.
Zuviría, José María. *Anales contemporáneos. Sarmiento, 1868–1874; estudios sobre política Argentina*. Buenos Aires: J. Peuser, 1889.

## Government Publications

Congreso Nacional de Educación Primaria. *Informes presentados al Congreso Nacional de Educación Primaria por las delegaciones de los estados: del distrito federal y territorios en septiembre de 1910, al celebrarse el primer centenario de la independencia mexicana*. México: Impenta de A. Carranza e Hijos, 1911.
*Diario de sesiones de la Cámara de Diputados*. Buenos Aires: Argentina. Congreso de la Nación. Cámara de Diputados de la Nación, Issues 129–205, 1922.
United States Olympic Committee. *Report; Games of the Olympiad*. New York: United States Olympic Committee, 1928.

## Telegram

J. G. Reagan to Culberson, February 21, 1896, Records of Charles Allen Culberson, Texas Office of the Governor, Texas State Library and Archives.

## Web Articles and Miscellaneous Web Pages

http://mexico2010encalifornia.org/boletinenero2010z.htm. Accessed September 19, 2010.
http://www.time.com/time/specials/packages/article/0,28804,1883644_1883653_1884544,00.html. Accessed September 22, 2009.
"The Bicentennial Gives U.S. New Champions" Azteca Deportes. http://www.aztecadeportes.com/notas/box-azteca/20670/el-bicentenario-nos-regala-nuevos-Campeónes.
The Internet Movie Database. http://www.imdb.com.

# Index

abolitionism and abolitionists, 79, 81
*Afición*, 135–36, 212
*afrocubanismo*, 3, 19, 176
Aguilar, Cuauhtemóc, 53, 55, 63, 73
Aguilar Reyes, Alejandro, 135, 158
Allen, Steve, 10, 214, 216, 240–41, 263
Amorós, Francisco, 82–83
Anderson, Benedict, 9, 17, 263
Anglo-Saxon: as a racial or cultural designation, 21, 24, 35, 42, 58, 104
Aramburu, J. R., 100–101, 106, 172–73, 263
Arbena, Joseph, 14, 263
Arena Nacional, 135–38
Arizmendi, Alberto "Baby," 141–42, 159
atavism, 22, 83, 98
athletic clubs, 54, 175, 184, 195
Atlantic Revolutions, 77

Bartra, Armando, 160–61
Bartra, Roger, 162, 213
baseball, 7, 11, 80, 95, 143
basketball, 136, 143
Battle Royale, 55, 67, 68, 124–125
Beattie, Peter, 7, 214
Bederman, Gail, 13, 193
Beezley, William, 21, 54
Belém Prison, 31, 32, 47
*Birth of a Nation*, 113
Bloch, Marc, ix
bodybuilding, 65, 77, 184, 210
boxing films, 5, 50, 58, 98, 102, 114

Bradt, George, 67, 110, 119–128
Byran, William Jennings, 128
Budinich, Juan, 105–107, 233
Buenos Aires, x, 66, 107, 115–17, 123
bullfighting, 22, 25, 29, 33, 80, 93, 97, 133
Buffington, Robert, 8, 23, 214, 265

Cabrera, Raimundo, 92
Cameron, Lucille, 122–23
*Campeón Sin Corona* (1945), 168–69
Campos, Isaac, 16–17, 265
*Caras y Caretas*, 116
Cardenas, Lazaro 135, 144
Carpentier, George, 187, 195
Casimir, Enver, 201
cartoons, (of boxing), 1–3, 60
Carranza, Venustiano, 111
Carroll, James, 22, 28, 32, 43
Casanova, Rodolfo "Chango," 4, 140, 168
Castellanos Mena, Manuel, 186
Carpio, Manuel, 39
censorship, 22, 48, 58, 77–84, 95, 144–45, 162
Chamber of Deputies (Mexico), 133–34
Charles, Mister, 85–87
Chaumont, Amadeo, 90–94
Cienfuegos, 100, 119, 195
Ciudad Juárez, 111
civic or civil society, vii, 3, 17, 84, 133, 142
comic books (*historietas*), 159–65
Clarke, Billy A., 22, 27–38

285

Club Atlético de Cuba, 120
Club Atlético Internacional, 54–56
Club Olímpico, 38, 65
Club Ugartechea, 38–39, 41–42
cock fighting, 5, 33, 80, 86, 100, 133
Colín, Fernando, 37, 42–49, 64, 166
color line, 13, 43, 47–48, 50, 52, 109
Corrales Mateos, Juan, 87
Cosmopolitan Club, 37, 48, 221
Cravioto, Rafael, 28, 30
*Cuba News*, 121–22, 131

De Castro, Rafael, 81–84, 89
De Castro Vicente Antonio, 82–83
Debord, Guy, 12, 215
Dempsey, Jack, 10, 15, 87, 133, 146–47, 185
*Diario de la Marina*, 5, 85, 89, 93, 99, 182, 196, 201, 204
Díaz, Porfirio, 3, 21–26, 25, 30, 57
Díaz Quesada, Enrique, 112
dueling, 31, 33, 53, 86, 103, 210, 228
Dulce, Domingo, 79

Edgren, Bob, 140, 235
*El Arte de los Puños*, 174, 179–88, 233
*El Diario*, 58–60
*El Diario del Hogar*, 39, 60, 62
*El Imparcial* (Mexico City), 17, 23, 43–45, 58
*El Moro Muza*, 90, 92, 229
*El Mundo* (Havana), 29, 65, 68, 99, 107, 119
*El Mundo* (Mexico City), 30, 45–46
*El Mundo Ilustrado*, 42, 45, 64
*El País*, 23, 42, 44, 57
*El Siglo*, 94–95
*El Tiempo*, 41, 45, 71
Elsey, Brenda, 7, 213, 268
Escuela Nacional Preparatoria, 26, 42, 218
Esperón, Salvador, 5–6, 37–49, 53, 164–66, 214
Esténoz, Evaristo, 121
Estrada Palma, Tomás, 99

eugenics, 4, 11, 18, 47, 110, 178, 181, 188, 209, 216

Febles, Miguel (Mike), 120, 156, 165–67, 248
Firpo, Luis Ángel, 133, 146, 174, 189–200
free trade, 78
freedom of association, 79, 81, 227
freedom of the press, 16, 79, 83–84, 95
Fitten, James, 136–37, 154, 240
Freyre de Andrade, Fernando, 120, 124

*Gaceta de Policía*, 37, 44, 46–47
Galindo, Alejandro, 168
gambling, 53, 97, 107, 129, 136
Gamboa, Federico, 13, 34, 53, 144–45, 211, 269
Geertz, Clifford, 8, 241, 270
Gimnasio Rafael Trejo, vii
globalization, 19, 140, 212
Gramsci, Antonio, 12
Great White Hope, 1, 6, 58–59, 63, 70, 103, 109, 112, 127
Guillén, Nicolas, 13, 175, 204
Gutmann, Matthew, 12, 215, 271

Habermas, Jürgen, 23, 53, 271
Haitian Revolution, 78, 120
Hajdu, Aladar, 9, 214, 249
Havana Circus, 85, 89, 93
*Havana Post*, 110, 121, 128
Heenan-Sayers bout, 93
Helg, Aline, 2, 101–2, 271
Hidalgo (Mexican state), 28, 30, 74
Hobsbawm, Eric, 11, 141, 212, 224, 231, 271
Hotel Plaza, 122

*indigenismo*, 3
Iturbide Hotel, 32, 43
Iriye, Akira, 12

Jeffries, Jim, 58–61, 71, 97, 101

Johnson, Jack, 1, 58, 101–110; Young Jack Johnson, 4, 63
Juárez, Benito, 78
jujitsu, 16, 19, 40, 57, 147, 152–53, 181

Kirkwood, Kid, 51

*La Lucha*, 98, 103, 120–21
*La Voz de México*, 30–32
Landa y Escandón, Guillermo, 44, 54, 56, 58
Larraín, Jorge, 139, 143, 241, 274
Lersundi, Gabriel, 183, 252
Levigne, Kid, 38–39, 51–52
literacy, 17–18, 160
Linares, Abel, 102, 121
Lobato, Emilio, 26–27, 218
London, Jack, 44, 225
L'Ouverture, Toussain, 120
lucha libre, 135
lynching, 4, 24, 29, 37, 71, 96, 101, 115, 123, 125

Maceo, Antonio, 104, 124, 172, 184, 202
Macías González, Víctor, 13, 215
Madán, Eligio, 112, 126–27, 238, 275
Maeterlinck, Maurice, 57
Maljoy, Joe, 38, 43, 64
Mañach, Jorge, 177, 251
Mangan, J. A., 14, 266
Marroquín, José, 180, 252
Martínez Arredondo, Patricio, 53, 145, 154, 163–67
Martí, José, viii, x, 4–6, 96, 104, 205, 211
masculinity, vii, 2–3, 6, 10–13, 21–24, 36, 49, 54, 65, 212
Massaguer, Conrado, 1, 69, 111, 113, 122
Massaguer, Joe, 196–97
Matanzas, 89, 92, 100, 185, 197, 199
McVea, Sam, 65, 115, 130, 194
Menocal, Mario, 110, 119, 124, 128, 238, 249
meritocracy, 3, 6, 130, 139, 158, 176, 211
*Mexican Herald*, 36, 38, 47, 48, 144

Mexican Revolution, 1, 16, 22, 27, 46, 52, 63, 73, 111, 223
*Mexican Sportsman*, 27
Mitchell, Kid, 18, 39, 43, 48, 50–52
modernity, 77, 83, 85, 95, 97, 134, 151, 155, 171
Monroe Doctrine, 78
Mora, Carl, 10, 248
Monsivais, Carlos, 144, 276
Moore, Robin, 203, 213, 276
Mosse, George, 13, 276
Muñoz, Victor, 2, 118, 122–23, 125, 128, 130–31
Muñoz Bustamante, Mario, 129, 236

Nájera, Jesus "Chucho," 135–37
NAACP, 120–21
*negrito*, 7, 10, 89, 100, 202, 205, 210
Nervo, Amado, 53, 224

Oriental Park, 109
Ortiz, Fernando, 172, 226, 230
Ortiz, Fidel, 163, 246

Partido Independiente de Color, 1, 102, 104, 121, 127, 182, 214, 232
Payret Theater, 100, 126, 231
Paz, Ireneo, 13, 34, 220
Peñalver, Anastasio, 68, 105, 130
Pérez Jr., Louis, 7–8, 79–80, 85, 95, 277
Piccato, Pablo, 8, 16–17, 23, 155, 216, 223, 277
Porfirian Persuasion, 21
Portantiero, Juan Carlos, 17
Portes Gil, Emilio, 133
Posada, José Guadalupe, 8, 22, 30, 74, 245
prostitution, 25, 114, 178
public sphere, 2–3, 17, 22, 41, 52, 79, 86, 92, 101, 113, 142, 158
public spectacle, 11, 22, 29, 89, 101, 149
*Puck*, 74, 97
*pulquerías*, 10, 147, 243

racelessness, 6–7, 104, 173, 250

racial segregation, 7, 25, 56, 122, 184, 194, 250
radio broadcasts, 199, 200, 211
Rama, Ángel, 18, 278
Remedios, 88
Reyes Spindola, Rafael, 45
Rickard, Tex, 146–47, 153, 278
Rivero, Ignacio, 98, 104, 232
Roberds, Asa Daniel, 121–22, 131, 237
Rodó, José Enrique, 153, 244
Romero, Baldomero, 149
Roosevelt, Theodore, 106, 193
Rough Riders, 56
Romero, Baldomero, 54–55, 58, 149, 154, 165
Rubenstein, Anne, 13, 142, 279
Runstedtler, Theresa, 10, 12, 279
Ryder, Jeannette, 129

samba, 7, 282
San Martín, Bernardo, 7, 177, 233
Santos y Artigas, 105, 128, 186, 233, 253
Sardiñas, Eligio "Kid Chocolate," 4, 7, 9, 159, 171–79, 201–8, 249
Schwartz, Vanessa, 12, 280
Sierra, Justo, 4–5, 40
Singer, Al, 200
Sixto de Sola, José, 13, 177, 188, 282
slavery and slave revolts, 19, 34, 51, 78, 81, 89, 112, 127
Smith, Jim, 16, 51, 164–65, 167, 215
*Social*, 9
Social Darwinism, 23, 55–56, 106, 110, 209–10, 271
*Sociedad Económico Amigos del País*, 82
Sotelo, Francsico "Paco," 135–41, 240–41
Sotelo Regil, Luis, 133–37
South Africa, 52, 103–4, 231
Spanish-American-Cuban War, 97
*Sport* (magazine), 95

sportsman: meaning of, 7, 10–11, 13, 192
Stepan, Nancy, 11, 178, 215, 251, 281
Sullivan, John L., 23, 272

Tablada, José Juan, 13, 38–40, 49, 53–54, 134, 149, 151–53, 221, 224, 281
Talán, Raul, 159, 188, 281
tango, 7, 35
Teatros (theaters), Colón, 125; Marianao, 97; Payret, 126; Villanueva, 89, 94
Tenorio-Trillo, Mauricio, 53–54, 151, 155, 224, 281
Tepito, vii, 169, 242
Thomas J. Watson Fellowship, viii
*Todo un Hombre* (1935), 159–60
Turnbull, David, 82

Ugartechea, Enrique, 38–39, 4–43, 50, 53, 247–48
Uncle Sam, 64, 74, 97–98, 103
University of Havana, vii, 106
Urbina, Luis, 38, 221

Valdés, Eladio "Black Bill," 4, 171, 186, 193, 201
Valdés, Gerónimo, 80
Vasconcelos, José, 148, 155, 178, 244, 282
Vedado Tennis Club, 15, 120, 252
Villa, Pancho, 111–12, 167, 273
Villanueva, Luis "Kid Azteca" 4, 140–41, 161–62, 242

Willard, Jess, 1–2, 19, 65, 70, 109–19, 125, 131, 186

YMCA, 26, 195, 218, 278

Zayas, Alfredo, 100, 188, 231
Zaydin, Ramón, 156